Romanticism in National Context

BA ___ COLL ___
N ___

ROMANTICISM IN NATIONAL CONTEXT

Edited by

ROY PORTER

Senior Lecturer in the Social History of Medicine, Wellcome Institute

and

MIKULÁŠ TEICH

Emeritus Fellow, Robinson College, Cambridge

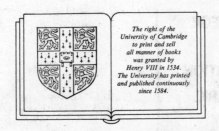

The right of the
University of Cambridge
to print and sell
all manner of books
was granted by
Henry VIII in 1534.
The University has printed
and published continuously
since 1584.

CAMBRIDGE UNIVERSITY PRESS

Cambridge

New York   New Rochelle   Melbourne   Sydney

Published by the Press Syndicate of the University of Cambridge
The Pitt Building, Trumpington Street, Cambridge CB2 1RP
32 East 57th Street, New York, NY 10022, USA
10 Stamford Road, Oakleigh, Melbourne 3166, Australia

First published 1988

Printed in Great Britain at
the University Press, Cambridge

British Library cataloguing in publication data

Romanticism in national context.
1. Romanticism – Europe
I. Porter, Roy, 1946–
II. Teich, Mikuláš
700′.94   PN751

Library of Congress cataloguing in publication data

Romanticism in national context.
1. Romanticism. I. Porter, Roy, 1946– .
II. Teich, Mikuláš.
PN603.R57   1988   809′.9145   87–26884

ISBN 0 521 32605 2 hard covers
ISBN 0 521 33913 8 paperback

Contents

Notes on contributors   *page* vii

Introduction   1

1   Romanticism in Wales   9
GWYN A. WILLIAMS

2   Romanticism in England   37
MARILYN BUTLER

3   Haunted by history: Irish Romantic writing 1800–50   68
TOM DUNNE

4   Romanticism in Greece   92
RODERICK BEATON

5   Romanticism in Germany   109
DIETRICH VON ENGELHARDT

6   Romanticism in Switzerland   134
CLARISSA CAMPBELL ORR

7   Romanticism in Scandinavia   172
GUNNAR ERIKSSON

8   Romanticism in The Netherlands   191
NICHOLAS A. RUPKE

9   Romanticism in Hungary   217
    MIHÁLY SZEGEDY-MASZÁK

10 Romanticism in France   240
    STEPHEN BANN

11 Spanish Romanticism   260
    SUSAN KIRKPATRICK

12 Russian Romanticism   284
    JOHN MERSEREAU, JR, and DAVID LAPEZA

13 The Agony in the Garden: Polish Romanticism   317
    DONALD PIRIE

    Index   345

Notes on contributors

STEPHEN BANN is a Reader in Modern Cultural Studies at the University of Kent. He has published widely on the history and theory of modern art (*Experimental Painting*, London, 1970; *The Tradition of Constructivism*, London, 1972), and, more recently, on the representation of history in the nineteenth century (*The Clothing of Clio*, Cambridge, 1984). He was Deputy Editor, then Editor, of *20th Century Studies* (1969–76) and is at present on the Advisory Committee of Cambridge Studies in New Art History and Theory, and the Editorial Committee of *Word and Image*.

RODERICK BEATON studied English Literature at the University of Cambridge before turning to Modern Greek for the subject of his doctorate. During the 1970s he lived for three years in Greece and is now Lecturer in Modern Greek Language and Literature at King's College, London. He has published *Folk Poetry of Modern Greece* (Cambridge, 1980) and several articles on Greek literature from the twelfth century to the twentieth and on Greek oral tradition. His next book, entitled *The Medieval Greek Romance*, is to be published shortly by Cambridge University Press.

MARILYN BUTLER is King Edward VII Professor of English Literature at Cambridge. Her books include *Jane Austen and the War of Ideas* (Oxford, 1975), *Peacock Displayed* (London 1979), *Romantics, Rebels and Reactionaries: English Literature and Its Background, 1760–1830* (Oxford, 1981), and a selection of polemical prose of the 1790s, *Burke, Paine, Godwin and the Revolution Controversy* (Cambridge, 1984).

TOM DUNNE lectures in Irish History in University College Cork, where he was Oliver MacDonagh's research student, before going to Peterhouse, Cambridge, to work on the Irish question and imperialist ideologies with Jack Gallagher. His main interest since then has been in using literary sources to explore Irish cultural history, and he has edited and contributed to a volume entitled *The Writer as Witness: Literature as Historical Evidence* (Cork, 1986), as well as publishing various articles on early nineteenth-century writers.

DIETRICH VON ENGELHARDT was born on 5 May 1941 in Göttingen, and studied philosophy, history, and Slavic languages in Tübingen, Munich, and Heidelberg. He was active in a criminological research project, 'The Criminal Career', combined with Reality Therapy for prisoners (Institute for Criminal Science, Heidelberg). He was Assistant in the Institute for the History of Medicine (Heidelberg) from 1971 to 1976; Professor for History of Medicine and Natural Sciences from 1976 (Heidelberg); Director of the Institute for History of Medicine and Natural Sciences at the Medical University of Lübeck from 1983. He has published *Hegel und die Chemie* (Wiesbaden, 1976); *Historisches Bewusstsein in der Naturwissenschaft von der Aufklärung bis zum Positivismus* (Freiburg and München, 1979); *Mit der Krankheit leben* (Heidelberg, 1986); *Wissenschaftsgeschichte auf den Versammlungen der GDNÄ 1822–1972* (Stuttgart, 1987); *Kriminalität und Verlauf* (with S. W. Engel) (Heidelberg, 1978), and *Die inneren Verbindungen zwischen Philosophie und Medizin im 20. Jahrhundert* (with H. Schipperges) (Darmstadt, 1980).

GUNNAR ERIKSSON is Professor of the History of Science and Ideas at the University of Uppsala, Sweden, and head of the department. His books, mainly in Swedish, include two on the connection between science and Romanticism in Sweden, a history of botany in Sweden until 1800, a study of Swedish science during the beginning of the industrial era in Sweden (1870–1914), and, most recently published, on the popularization of science, its theory and history. He is one of the contributors to the volume *Linnaeus, the Man and his Work*, ed. T. Frängsmyr (Berkeley, California, 1983).

SUSAN KIRKPATRICK was a Fulbright Fellow at Cambridge University, then completed her doctorate at Harvard University in 1972. Currently an Associate Professor of Spanish and Comparative Literature at the University of California, San Diego, she has published *Larra: El laberinto inextricable de un romántico liberal* (Madrid, 1977) and articles on Larra, Valle-Inclán, Fernán Caballero, and Galdós. A Guggenheim Fellow for 1986–7, she is finishing a book on Romantic subjectivity and female authorship in Spain.

DAVID LAPEZA (b. 1950) is currently a Professor of Russian Language and Literature at Kenyon College, Gambier, Ohio. His translations of nineteenth- and twentieth-century Russian prose include Vladimir

Voinovich's *The Ivankiad*, for which he was nominated for the National Book Award in 1978. A Fulbright fellowship at the Soviet Academy of Sciences allowed him to complete his recent doctoral dissertation on the popular Romantic novelist, Alexander Veltman.

JOHN MERSEREAU, JR (b. 1925), received his PhD. degree in Slavic Languages and Literatures from the University of California at Berkeley in 1957. He has taught at the University of Michigan for the past thirty years, specializing in nineteenth-century Russian literature and problems of Romanticism. Four books and many articles are the fruit of research at Berkeley, Michigan, Yale, Helsinki University, the New York Public Library, the Bibliothèque Nationale in Paris, and the Saltykov-Shchedrin Library in Leningrad.

CLARISSA CAMPBELL ORR graduated from Girton College, Cambridge, in 1972, with a degree in Literature, and History and Philosophy of Science. She is a Lecturer in History at Cambridgeshire College of Arts and Technology, where she specializes in the History of Ideas, and has taught on both the Enlightenment and the Romantic movement. She is working on studies of a friend and disciple of Rousseau, Jean-André Deluc of Geneva and of Mme Albertine Necker de Saussure, educationalist and cousin by marriage of Mme de Staël.

DONALD PIRIE was educated at the School of Slavonic and Eastern European Studies, University of London, 1975–9, and Emmanuel College, Cambridge, 1980–3. He has been Stepek Lecturer in Polish Language and Literature at Glasgow University since 1984. He is joint editor with Rosemary Hunt of *Campania*, a journal of Polish culture. His primary research interests relate to the development of Protestant culture and religiosity in sixteenth- and seventeenth-century Poland-Lithuania, and is currently writing a history of twentieth-century Polish literature, *The Prison of Myth: Polish Literature from Modernism to Post-Modernism*.

ROY PORTER was educated at Cambridge where he took his Ph.D. in 1974. He was University Lecturer in European History and Director of Studies in History at Churchill College, Cambridge, before moving to the Wellcome Institute for the History of Medicine in London in 1979, where he is Senior Lecturer in the Social History of Medicine. His publications include *English Society in the Eighteenth Century* (Harmondsworth, 1982), *Mind Forg'd Manacles* (London, 1987) and *A Social History of Madness* (London, 1987). With Mikuláš Teich he has also edited *The Enlightenment in National Context* (Cambridge, 1981) and *Revolution in History* (Cambridge, 1986).

NICHOLAS A. RUPKE is a Dutch geologist and historian of science and medicine, with a Ph.D. from Princeton University (1972). He has held research fellowships at the Smithsonian Institution, the University of Oxford, the University of Tübingen, the Netherlands Institute for Advanced Study, and the Wellcome Institute for the History of Medicine. His publications cover topics in marine geology and the history of the earth and life sciences, and include a scientific biography of William Buckland, *The Great Chain of History* (Oxford, 1983).

MIHÁLY SZEGEDY-MASZÁK is Associate Professor of Cultural History at Eötvös University, Budapest. In 1985 and in 1987 he was Visiting Professor at Indiana University. He is the author of three books in Hungarian: *Világkép és stílus* (*Studies in Historical Poetics*) (Budapest, 1980), *A regény, amint írja önmagát* (*An Introduction to Narratology*) (Budapest, 1980; 2nd edn 1987), and *Kubla kán és Pickwick úe* (*Romanticism and Realism in English Literature*) (Budapest, 1982), and a great number of essays, several of which have been published in the United States, France, Germany, and Holland. His main fields are narratology and comparative literature.

MIKULÁŠ TEICH first studied medicine in Prague. Thwarted by Hitler he eventually obtained a Ph.D. in chemistry (Leeds, 1946), and a C.Sc. in history (Prague, 1959). He is now Fellow Emeritus at Robinson College, Cambridge. His publications deal with wide-ranging topics of scientific history in different periods. Returning to Britain in 1969, he has edited (with Robert Young) *Changing Perspectives in the History of Science* (London, 1972), and (with Roy Porter) *The Enlightenment in National Context* (Cambridge, 1981), and *Revolution in History* (Cambridge, 1986). His *A Source Book in Biochemistry c. 1770–c. 1940* (with Dorothy M. Needham) is completed. *Bier, Wissenschaft und Wirtschaft in Deutschland 1800–1914* is nearing completion.

GWYN A. WILLIAMS was born in south Wales in 1925 and read history at Aberystwyth and University College London. He taught Welsh history at Aberystwyth and history at York and Cardiff, was a Simon Research Fellow at Manchester, and held visiting fellowships in Brown and Pennsylvania in the U.S.A. and St Antony's College, Oxford. He retired as Professor Emeritus in 1985 and is currently working on Marx and the writing of his *18 Brumaire*. Among his books are *Artisans and Sansculottes* (London, 1968), *Goya and the Impossible Revolution* (Harmondsworth, 1976), *The Merthyr Rising* (London, 1978), *Madoc: The Making of a Myth* (London, 1980) and a one-volume history of Wales, *When Was Wales?* (London, 1985).

Introduction

In the Anglo-Saxon world, Romanticism is a concept still most commonly and most comfortably handled within the fields of literary studies and aesthetics. In their schooldays, students first become familiar with the term as a label for the English 'Lake poets', and grow used to associating the movement with the 'truth of the imagination and the holiness of the heart's intentions', with a love of nature in the wild, and with the spiritual discovery of the self. The relation of such poets – Wordsworth, Coleridge, and their contemporaries – to their society is seen as simple: they rejected it. They are the heroic individuals who repudiated Mammon, and turned their backs on the philistine world of the bourgeoisie, the world that was 'too much with us'. They 'wandered lonely as a cloud', in quest for the eternal, the ideal, pure truth and beauty, or what Coleridge in his less reverential moments called 'inner goings-on'.

Within this perspective it is easy to regard Romanticism as essentially arising out of the life experiences and activities of isolated individuals – indeed, as the very forging of individualism – and to study it mainly biographically in terms of a series of spiritual odysseys. To prevent that approach from becoming too fragmented, however, certain essential intellectual and artistic continuities are then commonly postulated, linking Romantic art and thought across Europe. The goal of the Romantic quest, we are told (and quite plausibly) lay in repudiating the culture of perfection in favour of that of process, abandoning design for desire. The Romantics valued the infinite above the finite, rejected order in favour of chaos, discounted the general in preference for the particular, the material for the spiritual, the mechanical for the organic, and saw art not just as a product of 'taste', 'imitation', and craftsmanship ('a work of art') but as the spontaneous outpourings of transcendent genius. As Wordsworth was to poetry, so Turner was to painting, Schelling to philosophy, Berlioz to music, and Stendhal to the novel, we are often told.

The contributors to this volume believe that it is indeed valuable in

1

suchlike ways to seek to identify and explain the overarching integrity of Romanticism. If we look around Europe, we see that Romantics from Uppsala to Madrid, and from Dublin to Moscow, shared a number of common *bêtes noires*. They revolted against shallow, narrow conventionality, the banal art of the academies, the prostitution of mind to the service of money, power, and polite taste. Prophetic visions of the overthrow of Babylon haunted the imagination of William Blake and his contemporaries, with their visions of future 'green and pleasant lands'. Even the more conservative amongst them despised at least those aspects of an *ancien régime* which had encouraged vulgar materialism and hypocritical mediocrity. These sympathies and antipathies reflect the attitudes to nature and society of some of the most influential artists, scientists, and philosophers alive between 1789 and 1848. That is, approximately the period which saw the sunrise and sunset of the Romantic movement in Europe. But do they represent the themes which gave Romanticism its unity?

Pondering this question, many eminent scholars have argued that the concept of Romanticism, seen as a unity, has degenerated into a Procrustean bed, until the very word means everything and nothing, being applied to quite disparate intellectual and cultural currents eddying in the late eighteenth century and the first half of the nineteenth. Amongst such doubters, Arthur Lovejoy celebratedly claimed that what had truly existed was not 'Romanticism' but a veritable 'plurality of Romanticisms'.

The point is well made. But it would be a mistake to push this nominalism too far, and to reduce Romanticism to nothing other than that most Romantic notion, the biographies of great heroes, typically wanderers, exiles, and outcasts. After all, the exile is himself a product of the society from which he is banished or banishes himself, and individualism is not asocial but an expression of a particular structure of feelings.

Critical of exclusively biographical, textual, or literary-historical approaches, this volume hopes to show that it is possible to establish some internal coherence to such expressions as 'German Romanticism', 'Spanish Romanticism', 'Polish Romanticism', and so forth. It further aims to explore how these different national Romanticisms coexisted in symbiotic relations to each other. Romanticism did not spread out from a single source, though some important growth points are identified here – the mid-eighteenth-century English bardic and gothic movements, Rousseauvian sentiment, German Sturm und Drang – and questions of media of transmission loom large, above all in Clarissa Campbell Orr's discussion of Switzerland. Overall, however, instead of concentrating on questions of *origins*, the essays here seek to elucidate how the diverse

Romanticisms took shape under the influence of the epochal upheavals that were shaking the foundations of the whole of Europe, the French Revolution and the British Industrial Revolution.

At first glance, the more spectacular of these was the French Revolution and its aftermaths – both the Europe-wide Revolutionary and Napoleonic Wars down to 1815, but, no less significantly, the heritages of revolution and revolt which became integral to many nations thereafter. Faced with such revolutionary traumas, no profound thinker or artist of the era of Blake and Châteaubriand, Kleist and Hegel – whether radical or reactionary – could proceed on the basis of 'business as usual'. Whether the generation of Revolution was just a 'monster' (as it was for Joseph de Maistre), or it was truly a matter of Wordsworth's 'Bliss it was in that dawn to be alive', the universe of symbolic meanings needed to be recreated once more out of chaos. This fact applies not just to ardent revolutionaries but no less to those more conservative Romantics for whom the real priorities were the resurrection of the past and the 'invention of tradition'. Myths of creation and recreation – Faust, Prometheus, Frankenstein, Christ – were central to the Romantic imagination.

Romanticism thus responded to, and created, the shock of the new. It was neither uniformly progressive nor reactionary, neither wholly liberal nor authoritarian, neither unequivocally republican nor monarchist. For one thing, it embraced diversity; it took many forms; it had its asynchronisms. Thus Romanticism blossomed quite late in France (after all, Romanticism itself elsewhere was in no small measure a protest against French cultural imperialism, both Classical and Revolutionary). In early nineteenth-century France, Romanticism was principally identified with a traditionalist nostalgia for the past, expressing the wish to expunge the memory of the irreligion of the Enlightenment and the primal Reign of Terror, that 'despotism of liberty'. From the late 1820s onwards, however – the era of Victor Hugo – it came to be utterly fused with the hopes of liberalism. The same story applies equally to the Dutch experience. For another, many individual figures changed their allegiances. In England, the erstwhile Jacobins, Wordsworth, Coleridge and Southey, all ended up Burkean pillars of reaction.

And, at bottom, the multi-faceted nature of politics is so complex as to turn the attempt to attach crude party labellings into a fatuous exercise. It may be plausible enough to call that arch-Romantic Shelley (advocate of free love, of vegetarianism, of Irish emancipation, of colonial freedom, and so forth) an unambiguous radical. Similarly, in the case of Spain, it is reasonable (as Susan Kirkpatrick argues in her essay below) to see liberal and Romantic forces united together against the restoration monarchy. But what of Hungary or Poland, for instance? There the scions of Roman-

ticism were typically discontented gentry who felt passionate disdain for
the absolutism and foreign rule under which they lived, but they had little
or no concern for the conditions of life of the peasants and serfs (though
they were not against forging myths of the virtuous 'people').

Likewise in Ireland, where the chieftains of literary and political
Romanticism (eventually to spawn the Young Ireland movement) came
from the very same Anglo-Irish Protestant ruling class who formed the
colonial oppressors; they protested against English overlordship in the
English language rather than in Gaelic, using English verse-forms, largely
for a mainland English readership, and shuddered with contempt at the
bog-ridden indigenous Papist peasantry. Romantics could see that the old
world was sickening unto death, and that new bodies politic, supported by
new societies and cultures, had to be born. But just how to conceive
national movements from the marriage of idealities and practicalities
baffled even the most thoughtful amongst them.

There is thus something intrinsically and astonishingly complex about
Romanticism. Here the contrast with earlier movements, combining
thought and action, is revealing. For all its local differences, the Reformation had possessed a substantial unity, grounded upon a common core
of beliefs (the truth of Scripture, the primacy of faith, etc.), and is readily
enough identified with social forces which overall can be called historically
'progressive'. The same is true of the Enlightenment. The aspirations and
programmes of *philosophes* in London and Paris, Turin and Berlin
espoused common criticism of the ignorance, superstition, bigotry, and
injustice of the *ancien régime*, and a shared confidence in the powers of
reason to build a better world. In that cosmopolitan climate, it is not too
difficult to think of Hume and Diderot changing places, or to imagine
Joseph Priestley writing in Geneva (after all, Gibbon was scribbling away
just down the road in Lausanne). When the *philosophes* migrated, they
saw themselves more as cosmopolitans than as exiles. At least at some
level, all the leading Protestant Reformers, and all the Aufklärer were
clearly ranged on the same side, and they characteristically shared a
profound belief in both the duty and the possibility of public activism.

At once drawing upon and opposing the Enlightenment, Romanticism
presents a much more confused and contradictory picture. The degree to
which the Romantics were political animals must not of course be underestimated. Shelley quite explicitly spoke of poets as the unacknowledged
legislators of the world. The 'solitary' Wordsworth who 'wandered lonely
as a cloud' was the man who just a few years earlier had rushed off to
revolutionary Paris, and then, in disillusionment, had changed colours,
and wrote counter-revolutionary propaganda. As Dietrich von Engelhardt
emphasizes in his essay below, the metaphysical transcendentalism of

Schelling or Schlegel was not apolitical or above politics, but essentially expressed political preferences in a different tongue. The crucial point, however, is that in the maelstrom of the Revolution and its aftermath, there were no longer the easy targets and ready solutions which had united the *philosophes* – indeed, the Revolution itself had proved the nemesis of such optimism. What was to be done appeared ambiguously different to European Romantics operating from within diverse national, social, and cultural climates.

While not a few of this *avant garde* could repudiate the dynasticism of the *ancien régime*, they had no stomach for the shady realities of the bourgeois present. Bourgeois society was by no means living up to its aims, expressed clearly and concisely within the slogans of 'liberty, egality and fraternity'. In line with this, as Nietzsche pointed out, the Romantics (very much thanks to a religious upbringing) found the atheism of the *philosophes* inadequate and their mechanical materialism one-sided.

One by-product of the concern with these bourgeois social and philosophical propositions was the Romantic passion for the pre-bourgeois past. It turned into a rich as well as a barren soil for the growth of the arts, sciences, and politics. For this the Romantics naturally looked within their own nations, seeking to put down new roots in history, in folklore and folksong, in pure, indigenous traditions of language, speech, and expression, in bards and ballads. Throughout a Europe recoiling from a French domination which could pretend to advance *universal* progress and rationality, Romantics aimed to uncover a national character and even 'racial' continuities through which the past, embodied in living memory, could speak to, guide, and nurture the present. Sometimes, as with the extraordinarily influential Ossianic writings or the Welsh epics 'edited' by Iolo Morganwg, the boundary between 'discovering' and 'inventing' became utterly blurred. In all such matters, national distinctions remain crucial. Take the burning topic of language reform. In newly independent Greece, for instance, the mother tongue being recovered and advocated by one group of enthusiasts was not any old folk dialect, but the very speech of Classical Antiquity itself! Even so, it may overall be said that one common thread to Romanticism across Europe was the forging of historical myths to bolster indigenous national cultures. (It was, of course, a 'uniting' feature destined itself to produce disunity.)

But no longer did there seem any unique rational blueprint for action applicable simultaneously to the Greeks, rebelling against the rule of the infidel, the Poles oppressed by Czarist Russia, the Dutch or the Spaniards so recently occupied by revolutionary France, or indeed the Welsh, irremediably enveloped within the overwhelmingly larger culture of England. Romanticism spurred patriotism and nationalism, but that in itself proved double-edged, creating across Europe a chaos of rival and competing Romanticisms; everywhere the oppressed were battling against oppressors who themselves were oppressed by larger empires. Did Swiss Romantics ever think of themselves as *Swiss*, or solely as Genevans, Vaudois, Bernese, or whatever?

Let us now move our eyes forward very briefly to the Congress of Vienna (1815). There are various viewpoints about its place in history which, obviously, cannot be discussed here. But whatever the viewpoint, the pursuit of individualism and liberty that animated the Romantics was emphatically not the concern of the rulers and statesmen who worked out the settlement of Europe after the defeat of Napoleon. There were amongst the Romantics those who responded by expressing detachment, irony, and nihilistic despair that signalled a growing conviction of the impossibility, irrelevance, or futility of direct social involvement. It was that hopeless sense of alienation from purposeful action produced by what Goya termed the 'desastres de la guerra' which encouraged the retreat of men such as Châteaubriand and Stendhal into a wistful solipsism and Hölderlin into *Weltschmerz*. Many saw themselves as strangers in their own society. Not by initial choice, but by necessity and anguished experience, Romantic thinkers and artists found the divide between the world of action and the world of thought, the real and the ideal, ever widening. Some hoped to transcend this dilemma, by making 'destiny their choice' – indeed, often national destiny (Pushkin, Mickiewicz); or by creating an intellectual and artistic *moi romantique* which celebrated the quest for a grail within, or which chronicled man at war with himself (Lermontov). Such Romantic experiences of 'polarity' – self and other – connect with the key concepts of the developing knowledge of electricity – attraction and repulsion. They clearly find widespread usage in the Naturphilosophie movement which proved such an influence on science and metaphysics in Germany and in other parts of Northern Europe.

Of course, more complex factors were at work in the growing ambivalence – alienation even – which men of letters felt towards their milieu. Heroic and anti-heroic Romantics ceaselessly lambasted the philistine petty-mindedness of their age. But they did so as a newly fledged intelligentsia, flexing its muscles, well aware that though they might be biting the hand that fed them, that hand would nevertheless not be withdrawn. For that age of chaos looked to writers and thinkers for guidance and example as never before. Poets and playwrights, critics, intellectuals, and journalists were themselves conspicuous beneficiaries of an increasingly literate culture, hungry for opinions, and clamouring to worship the Napoleons of the novel, of epic poetry, of the symphony or opera. The Enlightenment had proved the critical power of the pen. But it was during the Romantic age that living writers – Sir Walter Scott, Byron, Victor Hugo, Goethe, and so forth – became a new priesthood (Coleridge's 'clerisy'), the paramount shapers of contemporary culture and the creators of the allusions by which peoples lived, and the reflections of the realities in which they lived. Their own not seldom restless lives – *la vie Bohème* – mirrored and modelled their times. Writers and artists attained a cultural influence hitherto unthinkable.

But the consequences were deeply ambiguous. Romanticism offered avenues a-plenty to make sense of or mask the often distasteful realities of oligarchic societies undergoing traumatic capitalist development, industrialization, urbanization, and proletarianization. They conjured up myths of the glories of the past, the drama of the inner self as hero, spiritual voyages into the religious and the transcendental, and a communion with the mountains. Especially in Protestant nations such as Holland and Sweden, but also in Catholic Poland, Romanticism could ally with faith to generate the last great religious 'new awakening' of Western Christendom. Frequently the result was mere escapism. When fleshed out into nationalist and racial fantasies, it might not be so innocent. The Romantics liked to forge solacing ideologies for the developing bourgeois societies they so profoundly despised.

As will be perfectly obvious, this book has no pretensions to completeness. The inevitable limitations of space have meant that consideration of some nations has had to be excluded in order to make way for others. The reasonably familiar cases of Italy and Scotland, for example, are absent, as is North America; but the relatively little-known experiences of (say) Wales, Hungary, or Spain do receive extensive coverage. The written word receives most attention, but broader cultural considerations such as debates over language have been given considerable prominence, and some contributors have chosen to emphasize other cultural forms such as painting. The balance of subject matter has of course been dictated by national cultural differences. In Greece, for instance, Romanticism primarily took literary forms; in Sweden, by contrast, science, philosophy, and scholarship were the media through which Romantic outlooks were largely expressed. Where the actual literary or philosophical works of particular nations may well be relatively unfamiliar to most English readers – as, say, in the case of Poland or Hungary – our contributors have chosen to devote greater space to exegesis of the leading writings involved, or, as in the case of Holland, to the careers of the key individuals. Overall, the project has aimed, however, to bring out those most Romantic themes, diversity in unity, and unity in diversity.

READING SUGGESTIONS

Each chapter in this book is extensively footnoted or contains a substantial bibliography of works pertaining both to the nation in question and to the general problems of Romanticism. Any attempt to present a substantial general bibliography here would thus be otiose, particularly as recent general books, dealing with the conceptual problems of Romanticism, already discuss the critical, scholarly, and historiographical issues. For example Jerome J. McGann's *The Romantic Ideology. A Critical Investigation* (Chicago and London, 1983) offers a wide-ranging evaluation of current meanings of Romanticism. Earlier assessments are contained in A. O. Lovejoy's 'On the discrimination of Romanticisms', *Publications of the Modern Language Association*, 39 (1924), 229–53, and René Wellek, 'The concept of Romanticism in literary scholarship', *Comparative Literature*, 1 (1949), 1–23 and 147–72. On the history of the word, consult Hans Eichner (ed.), *'Romantic' and Its Cognates: The European History of a Word* (Toronto, 1972), and also Northrop Frye (ed.), *Romanticism Reconsidered* (New York, 1963).

For lucid, broad-ranging histories of the Romantic movement in the arts and literature, see Anthony Thorlby, *The Romantic Movement* (London, 1955); H. G. Schenk, *The Mind of the European Romantics* (London, 1966); L. R. Furst, *Romanticism in Perspective* (London, 1969); Jacques Barzun, *Classic, Romantic and Modern* (New York, 1961); Ugo Cardinale (ed.), *Problemi del Romanticismo* (Milan 1983); and Howard Mumford Jones, *Revolution and Romanticism* (Cambridge, Mass., 1974).

1

Romanticism in Wales

GWYN A. WILLIAMS

Romanticism in a 'Country in the World's back-side, where every Man is born a Gentleman and a Genealogist'[1] has come under the scrutiny of the recently published *Oxford Companion to Welsh Literature* (Oxford 1986). It detects some 'pre-romantic nostalgia' in the eighteenth-century verse of Evan Evans (Ieuan Fardd) who in terms of a genuine Welsh poetic tradition was a 'Classicist', and in that of the great Methodist hymnist William Williams Pantycelyn who virtually invented what has become a characteristically Welsh genre. It can scarcely fail to take cognisance of the literally epoch-making achievements of Iolo Morganwg (Edward Williams) who invented a history of the Welsh and bestowed on Wales a novel cultural institution which has since become virtually a symbol of its nationhood.

The *Companion*'s tone, however, is magisterial: 'It was not until much later, in the nineteenth century, that the Romantic sensibility could be clearly identified.'

Yet, in the late eighteenth century, Wales produced a Romantic hero second to none and produced him, moreover, in the context of an intellectual ferment which cries aloud for orchestration by Hector Berlioz – and which was, in truth, orchestrated in part by Franz Joseph Haydn and the Czech composer Koželuh with some assistance from Walter Scott and the Mrs Hemans who wrote 'The boy stood on the burning deck . . . '.

The hero emerged in the unlikely person of John Evans, a Methodist of Waun-Fawr near Caernarfon.[2] At the age of 22, John Evans threw up family and career in 1792 to embark on an epic journey of discovery and self-discovery in quest of an elusive Welsh grail and to suffer sorrows worthy of Werther. Moved by a sense of historic mission which had possessed him, he drove himself to London to seek the support of the vivacious Welsh society of the Gwyneddigion, then in the throes of rescuing a Welsh past and building a Welsh future upon it. Losing patience, Evans borrowed his passage money and crossed in the steerage to

Baltimore in the American Republic. After a spell among the American Welsh, he set off, alone, to cross the wilderness of Kentucky and Ohio, where Indian war was raging, to stumble into the Spanish territory of Louisiana in 1793 and find a home with a Welsh family in New Madrid. In the summer, losing patience again, he set out with a companion to make his way up the largely unexplored Missouri through hostile Indians. Lost, sun-baked and broken, he reeled back to the American side of the Mississippi, but after a stint with a Canadian fur company, he tried his luck again and around Christmas 1794 crossed into Spanish St Louis, to be jailed as a British spy.

Rescued by friends, he at last found an instrument for his mission in Spain's Missouri Company, launched by a Welsh West Indian. The Scotsman James McKay took on Evans as his second-in-command in the last, great Spanish imperial enterprise in North America. It was John Evans who became the first white man to make his way up the Missouri to its great bend, to find the Mandan Indians, the legendary 'white' and 'civilised' Indians whose ghost haunted the minds of white America. He lived with them through a Dakota winter, fought off the Canadians to hold them for Spain (and hence a few years later, for the USA). Forced to pull out, he returned to Louisiana, to be taken into the home of the Governor and to collapse into disillusionment, drink and destruction. Don Juan Evans, Sieur Evans of the Western Sea, aged 29, died in New Orleans in 1799.

What was the historic mission which turned this young Welsh Methodist (who, as a Jacobin democrat, duly defected to the Baptists and the Freemasons) into the last of the Spanish conquistadors and a pioneer of American exploration? His mission was to re-establish contact with the Lost Brothers of the Welsh Nation, those Welsh Indians who were descended from a colony planted on the Gulf of Mexico by the Welsh Prince Madoc who had discovered America in 1170, 300 years before Columbus.

The epic myth of Madoc had emerged in the sixteenth century from sketchy origins in medieval Welsh romance.[3] It was born together with the new 'Britain' invented by the Tudors, a dynasty regarded as 'Welsh' west of Offa's Dyke. This first Britain was built upon the elimination of Welsh distinctiveness. Hitherto a patchwork of jurisdictions derived from Marcher lordships and a principality which the Crown had acquired by conquest from Welsh princes, Wales was entirely absorbed into the shire, legal and political system of England, with English as its sole official language; local power passed to its emerging gentry who rode the tide of a new merchant capitalism. The native language was dismissed from official life, the native culture expelled to an unregarded margin, the Welsh guild of professional poets and its patronage structure was dislocated. In counterpoint, the Tudors were forced to authorise a Protestant Bible in Welsh, which proved to be the sheet-anchor of the language's survival; and the first massive intrusion of the Welsh into all levels of English society, notably into Humanist scholarship, buttressed a virtual take-over of Tudor 'national' ideology and mythology by the legendary Welsh vision of an ancient, lost 'Britain', which a dynasty claiming descent from Arthur found necessary and useful. This dialectic of identity reached a climax under Elizabeth, when the new 'British' Welsh enjoyed an unwonted prestige. Even as the last Welsh poets of the professional guild struggled to re-organise their dissolving order in the last of their *eisteddfodau* (competitive literary colloquia), Dr John Dee, a London-Welshman of the new Renaissance breed and *magus* to Elizabeth and her sea-dogs, was coining for his 'Welsh' queen the very expression 'British Empire' and launching an avidly welcomed and Arthurian Madoc at the Spaniards, to challenge their monopoly of the New World.

This 'Cambro-British' and imperial legend, despite its acquisition of a supplementary Welsh-Indian myth in the seventeenth century, went into eclipse during that century, even as Wales itself, its identity dribbling away after the Civil War, slumped, in English estimation, into a stagnant and often despicable, provincial obscurity. It revived in the America of the eighteenth century in a complex interplay of exploration, encounter with novel peoples, Welsh settlement and, not least, a conflict of rival imperialisms, British, Spanish, American, over the Far West and its furs. The legend in its novel form recrossed the Atlantic to penetrate Britain in a scurry of reports, to climax in a learned study by a London-Welsh divine in 1791. The impact on Wales was explosive. This was a Wales which, after a century of growth as an export sector of the new imperial economy of 'Great Britain' was driving into an abrupt crisis of modernisation. Heavy industry thrust into the coalfields of the east and capitalist agriculture disrupted the west, its rural cloth industry in particular. This acceleration of economic growth accompanied a harsh, generation-long war against France in a society already divided by its first serious conflicts of political ideology in the age of the American and French Revolutions and witnessing the remorseless and rapid sweep of populist evangelical, and particularly Methodist, religion which was to transform a people in little more than a generation.

One product of the crisis of the cloth country of the west was a migration movement impregnated with the Madoc myth and its mission impulse. It was through the handfuls of (sometimes rough-hewn) Welsh intellectuals that the myth had circulated and among them the effect was more general. In many ways, the Madoc and Welsh-Indian myths were serving discontented, dissident and radical Welsh people much as the contemporary myth of the Freeborn Saxons and the Norman Yoke was serving their English counterparts: 'a branch of the Welsh Nation has preserved its independence even to this day!'. The reception of the Madoc legend in late eighteenth-century Wales and its London-Welsh extension can serve as a paradigm for a wider phenomenon. It lodged among intellectuals who for two generations had been labouring at a difficult task of *revival*, of recovery of lost literature, lost history, lost language. They had worked in a style which, in Welsh terms, was and had to be 'Classical'. In the late eighteenth century, such people adopted, indeed sometimes seem to explode into, a style which one has no hesitation in labelling 'Romantic'.

The man who inspired John Evans, for example, was a man of the Enlightenment and an intellectual of the rough-hewn variety whom Antonio Gramsci would certainly have dubbed 'organic'. At one of the new *eisteddfodau* held in 1791 in Llanrwst, a north Wales centre of the upland stocking trade, the crowds had thrust upon them a remarkable address *To All Indigenous Cambro-Britons*. This announced the discovery of the Welsh-Indians who 'are at this time a free and distinct people and have preserved their liberty, language and some traces of their religion to this very day', called for someone to be sent to establish contact and floated the idea of a Welsh liberty settlement in America alongside the Old Brethren.

Its author was William Jones of Llangadfan, a Montgomeryshire cloth parish in that upland core of Wales trapped in a bleak and unremitting poverty, where the farm-based cloth trade offered the only escape into a tolerable existence.[4] William Jones could certainly be counted a 'Romantic'. In the first place, convinced that the Welsh musical tradition was dead, he was an assiduous folksong collector – the very hallmark of a Romantic 'discoverer of the people' in his time. Most of the latter were, or tried to be, upper class. Thomas Percy the Northamptonshire cleric, for example, changed his name from Pearcy to sound more aristocratic and in his deliberately archaic *Reliques* of English song in 1765, spoke of 'minstrels' enjoying high status in medieval courts (which would certainly evoke echoes among the genuine historians of the Welsh).[5] He was typical. There were, however, folksong collectors who were truly 'of the people': the German Ludwig Tieck was the son of a ropemaker, the Finn Elias Lönnrot the son of a village tailor, the Serb Karadžić the son of a pesant. William Jones was of their company.

Born around 1729, he was said never to have left his native parish for more than a fortnight, trapped there by the desperate circumstances of his family. A country healer, he ran a school, but his pugnaciously rational and sceptical temper made him enemies wholesale. Undeterred, he built himself into an accomplished poet and musician, a sharp critic and a skilled antiquarian. He learned enough Latin to translate Horace and Ovid into tolerable Welsh verse and he was an amateur astronomer and physicist. During the anti-Jacobin witch-hunts of the 1790s, his mail was opened and he was leaned on; he died as poor as he had lived.

William Jones was as 'Romantic' as any of his European confrères. He created a legendary Madocian America to rescue his people from the Egyptian slavery of the English. He created an imaginary history of Wales which was one endless struggle against English oppression, from Edward I's legendary 'massacre of the bards' to the insufferable English arrogance of bishops who were destroying the Welsh Church which dated from Joseph of Arimathea. He wrote a Welsh national anthem *Toriad y Dydd* (*Daybreak*) to loosen the grip of *The Roast Beef of Old England*.

Yet William Jones was better informed on America than many of His Majesty's Ministers. His proposals for an Incorporated Company, to arrange the wholesale transfer of the Welsh to the Missouri, are actuarially sound. His scholarly work is scientific. To the end of his days, this man was a devoted admirer of Voltaire. Confronted with him – and he was in several ways exemplary – one is tempted to suggest that in Wales, and in any country like Wales, the very Enlightenment was itself 'Romantic', of necessity.

The *eisteddfod* at Llanrwst where William Jones circulated his address, was in no sense some archaic survival.[6] The new *eisteddfodau* of the 1790s were an innovation grounded in that sober and sustained research which had been made necessary by the disappearance of any poets' assemblies which could be considered traditional. While medieval Wales was rich in verse forms, often closely associated with quite complex song, the central tradition had been that of professional poets who had also served as genealogists and historians – remembrancers in brief – to princes, nobility and gentry. They had been a strictly disciplined guild, close and secretive, with examinations in the complicated 24 classical metres and their elaborate systems of alliteration and internal rhyme (*cynghanedd*). Assemblies to regulate the guild had been held periodically, oral 'statutes' promulgated. Two *eisteddfodau* of this kind were held in the sixteenth century, at Caerwys in 1523 and 1567, but they were in fact symptoms of disintegration. Despite the efforts of the Tudor Humanists, the guild would not or could not modernise itself and its structure of patronage collapsed with the advance of merchant capitalism and the English language. During the seventeenth century the *eisteddfod* tradition disappeared, its records buried away in manuscript collections known to none save a Gideon's Army of dedicated copiers.

Many relics and echoes of this tradition survived among the amateur poets scattered about the country and pub competitions were sometimes staged under the name of *eisteddfodau*, but when Siôn Rhydderch of Machynlleth tried to revive the more rigorous form, wrote a grammar to explain it and hawked it all over Wales in the early eighteenth century, he found it very hard going. From the 1770s, no doubt because of the slow seeping of knowledge from private collections, there are signs of greater ambition. Glamorgan, around its poets' clans near Bridgend and among Dissenting ministers in its hill country, Unitarian in persuasion and antiquarian in passion, generated a society of poets at Llantrisant which attracted the young Iolo Morganwg when he was still plain Ned Williams the stonemason. Under his impulse this tried, in vain, to set itself up as a kind of academy under the name of the Gwrth-Hengistiaid (Anti-Hengistians, Anti-Saxons).[7]

The breakthrough came in north Wales, characteristically in response to Thomas Pennant's celebrated *Tours* which paid much attention to the Caerwys *eisteddfodau* of the sixteenth century. Along with Pennant and after him came a swelling tide of English, gentlemanly and scholarly tourists in search of the 'sublime' and the 'grotesque'. The first of the new *eisteddfodau* in 1789 were held in towns on the tourist route, Llangollen, Corwen and Bala. What gave the movement power, however, was the commitment to it of the active and enthusiastic London-Welsh society of the Gwyneddigion which from the 1780s took over the lead given earlier by the Augustan circle of the Morris brothers of Anglesey, the poet Goronwy Owen and the London society of the Cymmrodorion. The Gwyneddigion were able to build on that earlier research and, infinitely better equipped than predecessors, to exploit the very modernisation of Wales. Moreover, these men were seized of a wider vision; they were acutely aware of the antiquity of the lost tradition. They were even more aware of the challenge to regenerate an old people which the American and even more the French Revolutions were posing to all the little, lost peoples of Europe. The first of their *eisteddfodau* were held as the Bastille fell; the first competition titles resound to the call of Liberty: their prize medals were struck by M. Dupré who was to become official engraver to the French Republic. They were well on the road to a romantic millenarianism when they were engulfed by Iolo Morganwg with his extravagant but breath-taking claims to an antiquity of Welsh tradition stretching back through Druids to the very Patriarchs, with his elaborate structure of ritual, philosophy and cabalistic practice Barddas (Bardism), with his brand-new if 'ancient' Order of Bards of the Island of Britain.

Yet Iolo Morganwg, very arch-demon of this transformation, himself exemplifies the trajectory.[8] He was the man to whom John Evans directed his mission, the man who took over the Madoc myth and made it an 'idea-that-walks'. He went into total immersion in the historical record from the summer of 1792, creating his *Padouca Gazette Extraordinary*, as he shuttled between London, Bristol and his cottage at Flemingston in the Vale of Glamorgan. He emerged with an astonishing document, composed of some isolated facts elaborated into a coherent but utterly imaginary vision in his own 'improvements'. He duly delivered the text to the Royal Society. He coupled it, however, with a plan, circulated to friends and the American Ambassador, for a Welsh liberty settlement to be located near the Lost Brothers, the Mandans on the Missouri. It was to be run by an intellectual elite not unlike his Order of Bards and he was able to enlist the hard-headed support of a St Louis merchant. Moreover, the work on the project which he did, which we can follow from his copious notes, in fact used the best scientific sources of his age. Iolo Morganwg was working like a dedicated scholar of the Enlightenment in the service of a Romantic delusion.

The particular bundle of sensations and ratiocinations which consti-tuted the mind of these men may defy neat categorisation but it is not unfamiliar. It finds a European exemplar, whose resonance was no less European, in the celebrated Constantin François Chassebeuf de Volney and his *Ruins of Empires*.[9] An Orientalist who haunted the salons of d'Holbach and Madame Helvétius, a man of 1789 who became a Napoleonic Count, Volney published *Les Ruines, ou méditation sur les révolutions des empires* in 1791. Its hero, meditating in melancholy on the fate of mankind at the site of an ancient ruin in the East, is wafted into outer space by a painfully rational Génie, there to survey the progress of the human race towards emancipation. The most recent scientific interpretations are skilfully communicated and all the religions of earth mercilessly dissected and discarded. It is virtually a populist climax to the Enlightenment. Yet the whole book is drenched in the new Romanticism; it had a profound influence on Chateaubriand; with its powerful, terse, evocative prose, it is a *tour de force*.

Not only does Volney himself, in his own genre, exemplify the dichotomy which characterised many Welsh intellectuals; he gained a European reputation. In England, there were at least eleven different editions of Volney between 1792 and 1822. In particular, Volney's *Ruins* became a classic text for the new working-class movements, especially their Infidel, freethinking core. More striking, the politically critical chap-ter 15 of this work, a celebrated Dialogue between the People and the Privileged, appeared in Welsh a good three years *before* the first effective English translation (though, for that matter, both Goethe's *Werther* and a Beaumarchais play were broadcast in Wales within a year of publication). More striking still, the Welsh translation appeared in the *Cylchgrawn*

Cymraeg (*Welsh Journal*) of 1793, the first Welsh periodical to discuss political issues. Its editor was Morgan John Rhys, a Baptist minister of Pontypool who was of liberal and rational bent, though he shared in the scholarly millenarianism characteristic of liberal Dissent at the time, of which Dr Joseph Priestley was an ornament.[10] But he was possessed of the need to 'raise up an old people'. When the Revolution broke out, he crossed to France to preach the rational liberty of a purified Protestant tradition. Driven home by war in Europe, he tried to organise mass translations of a Puritan Bible into French. He launched his Welsh journal in the same cause. It was a thoroughly Enlightened production in the best rational-religious style. Yet it printed not only Volney, but a summons to the renaissant Welsh by a liberal and democratic shade of Prince Madoc – *Dyma ni yn awr ar daith ein gobaith*. Here we are now on the journey of our hope.

Driven out by the reaction, Morgan John Rhys appointed himself Moses to a regenerated Welsh nation, crossed to America in John Evans's footsteps, went on an epic horse-back tour of the new republic, fought for a black church in Savannah and for Indian rights at the peace talks in Ohio and finally launched a Welsh settlement in Beula, Pennsylvania. He left behind him a potent dynasty of Jeffersonian Democrats.

The kind of 'Romanticism' displayed in this trajectory had strict limits. While many of its symptoms are familiar and individuality abounded, of 'individualism' there was little. There was hardly any scope for it in an enterprise directed at saving, restoring or asserting a people and its culture against the odds. This is even more true of that Other Face of Romanticism which some have detected in Methodism. The peculiar personal intensity of Methodism in particular and of Welsh evangelicalism in general did not lack the attributes of Romanticism as generally defined, including its displaced eroticism, but the Biblical and missionary discipline and field of reference, for all the abundance of its vivid imagery, denied uninhibited individualism any effective autonomy. Both tendencies reflected not only the exigencies of their respective missions, but the particular predicament of the people to whom they self-consciously directed themselves.

For the Welsh in the eighteenth and early nineteenth centuries fit with a disconcerting neatness into that category of peoples whom Marx and Engels, in the bitterness of defeat over 1848–9, brutally classified as 'non-historic': small, of no account, the debris of a past – a people whose history and traditions had been disrupted, whose language had lost status and threatened to dissolve into a mess of patois, a people without historical memory or an educational structure or a commercial or academic system to nurture scholarship, criticism, even conventional publication, a people which lacked even the vestiges of a state and was doomed to disappear.

It was precisely among peoples so designated (and so prematurely discounted) that the tendencies towards revival and re-assertion, so abruptly accelerated in response to the French Revolution, generated many of those sometimes startling phenomena which can be identified as 'Romantic'. Certainly anyone at all familiar with contemporary movements among Europe's 'non-historic' peoples is transfixed when he turns to Wales and encounters what, at first sight, seem movements which are identical. Finns, Serbs, Czechs, Slovaks, Catalans – and Welsh – all seem, on first hearing, to speak with the same range of voices. In my own case, the 'shock of recognition' came with work on the Czechs and Slovaks under the Habsburgs where the ubiquitous *presence* of a dominant, indeed hegemonic, external culture seemed to mirror with uncanny precision that of English in Wales. So powerful was this sense of kinship that in one essay on eighteenth-century Wales, I was driven to exclaim that if Welsh people as a whole behaved like Slovaks, their intellectuals behaved more like Czechs!

Second readings brought second thoughts, since the Welsh experience (no doubt like all the others!) was *sui generis*. The European dimension remains critical, not least because before the novel invention, 'Great Britain', moved away from Europe into world empire, dragging its Welsh province with it, Welsh cultures in their native form had in truth been more 'European' than 'English' in style. An entry into the labyrinth can perhaps be effected through Peter Burke's account of the 'discovery of the people' in late eighteenth-century Europe, which prefaces his encyclopedic survey of popular culture in earlier centuries.[11] To what extent, if any, does Wales follow a common pattern in this continent-wide shift in sensibilities which generated so much of what we call Romanticism?

Peter Burke suggests that 'popular culture', considered as something remote, even exotic, particularly pure and on the very lip of extinction, 'was discovered – or was it invented? – by a group of German intellectuals at the end of the eighteenth century' – among a people who were dispersed and lacked specifically national institutions. He cites the familiar and fertile source of Herder, in his prize essay of 1778 on the broken bond between poetry and morals, the loss of a genuine popular poetry, the need to recover the pure poetry of an 'organic community' among peoples considered 'wild' and 'primitive'. Herder's stress on folksong, *Volkslied*, in his collections of 1774 and 1778, taken up by the Grimm brothers in the next generation, echoed across Europe, among Russians from 1804, Germans from 1806, Serbs and Swedes from 1814 (in England the search had started earlier with Thomas Percy in 1765). From song, the seekers were led to folk-tale, *Volkssage*, which the Grimms called 'children's tales' (echoed in the Welsh title *Mabinogion* which Lady Charlotte Guest gave to her translations of early Welsh stories from 1836), to folk-writing, *Volksbuch* (the English chapbooks and the Welsh almanacs), to folklore, *Volkskunde* (not rendered into English until 1846), to popular religion and superstition and to efforts to write the history of 'peoples', culminating in the early nineteenth-century work of such as Michelet and the Czech Palacký (who had gone folksong collecting in his youth, but who wrote in respectable German). The search transformed much of the tourism of the time into a search for the popular, the wild, the simple – Alberto Foris among the Dalmatians, Samuel Johnson and Boswell among their 'American savages' of Highlanders.

Burke detects some basic drives in this movement. There was a characteristically Romantic revolt against 'art' and the 'artificial', against the prison of classicism. It hungered for the exotic, the wild, the natural. Hence, he argues with reason, the extraordinary popularity of *Ossian*, the Gaelic poet allegedly of the third century, 'translated' and largely created by James Macpherson in the 1760s, who was translated into ten European languages and echoed through heads as diverse as those of the Mendelssohn of Fingal's Cave, of Goethe, Napoleon and Chateaubriand. What caught their imaginations was the image of a Celtic Homer in all his 'simplicity, sublimity and fire'. The cult of 'The People' grew out of a pastoral tradition which cherished primitivism. It inevitably became a revolt against the Enlightenment and to some extent against Reason itself. This easily translated into a revolt against France – which nevertheless imitated French modes – and an assertion of nationalism. The surge in Sweden seems to date from its loss of Finland to Russia in 1809. The Finns had to assert themselves against both Swedes and Russians. H. G. Porthan's Latin essay on Finnish poetry came out in 1766, but this search took on a deeper meaning after 1809. When Elias Lönnrot went up to Turku university, his professor urged him to collect folksongs and out of this enterprise grew the national epic of the Kalevala. Examples could be multiplied among the Slavonic peoples. Even where, as Burke puts it, 'it was too late', there was a nativistic effort to revive traditional culture in the teeth of alien domination – the Scotland of Walter Scott for example. What lent the movement force was that it could build on a much older antiquarian tradition which in the eighteenth century took on a sociological and anthropological character. What lent it passion was the sense of a culture on the very brink of extinction. The movement therefore centred on what Peter Burke misleadingly calls a 'cultural periphery' of Europe, which was rather the Europe of peoples who were fragmented, displaced, subjected or submerged. Germany was a heartland. In Spain, Andalucia was the focus. Folksongs were unearthed late in France and then primarily by Bretons. In Britain, popular culture was discovered by Scots rather than English.

Conspicuously absent from Peter Burke's 'periphery' are the Welsh. There is a brutally simple explanation: most of the relevant texts, past and present, are in the Welsh language, which few bother to learn. Indeed, one could argue that the very survival and development of Welsh has itself been a Romantic Odyssey of the first order! This primal disqualification has distorted the perception of the history of the Welsh which is common beyond Offa's Dyke. For the experience of the Welsh in some respects diverges quite sharply from the pattern sketched by Peter Burke. Only in one area can they be located with any security in this European jigsaw – music and the related theme of landscape-as-history. And here, Welsh self-expression was largely a response to, and was shaped by, the changing image of Wales cultivated by the utterly dominant and all-pervasive culture of England. One is strongly reminded of those later Welsh writers who tried desperately to live up to the idea of a Celtic Twilight after Matthew Arnold had invented it (traditional Welsh poetry, brilliant as a jewelled mosaic, terse and epigrammatic, is anything but 'twilit'), or of that celebrated French discovery of 'Spanish' music (essentially Andalucian and alien to most Spaniards) which became so all-embracing that, by the end of the nineteenth century, Spaniards were writing this kind of music themselves because, obviously, this was the 'natural' way for Spaniards to compose!

All the evidence suggests that traditional Welsh music disappeared in the late seventeenth century, along with the professional poets' guild (precisely the time when the new 'Great Britain' was taking shape).[12] Old Welsh instruments, the *crwth* (crowd), the *pibgorn* (hornpipe) vanished from common sight; the original, small and rather simple Welsh harp was displaced by the triple harp, a variant of the Italian baroque instrument. Robert ap Huw, who had been harpist to James I and died very old in 1665, left a large, manuscript album of traditional music; by the early eighteenth century, no scholar in Wales could decipher it. Wales was full of song, of *noson lawen* (folk-nights), competitions between players and singers, of *penillion*, impromptu, often witty or satirical stanzas sung to the harp, with competing singers struggling to keep up with the harpist's switches in melody. But the vast majority of the songs seem to have been English. The scholarly Morris brothers of mid-century, in some embarrassment, suggested that Welsh titles be invented for them as a disguise! Wales, like most places, had duly succumbed to the new harmonic music pouring out from the courts of Europe.

Yet there persisted some sense that Welsh music was very ancient. A major figure in what came to be regarded as a 'revival' was Blind John Parry (died 1782), a harpist employed by the magnate family of Williams Wynn in north Wales who became harpist to the Prince of Wales. A brilliant artist, veteran of competitions, known in London, Oxford and

Dublin, Parry was also versed in the 24 classical metres of Welsh poets and believed Welsh music to date from the Druids. He published the first wholly Welsh song collection *Antient British Music* in 1742. His major contribution was indirect. In 1755, the poet Thomas Gray read in Carte's history of England the story of the 'massacre of the bards' by Edward I after his conquest of Gwynedd (a legend derived from penal legislation against the poets' guild and loosed on the world by one of the arriviste gentry of Tudor times). He was moved to write a long poem on the theme, but suffered a writer's block. What unblocked him was a concert by Blind John Parry in Cambridge: 'Mr. Parry has been here, and scratch'd out such ravishing blind Harmony, such tunes of a thousand year old with names enough to choak you, as have set all this learned body a'dancing.'

Gray's *The Bard* set half of Europe a'dancing. The image of the last bard clutching his harp in defiance of the English king struck the resonant frequency of a generation. János Arany wrote his *The Welsh Bards* to capture the imagination of Hungary, where it still figures in the canon.[13] The word 'bard' had been in currency earlier, but it was now that *The Bard* began to tower over writing about Wales, not least by Welsh people (*bardd* in Welsh simply means poet). The drama soon penetrated painting. It was about the same time that the landscape of Wales, viewed as something peculiarly spiritual and historic, entered English consciousness. It was in 1750 that the painter Richard Wilson (1714–82) began to draw the rugged landscape of north Wales which so transformed his work, to evoke pity in Sir Joshua Reynolds but admiration in Constable. English gentlemen tourists who had read Gray responded more immediately. They sought out 'Wilson's Pools' and the site of 'The Bard's Last Stand'. Natives, more especially hotel-keepers, obligingly located them.

For this registering of a Romantic Wales in the sensibilities of the cultivated and fashionable coincided with a wave of tourism which, during the Napoleonic Wars when the continent was cut off, became a flood, a Petty displacing the Grand Tour. William Gilpin's tours of 1770 and 1773 set the tone, with their misty landscapes and their 'venerable substitutes of the ancient Cambrian bards'. The Welsh had shown little interest in their own landscape and the first advance guard of tourists left them stupefied: 'Have you no rocks or waterfalls in your own country?' By 1833, a grammar of Welsh published a century earlier had to carry an additional tourists' phrase-book in familiar style: 'Is there a waterfall in this neighbourhood? I long to see the monastery. I will take a gig to go there.' By the 1790s the Welsh were already drowning in a flood of travel literature which ranged from the biliously racist to the embarrassingly effuse.

Nothing could stand against the flood, for towering over it was the renowned figure of Thomas Pennant, the Welsh gentleman of Flintshire who made himself a naturalist of world repute. A serious antiquarian, Pennant, in his *Tours* of 1778–81, recreated a Wales genuine enough to stand scrutiny, but Romantic enough to be vulnerable to legend. His achievement was clinched by the magnificent landscapes of Turner on his tours of the 1790s. By the 1780s, portraits of Owain Glyn Dŵr (Glendower), rescued by Pennant, were already figuring in proud armour on hotel bills in Corwen and along the tourist Dee.

Accompanying this commandeering of a Welsh past and powering it, was another surge of interest in Welsh music, personified in Edward Jones, Bardd y Brenin (King's Bard), harpist to the Prince Regent, a brilliant artist for whom J. C. Bach wrote pieces, with his *The Musical and Poetical Relicks of the Welsh Bards* of 1784, its supplement in 1794, his *Bardic Museum* of 1802 and his *Hen Ganiadau Cymru* (*Old Songs of Wales*) in 1820. Jones briefly befriended Iolo Morganwg and dubbed this music 'Druidic'; after he, a royalist, had quarrelled with Iolo, 'The Bard of Liberty', he abandoned the Druids and settled for a simple 'Bardic' (reducing this music's ancestry to a mere 2,000 years or so). After Jones came John Parry, Bardd Alaw, who became director of music at Vauxhall Gardens in 1809 and who could, by this time, call on a network of the new *eisteddfodau* and a few musical societies. What seemed the ultimate warrant appeared in the energetic person of George Thomson, an Edinburgh publisher who had already commissioned Haydn to arrange Scottish folksongs. Thomson mobilised a small army of writers, most of them non-Welsh and including Walter Scott and Mrs Hemans, to compose suitably historic and heroic lyrics in English to Welsh airs, in what became the most celebrated of the collections in 1809. Among the most beautiful is *Eryri Wen* (*White Snowdon*) which in 1803 Franz Joseph Haydn in Vienna arranged to fit a ballad written by the Hon. W. Spencer around the famous and moving story of Gelert, the faithful hound of Llywelyn the Great in the early thirteenth century. That story had been invented in the 1790s by a hotel-keeper in Beddgelert (Gelert's Grave) to put his little village on the new tourist map.[14]

By the early nineteenth century, this drive had mobilised new talents in Wales to create an abundant corpus of song, which was as 'authentic' as anything could be, but which was steeped in the belief that the Welsh musical tradition was the oldest in Europe, with an aura about it derived from a very ancient, indeed to some minds Patriarchal, order co-eval with the birth of humankind. It was probably in the same period that *penillion* singing acquired the complex, contrapuntal, difficult form (not unlike the more sophisticated versions of the *cante jondo* of the Andalucians) of the present (perhaps because John Parry of Vauxhall wanted to make his competitions harder).[15] The process climaxed in the great Welsh collections of the 1840s and in the writing of a song which was to be accepted as the Welsh national anthem, *Hen Wlad fy Nhadau* (*Land of My Fathers*). The first attribute which its national anthem confers on Wales is its character as *gwlad beirdd a chantorion* – a land of poets and singers.

Prys Morgan has described this new departure in Welsh music as 'something simple and artless, either old or new, transformed into something highly self-conscious, elaborate and uniquely Welsh'. The music had acquired historical status, it was hugely enjoyable, it was intended for the people and it was deeply Welsh – it was an innovation derived from a Romantic re-reading and appropriation of a reconstructed past. Central to its emergence was the overpowering hegemony of English and its directive elite. It is perhaps for this reason that it is here that Welsh Romanticism most closely approximates to that of other 'non-historic' peoples in Europe.

In many other respects, it differs profoundly. Peter Burke has identified the three dynamic drives of this Romanticism derived from a 'discovery of the people' as communalism, purism and primitivism. Commenting on the weakness of their scholarship, their innate tendency towards 'improvement' and high-minded fabrication, he notes that this was an age when poets were antiquarians and antiquarians poets, adding that 'poets make poor editors'. True enough, no doubt, but Welsh poets *had always been* antiquarians. Welsh poets had not been poets as English uses the term; they had specific duties in and to society, a specific status, that of *remembrancer*, privileges, salaries, responsibilities. The spirit of this order survived the deaths of princes and, to a degree, the loss of gentry patronage, to haunt even the beery *eisteddfodau* of the eighteenth-century amateurs. When Welsh poet-antiquarians reached back beyond the great divide to re-discover the classical tradition, they were renewing contact with spiritual kin. Of communalism, the notion of communal creation – *das Volk dichtet* – they had nothing. They revelled in anonymous folksongs and no doubt felt that they expressed the innermost meaning of a people, but they cherished no illusion that they had grown out of the soil like a mountain mist. They knew that poems are written by poets and they delighted in tracing them and their inter-connections. Nor did they nurture any misty perception of one, undifferentiated and remote 'past'. However legendary the 'history' they believed in, it was a *history* they believed in, which they thought they could trace through the princes of the Middle Ages, back through Arthur and the emergence of a Wales out of Romano-Celtic Britain, back through the Britons into a remote 'Celtic' origin. This kind of Romanticism could be buttressed by a kind of rationalism.

Purism there was in abundance, but this was a purism which found expression in horror at the 'degeneration' of Welsh from an illustrious past, and a past more illustrious and 'copious' (a favourite word) than England's. In some parts of Europe at this time, the publication of a dictionary could be a revolutionary act. In Wales, dictionary-making became something of a national obsession, as these people modernised Welsh with a marvellous abandon (while working, of course, to the strictest of 'ancient principles' as they understood them). For this reason, primitivism was precisely what they did *not* embrace. On the contrary, they embraced all the conveniences of modernity with enthusiasm; they were 'restoring' and re-equipping a culture which had been elaborate, sophisticated and superior. What drove them on, above all, was enormous resentment at the denigration of all things Welsh by many English – the Gibberish of Taphydom. They were going to prove and then re-establish at least the equality of their own culture, with its ancient roots. They had no truck with any Luddism or worship of the uneducated. 'Counted among the uneducated' was Iolo Morganwg's description of the inheritors of Welsh tradition whom English civilisation had turned into 'un-persons'; his intention was to pillory that civilisation for its ignorant rejection of some of the most educated men on the Island. He hated the university of Oxford as cordially as he hated Methodists, but his Order of Bards was in effect a convocation for the award of bardic degrees. The preface to his *Poems Lyrical and Pastoral* of 1794 is a classically Romantic exercise in its portrait of a lonely, melancholy youth shunning the concourse of men and cultivating Mother Nature. It was of course poppycock, he spent his youth in total immersion in the uproarious and bilingual popular culture of Glamorgan; it was a product shrewdly geared to a new market. He might revel in his reception among the Romantic English poets as an Original Wild Welsh Bard (an image he unscrupulously cultivated, as Southey hailed him as Old Iolo, He Who Knows and crafted his backbreaking verse epic *Madoc*) but he revelled no less in the company of learned men and antiquarian Anglican bishops busily creating Wales's first university college in Lampeter – and woe betide anyone who treated him as some wild untutored Phoenix!

Iolo reminds one forcibly of the Serb Karadžić who, after the defeat of the Serb rebellion by the Turks in 1813, fled to the Habsburg lands, to be taken up by Kopitar, the Slovene imperial censor for Slavonic languages who showed him Herder's collection and urged him to collect folksongs. Karadžić brought his out in 1814, with a preface worthy of Iolo, full of simple, innocent hearts and songs learned at the feet of goatherds. When he was promptly taken up as an illiterate genius of a goatherd himself, he exploded in rage. He was in no sense in revolt against classicism or reason or the literary: 'Whatever man may have invented in this world, nothing can be compared with writing.' He wrote a Serbian grammar, spelling book and dictionary and his dearest ambition was to be awarded an honorary degree by a good German university. *Mutatis mutandis*, it is Karadžić who is the closest European parallel to the organic intelligentsia of the new Welsh.[16]

For this is precisely what they were. There were among them some, like Pennant, who could be counted top drawer; there were several 'gentlefolk in diminished circumstances', who made their way through the patronage of less diminished kin. But the London-Welsh were generally a bohemian intelligentsia living by their pens and wits and presided over by a currier turned fur merchant. Many came from the poverty-stricken Welsh clergy denied preferment by English bishops and many from the multiplying ranks of the cultivated but often artisan ministers of the Old Dissent; Iolo himself was a stonemason. They emerged precisely from those 'middle and lower orders' who in the late eighteenth century throughout Europe (and much of the Americas) generated not only this Romantic nationalist thrust, but the democratic ideology itself. They were members of a novel organic intelligentsia which the growth of imperial Great Britain created in its Welsh province. For, whereas in Europe, the logical terminus of this kind of Romantic movement was an idealisation of 'The Peasant', it is doubtful whether, outside a few isolated, mountainous districts, there *were* any 'peasants' in eighteenth-century Wales.[17]

Half a million people, many of them poor, many of them trapped on traditional small farms, many tramping seasonally, as skinny as their cattle, into England to be fed, many still pinned to the mountain core of Wales's hollow heart, were in the eighteenth century recruited into an export sector of the new Great Britain. Of British copper production, 90 per cent was concentrated around Swansea and Neath, linked to the mines of Anglesey, with virtually a world monopoly, directed to the Atlantic. Iron and related industries, a sixth of basic British production in the earlier years, had commandeered two-fifths of it by the 1790s, with rapidly growing concentrations on the coalfields of north-east and south-east. Lead and every usable mineral were worked with increasing intensity and there were the beginnings of another British monopoly in slate. The cloth trade, having migrated to mid- and north Wales, was turning whole tracts of apparently rural Wales into something like a factory-parish whose output, even that of the poor stockingers in the hills, was directed to Atlantic export. A network of tiny but lively towns, overstaffed with artisans, printers and professional people, buttressed a brisk fraternity of seamen and shipmasters along the western coasts. As the population explosion registered in rural districts, to spill over into accelerating urban growth from the 1780s, there was a measured but remorseless increase in the numbers of artisans, craftsmen, agents of the service trades, shopkeepers, teachers, lawyers, doctors, the 'lower-middle classes' conjured up by merchant capitalism, even as the multitudinous lesser gentry stumbled and lost footing.

Above them, from mid-century, those gentry and magnates who regulated much of their lives experienced a radical transformation. This was most unhinging in regions geared to the new economy like Glamorgan whose notables, wealthier by far than their European equivalents and in demographic crisis, with a rapid turn-over in families, had located their societies squarely within the 'blue-water' strategy of mercantile Britain and prepared them for the imminent and explosive entry of industrial capitalism. Glamorgan had its counterparts in Monmouthshire, Denbighshire and the north-east, in modernising Anglesey, and the same impulses could be sensed within the more traditional societies west of the central massif. It was from the middle years of the century that the language barrier between masses and classes hardened, to be reinforced by religious differentiation, that complaints multiplied that the leaders of Welsh society had abandoned their traditional role as protectors and patrons of the nation's culture. Under their leadership, Wales, shedding the last vestiges of its peculiar identity, seemed to be disappearing into the hegemonic culture of England almost as completely as the Slovaks seemed to have disappeared into the Magyar culture of Hungary.

Into this vacuum flowed a rising tide of popular literacy in Welsh. Over the late seventeenth and early eighteenth centuries, the culture of the printed book had rooted itself in Wales and the Welsh language in a dedicated enterprise powered by the religious zeal of displaced Puritans and the more evangelical Anglicans.[18] It developed through a series of school-building enterprises, to climax in the circulating schools of Griffith Jones, intensive courses aimed at adults as much as children, employing a monitor system, using the Bible as sole text, and geared to the rhythms of living and working of hill communities of the poor. Jones's schools were a stunning success; they attracted the attention of Catherine the Great of Russia. By the third quarter of the eighteenth century, they had probably made a majority of a still largely monoglot people (though an instrumental knowledge of English was widespread and growing) technically literate in Welsh. The Welsh people learned to read in terms of the Bible and Protestant sectarianism.[19]

This was one root of the Welsh Methodist movement, which started independently of that in England, from young Anglican converts who started to preach in the 1730s, to build up small societies of earnest people, at first concentrated in areas where the Old Dissent was already a presence, in south and east. There was a second wave, powered by the hymns of William Williams Pantycelyn from 1762, as Dissent itself began to catch the fire. A third wave followed in the next generation as the movement penetrated north and west and a climax came in the 1790s, as the new industrial capitalism thrust into Wales, to create novel societies in the east and disrupt old ones in the west, and as the long wars against France became a forcing-house of change. In 1811, the Methodists were compelled to break from the Church of England, to join Dissent and enroll perhaps 15 per cent of the population in Nonconformity. By 1851 and the first religious census, Nonconformity embraced 75 per cent of the Welsh. This is one of the most remarkable and swift transformations in the history of any people. In a very real sense, it marks the emergence of a new and alternative Wales which, by the middle of the nineteenth century, was to win its political triumph.

Many have seen a kind of Romanticism in this form of evangelicalism. William Williams Pantycelyn (1717–91) was called the last lyric poet of south Wales at the time and the first Romantic poet by Dr Saunders Lewis in our own century. Certainly in his huge output and especially in his hymnal *Mor o Wydr* (*Sea of Glass*) (1762), there is a passion, conviction and sincerity, expressed in an accessible yet vaulting Welsh, which make his hymns lyric or tragic poetry of a high order. They were, moreover, aimed at the people and they reached the people. The hymn, the singing festival (which could run for hours, even days), swept over all the sects and Pantycelyn was foremost in that cultural obsession which has made hymns in general, and his hymns in particular, central to a 'Welsh Way of Life'. Coupled with these and a legion of teaching tracts, was his *Theomemphus*, a long allegorical novel in verse on the spiritual odyssey of an individual. This deeply personal outpouring does bear the imprint of sensibilities of a more secular familiarity. Yet it is difficult simply to accept them as 'Romantic'. The discipline of the Bible, of Calvin, the remorselessly didactic character of the writing, in fact imprison the individual. The release, notably in communal hymn-singing – which could develop into a form of mass possession, with much holy rolling and jumping and speaking with voices – may have been 'ecstasy', but it would be rash to classify it as 'Romanticism', except in a displaced, indeed, distorted, form. A better case can be made, perhaps, for Ann Griffiths (1776–1805), a convert who came from a family of poets, whose prose was a classic religious masterpiece. Her 74 hymns are an extraordinarily powerful evocation of intensely personal religious experience – and they were not meant to be sung in congregation. In a sense, they could be counted a 'Romanticism' of social withdrawal.[20]

In a wider sense, this term could be applied to the movement as a whole. Alongside the hymn-festivals and the mass ecstasy went a relentless growth of highly organised societies ranked in a rigid hierarchy, controlled by men like John Elias, who could be called a Pope with his Bulls of Bala; the discipline was an iron Calvinism, complete with heresy-hunting and an often narrow-minded bigotry. The high intellectual level of the first generations was not maintained in the bleak early years of the nineteenth century, a time of *crach-pregethwyr* (quack-preachers), a 'revival every seven years', and a mind-bending philistinism which could be not merely anti-intellectual but hostile to all forms of spontaneity. There was nothing very 'Romantic' about this species of practice which virtually 'withdrew' thousands of people from society – to such an extent that the radicalising of the Methodists, when it came, was experienced as a kind of 're-entry'.[21]

What is certain is that Methodism and the kind of Old Dissent which responded to it was regarded by these recoverers of a people's past, who generated their own form of Romanticism, as a deadly enemy. Methodists they blamed for the disappearance of the old, free-and-easy Wales they cherished. To the born-again Christians, the past was a tale told by an idiot. They had no truck with any search for purity in language; Pantycelyn addressed the Almighty in the ordinary spoken Welsh of Carmarthenshire. The Methodists and their kin were cutting the people off from their past and were concerned with the present only as preparation for Eternity. This was anathema to the Romantic nationalists, who found friends rather in that minority sector of Dissent which embraced the Enlightenment and moved, in extreme cases, towards Unitarianism and even Deism, and which responded to the challenge of the 1790s, when Wales became a cauldron of competing ideologies, in much the same manner as the nationalists. Some of the earlier leaders of Methodism were friendly with the leaders of the Welsh revival and displayed a mild interest in history. When Howel Harris, a giant among them, set up a community in Trefecca, Breconshire, modelled on the Moravian Brethren, he indulged in the newly fashionable styles of Chinese and Gothic. But these flickers, wan at the best of times, soon snuffed out. To the men engaged in what was, in practice, an enterprise in 'rescue archaeology' on Welsh tradition, evangelicalism, and Methodism in particular, the unspeakable and dreadfully successful rival, presented a face of brass. When Iolo Morganwg wrote to William Owen from north Wales in 1799, he was in despair: 'North Wales is now as Methodistical as South Wales and South Wales as Hell!'

The relatively abrupt take-off into a Romantic mode which characterised Iolo's generation took its rise from two generations of slow, painful labour against the odds to re-establish the language and recover its lost literary tradition.[22] It had a firm grounding in the magnificent and subtle scholarship of Edward Lhuyd, keeper of the Ashmolean Museum in Oxford, in the first and only volume of his *Archaeologia Britannica* of 1707. Among a wealth of other riches, this offered Welsh, in a discriminating, comparative study of Breton, a distinguished and ancient pedigree among a cluster of Celtic tongues whose origins seemed to lie a few centuries before Christ. Already, however in the Abbé Pezron's *Antiquités de la Nation des Celtes* of 1703, translated into English in 1706, they were being offered, in a much more speculative form, cultural descent from a single and powerful 'Celtic' language which might date from the Patriarchs and the very origins of humankind, a vision which lurked behind Henry Rowlands's influential essay on Anglesey as a heartland of Druidism, his *Mona Antiquata Restaurata* of 1723.

The crucial work was done in mid-century under the auspices of the genial, industrious, enormously influential but often frustrated circle of the Morris brothers of Anglesey, civil servants, Lewis a cartographer, land-surveyor and government agent, Richard a clerk in the Navy Office in London, William a customs collector in Holyhead. Through their personal efforts, the creative work they inspired, the London society of the Cymmrodorion they founded, something approximating to a Welsh classical tradition was restored, at least among an active minority of intellectuals. But already, what was to become a characteristic tone of voice begins to register. One of the men they stimulated was the poet and scholar Evan Evans (Ieuan Fardd). Like so many of them, an embittered and alcoholic clergyman denied preferment, Evan Evans discovered in 1758 the poetry of Aneirin, the first known poetry in the Welsh language, which may date from the sixth century – 'an epic Poem in the British called Gododin, equal at least to the Iliad, Aeneid or Paradise Lost', in the exultant words of Lewis Morris. He went on to publish a fine and scholarly collection of early Welsh verse in his *Some Specimens of Antient Welsh Poetry* of 1764, followed by a Welsh equivalent, the *Gorchestion Beirdd Cymru* (*Achievements of the Welsh Poets*) of Rice Jones in 1773.

Yet at this, a climax for 'classical' Welsh learning, there was an irony all too characteristic of the Welsh predicament. Evan Evans launched his book as a contribution to the controversy raging over Macpherson's *Ossian*, which he regarded as a forgery. His cry was taken up by the next generation who, to demonstrate that Wales needed no *Ossian* forgeries, published a massive three-volume *Myvyrian Archaiology* which was in fact dominated by the fabrications of Iolo Morganwg! Evans's own book stimulated his friend Thomas Gray of *The Bard* and was a major factor in the 'Celtic Revival' in England which distorted Wales's own perception of itself. Evan Evans himself, in his evocative verse on the ruined mansion of a patron of the medieval poet Dafydd ap Gwilym and in his English poem *The Love of Our Country* in which he resurrected Owain Glyn Dŵr (Glendower) to stand alongside Druids, princes and Tudor scholars as defenders of all things Welsh, registers the advance of a Romantic sensibility. And alongside his work came a flurry of books which seized on the wilder aspects of Pezron's Celts and drove the vision of the past into paroxysms of lunacy.

Into this cacophony came the advancing tramp of the great dictionaries. In the beginning, after all, was the word, and 'degenerate' Welsh was in need of words. They were provided. In 1755 Thomas Richards, rector of Coychurch, published his dictionary, to be followed, between 1770 and 1795, by John Walters, a rector near Cowbridge, in an enormous compilation which, working from current English, equipped Welsh as a modern tongue and in fact laid the foundations of the modern language (though we are in the throes of a similar enterprise in our own day). To accompany his dictionary, Walters published a *Dissertation* on the language which was a manifesto, designed to prove the *amlder*, copiousness, of Welsh and its superiority to the all-powerful English. An ardent lieutenant to Walters was the young Iolo Morganwg who, in characteristic style, went on to revitalise Welsh, re-discover the Glamorgan dialect and to stretch the old language to embrace the whole of past and present, in a typical mixture of genuine scholarship, ingenious coinage and sheer fantasy. Everybody concerned with Welsh at the time had a chip on the shoulder over English; these men carried a plank and in Iolo's case, it was a veritable platform!

It is notable that these dictionaries came out of Glamorgan – which disconcerted traditionally superior north Walians with their scorn for the 'Hottentot' Welsh of the south. In all probability, it reflects the quickening pace of change in one of Wales's most economically advanced regions and it finds a parallel in the displacement of the Cymmrodorion society of London by the Gwyneddigion which, despite its title (it means men of Gwynedd in north-west Wales) was largely staffed from Denbighshire, the Glamorgan of the north.[23]

The Gwyneddigion, who took the lead from the 1780s, were much more populist and active than the rather staid Cymmrodorion. They could build on earlier scholarship but were possessed much more fully by the vision of an ancient past. They were no less possessed by a vision of an attainable future, in the age of the American Revolution (which started 'politics' in Wales) and of the millenarian dreams inspired by the Revolution in France. A genial crew, meeting uproariously but creatively in London pubs, these men, at once the last, warm glow of a populist Enlightenment in Wales and her most characteristically Romantic spokesmen, poured out transcriptions, translations, word-lists; they revived the *eisteddfod* and through it, through journals, endless correspondence, repeated and adventurous enterprise, thrust a new vision of Wales before their frequently bemused stay-at-home compatriots.

A leading figure among them, William Owen (who, later in honour of a benefactor, added a Pughe) symbolises them.[24] A Merioneth man who worked as a teacher in London, he was something of a polymath under the patronage of the central figure, Owen Jones (Owain Myfyr), a furrier. He edited a volume of the poems of Dafydd ap Gwilym (1789), another on the ancient texts of Llywarch Hen (1792) and was a prime shaper of the big collection of early material, the *Myvyrian Archaiology* (1801–7). Amid many other enterprises, he composed the greatest dictionary of them all (1803) which contained over 100,000 words (40,000 more than Johnson's classic English work), following it in 1808 with a Welsh grammar. But his genuine scholarship was made to serve Utopian visions (he became a devoted follower of Joanna Southcott the Prophetess). In spirit kin to the Noah Webster who wanted to turn old Gothic English into an American Language of Liberty, Owen set out to rescue a Welsh which had degenerated into a lingo of servitude. He collected huge numbers of old Welsh words, broke them down into particles like atoms and then 'reconstructed' the language. In co-operation with Iolo Morganwg, he invented a new orthography for Welsh, derived from the 'Druids'; he packed Iolo's dream-world of Bards and Druids into his genuine erudition. For he, like all of them, responded to Iolo; the Gwyneddigion and their kin were the very seat of the first Welsh Romanticism.

The demi-urge himself, Iolo Morganwg, was born Edward Williams in 1747 in the Vale of Glamorgan, son to a stonemason and a woman who was at once the poor kin of a gentry family and a descendant of one of Glamorgan's dynasties of Welsh poets – and from whom Ned Williams inherited his demon.[25] A working stonemason, he went on epic journeyman tramp, collecting and copying manuscripts compulsively. He built himself into the most learned man on Welsh antiquities, literature and history in Wales (perhaps in Britain). He was one of the country's first and best folklorists and topographers; he was the first to call for a Welsh national library, museum and university. A polymath himself, he was a first-class poet (and had the makings of a historian). The demon which drove him was first resentment – a Welsh resentment against arrogant English, a south Wales resentment against arrogant northerners, a Glamorgan resentment against the rest and a Iolo resentment against any who snubbed him (in the end, he was to call himself the Last Bard in Europe). But secondly, he had a genius for mimicry, particularly of the language and literature of the late Middle Ages which became his spiritual home, and a total impatience with the exigencies of sparse evidence and its interpretation – all no doubt wreathed in the laudanum which he took for his asthma and to which he became addicted.

He would often, in his laborious research, come across a truth and then another (often truths which, in his own day, he alone was capable of identifying). He might perceive a possible connection between them (and recent scholarship has often confirmed his insights). If there was not enough evidence to warrant the connection, he supplied it, like an inspired ventriloquist. To him can be applied the words which the Highland Society used in 1797, when they passed judgement on *Ossian* – Macpherson, they said, 'was in use to supply chasms and to give connection, by inserting passages which he could not find'. Iolo strode over chasms in seven-league boots, inventing chronicles, poets, traditions the world had never seen. But so embedded were these fabrications in his genuine research that few could challenge him; it has taken the Herculean labours of a modern Welsh scholar to cut Iolo free from his fantasies – and in the process, Iolo's personal stature as a creative writer has in fact been enhanced! Peter Burke has pointed out that the line between Macpherson, generally considered a 'forger' and others like Percy, Scott, the Grimms, usually considered 'editors', is a blurred one.[26] Iolo, without doubt, was firmly on the Macpherson side of the line, but in his time he gave a neglected, despised and often self-despising people a new vision of history and a new sense of the relevance of that history to their present and future, which proved compelling and whose after-effects have proved permanent. In this sense, he can stand with those great Romantic poets who have been 'movers and shapers of a nation's destiny' and who loom so large in the history of Europe's 'non-historic' peoples.

Active from an early age, he assisted John Walters with his dictionary, tried to launch the Anti-Hengistian academy in Llantrisant and succumbed to the charms of Dafydd ap Gwilym, whom he assiduously mimicked, as he did so many other early writers. Failed architect, shipper, farmer, he was jailed for debt in Cardiff over 1786–7, to emerge as 'Iolo Morganwg', a man with a mission. He made contact with the London-Welsh, sent them an appendix of 'lost' Dafydd ap Gwilym poems which he had 'discovered' – and which they promptly published (understandably, since they are as good as anything the master himself wrote!) and moved to join them in the 1790s, the springtide of hope in the French Revolution. He drenched them in his vision, which he elaborated piecemeal in the preface to their 1792 edition of Llywarch Hen, in his own poems of 1794, in the second and third volumes of the *Myvyrian Archaiology* and in his own copious manuscripts which were to pack his Glamorgan cottage, to which he withdrew, and which were published only after his death in 1826.

Iolo offered the Welsh many visions. Some were false and disabling; others were full of insight. Characteristically, many were both simultaneously. His central vision was of Bardism, Druidism and the Gorsedd. Alert to the antiquity of the classical tradition, in his London years he became possessed of a much more coherent if imaginary interpretation of it. He was fully aware that Welsh poets were not as the English were – they had been remembrancers. He recreated that world in a Gorsedd (Order) of Bards of the Island of Britain dating from Arthur's time, with its distant roots among the Druids. He supplied that Gorsedd with ceremonies, rituals, a whole philosophy. In his London years, he recaptured the British Israelism of his distant compatriot, that Dr John Dee who had been 'philosopher' to Elizabeth I and whose Hermetic philosophy, reaching back to an order co-eval with the birth of humankind and pre-dating both Christianity and Judaism, had gone underground as Rosi-crucianism, to re-surface in the Enlightenment on the fringes of Free-masonry in those societies of Illuminés whom Burke and Barruel denounced as agents of a revolutionary conspiracy and whom the Sweden-borgians of London's radical artisanry had recently contacted.[27] The London-Welsh moved in the circle of William Blake and his friends, and in Iolo's mind now, those far-off Druids emerged as libertarians and unitarians, with a creed of Humanity which had been driven underground into Freemasonry. He duly became a Unitarian and a Freemason and when he launched the first Gorsedd at the summer solstice of 1792 (on the some-what un-Druidic slopes of Primrose Hill, London), he launched it as an Order of People's Remembrancers to a Welsh Republic. It was his vision, avidly received by a pre-disposed London-Welsh community of 'people's remembrancers', which charged the Welsh revival in the 1790s, the quest for Madoc, the subsidising of periodicals, the attempts to revive the Gorsedd. In the eyes of authority it also charged it with Jacobinism; they turned the yeomanry loose on the Gorsedd and a populist witch-hunt on its exponents. Iolo withdrew from public life into his own form of religion and helped to launch the Unitarian Association of South Wales in 1802, equipping it with two volumes of hymns which are, characteristically, hymns to Reason, as is his Gorsedd hymn.

He and his friends were struggling against the odds. As early as 1800, Owen, Iolo and rest were beginning to look like creatures from another time. The rapid advance of industrial society and of Nonconformity was shunting them off into the margins. This first Welsh Romanticism, with its paradoxical but living relationship to a rational Welsh classicism, was bubble-brilliant but brief.

In the next generation, the growth of the new Wales accelerated, cutting more and more people loose from their past. The Romantic perception of Wales was taken up by the people most seriously threatened by the change, the people the Welsh call 'Hen Bersoniaid Llengar', literally the Old Literary Parsons, in practice, patrons and intellectuals from the world of Anglicanism and the squirearchy, now becoming daily more 'traditional' and in the minds of some, archaic.[28] It was they who cultivated a Romanticism most visibly parallel to that of the Europe of the time, in that it was quite literally 'reactionary', and in which excess was unrestrained. After the Napoleonic War, it was clergymen led by such as Bishop Thomas Burgess of St David's, a prime mover in the creation of a university college in Lampeter as an Anglican bastion, who also created Cambrian societies and wrested the *eisteddfod* from Infidels. At the Carmarthen *eisteddfod* of 1819, the bishop invited Iolo himself, now old, to attend and here, for the first time, Iolo's Gorsedd entered the *eisteddfod* itself. It had some difficulty finding a secure lodgement there, but in the same period, persons associated with this movement, with the aid of Iolo's son Taliesin, published to the world that incredible mass of documents from his Glamorgan cottage with its corpus of ritual, philosophy, cabalistic signs, alphabet and mysticism, to bemuse and captivate successive generations. By the 1850s, the *eisteddfod*, now a great popular and national festival, serviced by railways, finally accepted the Gorsedd which, endowed with lavish ceremonial and, from the late nineteenth century, with robes and regalia designed by Sir Hubert von Herkomer and Goscombe John, came to dominate it. The same Anglican generation saw Lady Charlotte Guest's *Mabinogion*, Maria Jane Williams's collection of national airs and most blood-curdling of all, the invention of a Welsh national costume for women by the indefatigable Lady Llanover, wife to the industrialist Benjamin Hall (who gave his name to Big Ben). Lady Llanover was almost frenetically active in collecting Welsh manuscripts, popularising old Welsh customs, encouraging *eisteddfodau* (one at Beaumaris in 1832 graced by the presence of the Duchess of Kent and her daughter, later Queen Victoria). She seized on a witch-like costume, actually a seventeenth-century English fashion which had come late and lingered long in a few districts in Wales, and by ceaseless activity and exemplary performance, succeeded in inducing many Welsh people, even as their genuine 'folk costumes' vanished before industrial standardisation, to accept her invention as good 'national costume' in best peasant and picturesque manner. (Fortunately, perhaps, for Welsh males, Big Ben himself was uninterested.)

This distinctly comic and at times grotesque 'Welsh' Romanticism, increasingly marginalised, also had its term. After the uproar provoked by a hostile education report of 1847, which pilloried the Welsh language and Welsh Nonconformity (promptly dubbed 'Brâd y Llyfrau Gleision', the Treason of the Blue Books, in parody of 'Brâd y Cyllyll Hirion', the Treason of the Long Knives, an epithet for the legendary Saxon massacre of British leaders in Vortigern's time – a conceit which would itself, in all probability, have been unthinkable without the revival) generations of Welsh intellectuals set themselves to modernise Welsh culture and prove its

respectability. Out of intellectual circles in Merthyr Tydfil, the largest
town in Wales and centre of the iron, steel and coal trades, came Thomas
Stephens, a literary chemist who demolished the Madoc legend (to cause
an *eisteddfod* scandal), to write the first critical history of Welsh literature,
and to start the process whereby the study of Welsh history, literature and
language became a matter for academics, even as society as a whole settled
into an overpowering Nonconformist–Liberal regime grounded in an
industrial society, to which the concerns of the Romantics were irrelevant.
This was the Wales which at the end of the century witnessed the intrusion
into the *eisteddfod* of the New Poets, as they were called, who in their
intense, personal introspection, expressed the kind of Romanticism which
the *Oxford Companion to Welsh Literature* has no difficulty in
identifying.

Along with much dross, the fables and fantasies and, indeed, many
clouded realities survived, though only in the world of popular songs,
tourist guide-books, children's verse and after-dinner rhetoric. The
Romantic spasm, however, left some permanent, audible and all too
visible memorials: a national institution, a national anthem, and a national
costume.

Most intriguing of its legacies was that to the early working-class movements, normally indifferent to such matters. Iolo Morganwg spent many
of his later years in Merthyr Tydfil among its 'sturdy old republicans'; his
son Taliesin ran a school there. It was Iolo's Unitarians who took the lead
in the new democratic and working-class movements which made Merthyr
their focus. One of them was John Thomas (Ieuan Ddu), trained as an
artist in Carmarthen, who followed Taliesin as a schoolmaster. A composer and collector of folksongs, a brilliant and often caustic critic of the
eisteddfod, he was central to the emergent choral tradition and was the
man who introduced Handel's *Messiah* to Welsh choirs (with devastating
effect). Appalled that the only songs sung at weddings were hymns, he published a song collection *The Cambrian Minstrel* within a year of Maria
Jane Williams's and in a very different spirit. This man had helped to
launch Infidel, freethinking *eisteddfodau* in Merthyr on the eve of the
Rising of 1831. He was one of the editors of the first Welsh working-class
journal *Y Gweithiwr* (*The Workman*) of 1834. His fellow-editor was
Morgan Williams, who came from a family of harpists. Morgan Williams
went on to become the foremost Chartist leader in Wales and to be one of
the editors of its distinguished journal *Udgorn Cymru* (*Trumpet of Wales*),
published in Merthyr between 1840 and 1842.[29]

This was a journal of quality; it became a fully-fledged stamped newspaper before it was cut down in the general strike of 1842. It has everything
one might expect from a moral-force Chartist paper. But it has something

else. It has long essays, by cobblers, ironworkers, colliers, shopkeepers, on the history of the Welsh language, on significant events in Welsh history, on the true meaning of Welsh traditions. It is in fact steeped in the style not of the relentless and patronising effusion of Lady Llanover but of the earlier, more ambivalent but also more serious Romanticism of the 1790s.

And when Merthyr became a county borough (to acquire a coat of arms, also designed by Goscombe John), it blazoned a motto attributed to an ancient saint, Cadoc, but whose real author was Iolo Morganwg – *nid cadarn ond brodyrdde*, no strength but brotherhood.[30]

It is a paradox, but it is not inappropriate, that it was The Last Bard in Europe who gave its motto to the gritty capital of the new and distinctly un-Romantic Wales.

NOTES

1 Vanbrugh's description of Wales in his play *Aesop* (c. 1697) quoted in Prys Morgan, *The Eighteenth Century Renaissance* (Llandybie, 1981); Prys Morgan's crisp and entertaining monograph is a volume in *A New History of Wales*, ed. Ralph A. Griffiths, Kenneth O. Morgan and J. Beverly Smith. I have found it invaluable and cite it henceforth as Morgan.

2 On John Evans, see my 'John Evans's mission to the Madogwys, 1792–99', *Bulletin of the Board of Celtic Studies*, 27 (1978), and more generally, my *Madoc: The Making of a Myth* (London, 1980), esp. chs. 8–11.

3 On all this, see my *Madoc*.

4 On William Jones, Llangadfan, my *Madoc*, chs. 5–9, and Morgan, pp. 28, 40, 49, 124.

5 Peter Burke, *Popular Culture in Early Modern Europe* (London, 1978), p. 5 (henceforth Burke).

6 Hywel Teifi Edwards, *Yr Eisteddfod* (Llys yr Eisteddfod Genedlaethol, Court of the National Eisteddfod, and Welsh Arts Council, Llandysul, 1976); Dillwyn Miles, *The Royal National Eisteddfod of Wales* (Swansea, 1977); Morgan, pp. 63–6.

7 G. J. Williams, *Iolo Morganwg*, vol. 1 (Cardiff, 1956), pp. 124–8.

8 The major study of Iolo Morganwg is by the late Griffith John Williams (*ibid.*), who died before he could complete his second, critical volume in Welsh; there is an essay on him in English by Prys Morgan in the University of Wales/Welsh Arts Council 'Writers of Wales' series – *Iolo Morganwg* (Cardiff, 1975); Iolo figures prominently in my *Madoc*; on this issue, see ch. 7.

9 J. Gaulmier, *L'Idéologue Volney* (Beyrouth, 1951), and *Volney* (Paris, 1959).

10 My 'Morgan John Rhys and Volney's *Ruins of Empires*', *Bulletin of the Board of Celtic Studies*, 20 (1964), and on Rhys generally, my *The Search for Beulah Land: The Welsh and the Atlantic Revolution* (London, 1980).

11 Burke.

12 Osian Ellis on Welsh music in *Transactions of the Honourable Society of Cymmrodorion 1972–73* (1974); Morgan, pp. 124–32; my *When Was Wales?* (London, 1985), ch. 7.

13 Gwyn Williams, 'Gweledigaeth J. M. W. Turner, 1775–1851', *Barn*, 148 (1975); Morgan and Burke, *passim*.

14 J. P. Larsen, *Haydn*, New Grove Series (London, 1982), worklist by Georg Feder, p. 195; Morgan, p. 126.

15 Osian Ellis in the essay in *Transactions*, and Morgan, pp. 129–32.

16 On Karadžić, D. Wilson, *The Life and Times of Vuk Stefanović Karadžić* (Oxford, 1970); summary in Burke, p. 13.

17 For the social analysis which follows, see my *When Was Wales?*, ch. 7.

18 Geraint H. Jenkins, *Literature, Religion and Society in Wales 1660–1730* (Cardiff, 1978); a seminal study.

19 A mass of secondary material is analysed, from different points of view, in Morgan and my *When Was Wales?*.

20 Saunders Lewis, *Williams Pantycelyn* (London, 1927); Glyn Tegai Hughes, *Williams Pantycelyn* (Cardiff, 1983); A. M. Allchin, *Ann Griffiths* (Cardiff, 1976).

21 Vivid picture in R. T. Jenkins, *Hanes Cymru yn y Ddeunawfed Ganrif* and *Hanes Cymru yn y Bedwaredd Ganrif ar Bymtheg* (Cardiff, 1928 and 1933, with reprints; a history of Wales in the eighteenth and early nineteenth centuries).

22 The best summary account of this intellectual movement is Morgan, esp. ch. 3.

23 R. T. Jenkins and Helen T. Ramage, *A History of the Honourable Society of Cymmrodorion and of the Gwyneddigion and Cymreigyddion Societies* (London, 1951); I write on the Gwyneddigion in 'Druids and democrats: organic intellectuals and the first Welsh nation', in my *The Welsh in Their History* (London, 1982) and in *Madoc*, ch. 6.

24 Glenda Carr, *William Owen Pughe* (Cardiff, 1983), a fascinating study, in Welsh.

25 On Iolo, G. J. Williams, *Iolo Morganwg*; Prys Morgan, *Iolo Morganwg*, and my *Madoc*.

26 Burke, pp. 17–18.

27 On Dr John Dee in this context, my 'Welsh Wizard and British Empire: Dr John Dee and a Welsh identity', in *The Welsh in Their History*. On Dee in general, the many volumes of the late Dame Frances Yates, especially her *The Occult Philosophy in the Elizabethan Age* (London, 1979) and P. J. French, *John Dee: The World of an Elizabethan Magus* (London, 1972).

28 Morgan, chs. 4 and 5.

29 My *The Merthyr Rising* (London, 1978), and 'Locating a Welsh working class: the frontier years', in *The Welsh in Their History*: I am engaged in an analysis of *Udgorn Cymru*.

30 My 'Dic Penderyn: myth, martyr and memory in the Welsh working class', in *The Welsh in Their History*.

2

Romanticism in England

MARILYN BUTLER

English Romanticism is impossible to define with historical precision because the term itself is historically unsound. It is now applied to English writers of the first quarter of the nineteenth century, who did not think of themselves as Romantics. Instead they divided themselves by literary precept and by ideology into several distinct groups, dubbed by their opponents 'Lakeists', 'Cockneys', 'Satanists', Scotsmen. It was the middle of the nineteenth century before they were gathered into one band as the English Romantics, and the present tendency of textbooks to insist upon the resemblance to one another of (especially) six major poets – Blake, Wordsworth, Coleridge, Byron, Shelley and Keats – dates only from about 1940.[1]

With the partial exception of Coleridge, English creative writers were not in close touch with the German literary men who *did* call themselves Romantics at this time, nor was any German counter-revolutionary writing, whether poetry, philosophy, theology or literary criticism, much studied in England between 1800 and 1824. (Far more popular through translation in the 1790s were the pre-revolutionary writers, the Sturm und Drang dramatists including Schiller and the young Goethe, balladmongers like Burger, and writers of Gothic fiction; while translation from German began again with Carlyle's generation from the mid-1820s.) Yet English poetry written in the generation before and especially after 1800 has usually been thought of as entering upon a golden age, remarkable not only for its innovativeness, seriousness and, at its best, profundity, but for being read by the general public. And, whatever its awkward resistance to preconceived description, much of the English poetry and prose fiction of the period *has* after all distinguishing preoccupations which connect it with other European cultures and events, including its concern with class, social change, natural religion, regional and national pride, and world revolution.

The need to distance the English writers from their label arises because the term Romantic comes supplied with its own bibliography and history. It originated in a series of texts which emerged in Jena and Berlin, from 1797. It grew quickly in Germany over the next three decades, and only relatively slowly and intermittently in other European cultures. Like all intellectual artefacts, this theory has the preoccupations and the partisan interests of its time and place. For example, it opposes Romanticism to French materialism, identifying it instead with religious revival, idealism, aspiration, introversion and with literary techniques embodying a religious view of the world, such as myth and symbol. That this is an unhelpful angle from which to approach the English poetic output of the period can be illustrated from the case of Shelley. A poet interested in philosophy, working in the second decade of the nineteenth century, when German Romantic philosophy was in full flower, Shelley associated it with counter-revolutionary thinking, and only very belatedly began to learn German, primarily in order to read Goethe. He has been described by his more modern admirers as an idealist and a mythmaker, but contemporaries knew him as a freethinker and a materialist. His theories were shaped not by the post-Kantians but by Hume, Rousseau, Gibbon, Holbach, the French Revolutionary ideologues, and by the latter's English sympathisers, Erasmus Darwin and William Godwin. Shelley has more in common with Enlightenment thinkers, and indeed with Karl Marx, than with the thinkers we normally deem the European Romantics. This does not mean that poetry in England does not cross-refer to European poetry, but it does mean that a Romanticism defined in terms of German thinking of the time should not be allowed unexamined privileges as a tool of analysis.

Let us take, for example, the frequent use of the appearance of Friedrich Schlegel's Romantic manifesto in 1797 as an approximate starting-point. This date, or its convenient nearby English points of reference – Blake's *Songs of Innocence* (1789) or Wordsworth's *Lyrical Ballads* (1798) – is far too late to begin tracing the significant points of innovation in English literature. Its lateness is indeed itself interested – it implies, of course, that a fresh start had to be made *after* French classicism and materialism had brought Europe to revolution and the Terror. Rather than treating ideas, especially books advocating new ideas, as though they were necessarily key historical events, we might do better to enquire more dispassionately into the general range of books of literary interest in circulation, and into the material circumstances that shaped their content and style, or even enabled them to appear when they did. If late eighteenth-century English poets and indeed novelists seem original and surprisingly numerous, it may be because they were in a new situation; but the world of books, publishers and writers had already changed before 1750. The revolutionary factor was the new audience for imaginative literature. More English people were literate, and they were wealthier than before, giving them the means to own books and the leisure to read them. More books were published, and they were better distributed, and better publicised, usually through being reviewed in journals; through improved roads, they reached out into the provinces, where most of the population still lived. The eighteenth-century reader was likely to be 'of the middling sort', what would later be called bourgeois: provincial rather than metropolitan; at least as likely to be female as male.

English 'Romanticism', or whatever term we prefer for the era's cultural revolution, has to be dated from about 1740, when the new readership was felt to have emerged, to somewhere in the mid-1820s, when the conditions of publication underwent a further change. By lowering the price of books from 1825, publishers greatly enlarged the readership once more, and thus produced the conditions for Victorian middle-class literature. Within those dates, literature displays consistent characteristics, or rather it evolves through a number of phases which are sometimes antithetical rather than akin. The notional readership addressed will be literate but not perhaps well-educated: there is more emphasis on feeling and on life-experience (or a hunger for it) than on prior knowledge gained from reading. The great majority of new readers were necessarily excluded from direct political power, which remained in the hands of an oligarchy in the capital. Apparently the new poetry and fiction was less political than the court poetry of earlier periods, which circulated among a smaller elite; but latently the eighteenth-century mode had a political content, for it tended to oppose the central British state and its institutions. This underlying civic preoccupation was one of the features of English Romanticism which was most excitingly new.

The common impression in England of the politics of Romanticism has derived from English poetry, and is quite different from the German impression derived from German criticism and creative writing. The British, from the late eighteenth century on, have tended to associate the poetry we now call Romantic with social change and even revolution. This is because the English poems thought most typical visibly appeal to a democratised audience, either in taking up themes favourable to the lower orders or hostile to the powerful, or in employing diction, metres and (as we shall see) symbols with popular connotations. Blake's *Songs* and *The Lyrical Ballads* of Wordsworth and Coleridge retain their populism and accessibility even in the twentieth century. They are in this sense modern, but it is not a sense which embraces the literary term modernist, for modernist art was not populist and accessible.

Some of the most influential and eloquent twentieth-century admirers of

these poets have found some common sources, for example a hostile
reaction to modern urban life, and thus some common features, in Romantic art and modernist art. Since the middle of the twentieth century,
especially in America, English Romantic poetry has been more and more
seen as grouped around one great autobiographical statement, Wordsworth's long blank-verse poem *The Prelude* (1850) and the most influential criticism of *The Prelude*, for example that of Geoffrey Hartman, has
played up its self-referentiality, while playing down its dealings with men,
with nature and with God.[2] Similarly, *fin de siècle* nineteenth-century
critics claimed that their aestheticism, self-absorption and social alienation
was the essence of Romanticism. As we shall see, these generalisations can
be sustained only by concentrating on a small proportion of even the best
and most innovative English writing of the period. What they really reveal
is the interesting affinity some groups of later intellectuals have felt for the
manner, the self-description and the ideology of that first group of critics
to style themselves Romantics, or for post-Kantianism more generally.
Many later commentators on Romanticism have taken up the subject for
the reason Schlegel did, to write a manifesto for the writer's autonomy,
most immediately for the critic's own. Criticism *of* Romantics has frequently been rhetorically more Romantic, and certainly more partial, than
English Romantic writing itself: most notably, in the claim that it entails a
step in the arts that is new and irreversible. That is why this survey of the
period in England centres on the issue of whether innovation and Romanticism were the same thing.

In several West European literatures, certainly the English and German,
the impulse to innovation in the arts preceded the French Revolution. The
literal, political revolution was thus not the agent of cultural change, and
post-revolutionary Romanticism must be recognised as at most a secondary phase within a series of innovations. Alternatively we can extend the
scope of the term, and conclude that it was an early, civic form of Romanticism that had priority in England, and was itself a factor in creating the
post-revolutionary mood of introspection that for some moderns is *the*
Romanticism. According to their adoption of public themes, English poets
of the period fall into three groups. The first expresses a challenge from the
still disenfranchised middle and provincial classes in the half-century
before the French Revolution: it includes Blake and the early Wordsworth
and Coleridge. The second, from the mid-1790s to about 1815 (the years
when Britain was at war with post-revolutionary France), continues to use
similar provincial landscapes and an accessible 'natural' tone, but
drastically revises the oppositional message in favour of a religiously
orthodox, politically loyal one. This phase includes the mature work of
Wordsworth and Coleridge. The third, from about 1812 to 1824, is much

less distinctively provincial and democratic; indeed, the poetic modes of Byron and Shelley are as aristocratic as their social origins, though this does not prevent them from challenging the policies of the British government more boldly and directly than their predecessors. The purpose of this summary of all three phases is to explore their reactiveness – to other texts, to war, dearth and unrest, to images of citizenship, of nationhood and of power. It will be followed by a conclusion dealing largely with the transitional 1820s, which considers whether the arrival of common or solipsistic Romanticism was not postponed, in England as in France, until that decade.

THE COUNTRY MOVEMENT

The word 'country' in English puns on two quite different, even incompatible concepts: the countryside, a part or even a negation insofar as it is undeveloped, not-town; and the nation, which implies the whole rather than the part. Eighteenth-century poets beginning with James Thomson (1700–48), and going on through Thomas Gray (1716–71) to William Blake (1757–1827) and William Wordsworth (1775–1850), replace the 'court' or London or aristocratic discourse of Dryden, Pope, Swift and Gay with a symbolic language exalting provincialism. By keeping in view the term country in both its possible senses, they express, and further shape, attitudes which are representative of the attitudes of some of the gentry and much of the 'middling orders', especially of the commercial and entrepreneurial classes in eighteenth-century London and the provinces.

The term in use at the time for the sentiments I am describing, and for those who upheld them, was 'patriot'.[3] Both the sentiment and the word patriot as a descriptive term for it go back into the seventeenth century, especially the civil war period, when two of its strands were already visible: (1) a coherent sense of nationhood, and (2) a tendency to cite 'the nation' in selective contexts, e.g. when a Stuart monarch's right to levy taxes was being challenged. In other words, 'patriot' was often used in opposition to 'Crown' and the centralised bureaucracy at Westminster. Though early in the eighteenth century a Tory aristocrat such as Bolingbroke would deploy the term, as in his essay *The Idea of a Patriot King* (1740), it became much more commonly associated with liberal or radical thinking. This is why the Tory Dr Johnson opined that 'Patriotism is the last refuge of a scoundrel.' Patriot writing generally sounded chauvinistic, expansive and aggressive: France and Spain, Britain's chief trading rivals, were the favourite enemies, and the government was much criticised for its reluctance to go to war with them.

The eighteenth-century English patriot liked war, but not war against

Americans, whom he regarded as sturdy British provincials like himself. Though he had advocated war against old-regime France, war against the new France was another matter. The French Revolutionary wars which began on the 1st of February 1793 embarrassed and divided English radicals, and enabled the government's supporters to capture the old patriot rhetoric for national purposes. It is because of this war that creative writers, like other middle-class people, tended to move just before 1800 from an oppositional patriotism to a more modern form of nationalism that now looks decidedly conservative.

Creative literature, like the graphic arts, gives to attitudes an emotive, symbolic imagery, an iconography that works on opinion at a level deeper than slogans and far more universal than argument. Through literature 'country' becomes an image to inspire emotion, idealism and loyalty, and an eighteenth-century reality, not a term read about in books by Cicero, Machiavelli or Harrington. It is poets like James Thomson, Thomas Gray and Oliver Goldsmith who make the actual physical countryside both beautiful and familiar, and the same poets who give the country a quite new historical past, going back, importantly, into pre-history. Until this period poets had tended to write as though the metropolitan centres, the courts, the worlds of learning held all the keys to written historical records, and thus all the claims to legitimacy. Named heroes, precursors of kings, conquerors, founders of royal houses, were also conventionally the makers of nations. Mid-eighteenth-century poets became interested in a more generalised and remote people's history, and thus history like the similarly revised terms 'country' and 'nature' acquires an oppositional potential and an appropriate set of symbols.

James Thomson, a new man in London literary society when he arrived from Scotland in 1725, quickly made his name, and enlarged the meaning of 'country', with a long poem that remained a classic for a century, *The Seasons* (1725–30). The whole point of the seasons viewed as a natural phenomenon is that everyone experiences them; in the most fashionable poetry of that decade by Pope, Swift and Gay, individual Londoners, courtiers, writers, aldermen, bawdy-house keepers are listed by name, and the unfashionable reader is thus largely excluded from equal participation in the poem's code. Thomson's attitudes in the 1720s were not so much anti-aristocratic as sympathetic to middling and common people. The benignity of his best-known poem made it an accessible middlebrow classic, which could be recruited by relative liberals of the French Revolutionary period, like the Earl of Buchan and William Wordsworth, and was still thought to have a populist message in the 1830s and 1840s. By 1740 Thomson had thrown in his lot with the political opposition (though in the 1730s this still entailed patronage by aristocrats), and his last poem, *The Castle of Indolence* (1746), speaks eloquently to a middle-class provincial readership. It is an imitation of *The Faerie Queene* of the Elizabethan poet Edmund Spenser, who was now interpreted as an ultra-Protestant patriot. The first canto allegorically represents Robert Walpole's oppressive, sybaritic, aristocratic England, and the second imagines its replacement by a busy, modern commercial community, located in north-west England, the region where many of the new industries were. Nature isn't empty for Thomson, as it becomes for Wordsworth and other nineteenth- and twentieth-century writers. His 'country' is well-populated, productive and even technological.

Moreover, as a Scotsman himself, Thomson in all his later work tends to equate the nation's past with the story of all its peoples, which means going back beyond the arrival of the English to the cultures of the aboriginal Scots and Welsh. It is Thomson, in *The Castle of Indolence*, in his long blank-verse poem *Liberty* (1735) and in his patriot masque *Alfred* (1740), who introduces the symbolic figure of the Druid, as both the archetypal poet and the archivist of collective popular wisdom. And Druids, or their secular successors the bards, afterwards walk the pages of much early Romantic British poetry.

The next substantial poet after Thomson was Thomas Gray, a Cambridge academic and cultural historian whose *magnum opus* was to have been a history of *British* poetry. Gray traced a continuous literary tradition back not (as was and still is customary) through the Normans to Provençal and Latin literature, but to the Welsh and the Norse. He defined British poetry as poetry written by the people of the British Isles, an all-inclusive and de-centrist conception of literary history. The work was never written, though the notebooks survive.[4] Gray did on the other hand publish some of his translations from Norse and Welsh, and his two most celebrated original poems were perceived in the eighteenth century to belong to the patriot tradition.[5] One was the 'Elegy in a Country Church-yard', in which Gray compares the blameless, forgotten lives of the poor who are buried in the churchyard with the pompous memorials and destructive careers of the rich. The other was 'The Bard', in which the last of the thirteenth-century Welsh bards defies the invading English king, Edward I, before plunging to his death from a Snowdonian crag. 'The Bard' remains an important work in Romantic poetry, because it puts in its most memorable form the series of connections English poets henceforth made. Historical Welsh resistance to London legitimises not armed rebellion, of course – no one could be more blamelessly pacific than Gray – but the rights of provincial men to civic esteem and some access to power.

The two most brilliant and imaginative mid-century poets, certainly the two who used history most creatively, are seldom now studied as serious writers. The simple reason for this is that their enemies, whose motives were often more political than literary, succeeded in pinning on them the charge of forgery. Read literally, Macpherson and Chatterton certainly were forgers, but their partisans urged that they should be read imaginatively, and posterity has lost the key to the most exciting strand of mid-eighteenth-century poetry by not following this advice.

James Macpherson (1736–96) grew up a Highlander in a Jacobite region of Scotland, and was ten when Bonnie Prince Charlie's rebellion was crushed at Culloden, a few miles from his home. The Scottish culture he encountered as a university student at Aberdeen, and later as a school-master and minor poet, was not in rebellion against Scotland's political union with England of 1707. But articulate university men did resent the centralising of power and professional opportunities in London, the cultural snobbery of the English and the national insult to Scotland administered in 1756, whereby, during a new war with France, the pro-Hanoverian Scottish gentry were not permitted to arm. Encouraged by well-known Edinburgh professors like Adam Ferguson and Hugh Blair, Macpherson 'discovered' two Gaelic epics, *Fingal* (1761) and *Temora* (1763). By this 'find', he demonstrated the heroic and warlike character of Scotsmen, along with the legitimacy of their claim to the soil, and the age of their culture. The symbolic point was at once seized upon, for example, by enthusiastic Scottish patriots like Blair, and by incensed defenders of orthodoxy in London. James Boswell, a Scotsman in heated rebellion against an Edinburgh culture he associated with his enlightened, Whiggish, lawyer father, quickly identified Macpherson's subversive aims. He described him to Samuel Johnson, who soon became Macpherson's arch-enemy, as 'an impudent fellow from Scotland, who affected to be a savage, and railed at all established systems'.[6]

But it was precisely Macpherson's elemental reduction of provincial patriotism to cultural and historical first principles that made him re-usable elsewhere. Just as he became an inspiration to provincial and iconoclastic British poets in the next half-century so, perhaps more importantly, he became a force in revolutionary America and successively in different parts of Europe. His translation was retranslated into Italian (1763) and thereafter into German, French, Spanish, Danish, Dutch, Swedish, Russian, Czech and Polish. Macpherson made a very large contribution to the great upsurge of purchases of English books recorded in Germany in the early 1770s and again in the late 1780s and early 1790s.[7] Part of the appeal of English was that it was not French; the more resentfully French cultural hegemony was felt, the more popular another 'northern' literature was likely to be. But the source of Macpherson's charm was more specific than this. He was himself an articulate cultural nationalist on behalf of a small nation.

Fingal, a third-century Scottish tribal chief, goes to help defend his Gaelic kinsmen in Ireland, first in *Fingal* from an invasion of Norsemen, afterwards in *Temora* against the treachery of a southern Irish tribe. These plots support a series of contrasts between one people and another, and the notes and introductory material develop them further. The reader is prompted to read the poem comparatively and analytically, to see it as a model heroic poem, an expectation Macpherson satisfies with his brilliantly simplified settings and situations, and his use of a vocabulary, rhythm and imagery which appear to be literally rendered from ancient originals. Ultimately it is not the individual characters who hold the attention, Fingal and his son, the bard Ossian, but their people, who have been submerged by political destiny but never fully assimilated by their powerful neighbours. Eighteenth-century historians already tended to idealise the people of northern Europe for their symbolic resistances to southern empires – ancient Rome, and its successor, the Catholic Church. Macpherson's band of brothers, whose idealised society has no courtiers, no priests, no hierarchy of church or state, implicitly made a case on behalf of any marginalised group; not specifically against London, but equally well against Bourbon or Napoleonic France, Austria or Russia.

Macpherson's immediate notoriety in England is partly a tribute to the effectiveness as a spokesman for orthodoxy of Samuel Johnson (1709–84). Though a provincial himself, Johnson sturdily upheld mainstream metropolitan culture, its Latin roots and its link with the Church of England. The problem with nineteenth- and twentieth-century textbook accounts is that they exaggerate Johnson's typicality, and underplay the extent to which his values were contested by other able writers in his lifetime. The most drastic opposition offered to Johnson's London-centred literary values came from the Bristol poet who killed himself before his eighteenth birthday, Thomas Chatterton (1752–70), the author of an entire corpus of allegedly fifteenth-century poetry and prose. These manuscripts all appeared to have been written in and around Bristol, or to have Bristol connections. Significantly, a handful emanated from Wales or the Isle of Man, and were supposedly contemporaneous translations from the respective Celtic languages; others dated from about 1100, and related details about the Bristol region before the Norman Conquest. In this way Chatterton associates culture and the true civic spirit with everywhere that is not London, for Londoners, he insinuates, have been half-foreign and pro-foreign in all periods.

It is for the comprehensiveness of his civic claims, not merely on account of the pathos of his early death, that Chatterton remains a hero to three succeeding generations of poets, notably to Blake, Wordsworth, Keats and Browning. Chatterton no less than Macpherson had a clear theoretical understanding of the spirit of an incipient nationalism that would apply everywhere, not merely in the British provinces. Shortly before his death, he wrote three brilliant 'African Eclogues', the first of which, 'Heccar and Gaira', describes a tropical Eden, simple, sensuous and primary. The idyll of two lovers in interrupted by the arrival of European slavers, who carry off the woman, Cawma; it is both a personal and a tribal or national rape. In the last of the eclogues, 'The Death of Nicou', Chatterton brilliantly imagines a 'national' religion, similar in structure and incident to the Hebraic. It includes a war in heaven and a fall, implying that these are universal myths, not peculiar to Hebraism. Again, however, the vividly colourful detail also particularises the world of the poem, along with its religion, as specifically African. Chatterton writes here as a sympathiser with cultural autonomy worldwide. Bristol was a slavetrading port: by moving his ground and his angle of vision to Africa, Chatterton suddenly represents his own whiteskinned people and their religious traditions as ugly and alien. This is a transference of the goals of provincial patriotism to another people which has parallels in the humanitarian literature of the late eighteenth century, and as we shall see recurs impressively in the early nineteenth century too, but nowhere with more respect for the otherness of the east and south than in Chatterton.

Macpherson and Chatterton were unorthodox members of a network of scholars engaged in the distinct history of peoples, and thus with characteristic localised traditions in poetry, in historiography, in religion and in language. It is a form of historicism we now associate more readily with Herder's Germany in the 1770s, but from the mid-1730s to the 1770s the cultural history of heroic-age societies such as Homer's Greece, republican Rome and Gaelic Scotland was a leading preoccupation of Scottish academics such as Thomas Blackwell (1701–57), Adam Ferguson (1723–1816) and Hugh Blair (1718–1800). By the era of the American Revolution, 1775–82, Scottish academic and professional opinion was more reconciled with the *status quo* and the many opportunities it offered to well-educated young Scotsmen in London and in the expanding possessions overseas. Even if the well-orchestrated English campaign against Macpherson as a forger had not done much to discredit Gaelic-based cultural nationalism, the Scottish professoriate now had more to gain from identifying with mainstream English interests, including the central literary tradition.

Even before the French Revolution, Scots professors like Blair, who (seventy years before the first English university) offered university-level courses in literature, were presiding over the formation of a more limited, confined, academicised and gentrified concept of Literature as, in a fairly full sense, a discipline. Blair was the first professor in Britain of 'belles lettres' or polite letters (1762), and his lectures, published in two volumes on his retirement in 1783, show that he taught the subject synoptically as a continuous world tradition incorporating the European (but not the Asiatic) ancients, and modern texts written in standard southern English rather than in regional dialects. At the same time the new sub-field of aesthetics was emerging, strengthened by Scottish medicine's empirical work in psychology. As for a literary syllabus, the poetry in English fittest for study was reissued in a convenient form by two Scottish anthologists who, as the latest editor of the *Oxford Book of Eighteenth Century Verse* has observed, have had a surprisingly strong influence on modern conceptions of what eighteenth-century English poetry is like.[8] Anderson and Chalmers, making their selections in the post-revolutionary years of 1795 and 1810, confined themselves to dead authors whose collected works had been published, which meant that they also chose men and not women, the established and not the occasional – those who found favour with publishers and with received opinion, both in the public and in the rapidly defining profession of letters.

By the same process of literary natural selection, certain late eighteenth-century notions of literature and literary history have had a better chance of survival than others. The views of the Johnson circle in London and of the Scottish professoriate have received ample attention in the late twentieth century.[9] Less visible now, but through journals a more familiar component of the literary scene at the time, were the 'popular antiquarians' who, by exchanging ideas, discoveries, manuscripts and books, between them opened up the field of folk or people's history and culture. Thomas Gray's network, involving the Wartons, Thomas Percy, Horace Walpole, Richard Hurd, is well-remembered; another of Gray's correspondents, the Welshman Evan Evans, who found a genuine sixth-century long heroic poem, the *Gododdin*, has had less notice. Equally, Percy's collection of ballads, *The Reliques of Ancient English Poetry* (1765), now outshines the collections made in the 1780s and 1790s by the tough and relatively rigorous Northumbrian, Joseph Ritson, who was not only more scrupulous in his editorial procedures, but far more accurate than Percy in locating the origins of ballads in an oral tradition emanating from the illiterate masses.[10]

Especially between 1760 and 1800, studies of popular language burgeoned. Dictionaries of English slang and provincialisms appeared to challenge Johnson's great dictionary of the *written* English language (1755).[11] Revisionist grammarians, who in the middle of the century were generally Dissenters addressing middle-class readers, but in the 1790s were sometimes radicals speaking for the half-lettered, challenged a tradition in writing English which insisted upon 'correctness' and upon a knowledge of Latin, for, in effect, such rules ensured that written discourse was controlled by the expensively educated.[12] Meanwhile the two greatest literary geniuses of the 'mainstream' tradition, Shakespeare and Milton, were reclaimed for the popular side. The Shakespearean scholars Francis Douce and George Steevens interpreted the comedies and histories, especially, as a product of Elizabethan popular culture, and the influence of this type of work is plainly seen in the paintings and engravings done in the 1790s for Boydell's exhibition-room in London, the Shakespeare Gallery.[13] In 1790 a similar project was begun for Milton, who as the 'great republican', a participator in England's own revolution, was an even more apt subject for canonisation in the stirring new times. Fuseli and Blake worked together on illustrations to Milton, and for Blake this meant a doubly significant apprenticeship, to a continental-trained, Michelangelesque painter and to the most exalted of English poets. But then it is hard to exaggerate the central significance of Milton, the outspoken prophet-poet and religious iconoclast, as a prototype for every major English poet who passed through a liberal phase during the Romantic period.

Of all British poets, it is William Blake, the working-class engraver, never normally thought of as typical, who straddles the radical ideological chasm of the 1790s, and manages even after that date to develop populist insights. Blake's juvenilia uses the standard pastoral and historical emblems of patriotism. In his poetry and prose of the 1770s and 1780s he imitates Spenser, Shakespeare and Macpherson, and he writes a patriot historical drama of a type familiar since Thomson's day, *Edward III*. Blake's first mature illuminated book, the *Songs of Innocence* (1789), idealises both the simplicity of the child and the simplicity of the pastoral world, and sets them up in opposition to the corruption of advanced adult society, a world most savagely delineated in the poem 'London' in the complementary series, *Songs of Experience* (1794):

> In every cry of every Man,
> In every Infants cry of fear,
> In every voice: in every ban,
> The mind-forg'd manacles I hear.

From 1790 on, Blake, a fervent sympathiser with the French Revolution, is engaged in imaginative world histories which are also projections of a revolutionary millennium. He writes a series of 'prophecies', *America* (1793), *Europe* (1794) and, in *The Song of Los* (1795), a Part I called

'Africa' and a Part II called 'Asia'. *America* is another great primitivist epic like Macpherson's *Fingal*, which Blake admired, though it is set in the present, in that wider Atlantic community the patriots were so keen to exalt. *Europe*, an attack on the European super-states, France and Britain, anticipates the work of the next generation of liberal poets, whose pre-occupation with the aristocratic state is the subject of the third section of this essay. The untypical feature of Blake's career is that he never clearly takes the step common to the middle-class poets of his generation, which is to become a nationalist loyal to the war effort against the French. Instead, Blake reverts after 1800 to a familiar type of patriot historicism, unfamiliarly crossed with a religious fundamentalism that has even older popular and radical credentials.

Between 1800 and 1803 Blake conceived the plots of his last two epics, *Milton* (1810) and *Jerusalem* (1820), which each synthesise two strands of popular thought significant among working-class radicals in the 1790s. One is the prophetic strain apparent even in Anglican preaching, but most sensational in the claims of Richard Brothers, ex-naval officer, religious enthusiast, and self-styled Prince of Israel: that the revolutionary wars were millenarian events which would enable the poor and meek to inherit the earth, and Brothers himself to convert the Jews to Christianity. The other is the 'revived' Druid or ancient British religion, as expounded by the Welshman Edward Williams, or Iolo Morganwg.[14] Blake knew of the Welsh nationalists' poetic claims early in the next century, but we do not know when and by what means he came on them. More likely perhaps than the translations by William Owen Pughe and Iolo Morganwg of 1789 and 1792, or than Iolo's own collection of poems of 1794, was Iolo's 'reinstitution' of the Druid ceremony of celebrating the autumn solstice on Primrose Hill in 1792, which was reported in the press. As for the nature of the appeal his work had for Blake, this was likely to have been his advocacy of a universal popular religion uncontaminated by priestcraft, mystification and a church hierarchy, and the role in his system of the bard, as a prophet and leader.

By 1808 Blake had achieved a number of works, both graphic and literary, which are plainly beholden to recent radical Welsh cultural nationalism. In describing his paintings on British mythological subjects (now lost) which he intended to exhibit in the forthcoming exhibition of his work, Blake claims to have studied British history, and he plainly perceives it as heroic in the older patriot style. 'Adam was a Druid, and Noah . . . '; Arthur's period was a time of 'ancient glory', when Britain was 'the source of learning and inspiration'.[15] The most famous and memorable of all Druidic doctrines, certainly in Iolo's descriptions of them, was the transmigration of souls. As a political activist and a revolutionary sympathiser at this time, Iolo plainly discerned the potential for a modern leader of the popular will to believe that a dead hero may return. He hints at his own bardic identity with previous bards, great spirits and benefactors of mankind, who had 'again assume[d] the earthly state, to restore the knowledge of truth'. Above all, Iolo invokes the memory of the sixth-century poet Taliesin, whose poetry speaks of the previous transmigrations his soul has passed through, ascending to heaven and returning to earth.[16]

The conception of a Taliesin who has witnessed the creation and is also magically identical with his Bardic son Iolo comes remarkably close to the central action of *Milton*. In Blake's poem the dead poet, the republican John Milton, benevolently chooses after a hundred years to re-enter the earthly life, in order to bring prophetic truths gathered in eternity down to his own people. He does this through the new inventions of Blake, the author of the present poem; he enters or merges with Blake. similarly, Blake's *Jerusalem* reflects the Welsh nationalists' claims to cultural seniority – or, rather, it exaggerates them greatly. In Blake's poem the British are symbolised by the male Albion, the Jews by his female emanation, Jerusalem. One meaning of their eventual reconciliation is plainly the conversion of the Jews to Christianity, the Jewish religious tradition being more corrupt than the British. Chapter 2 opens with Plate 27, an address 'To the Jews' in which Blake insists on British primacy:

Was Britain the primitive seat of the patriarchal religion? . . . It is true and cannot be controverted . . . Your ancestors derived their origin from Abraham, Heber, Shem and Noah, who were druids . . . Albion was the power of the druids.

In the last stages of writing *Milton*, and while still in the middle of *Jerusalem*, Blake seems to have come upon a much more conservative interpretation of Druidism as itself a degenerate 'state religion'.[17] Possibly under the influence of this more orthodox view, Blake in his epics as published no longer seems to boast of the purity of the native British inspirational tradition, as he certainly does in the passages quoted above. Yet in their fervour and their moments of pristine simplicity, especially when they fall into hymn-like metres, the two epics still evoke the older type of patriotism:

> The fields from Islington to Marybone,
> To Primrose Hill and Saint Johns Wood:
> Were builded over with pillars of gold,
> And there Jerusalem's pillars stood.[18]

Blake's introductory verses in *Milton*, confusingly well-known in modern times in Parry's setting as 'Jerusalem', sing of a millennium in which Jerusalem will be rebuilt 'in England's green and pleasant land'.

Modern patriotic conservatives have adopted the song as their own, but Blake around 1810 came nowhere near making a respectable upholder of the national effort. His *Jerusalem* celebrates Albion the Giant Man, the archetypal Briton, and it names the places, from London suburbs to Welsh mountains, where ordinary people live. But the poem as a whole still rejects the institutional aspect of Britain-in-history – the court, the law, and the state religion – which in Blake's idiom became 'stony laws' and 'serpent temples'. And it is wholly in line with the older, oppositional conception of patriotism to suggest, as Blake does, that the line back to earliest wisdom has been in the keeping of marginal, despised, half-visible elements in the present population, its Celtic fringe and its Bible-based antinomian sects.

PATRIOTS INTO NATIONALISTS

Though it is common to think of Romanticism as an artistic expression of the French Revolution, this cannot be correct in any simple sense if, as the previous section argued, a symbolic language of liberty, equality and popular nationhood had been evolving in England over the previous half-century. The political effect of the French Revolution was to provoke counter-revolution in England, at least in the propertied classes, and thus to scale down and muffle the rhetoric of liberty and nationhood in a literate pursuit like poetry. Concepts such as Nature and national history had to be divested of much of their recently acquired meaning, or they would remain oppositional and socially divisive. One of the commoner responses to the political crisis of 1790–1800 was to make both concepts more detailed, literal and particularised, so that their uncomfortable associations with the populace were lost.

George Crabbe (1754–1832) represents nature in a way that becomes characteristic of the nineteenth century. Even his early poems of the 1780s, such as *The Village* (1784), stand out for their unprecedented fidelity to a single locale, the bleak eastern seacoast around his native Aldeburgh in Suffolk. Crabbe himself represents the innovation as a change from the highbrow and idyllic literary pastoral of Virgil and Theocritus to an accurate imitation of the grim, prosy realities of modern life:

> . . . Cast by Fortune on a frowning coast,
> Which neither groves nor happy valleys boast . . .
> By such examples taught, I paint the Cot,
> As Truth will paint it and as Bards will not.
> (I.49–54)

Like so many eighteenth-century poets after the first quarter of the century, Crabbe was himself an isolated provincial from humble stock, the

son of the village exciseman. It is in fact now common to regard him as an
eighteenth-century poet, old-fashioned in his day and left behind by
Romanticism. But, as the word 'bard' hints, Crabbe is also rejecting a
much newer kind of poetry which idealised the countryside in terms different from those of the classical pastoral. His flat marshlands, peopled with
struggling, sinning individuals, also question the countryside of Gray in
'The Elegy in a Country Churchyard' (1751) and of Oliver Goldsmith in
'The Deserted Village' (1770), since in both these famous and representative eighteenth-century poems the poor villagers appear morally superior
to rich town-dwellers, and sympathetic because they are also implicitly the
victims of 'the mighty'. It is no accident that Crabbe had already attracted
the notice and patronage of the Whig statesman Edmund Burke, who
introduced him to the wealthy Duke of Rutland: Crabbe was first chaplain
to Rutland, then a parish clergyman in one of the duke's livings for the rest
of his life.

From the beginning, Crabbe drops the divisive social message. As he
develops his art, that of the verse short story, in collections such as *The
Borough* (1810) and *Tales* (1812), his characters become as isolated and
individual as his plots. What goes wrong in their lives, and often a lot goes
wrong, is no one's fault but their own. The brutalised fisherman Peter
Grimes, the comfortable, respectable, snobbish spinster Dinah, are more
believable and lifelike than eighteenth-century country-dwellers in literature, but they are not in the same degree 'the people'. Nor do Crabbe's
mudflats and weed-choked estuaries evoke 'the country': instead they have
been seen plausibly as interiorised landscapes, desolate images for personal alienation, among the earliest of modern poetry's waste lands. In one
sense Crabbe is anything but limited in his perspective, for he is a geologist,
a student of flora and fauna. Yet, paradoxically, the kind of generalisation
which that pre-Victorian interest leads to also has the effect of deflecting,
because it dwarfs, the social, humanitarian aim of making this world
better.

On nationhood, or history, a similar process of particularisation is
carried out by Walter Scott (1771–1832). Just as Crabbe's specific nature
counters the country party's generalised nature, so Scott's Scottish history
of the last three centuries, conveyed in his long narrative poems, beginning
with *The Lay of the Last Minstrel* (1805), and in the novels, beginning
with *Waverley* (1814), supersedes Macpherson's primitive and nationalist
epics. Scott should not be seen as initiating historical poetry or fiction, any
more than Crabbe or Wordsworth are the pioneers of nature-poetry. His
well-documented studies of relatively recent Scottish history serve the purposes of making his characters and communities familiar and likeable, and
of connecting them with English history. By beginning with the English–

Scottish border he draws on stories already familiar to the English reader, since the rivalry of the English Percy and the Scottish Douglas appears in Shakespeare's *Henry IV* Part I, and in the famous traditional 'Ballad of Chevy Chase'. Until well after the end of the Napoleonic Wars, Scott writes works which preach reconciliation, national solidarity, acceptance of a present-day world which history seems to have created by an inevitable process. In doing so he helps to erase the memory of a version of Scottish history which belongs to the literature of protest.

Again, Edmund Burke is often praised for his great polemical work, *The Reflections on the Revolution in France* (1790), because he is felt to have initiated the concept of a nation growing through history organically like a tree. It is true that the idea of a process leading to the present is far more important to Burke and to Scott than it is to their patriot predecessors. Yet, viewed against the whole-island and primitivist perspectives of, say, Thomson, Macpherson and Gray, Burke seems to have pared down the vision he found. He has shortened English history to the medieval Plantagenet kings and their successors, and moreover narrowed the social perspective from the past lives of the populace to the heroic deeds of an elite. It is Burke's literary achievement that he preserves the patriot sense of common humanity through the homely detail of his imagery and idiom; but his sense of the familiar and the family fits into a framework of customary law and social hierarchy, an elaborate system-as-it-is. So mixed was Burke's medium that the book at first embarrassed both sides. It was only by the end of the 1790s that the *Reflections* really began to elicit admiration from the type of reader Burke surely aimed for, the middle-of-the-road patriot, and to become a comfortable staging-post for middle-class liberals on the way to conservatism.

Samuel Taylor Coleridge (1772–1834) and William Wordsworth (1775–1850), both 'Jacobins' between 1791 and 1795, begin to sound like Burkeans before 1800. Of the two it is Coleridge who resembles Burke in his interest in history. As late as 1804, Coleridge and his former Jacobin friend, the poet Robert Southey (1774–1843), still planned to write a complete history of the literature of the British Isles, including the writings of the Celts and Anglo-Saxons, a project that does not sound very different from Thomas Gray's half a century earlier. When in 1797 Wordsworth and Coleridge divided the subject-areas of *Lyrical Ballads* (1798) between them, it was Coleridge who chose to imitate a historical ballad, while Wordsworth adopted the language and concerns of present-day rustics. Coleridge in *The Ancient Mariner* achieves the same shift of perspective that Burke and Scott do. He takes an incident – the mariner's slaying of the albatross – which must have happened in a remote age, barely imaginable, semi-pagan, pre-Reformation, and focuses upon what happened later: not merely the mariner's personal, spiritual journey through guilt, repentance and atonement, but the transformation of the remembered episode's symbolic significance over centuries, as an entire culture grows in religious understanding.[19] The folk-collectors and ballad-editors of the 1770s and 1780s, notably the Northumbrians John Brand and Joseph Ritson, rejoice when they find traces of paganism in some legend; Coleridge, on the contrary, emphasises the Christianising of his tale, its presumably ancient or gradual modelling to become a tale of redemption. In a later version, in 1817, he even adds a new layer of interpretation, a series of prose glosses in the margin, in the manner of a seventeenth-century Bible. History, a discourse which had so recently been used to challenge legitimacy, becomes an instrument to legitimise a present-day order.

Wordsworth's ballads of peasant life often seem similarly prone to preach acceptance of the current system. Like Crabbe, he tells stories about particular individuals. Many of them are very poor, but Wordsworth drops the type of explanation for their poverty that would have made the poem a social protest. It was fashionable in the 1790s to write poetic laments about beggars who were also victims of the government's policy of war with France, as Robert Southey had done, and Wordsworth himself in his still unpublished 'Salisbury Plain' of 1794. But Wordsworth in the *Lyrical Ballads* (1798) goes out of his way to insist that his impoverished sufferers are not evidence of the heartlessness of any section of society, still less of a particular policy, such as war. Perhaps the most striking example in the *Lyrical Ballads* of Wordsworth's changed views is the beautiful, meditative nature-poem 'Tintern Abbey'. A few years earlier Wordsworth had himself visited the ruins of the abbey, in the Wye valley on the Welsh border, and he also knew William Gilpin's *Observations on the River Wye* (1792). Gilpin's book, like other contemporary accounts, protests at the intrusion of industry and the presence of homeless vagrants in the ruins and in the surrounding woods, many of them dispossessed by the enclosure and reapportionment of village land. It is a peculiarity of Wordsworth's poem that its meticulous descriptions record the evidence for the displacement of the population: thin lines of smoke rising from the woods come from poor people trying to live as charcoal burners, a cottage 'green to the very door' may well have been abandoned. But Wordsworth on rural suffering, like Coleridge on paganism, prefers now to look elsewhere, at what is socially harmonious and consolatory: in this case, at his affection for his sister, and at the processes of memory that make the landscape a living presence and a moral influence years after he has seen it. For this purpose, it is an aesthetic landscape, empty of people, that apparently serves best; though the Wye valley's power to haunt him for so long may derive from his suppression of its troubling human features.[20]

Many critics now agree that Wordsworth had adopted the conservative line on key political and social questions by 1798. James Chandler illustrates this well by examining a poem of that year on a typical Wordsworthian subject, 'The Old Cumberland Beggar'.[21] Many of Wordsworth's derelicts are met by chance on a lonely country road or in London, but this old man belongs to the neighbourhood, and calls regularly at different houses to beg for money or good. Wordsworth sees him take out what he has been given:

> From a bag
> All white with flour, the dole of village dames,
> He drew his scraps and fragments, one by one;
> And scanned them with a fixed and serious look
> Of idle computation. In the sun,
> Upon the second step of that small pile,
> Surrounded by those wild unpeopled hills,
> He sat, and ate his food in solitude:
> And ever, scattered from his palsied hand,
> That, still attempting to prevent the waste,
> Was baffled still, the crumbs in little showers
> Fell on the ground; and the small mountain birds,
> Not venturing yet to peck their destined meal,
> Approached within the length of half his staff.

At the bottom of the human social chain, the beggar in turn nurtures the birds, while he prompts his betters to charity:

> The mild necessity of use compels
> To acts of love; and habit does the work
> Of reason.

The social hierarchy contributes naturally to maintain a moral order; all is for the best. But the resonance of the old idea of nature is too strong to be fully deflected and socialised. At the very least, Wordsworth in his language and his imagery goes on sending our conflicting messages. A good example is his prose Preface to the *Lyrical Ballads*, first added to the volume in 1800, and then amplified in 1802 with a number of phrases that could not have sounded other than democratic in the sensitive war climate. 'What is a Poet? . . . He is a man speaking to men . . . Nor let the necessity of producing immediate pleasure [i.e. submitting to the reader] be considered a degradation of the poet's art. It is far otherwise . . . it is a homage paid to the native and naked dignity of man.' Among his poems, for every humble, accepting Cumberland beggar, there is at least one stranger and less reassuring figure. Wordsworth, or rather his persona the Poet, meets one of the latter on the moors in *Resolution and Independence* (1807). The narrator has been thinking egotistically of his own sophisticated profession and its troubles; oddly, of two poets, dead tragically young, who also happen to belong to the patriot tradition of Wordsworth's own youth:

> I thought of Chatterton, the marvellous Boy,
> The sleepless soul that perished in his pride;
> Of Him who walked in glory and in joy
> Following his plough, along the mountain-side . . .

The sight of an old man, resembling a huge stone, or a sea-beast emerging from a pool, again brings his thoughts back to Chatterton and Robert Burns. The leechgatherer is a Scotsman and, like so many of the unorthodox sages encountered in Wordsworth's poetry, talkative, wise, but barely comprehensible. Some of Wordsworth's best poems, of which this is one, preach not acceptance of what is, but the painful loss of the past. There is a gap between the educated modern practitioner in the written culture, and a half-understood, fading oral wisdom, that of the child or sage or Druid, which temporarily abashes the self-confident modern man:

> In my mind's eye I seemed to see him pace
> About the weary moors continually
> Wandering about alone and silently.

It is because he could still write the Preface and a poem about a leech-gatherer that Wordsworth went on being associated into the second and third decades of the century, especially by some of his more liberal readers, with his old 'levelling Muse'.[22]

INTERNATIONALISM AND THE NATIONALISM
OF OTHER NATIONS

Two of the best-known poets among the next literary generation are Lord Byron, an impoverished hereditary peer, and Percy Bysshe Shelley, the estranged son of a wealthy baronet. Their rank makes them unusual among English poets, and Byron's contributed importantly to his fame in his own day; but there were general social factors behind the recruitment of fashionable men to poetry. After half a century of expansion, the literary profession had become better defined. By about 1800, biographies of men of letters were one of the staples of much-read journals like the *Gentleman's Magazine*; dictionaries of writers, and encyclopaedic collections of their works, were issued; poets and leading novelists became sought-after guests at smart parties. Thwarted from travelling in Europe to collect art-works because of the 22-year-long war, the upper orders established a new terrain to cultivate, that of highbrow literature. After two generations in which it seems unusually provincial, literature from the middle of the war on looks like a centralised, aristocratic pursuit. There was nothing originally aristocratic about the more important friends and acquaintances of

Byron and Shelley – Mary Shelley, Thomas Love Peacock, Leigh Hunt, William Hazlitt, Tom Moore. But they worked in London, met in drawing-rooms, and alluded richly to literature in learned languages and to that metropolitan pursuit, politics. Even if the brilliant Regency period was shortlived – the period of the 'younger Romantics' is roughly 1812–22 – it marked the end of the remarkable provincial phase that preceded it.

The real intellectual inspiration for the younger Romantics and for their metropolitan readers lay in the period leading up to the French Revolution, the 1770s and 1780s, when British upper-class culture had been markedly liberal and pro-French. Wealthy aristocrats, who were often enthusiastic buyers of paintings, sculpture and other artefacts, looked to Rome as the current European art-capital, or travelled further afield in the Mediterranean, the Near East, Egypt and Abyssinia. Scholars and scientists corresponded particularly with the French, though theologians and Bible-scholars were in touch with Germany. The prevailing tone of most of this scholarly industry was liberal and secular. Appropriate fields – including classicism, Bible-criticism, the study of the world's religions or myths – served the purposes of critics of the political establishment, in France particularly but also, in more generalised terms, in England. Thus two of the most admired and influential of British intellectuals in the second half of the eighteenth century, the philosopher David Hume and the historian Edward Gibbon, each spent much time in France or Switzerland, and helped to bring the characteristic French qualities of irony and irreligiousness into fashion in Britain. Gibbon's magisterial *Decline and Fall of the Roman Empire* (1776–88) established not only the tone of aristocratic intellectualism, but also two of its favourite topics: the injustice, inefficiency and bad government that accompanies an over-extensive empire, and the malign influence of religion in civic life.

Shelley (1792–1822), educated at Eton and (briefly) Oxford, absorbed the Enlightenment scepticism of Hume and Gibbon, made fiery by further reading in French revolutionary ideologues and their British sympathisers. Among the latter, for example, Shelley read the scientist, evolutionist and poet Erasmus Darwin, especially his annotated poem on natural history, *The Botanic Garden* (1791), and the anarchist philosopher William Godwin, whose *Political Justice* (1793) confronted the problem of how to unchain minds already moulded by law, custom and prejudice. Like many other English intellectuals, Shelley also read French 'mythologists', or anti-Christian students of paganism, and he was particularly beholden to Constantin Volney's *Ruins of Empire* (1791), a book translated into English in its year of publication. Volney had travelled in the Middle East in the 1780s, and his three books describing the current societies and ancient cultures he found encouraged French dreams of revolution on a world scale. The last chapters of *The Ruins* set out a bleak vision of the history of human society: successive empires, all of them similarly structured, ruled by despots with the help of small elites, had kept themselves in power by using religion as a tool of state. Religion had persuaded the masses either that it was their duty to obey, or that another world was more important than this one. Volney's imaginary 'Legislator' appears in his closing chapters as a spokesman for the French Revolution: now, at last, the masses may be released from imposition, once they can be persuaded to un-think their beliefs. Revolutionaries will re-tell the old charmed stories, the myths, in order to expose their falsity, and thus to break the people's mental chains. *Queen Mab* (1813), Shelley's first long poem, is a Volneyan vision-poem in which the Fairy Queen appears to a young girl, Ianthe, to re-instruct her in religion from a brutally materialist and atheist point of view.

The longest and most important of Shelley's mature poems also often meet Volneyan goals, including the most ambitious of all, *Prometheus Unbound* (1820). Here Shelley merges a plot found in Genesis and *Paradise Lost* with a plot found in Greek mythology and in Aeschylus; for in both myths, God the Father wars with an antagonist. In Shelley's re-telling, Prometheus, the Greek antagonist, becomes identified with Satan; but he is virtuous, and not only do we see him triumphing, we understand the hitherto orthodox, legitimising story from his rebel's vantage-point. Similarly, Shelley's charming mythological poem *The Witch of Atlas* (1820) begins as a pagan myth of creation and ends as a Volneyan satire on a corrupt ancient theocracy, Egypt. *Adonais* (1821) laments Keats's death by re-writing Milton's elegy for a dead youth, *Lycidas*, but in Shelley's version there is no consolatory doctrine of a personal afterlife.

Among the modern 'myths' Shelley revises and exposes are pro-Christian accounts of Eastern religions. Here his leading antagonist was the friend of Wordsworth and Shelley, Robert Southey. By 1801 Southey had given up his youthful Jacobinism, and was declaring his support of the British war effort with a romance epic nominally featuring Mohammedanism, but really exalting monotheism, *Thalaba the Destroyer*. More contentiously political and far more influential was *The Curse of Kehama* (1810), another readable verse romance, this time set in India. The theme, the cruelty and anarchy of Hinduism, supported Southey's serious journalistic campaign to persuade the British public of the need to impose a strong Christian government on India.[23] Southey's wicked, ambitious tyrant Kehama is an Eastern *alter ego* (and, it is hinted, a natural ally) of Napoleon. His epic's opening scene, a funeral at which sati, or widow-burning is practised, probably qualifies as the most frequently imitated scene in all Romantic poetry. Shelley for example invokes Southey's Hindu pyre twice in *The Revolt of Islam* (1818), an epic in which the French Revolution is relived in the Middle East. It ends not in triumph but in catastrophe: two cruel monotheists, the Turkish emperor Othman and his advisor, a Spanish Catholic priest, burn the hero and heroine, the empire's would-be liberators, in the final *auto da fé*.

To a remarkable degree, the favourite location of English poetry in the second decade of the nineteenth century becomes the Eastern Mediterranean and the Middle East, the route to India. Byron begins his career with a Spenserean epic, *Childe Harold* (1812), that is also a versified travelogue, and so goes one better than Southey, who got his learned annotations from books. The Christian Greeks seek liberation from an alien empire, that of the Turks, and in *Childe Harold* II, and especially *The Giaour* (1813), Byron depicts the cruelty and superstition of the master-race in no favourable light. But he also undercuts the foolish, bigoted Greek Christians: he seems afraid that the revolt, if it comes, may merely give the Greeks a new breed of tyrants. Byron campaigns for a secular liberation of the Greeks, not one on behalf of fellow-religionists: hence his zeal to glamorise, through figures like his Corsair, the real-life pirates and brigands of the Eastern-Mediterranean, equivalents in the period of the modern-day urban terrorist.

In introducing *The Corsair* (1814), Byron himself primed the public to expect an even more thorough-going poem on political and religious nationalism, *Lalla Rookh* (1817), by the Irish poet Tom Moore. In Moore's best-received episode, 'The Fireworshippers', a Persian hero, having failed in his attempt to resist an Arab, Moslem invasion, sets fire to his own citadel and so dies on an altar dedicated to the religion of his own people. This too was an appropriate riposte to Southey for his malignant representation of Hinduism. And so was the final curtain of Byron's magnificent Oriental drama, *Sardanapalus* (1821), when the civilised, agnostic Assyrian monarch, who believes in love, not war or empire, sets fire to himself and his palace. In all these cases, the monotheist imperialists behave a great deal worse than the local resisters. Liberal poets of the second decade of the nineteenth century question the religious generalisations which facilitate colonialism, and, especially, criticise Britain's own role in steadily annexing India.

Byron's Oriental poems need to be taken seriously, and set beside the great unfinished satirical epic, *Don Juan* (1819–24), which in the English-speaking world has become his chief claim to fame. For both the major themes he shares with Shelley – the assault upon institutional religion, and the representation of Western states as evil, oligarchic empires – can be read as metaphorical. The church is the means whereby the state cunningly imposes itself at home; the theme of empire shows it imposing itself by force abroad. The poets' selective, hostile portrayal of a tyrannous state coincides with a period of mass unrest and renewed radical polemic; from 1816, when the heyday of Byron and Shelley begins, William Cobbett, the greatest journalist of the day, was informing a popular readership more directly and bluntly of the iniquities of a political system he described as 'Old Corruption'. As metaphors, church and empire compare interestingly with pre-war nature and nationhood. There is a shift from positive to negative: early nineteenth-century poetry becomes blacker, more satirical. But the focus on the actual doings of the state tends also to be literal and detailed, to appeal to a knowledge of recent events, even personalities, while eighteenth-century poets engaged in a more generalised, fanciful, farflung search to give social body to the concept of country.

THE 1820s

The 1820s saw the end of the brilliantly productive post-war era of poetry. Posterity has tended to the view that the great epoch was rounded off by the early deaths of the three leading poets of the younger generation, Keats in 1821, Shelley in 1822 and Byron in 1824. At the time it was observed that poetry was becoming commercially less profitable. Already by the end of his short career the youngest of the poets, Keats, was moving away from the example of the slightly older fellow-liberals, his friend Leigh Hunt and his acquaintance Shelley, who both thought Keats ideologically one of themselves. A man of lower-middle-class origins, the son of an ostler, Keats had received a good secular education at a Dissenting academy, but was uninterested in the public sphere of power-politics which for Byron and Shelley was a natural habitat. He plainly found in Wordsworth a professionalism, a singleminded devotion to the craft of poetry, which he could respond to. And it is Wordsworth and Keats who have on the whole been regarded by English-speaking readers as the leading literary artists of the period, the prototypes of the modern writer absorbed in self, haunted by words, private, dedicated, specialised. Between 1818 and 1820, Keats turned away from Milton, an important earlier model but a public poet, and sought instead to recover the richness, warmth, dispassionateness and unintellectuality of Shakespeare. He was never drawn to the Shakespeare that more radical readers had read as a festive, near-anonymous poet of the people. Like the two great post-war Shakespearean critics, Hazlitt and Coleridge, Keats was interested in the tragedies, as private introverted dramas of individual character, rather than in the histories and comedies. He was similarly selective with other fashionable motifs. He took the mythological subjects which for the Shelley circle became the occasion for critiques of Christianity, and (in *Lamia* and in the epic fragment *Hyperion*, both 1820) turned them into the family dramas of realised human personalities. In these, in narrative poems such as *The Eve of St Agnes*, and above all in his *Odes*, Keats treats poetry as though its natural subject is not politics and civic morality but art and private feeling.

Keats constructed a separate literary sphere, in which Beauty alone ruled. It was a well-timed move, for the ever-growing middle-class reading public wanted books that treated the ideal in a religious or at least idealistic way, and avoided satire and profanity. Together with the high-minded and more directly consoling Wordsworth, Keats helped pave the way for the poetry of the second quarter of the century, ruled over by Tennyson, the idealist, aesthete and Christian moralist. At the same time the public acquired a taste for a new kind of literary celebrity, the essayist or journalist. Especially when writing strongly characterised confessional fragments of autobiography, informal versions of Wordsworth's lofty but still-unpublished *Prelude* (begun in 1797, published 1850), prose-writers now familiarised the public with an unequivocally Romantic genre, the self-portrait of an artist. Charles Lamb's humorous, melancholy reminiscences, *The Essays of Elia*, and William Hazlitt's often self-tormenting *Table-Talk* first appeared in the *London Magazine* early in the 1820s. Thomas De Quincey's more sustained fictionalised autobiography, *The Confessions of an English Opium Eater*, appeared in the same venue in 1820–1, and may have helped to provoke Hazlitt's strange masterpiece, the love-letters he issued as an epistolary novel, the *Liber Amoris* (1823).[24] When we think of English 'Romantic prose', we do not on the whole think of books or essays about literature, philosophy or aesthetics, such as are found in German, but of this type of occasional, informal writing aimed at the general public rather than at other intellectuals. An early European intellectual in England (to be followed in the next generation by Carlyle, Ruskin, Macaulay, Mill and Arnold) is Coleridge, who now after 1820 belatedly acquired a significant literary following. His polymathic reading and his profound religious sensibility bore fruit at last in an exalted vein of social criticism. His late books, especially *The Aids to Reflection* (1825) and *On the Constitution of the Church and State* (1830), impressed a student generation caught in the grip of the religious revival far more than his early political essays and mid-life literary criticism had impressed his contemporaries.

What academics now call the period of 'High Romanticism' in England had been and gone without making much impact on the nation's favourite literary form, the novel. The six major poets attempted drama but none completed a novel, except Shelley with two juvenile experiments with the Gothic, *Zastrozzi* and *St Irvyne*. Until 1814, when Scott's *Waverley* appeared, it seemed to be taken for granted that the novel was a woman's form, which treated daily life and domestic concerns by means of its favourite plot, a young woman's (or, more rarely, a young man's) preparation for marriage. The novelist whom English-speaking readers now rate supreme in the period, Jane Austen (1775–1817), uses this format and is not considered one of the Romantics. Nor are the other leading women novelists, Fanny Burney and Maria Edgeworth. But the man who intruded on their domain, the poet Walter Scott, has not struck most of his recent admirers as precisely Romantic either, for Scott opened with a brilliant series of social, national novels, portraying the Scotland of living memory, or only just beyond it.

Scott's commanding prestige as a novelist for more than a decade is an interesting example, among other things, of the effect that the early nineteenth-century professionalising of literature had on women's saliency as writers. He successfully introduced into his novels his own wealth of worldly knowledge, his interest in the nation's affairs, and his formidable antiquarian scholarship. Especially as practised by many women writers, the novel had not seemed to demand many qualifications in the way of experience or education, and one result of Scott's making the historical novel and the panoramic social novel fashionable was that women novelists became relatively less successful until the emergence after 1840 of Elizabeth Gaskell and the Brontës. But it is wrong to exaggerate the limited horizons of the woman's novel as Scott found it. Its ability to portray the irrational had been imaginatively extended by Ann Radcliffe in her dreamily-landscaped historical novels of the 1790s. The Anglo-Irish gentlewoman Maria Edgeworth initiated the regional novel with *Castle Rackrent* (1800), a remarkable technical experiment in which an Irish servant narrates in his own peasant accents the decline and fall of his master's dynasty. After this a number of other women novelists took up and excelled in similar genre-pieces, including Elizabeth Hamilton, Susan Ferrier and Lady Morgan (*née* Sydney Owenson).

Also before Scott, and also ambitiously, a type of novel-of-ideas, or *tendenz-roman*, was developed in the 1790s by, among others, William Godwin, whose masterpiece *Caleb Williams* (1794) borrows some Gothic settings and a thrilling suspense-plot to act out the conflict of class between the aristocrat Falkland and the plebeian Caleb Williams. M. G. Lewis's *The Monk* (1795), Mary Shelley's *Frankenstein* (1818), Charles Robert Maturin's *Melmoth the Wanderer* (1820) and James Hogg's *Confessions of a Justified Sinner* (1824) have come to be known collectively as 'Gothic' novels, and to be associated with Romantic irrationality, but this is to overlook their structural formality, and the one essential characteristic they have in common. All their protagonists are obsessives seized with a pernicious idea, a notion which leads to the disintegration not only of the hero but of his loved ones and of the entire civic order: they seem to have been read as, and intended for, allegories of revolution. And indeed Scott too, far more than has generally been recognised, tends to write on this theme, especially after 1820. In later novels such as *The Monastery*, *The Abbot* and *Redgauntlet*, he is drawn not to portray the medieval world for characteristics special to itself, but for the danger of breakdown it shares with the modern world. The theme, and the pessimism it induces, may resemble qualities in E. T. A. Hoffmann's brilliant German tales, but the differences are equally interesting, for by their intellectualism and their structural formality the English novels remain committed to identified rational positions – social progress and egalitarianism in Godwin's case, for example, or Protestantism as opposed to Irish Catholic Emancipation in Maturin's.

Movements, like periods, cannot be expected to begin or end tidily. Individual writers are often hard to classify. One of the most remarkable of English poets is the Northamptonshire labourer John Clare (1793–1864), who wrote prolifically through the 1820s and 1830s, poetry and prose, songs, ballads, loving observations of bird and human life, desolate accounts of himself; then, breaking down, he spent more than a quarter of a century in two asylums for the insane. Nothing could be more evidently Romantic, except that Clare also represents the perfect late flowering of the eighteenth-century English provincial or 'country' tradition. He even joined it consciously, by training himself to be a poet through reading Thomson and Burns. Like Crabbe, that other village poet, he was a meticulous and scientific observer, who kept notes of birds, their plumage, song, habitats and nests, and of village sports, customs and songs. Some he sent in to William Hone, the radical publisher, who brought out a large two-volume *Everyday Book* made up of such local records in 1829. Clare intended, he wrote in 1825, to compile a Natural History of Helpston, his village, and this is one way of summarising his oeuvre, though the poems especially convey an emotion outside the range of most anthropology, the alienation of the observer from the community he observes.

Coming late as he did to the ideal of creating popular, simple or universally human poetry, Clare was cursed with too much consciousness. Well-wishers like Lamb and Clare's publisher John Taylor, who had also published Keats, urged him to use the written language, standard metropolitan English, as the only fit medium for poetry. Taylor indeed, after initially tolerating Clare's provincialisms as curiosities, took to 'correcting' them wholesale. But when he tried to disallow the expression 'eggs on', Clare's reply shows his understanding that his language was not to be separated from all the features of place, time and class that made up his experience.

'Whether provincial or not I cannot tell; but it is common with the vulgar (I am of that class) and I heartily desire no word of mine to be altered.'[25] Like Ritson and Spence,[26] he went his own way with spelling, and when he came to treat a wintry morning, a familiar set-piece for eighteenth-century nature poets from Thomson on, his deployment of dialect powerfully conveys intransigence: it will not let the comfortable towndweller settle into the scene. The opening of Clare's sonnet seems almost impudently to parody Taylor's more biddable author, Keats:

> O for a pleasant book to cheat the sway
> Of winter – where rich mirth with hearty laugh
> Listens and rubs his legs on corner seat
> For fields are mire and sludge – and badly off
> Are those who on their pudgy paths delay
> There striding shepherd seeking driest way
> Fearing nights wetshod feet and hacking cough
> That keeps him waken till the peep of day
> Goes shouldering onward and with ready hook
> Progs oft to ford the sloughs that nearly meet
> Accross the lands – croodling and thin to view
> His loath dog follows – stops and quakes and looks
> For better roads – till whistled to pursue
> Then on with frequent jump he hirkles through.

The rage and loathing of the man and the dog for their element is duplicated by the rage of the poet, who, burdened and clogged with his rough vocabulary, can only contend with his medium. The smooth language of the rich belongs to the rich, and so, perhaps, does poetry itself, especially a form like the sonnet. A provincial poet in the nineteenth century who is also a labourer cannot be unaware of his own marginality.

What, then, of the later eighteenth-century poet? Labourers wrote verse then, but to become an established, professional poet, selling to the public, was a far more remote possibility. It was the public success of poetry and the general professionalising of literature in the early nineteenth century that opened doors to educated middle-class writers without patronage, but much less often and less widely to working men and to women. Clare's bitter sense of exclusion from London as from Helpston casts a curious light not only on the very different experience of his near-contemporary Keats, but also on the eighteenth-century country poet in the patriot tradition. Poets from Thomson to the Wordsworth of *The Lyrical Ballads* could claim to be speaking for the 'real' nation, that is for the majority of the people, by defining them in contradistinction to the minority who spoke for the 'official' nation in the capital. The sense of class was not yet so general or well-articulated that it exposed the fallacy of a middle-class writer's claiming an identity of interest with the illiterate masses.

For the purposes of writing poetry, it perhaps did not matter that such claims to representativeness were spurious, or that the poets' rhetoric was more radical than their practical politics, as the testing times of the 1790s showed. Merely to believe in a community of shared interests, in the reality of 'the patriot nation' or alternatively 'the republic of letters' was inspiriting enough, especially for individual writers who might in real life be isolated and socially obscure. The new, large and unjaded eighteenth-century audience created conditions which allowed, even demanded, the redefinition of the world and of the self. The newly devised figure of the common reader has a central role in this story, for it is to him and to her that we ultimately owe Romanticism, the most broadly accessible and powerfully activating of literary movements.

NOTES

1 Standard works on English Romanticism which have influenced perceptions of its important writers, its date of commencement and its place in the history of ideas include René Wellek, 'The concept of Romanticism in literary history', *Comparative Literature*, 1 (1949), and *A History of Modern Criticism*, vol. 3 (London, 1957); M. H. Abrams, *The Mirror and the Lamp* (New York, 1953), *Natural Supernaturalism* (New York, 1971), and his selections for the period in the *Norton Anthology*; Northrop Frye, beginning with his book on Blake, *A Fearful Symmetry* (New York, 1947); Harold Bloom, *A Visionary Company* (New York and London, 1962), and subsequent work. Among studies published in England are Basil Willey, *Nineteenth-Century Studies* (London, 1949), Graham Hough, *The Romantic Poets* (London, 1953), and the broad survey, including England, by H. G. Schenk, *The Mind of the European Romantics* (London, 1966).

2 Geoffrey Hartman, *Wordsworth's Poetry, 1787–1814* (New Haven, 1964).

3 For recent work by historians on the eighteenth-century patriot movement, see Hugh Cunningham, 'The language of patriotism, 1750–1914', *History Workshop*, 12 (1981), 8–33; Linda Colley, 'Whose nation? Class and national consciousness in Britain, 1750–1830', *Past and Present*, 113 (1986), 96–117, and J. R. Dinwiddy, 'Patriotism and national sentiment in England, 1790–1805', paper delivered Paris, Nov. 1985.

4 Gray's Commonplace Book, in three volumes containing a thousand pages, is in Pembroke College, Cambridge. He handed over some of his material to his friend and fellow-poet Thomas Warton, whose own *History of English Poetry* appeared in 1774–88. But, though Warton followed Gray's anti-French lead by representing English poetry arriving at maturity around 1600, he omitted Gray's Welsh and Norse researches, beginning instead in 1100.

5 Gray's 'Elegy' was much reprinted in both England and America as a popular, anti-aristocratic poem; cf. John Brand on Gray as 'the poet of humanity',

Popular Antiquities, ed. Sir Henry Ellis, new edn, 3 vols. (1895), p. ixn. (from Brand's Preface, dated 1795).

6 James Boswell, *Life of Johnson*, ed. R. W. Chapman (Oxford, 1953) p. 302.

7 For Macpherson's reception in Germany, see especially Bernhard Fabian, 'English books and their German readers', in Paul J. Korshin (ed.), *The Widening Circle: Essays on the Circulation of Literature in Eighteenth-Century Europe* (Philadelphia, 1976), p. 127. His impact on Europe in general is surveyed in Paul van Tieghem, *Ossian en France*, 2 vols. (Paris, 1917), and 'Ossian et l'ossianisme dans la littérature européenne au XVIIIe siècle', in his *Le Preromantisme* (Paris, 1924), pp. 195–287. Macpherson's achievement and significance have been thoughtfully reassessed by Howard Gaskill, 'Ossian Macpherson: towards a rehabilitation', *Comparative Criticism*, 8 (1986), 113–46.

8 Robert Anderson (ed.), *Works of the British Poets*, 13 vols. (Edinburgh, 1792–5), and Alexander Chalmers (ed.), *Works of the English Poets*, 21 vols. (London, 1810). 'It need be no surprise that moderation, decorum, restraint and propriety were the criteria controlling admission . . . , the very qualities which have helped to impart an air of remoteness and insubstantiality to much eighteenth-century poetry. There could be no place for the eccentric, the vulgar, the extravagant, the disturbing, the subversive.' Roger Lonsdale, *The New Oxford Book of Eighteenth Century Verse* (Oxford, 1984), p. xxxvi.

9 See for example Abrams, *The Mirror and the Lamp*, and Lawrence Lipking, *The Ordering of the Arts in the Eighteenth Century* (Princeton, 1970).

10 Ritson's most important single work was probably his *Select Collection of English Songs*, 3 vols. (London, 1783). Blake was one of a team of engravers who worked on the illustrations done for this book by Thomas Stothard: both the drawing and engraving styles aimed at reproducing the folk art effect of woodcut. Ritson prefaces the volume with his important 'Historical Essay on National Song', in which he censures Percy and Warton for carelessness and for a bias towards gentility. Even more popular and widely influential was his *Robin Hood: A Collection of All the Ancient Poems, Songs and Ballads, now Extant*, 2 vols. (London, 1795), in which he argues polemically and topically that the songs amount to the populace's own history of their experiences and attitudes, an element missing from official written history. See my *Burke, Paine, Godwin and the Revolution Controversy* (Cambridge, 1984), pp. 203–5.

11 E.g., Francis Grose, *A Classical Dictionary of the Vulgar Tongue* (1785) and *A Provincial Glossary* (1787).

12 Both Ritson and Thomas Spence (1750–1814), a self-educated pamphleteer who preached an agrarian communism, also campaigned for a simplified spelling. But the most celebrated single effort to challenge orthodox grammar in the interests of the radicals was John Horne Tooke's *Diversions of Purley*, 2 vols. (1786, 1805). See M. Cohen, *Sensible Words: Linguistic Practice in England, 1640–1785* (Baltimore, 1977), J. Barrell, 'The language properly so called', in *English Literature in History, 1730–1780* (London, 1983), and Olivia Smith, *The Politics of Language* (Oxford, 1984).

13 Though the prestigious painters of the day such as Reynolds and West were offered tragic or serious historical subjects, Winifred Friedman points out in *Boydell's Shakespeare Gallery* (New York, 1975) that illustrations for the comedies by Henry Fuseli and Robert Smirke attracted quite as much notice,

and were held to realise particularly well the distinct qualities of Shakespeare and of his characters. Smirke specialised in scenes of broad comedy set in low or middle life, for which he used a style of semi-caricature in the English tradition derived from Hogarth. Fuseli invoked a stronger, more grotesque and even horrific tradition of German folk art in order to realise the witches in *Macbeth* or the fairies in *A Midsummer Night's Dream*.

14 For Iolo Morganwg and his colleague William Owen Pughe, both of whom seem to have had an extensive but largely undocumented acquaintance among London writers, see Gwyn Williams, above, pp. 9–36. Accounts of Iolo's career which bring out the qualities that could have appealed to English writers have been given by Prys Morgan, *Iolo Morganwg* (Cardiff, 1975); *A New History of Wales: The Eighteenth-Century Renaissance* (Llandybie, 1981); 'The hunt for the Welsh past in the Romantic period', *The Invention of Tradition*, ed. E. Hobsbawm and T. Ranger (Cambridge, 1983).

15 William Blake, *A Descriptive Catalogue* (1809), *Complete Poetry and Prose of William Blake*, ed. D. V. Erdman (New York, 1982), pp. 542–3.

16 [Iolo Morganwg], *Llywarc Hen: Heroic Elegies*, ed. W. Owen [Pughe] (London, 1792), p. lviin.

17 Blake's probable conservative sources were two volumes by the Rev. Edmund Davies, rector of Bishopston, Glamorgan, *Celtic Researches* (1804) and *Mythology and Rites of the British Druids* (1809). Davies became outspoken about the ideological bias of Owen and Iolo, particularly in the *Llywarc Hen* volume. 'The principles here announced, seem to go rather beyond the levellers of the seventeenth century, and to savour of a Druidism which originated in Gaul, and was from thence transplanted into some corners of Britain, not many ages before 1792, when the memorial of Bardism made its appearance.' *Mythology and Rites*, pp. 56–7.

18 Blake, *Jerusalem*, ch. 2, Plate 27.

19 For a detailed study of the poem as a commentary on the processes of historical transmission, see Jerome J. McGann, *The Beauty of Inflections* (Oxford, 1985), pp. 135–72.

20 'Wordsworth's pastoral prospect is a fragile affair, artfully assembled by acts of exclusion.' Marjorie Levinson, *Wordsworth's Great Period Poems* (Cambridge, 1986), p. 32, in a discussion of 'Tintern Abbey' to which mine is indebted.

21 James K. Chandler, *Wordsworth's Second Nature* (Chicago, 1984), pp. 84–92.

22 Hazlitt, 'Mr Wordsworth', *Spirit of the Age* (1825); *Collected Works of William Hazlitt*, ed. P. P. Howe, 21 vols. (London 1931), XI.87.

23 See e.g. Southey, *Quarterly Review*, 1 (Feb. 1809), 217, and other reviews by Southey on missions to India in the *Annual Review* (1802 and 1803).

24 See my 'Long tradition of Hazlitt's *Liber Amoris*', in *English Satire and the Satiric Tradition*, ed. Claude Rawson (Oxford, 1984), pp. 209–25.

25 John Clare to John Taylor, quoted by John Barrell, *The Idea of Landscape and the Sense of Place* (Cambridge, 1972), p. 126.

26 See above, n. 12.

3

Haunted by history:
Irish romantic writing 1800–50

TOM DUNNE

The view that Romanticism was a richly confused and often contradictory phenomenon, with each local manifestation reflecting its unique social, cultural and political contexts, is well illustrated by the case of Ireland. It may seem surprising, for example, that German ideas had so little influence on Irish writers and cultural nationalists during the first half of the nineteenth century.[1] There were obvious similarities between the young and mainly bourgeois urban intellectuals of both countries, resentful at a degrading provincialism, the dominance of a foreign culture and the lack of opportunity and reward for their talents. In both, Romanticism developed partly as a social critique of corrupt state and oligarchical power, and featured historical genres which analysed the nature and consequences of imperial rule. However, while Germany produced a relatively coherent and self-confident Romanticism, with an impressive philosophical base and major creative dimensions, that of Ireland was confused and introverted, and stressed partisan rather than philosophical explorations of the past. This contrast reflected very different historical experiences, in particular of foreign rule, which in the Irish case involved the destruction rather than the erosion of indigenous culture and language, and, ultimately, total absorption into a major centralising and imperial state. What made Ireland unique in western Europe, and most shaped its culture, was its radical, traumatic and (in its modern phase) still recent experience of foreign conquest, followed by colonisation on a massive scale, which left victors and victims alike obsessed with its social, political and cultural legacies.

The Irish colonial experience was felt no less intensely because the country's colonial status was disguised, particularly since the early sixteenth century, by one legal fiction or another, and at the beginning of the Romantic period an important change took place in both the nature of the colonial relationship with Britain and its masking legal form. The Act of Union of 1800, an attempt to form a *cordon sanitaire* to prevent the contagion of European revolution, involved a change from indirect to direct rule, and from Ireland being characterised as an independent 'kingdom' to one having free and equal partnership in the new 'United Kingdom of Great Britain and Ireland'. However, the established pattern of perceptions and response, like those of power and wealth, endured among all the groups involved, whether 'native' Irish, colonist Irish or English; Irish society, like the Anglo-Irish relationship, remained fundamentally colonial. The change has been well described as making Ireland a 'metropolitan colony within the United Kingdom'[2] and the inevitable intensification of the contact between the two countries which it involved created an explosive context for the dual processes of modernisation and Anglicanisation in Ireland. W. J. McCormack's argument that the Union was of great importance in the formulation of Irish Romanticism emphasised its symbolic force and appropriateness in reflecting an unrealised aspiration to wholeness and healing.[3] More important, however, were its concrete consequences in the areas of cultural and political development, and in particular the reactive and often reactionary formulations of 'national' identity which it provoked. Ireland's accelerated absorption of English culture after 1800 ensured that whatever the influence of European Romanticism, it would be mediated mainly through England; and English Romantic modes, notably of the picturesque and the gothic, were an obvious feature of Irish writing in this period. However, these were transformed by the Irish context and by Irish needs, even when they were being exploited to reach English audiences.

Irish Romantic literature was intensely and undisguisedly political, and Irish politics during this period was dominated by Daniel O'Connell's attempts either to operate the new system for the benefit of the majority Catholic population, or to achieve its 'Repeal' – attempts met by Irish Protestant or 'unionist' commitment to the status quo, including the creation of new cultural frameworks for the maintenance of their 'ascendancy'. O'Connell's colourful rhetoric, fulminating against 'national slavery' and 'seven hundred years of oppression', was employed in the pursuit of very limited ends from a nationalist point of view, at most asking for a restricted autonomy within a different but still imperial framework. The very vagueness of O'Connell's nationalism was its main strength, and it lacked any coherent cultural or Romantic element. Repairing this deficiency was a major concern of Young Ireland, an ad hoc group of Romantic intellectuals, many of them liberal Protestants, within his Repeal movement, which produced the influential *Nation* newspaper, but was hampered by the almost ludicrous necessity of articulating cultural nationalism in the language of the imperial power. After the early death of its leading ideologue, Thomas Davis, Young Ireland felt driven to live up to its increasingly militaristic rhetoric and to imitate events in Europe by staging a purely gestural 'revolution' in 1848. This amounted to little more than minor skirmishes with the police, after attempts to rouse the peasantry of Munster foundered on famine and indifference. If the Romantic period ended thus, with a mock rebellion, its beginning had been overshadowed by a very violent one, that of the bloody civil war of 1798. In that year sectarian, class and political antagonisms produced an outbreak of stunning ferocity, such as had not been seen since the 1640s. It was all the more terrifying in being centred on the normally peaceful and prosperous south-east, and it induced most Catholic as well as Protestant leaders to accept Union with Britain as a guarantee of greater stability and necessary reform. The recurrence of such a conflict was the fear which inhibited the Irish Romantic imagination, as it did political development. It was a fear fuelled by the endemic poverty of the country, annually intensified by unprecedented population increase, and having its dreaded and dreadful apotheosis in the Great Famine of 1845–9. It was despairing poverty too which facilitated the final phase of the replacement of the Irish language by English, which came to be perceived as a vital means of economic survival even by the poorest classes in the decades of agricultural depression and high emigration before the Famine. The processes and traumas of this cultural revolution are still little understood. Some of its dimensions were captured in contemporary literature, notably its heightening of peasant vulnerability as well as peasant comicality, but its implications for the development of a coherent Romantic nationalism in Ireland were clearly immense.

The colonial character of Irish Romantic literature is particularly obvious in the treatment of its major themes – the historical past, conflict over the land or religious settlements, Irish lawlessness and alienation – and also in its perception of its audience as English rather than Irish. The nature of the Anglo-Irish tradition in literature has been too narrowly conceived by both historians and literary scholars.[4] Insofar as it concentrated on Irish themes (and leaving to one side the strong universalist tradition in writers like Swift, Goldsmith and Sheridan), it had three main, interconnected strands. (a) The 'Old English' (descendants of the early Norman colonists) emphasis on their cultural distinctiveness and political autonomy, and their role as interpreters and civilisers of the barbaric native Irish world – this was developed particularly when their role was threatened in the sixteenth century, and reworked again in the Romantic period for similar reasons by Lady Morgan and Thomas Davis.[5] (b) The 'New English' (Elizabethan and later) radicalisation of existing colonist perspectives, including a greater hostility to the Gaelic world, and the infusion of the political and religious dimensions of Protestantism – here the key figure is Edmund Spenser, and in the Romantic era, Maria Edgeworth.[6] (c) The assimilation by writers from the Gaelic, colonised population of colonist techniques of argument and presentation, in order to make the case for equality of treatment – examples being the Catholic antiquaries of the mid-eighteenth century, such as Charles O'Conor and Sylvester O'Halloran, whose literary descendants were Catholic novelists like Gerald Griffin and, to an extent, poets like Tom Moore.[7] The assimilation by all three strands of elements of the very different Gaelic tradition, initially through newly available translations of Gaelic poetry, was a central feature of Irish Romanticism and was to become the core element of the Anglo-Irish tradition by the end of the nineteenth century. However distorted by its translators, this poetry reflected the keynotes of the Gaelic response to annihilation – its pragmatism and fatalism, as well as its grief, alienation and nostalgia for a lost pre-colonial past.

Writers from all sectors of this complex Anglo-Irish tradition were published mainly in London, and had always written primarily for an English audience: to explain Irish realities, to urge support for favoured policies and to counteract the negative stereotype of the country and of the native Irish prevalent in England (which ironically was based in part on earlier colonist writings). The Union had given a new impetus to this by locating the centre of Irish political power even more clearly in Westminster, and by making Irish affairs of more direct concern to English politics and public opinion. As the horrors of Irish poverty and violence became ever more familiar through government commission reports, parliamentary debates and the revolution in travel and communications, the demand for literature with Irish themes grew. This was exploited by Irish writers in commercial terms, but also in order to educate enlightened English opinion to their view of the situation and its remedy. This perception of audience and role clearly shaped the literature. The need to please inevitably cut across the desire to instruct, although English sensibilities could also be exploited for Irish ends.[8] From the 1820s there was also a growing awareness of a new Irish audience for fiction and poetry, one which was predominantly urban, middle-class and Catholic by 1850, thanks to a dramatic growth in education, political agitation and a popular nationalist press. A new kind of Catholic writer emerged; more works were published in Dublin, or, like Moore's *Irish Melodies*, both there and in London. While the problems of catering for this dual audience were often solved in interesting ways, the English focus, like the English language and English literary genres, remained predominant.

Seamus Deane has argued that the 'incredulity' of English readers confronted by Irish writing was important in the development of Romanticism, which expanded the eighteenth-century concept of 'national

character' in order to explain the dramatic differences between the 'real'
English and 'surreal' Irish worlds.[9] Basic to the various and evolving
versions of this 'national character' were perceptions of the lost but lingering Gaelic world – and these form the key and most characteristic motif of
Irish Romanticism. This will become apparent when the manipulations of
the literature and history of this exotic past for a variety of political purposes by novelists, poets and political ideologues are examined. For those
from an Ascendancy or 'colonist' background the Gaelic world served
both as a warning and as the basis for creating new cultural foundations
for an eroding social and political hegemony; for the Catholic or
'colonised' writers it provided a vehicle for their burgeoning political self-
confidence, but also a necessary sublimation of trauma and loss. Such a
division may appear simplistic and crude, but it is at the heart of the
matter. It also suggests interesting connections between writers; between
Lady Morgan and Thomas Davis, who represent the Irish Whig and, more
dimly, the Old English reform traditions; between Maria Edgeworth,
Charles Maturin and Sir Samuel Ferguson who illustrate different but
related facets of the Irish Tory mind and have fascinating echoes of
Edmund Spenser; between James Hardiman, Gerald Griffin, Tom Moore
and James Clarence Mangan who exemplify Catholic exploitation of and
nostalgia for the past as well as the survival of older Gaelic perspectives. As
is clear in their scholarly footnotes and prefaces, as well as in their texts, all
of these writers found their raw material not only in the new and often
bowdlerised translations of Gaelic poetry and the works of colonist writers
like Spenser, but also in the heady mixture of fantasy and scholarship
which characterised eighteenth-century antiquarianism, and in the more
scholarly but still often partisan historical, ethnographic and archaeologi-
cal studies of the early nineteenth century. The contrast between the
remarkably modern philosophical and sociological history being written
in Scotland in this period and the traditionalism in theme and too often in
method of Irish historical scholarship helps to explain the success of Sir
Walter Scott in writing universally accessible historical novels which
delineated forces and trends in the very process of change, while the more
fractured and traumatised historical sense of his Irish imitators resulted in
more introverted and purely local fiction.

What all such manipulations of history had in common was a conservative intent, to aid the preservation or amelioration of the status quo and the
avoidance of revolution. The profound conservatism of Irish Romanticism
has been linked by literary critics with Edmund Burke's formulation of a
theory of community and tradition, emphasising custom and national
character, and its completion by Coleridge in an organic model, which
suggested a means of transforming ancient communal loyalties into popu-

lar acceptance of the state and economic systems.[10] Such ideas were certainly important for some writers, but they had their origins rather in the particular colonial experience of Ireland, and in an extension of the liberal Protestant tradition into the cultural sphere. The pervasiveness of the conservative mind is best illustrated by comparing the *Nation* (1842), populist organ of anti-Union cultural nationalism with its more intellectual, Tory, pro-Union rival, the *Dublin University Magazine*, founded ten years earlier. Both journals emerged from the more critical and 'national' atmosphere which characterised Trinity College Dublin after the Union and the Catholic Emancipation campaign, and neither fitted comfortably into the mainstreams of their opposing political traditions. The many contributors common to both had little adjustment to make in moving from one side to the other of the relatively narrow cultural spectrum involved. They shared a relentless didacticism and an emphasis on a popular education which featured reinterpretation of the historical experience and the production of a new 'national' literature. The latter, they believed to be 'in its very essence amalgamating, and may eventually become the great temple of concord'.[11] While it is valid to emphasise such common features, it also needs to be stressed that each of these remarkable journals featured interesting diversities in 'voice' and approach, and underwent significant developments as editors changed, and social and political tensions increased. In the key area of the Romanticisation of history, however, their most influential ideologues were Thomas Davis, who dominated the *Nation* until his death at 31 in 1845, and Samuel Ferguson, who began his long intricate colonisation of Gaelic literature in a series of articles in the *Dublin University Magazine* in 1834.

The colonist Whig tradition, to which Davis belonged, had produced previously a colourful and successful novelist in Lady Morgan, who first created a popular vogue in England as well as in Ireland for a sentimental view of the Irish past. Morgan's social and literary theatricality partly masked a serious political purpose. She viewed her Irish novels, published between 1806 and 1827, as 'a series of national tales', designed to promote reconciliation and reform, and, more specifically, the 'great national cause, the emancipation of the Catholics of Ireland'. This she sponsored, on prudential as well as humanitarian grounds, to promote the liberal Protestant leadership of the new Catholic democracy, and the consolidation of the imperial relationship. Her chagrin when Emancipation proved to be the beginning rather than the completion of a political revolution, confirming a more abrasive Catholic historical sense as well as a new political leadership, led to her abandonment in the 1830s of both Irish themes and Irish residence. Her description of her novels as 'my Irish histories' was justified, although they were not 'historical' in the sense that

Scott's novels were, that is, set in a past age. Instead, they were contemporary novels, dominated (like Irish politics) by historical awareness and
debate. Reflecting and exploiting the blurred boundaries between the new
literary genres of 'history' and 'fiction' which still obtained, she loaded her
novels with the apparatus of historical scholarship, providing a subtext of
learned references and notes which was designed to give authority to her
interpretation, and to guide the response of the reader. History served a
number of related literary and political purposes in Morgan's work. It provided atmosphere (most frequently that of melancholic ruin), it offered a
key to the present and it was often a dynamic element in the story. Thus,
the reading of history changed the direction of her heroes' lives, fortunes
depended on historical proofs, and, above all, by confronting the past,
traditional enemies were reconciled in marriages of symbolic healing.[12]

Morgan's unusual background helps to explain why she exemplified
with peculiar intensity that combination of fascination with, and hostility
to, the Gaelic world which characterised so much of the Anglo-Irish
tradition. Her father, Robert Owenson, a flamboyant actor-manager,
specialised in stage-Irish parts, but frequently complicated their effect by
the totally serious singing of traditional Irish songs in the Gaelic of his
native Connaught. His daughter mimicked his singing in Irish, and published an early collection of airs and translations, which influenced her
friend Tom Moore – yet she never learned the language, and identified
rather with the Protestant gentry tradition of her paternal grandmother,
who also played the harp, and had eloped to marry a Catholic tenant
farmer. Morgan's view of Romantic Gaelic Connaught, the setting for her
first novel, *The Wild Irish Girl*, is that of Longford House, residence of her
gentry Crofton relations, where she stayed while gathering materials for
the book. Her father's improvidence forced her to become a writer and the
family breadwinner, after the death of her English Methodist mother,
whose bourgeois business sense she inherited, along with a marked distaste
for the chaos and poverty of Irish life. A less confused legacy from her
father was that of involvement in Irish Whig politics, and it was Whig
patronage which made her an overnight social as well as literary success in
Dublin.[13]

The success of *The Wild Irish Girl* (1806) with Irish Whigs owed much
to its combination of fashionable antiquarian enthusiasms with an attack
on English stereotypes of Ireland as 'a country . . . semi-barbarous, semi-
civilised'. So its Anglo-Irish hero, Mortimer, expected to find it when
exiled to his absentee father's Irish estate in remotest Connaught, 'the
classic ground of Ireland', and home of 'the Irish character in all its
primeval ferocity'. Instead, he found the peasantry hospitable and hard-
working, especially those living under the last Gaelic 'Prince of Innismore',

whose ancestor had been killed and dispossessed by the original Cromwellian Mortimer. The Prince lived in his ruined Romantic castle a pathetic parody of the lifestyle of his ancestors, with antiquarian pride compensating for poverty and powerlessness. The hero's perspectives on Ireland were transformed mainly by reading its sad history, and by a series of lectures on the ancient glories of Celtic chivalry, music and learning by the Prince, and his beautiful daughter Glorvina. This novel was based heavily on the works of Catholic antiquaries like Sylvester O'Halloran, and reflected what Morgan soon came to recognise as their naivety and crude historical sense. Her later novels reflected the more critical judgement mainly of Protestant historiography after Ledwich, and never repeated the theme of a repentant colonialism. Even *The Wild Irish Girl* had interesting reservations and indicated the specific political orientation of Morgan's Romanticism. Its most interesting character was Glorvina, with whom the author identified strongly on many levels. Glorvina read Rousseau and other Romantic writers and was at odds with the traditionalism and prejudices of her father – a character based partly on Morgan's father, Robert Owenson. In a key scene, she intervened at the end of a long and learned defence by the Prince and his ultra-Catholic Chaplain of the Irish provenance of the Ossianic literature, popularised as Scottish in Macpherson's by now largely discredited translations. Under their barrage of historical proofs, Mortimer conceded, but claimed 'as an Englishman . . . an armed neutrality.' Glorvina also urged a compromise view, arguing that while Macpherson's originals were undoubtedly Irish, his translations were superior 'over those wild effusions of our native bards whence he compiled them'. Her pleasure in 'the sublimity of sentiment' in the originals was marred by their 'ridiculously grotesque' features, and she often preferred her 'English Ossian' – 'the refined medium of Macpherson's genius'.[14] Thus, even before her marriage to Mortimer, Glorvina had begun the process of adapting the Gaelic literary tradition to modern Romantic modes.

The idea that Catholic antiquarianism was potentially dangerous as well as anachronistic was stressed in the later novels, particularly in the sinister figure of Terence O'Brien, descendant of Brian Boru, and father of the Romantic hero of *The O'Briens and the O'Flahertys* (1827). 'Knowing nothing of modern Ireland but her sufferings and her wrongs', and 'little of ancient Ireland but her fables and her dreams', he hatched a bizarre plot to restore the ancient High Kingship in the Catholic cause.[15] Morgan showed no further enthusiasm, however qualified, for ancient Gaelic glories, and was clearly concerned in her second novel, *O'Donnel* (1814), to correct any mistaken impressions her first might have given. Its anaemic Gaelic hero, an honourable and sophisticated European, argued with a tired

fatalism 'that in Ireland, as in all nations, what is won by the sword becomes legitimate property', and that his ancestors the O'Donnels 'were not *even anciently* the original possessors of the land over which they reigned for centuries, which they won by the sword and which the sword partly won in turn from them'. This answered a major argument against Catholic Emancipation, and formed one basis on which Irish Whigs urged reconciliation – that the Catholic population had accepted the colonial land settlement completely. Complementing this was the historical explanation of majority alienation, into which the Anglo-Irish had always claimed a special insight. Morgan was in a long tradition in her heavy emphasis on 'the demoralisation of the people', who had been 'persecuted and brutified' by the searing experiences of the new colonialism in the sixteenth and seventeenth centuries.[16] This was an argument charged with moral judgement, and a certain impatience, even contempt. In *The O'Briens and the O'Flahertys* it was blended with Morgan's burgeoning anti-Catholicism. Repeatedly the 'degradation' of the Irish Catholic gentry was ascribed, not just to 'six hundred years of oppression . . . producing their moral effects', but also to that 'passive obedience with which . . . Catholics are accursed'.[17] Such perspectives determined the traditional colonial stereotypes which peopled these novels: the dangerous duality of the Dublin porter, who was 'debasingly acquiescent', yet 'preserved the vindictiveness of conscious degradation'; the peasant leader Owney Rabragh who typified 'qualities inherent in the lower Irish. Warm friends and revengeful enemies, inviolable in their secrecy, devoted in their attachments, inexorable in their resentments.'[18] Only enlightened Anglo-Irish leadership could save such a people from themselves, in alliance with Morgan's younger generation of Gaelic Irish heroes and heroines, who escaped degradation by education and experience of Europe, and whose role in the partnership was clearly subordinate, consisting mainly in the exploitation of the peasantry's hereditary loyalty.

In the preface to the new popular edition of *The Wild Irish Girl* in 1846 Morgan claimed that this 'first attempt at a genuine Irish novel' began a literary tradition 'founded on national grievances and borne out by historic fact'. Among the 'abler talents' who had succeeded her, she named not only novelists like Griffin and Carleton, but the 'exquisite literary historical essays' of Thomas Davis – although she rejected the advocacy of the Repeal of the Union 'indulged in by "Young England's" cadet-brother "Young Ireland"'. This approach to Davis (the guiding spirit of the *Nation*), as belonging to a particular Anglo-Irish literary tradition suggests some modifications to the usual view of him as a radical political ideologue, the creator of the Irish version of European Romantic cultural nationalism. Morgan's stress on the comparison with Young England was also perceptive and supported one element of Mazzini's judgement that Davis and his friends were not part of 'Young Europe', because their emphasis was more on good government than on national government. The *Nation* was, however, enthusiastically approved of by Samuel Smiles, who recognised the sentimental bourgeois utilitarianism and the preoccupation with moral improvement through education which overshadowed or infused its elements of Romanticism.[19]

Conspicuously absent from the *Nation* was any clear awareness, much less influence, of contemporary continental writing on the cultural basis of politics and society. In the only comprehensive analysis to date of Davis's ideology, Mary Buckley emphasised his ignorance even of contemporary European politics. There is no evidence that he had read, or was influenced by, Herder or Fichte, despite many shared preoccupations and ideas. One of his few references to Germany was to its success in halting 'the incipient creeping progress of French', thus liberating its own 'genius'. However, the German Romantic view of language as the touchstone of national identity was at the heart of the dilemma of the Young Ireland group, who came from outside what remained of the Gaelic tradition and did not even know the language. Among them, only Davis emphasised it as the key to Irish nationality, and even his attempts to learn Irish were half-hearted and were mocked by his friends. The strains involved in attempting to develop a cultural nationalism during a period of great cultural flux, and in the language of cultural domination, were all too evident in Davis's analysis, which had interesting echoes of Fichte's, with its view of language as the core and repository of communal consciousness and history; its contrast of the 'wild liquid speech' of the Celt with 'the mongrel of a hundred breeds called English'; and its emphasis on language as a barrier against foreign oppression. However, Davis's weak conclusion that 'a people without a language is only half a nation' fell far short of Fichte's view that such a people could not be a nation in any sense.[20]

This disjunction between the ideal and the actual ultimately provided a dynamic as well as a dilemma for Irish cultural nationalism. However, in the first half of the nineteenth century it led less to language revivalism, or the equation of 'Irish' with 'Gaelic', than to the formulation of a nationalism which would be inclusive of colonists and natives alike. This was also stressed particularly by Davis, whose mixed background – his mother came from a Cromwellian family which had intermarried with the Gaelic O'Sullivan Beares, and his father was English – clearly formed the basis of his guiding formulation, published in the 'prospectus' for the first number of the *Nation*. This repeated Wolfe Tone's Whiggish constellation of 'Protestant, Catholic and Dissenter', and added 'Milesian and Cromwellian – the Irishman of a hundred generations and the stranger who is within our gates' – all combined to form Irish 'nationality'. The unease of the next phrase of this manifesto – that this was 'not a nationality which would prelude civil war' – reflects the shadow of the collapse of 'united Irishmen' in the horrors of 1798. There was an obvious tension between Davis's wish, or need, to emphasise the distinctive Celtic element (his pen-name was 'The Celt', for example, and he claimed that 'probably five sixths or more of us are Celts'),[21] and his desire to form a new modern 'nationality' (the word he normally used) which, he insisted, 'must not be Celtic' but 'must be Irish'. He argued in several places that this would combine the strengths of its component parts, 'the cloudy and lightning genius of the Gael, the placid strength of the Sassenach, the marshalling insight of the Norman'. In any case, 'a Celtic kingdom with the names and the old language' was impossible, given 'the English Pale, and the Ulster Settlement and the filtered colonisation of men and ideas'.[22] Romantic nationalism had to have a different meaning in Ireland, to reflect the confusion of cultures resulting from its colonial past, rather than to assert a cultural and linguistic purity. It had to be created rather than simply articulated, and a primary creative agency was to be a new 'national literature', 'a literature which shall exhibit a combination of the passions and idioms of all' and which was to be 'racy of the soil'.[23]

To refashion history was a more difficult and more fraught endeavour, particularly as historical controversy filled the air and formed a major basis and battleground of Irish political divisions – but it was even more basic to Davis's projected national accord. His approach was to promote a type of history which emphasised colour rather than content and controversy – modelled on the pyrotechnics of Thierry rather than on the new scientific models of Ranke. Its function was to be inspirational rather than explanatory, and Davis's view of it was strongly pictorial. Apart from an early piece of original research on the 'Patriot' parliament, his historical writings were impressionistic and concentrated on a succession of military heroes, just as his historical ballads featured especially the exploits of 'the soldiers and chiefs of the Irish Brigade'. Davis's Romanticism was thus conventionally martial as much as philosophical or aesthetic, and he saw Irish history as a series of heroic but unavailing struggles against oppression. He argued that he did so to urge 'perseverance' rather than to 'paint despair', and that in any case, 'this *is* our history for three hundred years past and must be told'. He admitted privately that it was difficult to be optimistic: 'The weight of that past is upon us now, and sanguine as I am that this country could be rescued, I often doubt if it will, for history casts shadows on my hopes.'[24]

The most interesting and, on the face of it, most surprising of these shadows was that of the Gaelic world, towards which Davis exhibited traditional liberal Protestant ambivalence. This was well captured in his key phrase, 'the cloudy and lightning genius of the Gael' (the virtues of the English and Normans by contrast being unambiguous). The pre-colonial Celtic civilisation was for him also a 'glorious age', but one whose history was inaccessible, locked up in 'dry annals or stupid compilations'.[25] He rejected most of Gaelic literature as unsuitable for his proposed new 'national literature': 'There are great gaps in Irish song to be filled up. This is true even of the songs of the Irish speaking people', some of which were 'sweet and noble', but 'the bulk of the songs are very defective', especially those of the eighteenth century, 'their grief slavish and despairing, their joy reckless and bombastic, their religion bitter and sectarian, their politics Jacobite and concealed by extravagance and tiresome allegory'. Some of the better ones, he felt, might be sold as ballads in the 'cabins', together with simplified versions of the older Bardic poetry, 'without the clumsy ornaments and exaggerations'. Too many of the latter were disappointing, being 'national in form and colour, but clannish in opinion'. The traditional colonist stereotype, and view of native Irish degeneracy, was particularly apparent in his praise for recent translations from the Irish by Mangan, Ferguson and others, for being 'true to the vehemence and tendencies of the Celtic people and representing equally their vagueness and extravagance during slavish times'. There was a rich but wholly unconscious irony in his enthusiasm for a translation of Moore's *Melodies* into Irish as 'a noble attempt to supply this deficiency', and his proposal to turn the ballads of the *Nation* into 'racy and musical Irish'.[26] The attempted colonisation of Gaelic culture by Davis, in the interests of his hybrid brand of nationality, was as crude, as calculated and as pejorative as anything in Morgan. By comparison, Moore's exploitation of it was more sympathetic and more truly in the Romantic mode.

The still darker view of the Gaelic world in the novels of Maria Edgeworth reflects a rationalist rather than a Romantic response, but in its refashioning of a major tradition in colonist writing in a modern idiom, her work provided later Anglo-Irish Romanticism with a vital ingredient. Originally Elizabethan settlers, the Edgeworths had particular reason to be aware of the vulnerability of the colonial settlement, having had to flee their home during the upheavals of 1641, 1690 and again, interrupting the writing of *Castle Rackrent*, in 1798. She had come to Ireland as an impressionable 15-year-old, and a great strength of her Irish writings was that the country remained for her an exotic place, particularly in the colourful and calculated manipulation of the newly acquired English language by the peasantry. Her family history may have supplied the models for the improvident and ultimately pathetic Rackrents, but the real theme of her deeply ironic and pessimistic first novel was that of the peasant threat to a moribund Ascendancy, not by rebellion, but by the little regarded actions of a trusted family retainer. One of the first books given to her by her father after their arrival in Ireland was Edmund Spenser's *A View of the Present State of Ireland*, written during the even greater horrors of the 1590s, and advocating a ruthless military conquest as a prelude to a radical colonisation scheme, and the Anglicisation of every facet of Irish life. In *The Absentee* (1812), she had it recommended to the newly arrived Lord Colombre as a reliable guide to the country, and she quoted Spenser several times in her novels, most notably in the first footnote to *Castle Rackrent*, identifying the comical greatcoat of the servant/narrator, Thady Quirk, with the *brat* or cloak of the sixteenth-century Gaelic rebels, and even amending the quotation to suit the circumstances of Edgeworthstown in 1798.[27] Edgeworth, like Spenser, was a colonist writing in conditions of siege, and while his specific proposals had long been implemented, she retained his advocacy of thorough Anglicisation, and, like him, presented a stereotype of the native Irish which best suited her preferred approach – that of a benevolent, improving landlordism. This was composed in part by adapting a major Spenserian theme, the seductive as well as the hostile and degraded nature of the encircling native world. She, however, took a more optimistic view of the potential for loyalism and social deference in native Irish character, and in vestigial Gaelic social mores.

A striking and revealing feature of *Castle Rackrent* was the absence from it of the group with which Edgeworth most identified, the descendants of *English* colonists. The Rackrents were apostate native Irish gentry who changed their name and (less clearly) their religion for financial gain, but were ruined by stereotypical Irish characteristics associated with drink, litigation, fighting and extravagant hospitality. This theme of apostate native gentry was continued in her later novels, and, most tellingly, in *Ormond* (1817). In this, her last Irish novel, written for her dying father who was the model for its improving English landlord, Lord Annally, the main social focus was on the contrast between the corrupt politician and evil landlord, Sir Ulick O'Shane and his traditionalist Gaelic and Catholic cousin, 'King' Corny of the Black Islands, who despised Ulick's apostasy, and who, despite the ludicrous archaism of his own lifestyle, was more sympathetically portrayed by the author. There is more than a hint in all of this that Edgeworth regretted the failure of some of the old native gentry to survive and to adapt traditional loyalties to modern circumstances,[28] but she did not despair of remedying the situation, if in a different way. She rejected, however, the approach of Romanticised antiquarianism; entombing the Gaelic past mausoleum-like in Count O'Halloran's house, in *The Absentee*. Instead, she focused on the replacement of what she considered the false and dangerous servility of the peasantry by providing a new object for traditional loyalties.

In all her Irish novels after *Castle Rackrent*, Edgeworth balanced examples of the native Irish threat to the colonial settlement[29] with the figure of the loyal servant who exemplified their contrary tendency towards loyalty, once they were properly treated; and it was the quasi-feudal nature of this trait which constituted for Edgeworth both the dangerous seductiveness and the real potential of traditional society. In *Ennui* (1809), the hero was accepted by the people because he had been fostered with a peasant family according to Gaelic practice, and he was prevailed on to return from a dissolute life in England, to the excited welcome of his tenantry which 'gave more the idea of vassals than of tenants, and carried my imagination back to feudal times'. Similarly, at the end of *The Absentee*, the long-negligent landlord, Lord Clonbrony, was welcomed by his tenants, 'for he knows the nature of us . . . as well as if he had lived all his life in Ireland, and by the same token . . . will do what he pleases with us'. The temptation of the impressionable Harry Ormond to succeed to his uncle's feudal power was presented as a moral test, but while he modelled himself instead on the Edgeworthian figure of Lord Annally, he chose to live on the Black Islands with the intention, expressed in a fine Spenserian phrase, of 'further civilising the people'. His chances of success were enhanced greatly by his popular acceptance as the proclaimed heir of 'King' Corny, and the people's pleasure at 'his coming to reign over them'.[30]

A less optimistic view of the Gaelic threat was expressed in the Irish novels of the eccentric Protestant clergyman, Charles Maturin, beginning with *The Wild Irish Boy* (1808). This carried a quotation from Spenser's *View* on its title page, and contrasted the sordid realities of Irish life with its hero's first Romantic dream of it. In *The Milesian Chief* (1812), set in the period after the Union, Maturin's horrified fascination with Romantic sensibility was focused on the evils involved in glorifying and clinging to the Gaelic past. This ruined the life of his otherwise admirable young hero, ultimately forcing him into leading a large-scale rebellion, described by Maturin in terms which conflated the native Irish rebellions of Spenser's time with the still vivid anarchy of 1798. This apocalyptic view of the dangers of antiquarianism and the ignominious death by execution of the Romantic hero reflected the pessimistic side of the Irish Tory mind, as well as Maturin's commitment to following the logic of Romantic alienation to its conclusion. In *Melmoth the Wanderer* (1820), the Irish colonial nightmare is given its most memorable Romantic expression. Melmoth may combine elements of Faust, Mephistopheles and the Wandering Jew, but it should be remembered that he also belonged to an Irish Cromwellian

colonist family which he continued to haunt and whose concern to escape
from the burdens of its history paralleled and was reflected in his doomed
attempts to lift the curse of immortality.

Alone among these writers, Maturin offered no solutions to the Anglo-
Irish dilemma. Writing after Catholic Emancipation and with an even
greater sense of crisis, Sir Samuel Ferguson had no such inhibition. The
contrast with Maturin was great in other respects also: Ferguson was a
supremely confident and successful Ulster Scot, distinguished lawyer and
public servant, ultimately president of the Royal Irish Academy.[31] What
they shared was a Spenserian preoccupation with the 'Gaelic' threat and a
strong distaste for Catholicism. Ferguson is best known for his reworking
in the 1860s and 1870s of heroic Gaelic legends, so as to make their heroes
into prototypes of aristocratic leadership and artistic integrity in a world
in which the threat from below had become that of the democratic mob.
These ponderous productions are of interest now mainly because of their
role in the transformation of the Anglo-Irish literary tradition, but the key
to their political orientation can be found in Ferguson's series of four
articles in the Dublin University Magazine in 1834, on James Hardiman's
influential Irish Minstrelsy, or the Bardic Remains of Ireland with English
Poetical Translations, published three years before.[32] Ferguson later
became adept at disguising his colonist perspectives in the vague cultural
nationalist rhetoric popularised by Davis, but in these early reflections on
the nature and potential of the Gaelic tradition, written for an Irish Tory
audience, they were undisguised and in the vein of his earlier 'Dialogue
between the head and heart of an Irish Protestant' which had expressed the
angst and pride, as well as the dilemma, of his class with such memorable
vehemence.[33] The articles against Hardiman were addressed to 'the
Protestant wealth and intelligence of the country', and proposed a new
interpretation of the nature of the threat they faced, that 'their wealth has
hitherto been insecure because their intelligence has not embraced a
thorough knowledge of the genius and disposition of their Catholic fellow
citizens'. As well as remedies with which Davis was to become strongly
associated some years later – education, 'the reconciling strength of an
honest literature', and the creation of 'a green spot of neutral ground
where all parties may meet in kindness and part in peace' – Ferguson proposed denying to Irish Catholics 'the monopoly of native Irish sympathies'.
His acknowledgement of the 'genius', 'bravery' and 'pious love of country'
which Hardiman had 'vindicated to the meere Irish' was hardly enhanced
by the use of this dismissive description of the native population also used
in Spenser's View.[34]

Ferguson was already a respected Gaelic scholar, but his interpretation of Gaelic literature was shaped more by political considerations. In particular, his Romanticising of elements of 'the squalid and repulsive sketch given by Spenser or Moryson' was designed to meet the new threat involved in the replacement of the old Gaelic rebels, who at least 'when they had high treason in their hearts had arms in their hands and honest defiance in their faces', with 'the indolent brawler, the bankrupt and fraudulent demagogue, the crawling incendiary, the scheming Jesuitical ambitious priest' of 'the last quarter of a century'. Following Spenser's 'meere Irishman' back to his home environment, Ferguson discovered 'the old romantic life of the Irish nobleman' and found, especially in Gaelic poetry, evidence of a civilisation which, while still marked by 'strife, cruelty and desolation', was redeemed by hospitality and 'the ascendancy of the heart'. The distinguishing feature of Irish song was 'sentiment', and while this had unfortunate origins in 'languishing but savage sincerity' and 'the despondency of conscious degradation', it was capable of achieving acceptable modern forms in the hands of a supreme lyricist like Moore. One particular aspect of Gaelic culture, Ferguson argued, was equally adaptable to the political needs of Irish Protestants. This was 'the patriarchal spirit . . . that great unphilosophical allegiance' to the Lord which had been 'a great obstacle to the thorough conquest of Ireland' and was now being monopolised to the detriment of civilisation by the Catholic Church, or 'clan Rome'. In Coleridgean vein, he argued that Ireland must evolve from its disastrous hybrid of patriarchalism and feudalism by transferring these traditional loyalties to the sovereign, constitution and law of the modern state. Thus, 'the worthiest labour of the age' was 'to supply the lost links, to carry forward the untutored loyalty of the clansman, till the whole country become his faction and the king his chief'. The key to exploiting the fact that 'the national character so reverences hereditary obligation' was to understand Gaelic culture and to counter the 'petty anti-Anglicanism' of those who, like Hardiman, sought to equate Gaelic with Catholic.[35]

Ferguson had little difficulty in exposing his rival's translations as 'spurious, puerile, unclassical, lamentably bad', but his own versions, while superior in literary and linguistic terms, were as biased politically. Most dramatically, 'The Fair Hills of Ireland' was transformed from a Jacobite poem lamenting the exile of the native Irish lords, to one celebrating the entry *into* Ireland of her new 'captains'! Ferguson had indeed begun his series of articles by commenting on this poem and claiming that colonialism was proof of the truest patriotism. Addressing Ireland, Bardic fashion, he wrote, 'it was for love of you that we contended, for possession and enjoyment of you that we trampled down our rivals in your bosom'.[36]

The colonisation of Gaelic literature in the interest of the Anglo-Irish Ascendancy was a logical extension of this and was the basis of all Ferguson's later work.

The case against Hardiman was stronger than Ferguson realised. Not alone had his translators produced drawing-room travesties of the Gaelic texts, but some of the originals were clumsy modern forgeries in the Bardic style, written to provide a spurious aristocratic Gaelic background for an associate of Hardiman, and probably with the latter's connivance. Reflecting the fashion for things Gaelic among elements of the Ascendancy, many newly wealthy middle-class Catholics sought respectability and asserted their self-confidence by such means. Hardiman himself came from this class and was heavily involved in the often shady trade in Gaelic manuscripts. The introduction to his *Minstrelsy* was a Catholic-nationalist polemic, concerned to rescue the 'ancient literature of Ireland' from 'oblivion' (or from Macpherson!) but even more to prove that the ' "meere Irish" bards were invariably Catholics, Patriots and Jacobites'.[37] His collection, therefore, concentrated strongly on eighteenth-century texts, and began the tradition of ascribing an anachronistic modern nationalism to Bardic and post-Bardic Gaelic poetry.

Hardiman was a native Irish speaker and close to the tradition which he exploited so pragmatically. A more interesting and representative Catholic middle-class writer was the Limerick novelist, Gerald Griffin, who knew no Irish, but still felt inhibited about writing in English for an English audience, and was fascinated by the impact of linguistic change on the peasantry. In the introduction to *Tales of the Munster Festivals* (1827), he seemed to reject the Catholic antiquarian argument that the most 'potent restorative' for a 'ruined people' was to depict 'the Ireland that once was', and opted instead for a didactic realism designed to guide 'the statesman and the legislator'.[38] Yet, five years later he produced in *The Invasion* one of the few fully historical novels of this period in Ireland, and the only one which properly can be called 'Romantic'. Like Maturin, his work in the intervening years reveals a Romantic writer resisting the Romantic impulse on religious grounds, and this was particularly clear in his best novel, *The Collegians*, and in the awkward sketch, *The Rivals*, both published in the year of Catholic Emancipation, 1829. Reflecting the darker and less confident side of the middle-class Catholic mind, his main theme in those years was the threat of social chaos, in consequence of the alienation of the peasantry from the law and from the dominant official culture.[39] His heroes were hypersensitive tortured Romantics, like Hardress Cregan in *The Collegians*, a 'slave to his imagination', and instigator of a murder which had its origins in Romantic philosophy as much as in social divisions. The battle against evil passion was fought against the dramatic backdrop of Romantic mountain scenery in Kerry or Wicklow, and even Griffin's more tranquil landscapes were set-pieces of the picturesque. Yet he also attacked Romantic sensibility as evil and was dismayed when his readers preferred the dashing Cregan to his dull rationalist rival, Kyrle Daly, the epitome of refined middle-class Catholic virtues and intended by Griffin as the real hero of *The Collegians*. This tension in his work contributed ultimately to what John Cronin has called his 'decline into aesthetic paralysis', and abandonment of a literary for a religious life.[40] Before this happened, however, he had sought escape in historical research for 'a novel full of curious and characteristic traits of ancient Irish life', which became *The Invasion*. He had long wished to write a history of Ireland, and in an 1828 letter had outlined what its theme must be: 'a miserable and shocking succession of follies, excesses and tyrannies'. The main difficulty for the historian lay in detailing 'centuries consumed in suffering, in vain remonstrance, and idle though desperate struggles for change . . . [and] in painting the convulsions of a powerful people labouring under a nightmare for ten centuries'.[41] Hardly surprisingly, he shied away from such a distressing project and concentrated instead on another aspect of the Catholic historical consciousness, and one having its roots in Gaelic poetry, especially since the mid-seventeenth century – the celebration of the pre-colonial period as a Romantic golden age, when Ireland was 'the island of saints and scholars'. Set before even the Viking invasions, Griffin's novel is also in the tradition of eighteenth-century writing in seeking to counteract the English stereotype of the barbarous Irish by presenting an idealised picture of a sophisticated ancient native culture. If *The Invasion* survives the dead-weight of its painfully acquired and meticulously reproduced detail of ancient Irish dress and manners, it is only because of its gradual shift in focus to the hero, Kenric, another autobiographical essay in Romantic psychology.

The mood of golden-age nostalgia formed only a part of Tom Moore's complexly Romantic treatment of the Gaelic past, and his ten volumes of *Irish Melodies* (1807–34) wore their antiquarian learning more lightly and seductively. Moore's reputation still suffers from the Young Ireland charge that he had compromised his patriotic principles in his search for aristocratic and political patronage in England.[42] While Moore was a privileged Whig insider and propagandist, the most striking fact about his extraordinary English career was his studied financial and political independence. He lived mainly by his writings, especially the steady annual income from the *Irish Melodies*, and he was a trenchant critic of English policy towards Ireland. His writing on Ireland became more overtly political in the early 1820s with his pseudo-novel on agrarian rebellion, *Captain Rock* (1824), and in 1831 he published his sympathetic *Life of Lord Edward Fitzgerald* (the Romantic hero of 1798), despite the objections of his Whig friends. The key to Moore's politics, as to his writing, is to be found less in his career in England, than in his lower middle-class Catholic background in Dublin, which also inculcated techniques of concealment in both spheres. A tradition of masking resentment by a deferential rhetoric had marked Irish Catholic politics since the 1750s, and had contributed to the process of dismantling the Penal Laws from which Moore benefited. The Catholic mask would have been assumed automatically by him on his entry into Trinity College, 'among the first of the helots of the land' to go there,[43] and must have been a factor in his prudent avoidance of the United Irish movement in which some of his college friends were involved. Growing self-confidence and O'Connell's more abrasive articulation of Catholic resentment allowed him to drop the mask in the 1820s.

The audience for which the *Irish Melodies* were written was, above all, an English audience, and their main intention was the creation of a sentimental sympathy with Irish wrongs. In rededicating his poetry to the wrongs of 'loved Erin' in the 1810 'Oh! blame not the bard', it was his special concern that through it,

> The stranger shall hear thy lament on his plains,
> The sigh of thy harp shall be sent o'er the deep,
> Till thy masters themselves, as they rivet thy chains,
> Shall pause at the song of their captive and weep![44]

These songs of the 'captive' for his 'masters' were shaped also by the nature of Moore's fascination with Irish history. The colonial period he considered 'creditable neither to our neighbours nor to ourselves', and offered little to the poet, who must seek inspiration instead 'in those early periods when our character was as yet unalloyed and original, before the impolitic craft of our conquerors had divided, weakened and disgraced us'. Even if the glories of such timer were only 'inventions of national partiality', it was understandable that poets should 'fly to such flattering fictions from the sad degrading truths which the history of later times presents to us'.[45] Any indulgence in such self-conscious nostalgia, however, was balanced in Moore by his inventive and oblique approach to the 'sad degrading truths' of the colonial experience, that is, through music, the 'truest of all comments upon our history'. Irish music reflected the contradictions commonly ascribed to the national character as well as the traumas of national history.

The tone of defiance, succeeded by the languor of despondency – a burst of turbulence dying away into softness – the sorrows of one moment lost in the levity of the next – and all that romantic mixture of mirth and sadness which is naturally produced by the efforts of a lively temperament to shake off or forget the wrongs that lie upon it.[46]

The *Irish Melodies*, therefore, attempted to evoke a painful historical experience through a combination of sense and sound, of carefully pitched sentimental lyrics matched to a modified musical tradition. They were meant, as he said, 'rather to be sung than read', but the lyrics repay study, and help to establish Moore in a distinctively Gaelic as well as Irish Catholic tradition.

Moore's only access to Gaelic literature was through translations, but his access to the Gaelic-Catholic *experience* was another matter. The ways in which some of the perspectives of the old Gaelic elites became transmuted into those of the Anglicised gentry and middle-class Catholic leadership which ultimately succeeded them is, as yet, but dimly understood. Moore offers an interesting example, particularly in the comparison between his *Irish Melodies* and the Gaelic poetry of the late seventeenth and early eighteenth centuries. From the time of Dáibhí Ó Bruadair (died 1697) particularly, Gaelic poetry had combined nostalgia for past glories with a fatalistic acceptance of *fait accompli*; sorrow for the individual and collective tragedies involved in 'the ship-wreck', with a pragmatic appeal to whatever powers in the new order offered the best hope for the future. All of this was captured in a new way in the early *aislingí* (or vision poems) such as those of Aogán Ó Rathaille (died 1729), which also used sophisticated literary techniques to disguise their political message, a not-too-hopeful Jacobitism.[47] Moore's *Irish Melodies* encompassed the same range of feelings, and also developed a new literary mask, that of the Romantic lyric mode. This vital Gaelic element in Moore was the result less of conscious literary borrowings than of major continuities in historical and cultural perspectives. 'Let Erin Remember the Days of Old', for example, despite being footnoted with references to the celebratory writings of antiquaries, had a fatalistic and distanced tone. The 'glories' of the past were 'long-faded', its round towers those of 'other days' and submerged in 'memory' as beneath the waters of Lough Neagh. Those distant times, 'when Malachi wore the collar of gold' may be a matter of pride, but only in the context of Ireland having long been ruled by 'the stranger', and (another characteristic note of Gaelic poetry) betrayed by 'her faithless sons'. Similarly, the harp that had proclaimed the glory of native High Kings at Tara in 'former days' now told 'a tale of ruin'.[48] Moore identified himself strongly with the harp, the conventional if mistaken symbol of the Gaelic Bard – indeed in what was intended to be the last of the *Irish Melodies* he described himself simply as 'the wind passing heedlessly over' the 'dear harp of my country'. In an attempt to match the plaintive tone of the instrument, his lyrics sonorously emphasise sorrow, silence, death and, above all, the motif of slavery, so prominent a feature of the general political discourse of the age, but appropriated in a particular fashion by Irish Catholic politicians and writers.[49]

Other techniques of masking or disguise marked the very different poetry of James Clarence Mangan, particularly those of irony and of real or mock translation. His work, as David Lloyd has shown so well,[50] was subversive of nationalism and Romanticism, and yet shaped by both. Coming from a similar background to Moore's, he never left Dublin, despite finding it a wasteland, 'where man lives and doth not live / Doth not live – nor die',[51] and sought refuge in alcohol, drugs and eccentricity, as well as in playing complex games with his readers, including often fitting his work, chameleon-like, to the colouring of each of the eclectic range of journals to which he contributed. It seems likely that he too knew no Irish, and relied on the translations of others, but like Moore's lyrics, his 'translations' from the Gaelic, as well as many of his original verses, have fascinating resonances of the mood, even more than the sense, of Gaelic poetry. This went further than his restoration of the 'patriotic' or Catholic elements of such poems as 'The Fair Hills of Holy Ireland', or 'Lament over the Ruins of the Abbey of Teach Molaga', which Ferguson had excised.[52] It went further even than the elegaic tone and bleak fatalism of lines like 'And Erin, once the great and free / Now vainly mourns her breakless chain'.[53] His poetry, at its best, captured, above all, the sense of trauma, of being in the grip of an inexorable and hostile fate, which so marked Gaelic poetry from the mid-seventeenth century – the sense, as in Griffin, and later in Joyce, of history as nightmare. When Mangan tried to enter his 'Vision of Connaught in the Thirteenth Century', the result was a nameless 'terror', and as he left

> ... the sky
> Showed fleckt with blood and an alien sun
> Glared from the north,
> And there stood on high,
> Amid his shorn beams, a skeleton.[54]

His personal sense of trauma had by then (1846) been merged in the communal horror of 'blood-blackening plague and gaunt famine', of which he is the poet, and to which he fell victim. Another victim was this early phase of Irish Romanticism, which Mangan brought to an appropriately enigmatic close.

It had been marked, above all, by manipulations of elements of the Gaelic past, under various guises and for often conflicting political purposes. There was no 'Romantic era' in early nineteenth-century Ireland, only Romantic impulses which were absorbed into already established patterns of response to the colonial experience. It may be argued that

Romanticism developed properly only at the end of the century with the more strident cultural nationalism of the Gaelic League and the literary revival headed by Yeats, but by then it was a Romanticism permeated by Social Darwinism and modernist literary trends, even if its dynamic still lay mainly in being haunted by history and the colonial legacy.

ACKNOWLEDGEMENTS

I am grateful to Clare O'Halloran, Oliver MacDonagh, Kevin Barry, Pat Coughlan and Joe Spence for their help and encouragement, and to the Arts Faculty fund of University College Cork.

NOTES

1 Patrick O'Neill, 'The reception of German literature in Ireland 1750–1850', part I, *Studia Hibernica*, 16 (1976), 122–39; part II, *ibid.*, 17–18 (1977–8), 91–106.

2 W. J. McCormack, *Ascendancy and Tradition in Anglo-Irish Literary History from 1789 to 1939* (Oxford, 1985), p. 7.

3 *Ibid.*, p. 27.

4 J. C. Beckett, *The Anglo-Irish Tradition* (London, 1976); Seamus Deane, *Celtic Revivals* (London, 1985); McCormack, *Ascendancy and Tradition*.

5 Brendan Bradshaw, *The Irish Constitutional Revolution in the Sixteenth Century* (Cambridge, 1979); Tom Dunne, 'Fiction as "the best history of nations": Lady Morgan's Irish novels', in Tom Dunne (ed.), *The Writer as Witness: Literature as Historical Evidence* (Cork, 1987).

6 Edmund Spenser, *A View of the Present State of Ireland*, ed. W. L. Renwick (Oxford, 1970); Tom Dunne, *Maria Edgeworth and the Colonial Mind* (Dublin, 1984).

7 Ann de Valera, 'Antiquarian and historical investigations in Ireland in the eighteenth century' (M.A. thesis, University College Dublin, 1978).

8 E.g. John Banim, *The Boyne Water* (London, 1826), a historical novel on the period of the Williamite wars, pitched brilliantly to suit the English Whig sense of history.

9 Seamus Deane, 'Irish national character 1790–1900', in Dunne (ed.), *The Writer as Witness*.

10 McCormack, *Ascendancy and Tradition*, pp. 20ff; Seamus Deane, 'Edmund Burke and the ideology of Irish liberalism', in Richard Kearney (ed.), *The Irish Mind. Exploring Intellectual Traditions* (Dublin, 1985), pp. 141–56; D. C. Lloyd, 'The writings of James Clarence Mangan: a case study in nationalism and writing' (Ph.D. thesis, Cambridge University, 1982), chapter iii.

11 John Mitchel, 'The individuality of a native literature', *Nation*, 21 August 1847.

12 Lady Morgan, *O'Donnel. A National Tale*, 2nd edn (London, 1846), preface.

13 H. Hepworth Dixon (ed.), *Lady Morgan's Memoirs: Autobiography, Diary*

and Correspondence, 2 vols. (London, 1863); Lionel Stevenson, *The Wild Irish Girl. The Life of Sydney Owenson, Lady Morgan* (London, 1936).

14 Morgan, *The Wild Irish Girl*, 3 vols. (London, 1806), vol. 2, pp. 65–97.

15 Morgan, *The O'Briens and the O'Flahertys*, 4 vols. (London, 1827), vol. 1, pp. 30, 55–6; vol. 2, pp. 211–12.

16 Morgan, *Florence Macarthy. An Irish Tale*, 4 vols. (London, 1818), vol. 1, pp. 326–7; vol. 3, pp. 119, 271; vol. 4, p. 268; *The O'Briens and the O'Flahertys*, vol. 1, pp. 26, 68–9; vol. 4, pp. 283–4.

17 Morgan, *The O'Briens and the O'Flahertys*, vol. 1, pp. 68–71; vol. 4, pp. 244–6.

18 Morgan, *Florence Macarthy*, vol. 1, pp. 21, 92; vol. 3, p. 136; vol. 4, p. 8.

19 C. Gavan Duffy, *Young Ireland: A Fragment of Irish History, 1840–50*, 2nd edn (London, 1880), pp. 163–5; Nicholas Mansergh, *The Irish Question 1840–1921* (London, 1965), pp. 76–9.

20 M. G. Buckley, 'Thomas Davis; a study in nationalist philosophy' (Ph.D. thesis, University College Cork, 1980), pp. 83–123, 222–3; Duffy, *Young Ireland*, pp. 561–5.

21 Thomas Davis, 'Our national language', in *Essays and Poems, with a Centenary Memoir 1845–1945* (Dublin, 1945), pp. 70–7.

22 Davis, 'Songs of Ireland', in *Essays and Poems*, p. 103; 'Ballad poetry', in *ibid.*, p. 102.

23 Davis, 'Our national language', in *ibid.*, p. 103; Duffy, *Young Ireland*, p. 63.

24 Davis to Maddyn, n.d., in Duffy, *Young Ireland*, p. 289.

25 Buckley, 'Davis', pp. 323–4.

26 Davis, *Essays and Poems*, pp. 93–109.

27 Maria Edgeworth, *Tales of Fashionable Life* (London, 1812), vols. 5–6, containing *The Absentee*, vol. 6, pp. 4, 90; *Castle Rackrent, an Hibernian Tale. Taken from Facts and from the Manners of the Irish Squires before the Year 1782* (London, 1800), pp. 2–4 (fn); Dunne, *Edgeworth*, pp. 6–9.

28 Marilyn Butler, *Maria Edgeworth. A Literary Biography* (Oxford, 1972), p. 360.

29 Cf. especially *Ennui* (London, 1809), in which the subversive servant is revealed as the local leader of the United Irishmen, and a well-run estate is reduced to chaos when the new owner reverts to Gaelic traditions.

30 Edgeworth, *Ennui*, pp. 39, 76; *The Absentee*, vol. 6, pp. 456–63; *Ormond, a Tale* (London, 1817; Irish University Press reprint, 1972), p. 399.

31 Lady Ferguson, *Sir Samuel Ferguson in the Ireland of His Day*, 2 vols. (Edinburgh and London, 1896).

32 Samuel Ferguson, 'Hardiman's Irish Minstrelsy', part 1, *Dublin University Magazine*, vol. 3, April 1834, 456–78; part 2, vol. 4, August 1834, 152–67; part 3, *ibid.*, 447–67; part 4, *ibid.*, 514–42.

33 *D.U.M.*, vol. 2, November 1833.

34 *Ibid.*, vol. 3, 457; vol. 4, 516, 467; vol. 3, 465.

35 *Ibid.*, vol. 3, 457; vol. 4, 153, 161, 154–5; vol. 3, 471; vol. 4, 448–64, 516.

36 *Ibid.*, vol. 4, 532–42; vol. 3, 465; Lloyd, 'Mangan', pp. 161–79.

37 Colm O Lochlainn, 'Literary forgeries in Irish', *Éigse*, vol. 2 (1940), 123–36; James Hardiman, *Irish Minstrelsy*, 2 vols. (London, 1831), vol. 1, pp. i–xl.

38 Gerald Griffin, *Tales of the Munster Festivals*, 3 vols. (London, 1827), vol. 1, pp. vi–xxiii.

39 John Cronin, *Gerald Griffin 1803–1840. A Critical Biography* (Cambridge,

1978); Tom Dunne, 'Murder as metaphor: Gerald Griffin's portrayal of Ireland in the year of Catholic Emancipation', in Oliver MacDonagh and W. F. Mandle (eds.), *Ireland and Irish-Australia* (Beckenham, Kent, 1986).

40 Cronin, *Griffin*, p. 94.
41 William Griffin, *The Life of Gerald Griffin*, 2nd edn (London, 1857), pp. 231, 285–90.
42 Cf. Buckley, 'Davis', p. 187.
43 Thomas Moore, *The Poetical Works of Thomas Moore, Collected by Himself*, 10 vols. (London, 1840–1), vol. 1, p. xvii.
44 Moore, *Works*, vol. 3, pp. 264–6. The feelings that lay behind the lyrical mood pieces of the *Irish Melodies* were articulated more clearly in the satires, *Corruption and Intolerance. Two Poems, with Notes, Addressed to an Englishman by an Irishman* (London, 1808). Cf. also W. S. Dowden (ed.), *The Letters of Thomas Moore*, 2 vols. (Oxford, 1964); *The Journal of Thomas Moore*, 2 vols. (London, 1983).
45 Moore, *Corruption and Intolerance*, pp. 59–64.
46 Moore, *Irish Melodies* (London, 1810), preface.
47 Seán Ó Tuama, *Filí faoi sceimhle* (Dublin, 1978); Tom Dunne, 'The Gaelic response to conquest and colonisation: the evidence of the poetry', *Studia Hibernica*, 20 (1980), 7–30.
48 Moore, *Works*, vol. 3, pp. 252–4, 229–30.
49 *Ibid.*, pp. 354–5.
50 Lloyd, 'Mangan'.
51 James Clarence Mangan, 'Siberia', in D. J. O'Donoghue (ed.), *Poems of James Clarence Mangan* (Dublin, 1903), pp. 151–2.
52 Lloyd, 'Mangan', chapter iv.
53 Mangan, 'Lament for the Princes of Tyrone and Tyrconnell' in O'Donoghue (ed.), *Poems*, pp. 17–24.
54 *Ibid.*, pp. 94–6.

4

Romanticism in Greece

RODERICK BEATON

Greek Romanticism was born out of the war of independence which was waged against the Ottoman Turks from 1821 until 1828. The reasons for this go deeper than the tragic accident of the death of George Gordon, Lord Byron, at Mesolonghi in 1824. Before the creation of a nation state in 1821 Greek intellectual life had revolved around three focal points: the Ecumenical Patriarchate of the Orthodox Church in Constantinople; the aristocratic communities of the Ionian Islands off the west coast of Greece, ruled until the Napoleonic wars by the Republic of Venice and as a result closely in touch with Italian culture; and the Greek merchant communities of the 'Diaspora' – especially those of Odessa, Amsterdam and Paris. Insofar as the successful revolt was directed or inspired by intellectual ideas, these were the ideas of the French Enlightenment.[1] Romanticism becomes discernible only once hostilities had broken out. Along with Byron thousands of young idealists from England, France and Germany, most of them disaffected with the conservative regimes established in the wake of the Napoleonic wars, came to Greece to join in the struggle. Many died; a few such as Richard Church, Thomas Cochrane and Charles Fabvier, made significant contributions to the military success of the Greeks; many more returned home disillusioned. They were, in Greece, the first Romantics and it is to them that Greek Romanticism owed its real beginning.[2]

Byron's fate provoked a long, impassioned Ode from Dionísios Solomós, a young Italian-educated aristocrat from Zákinthos in the Ionian Islands. Solomós had already begun to establish himself, in the year before Byron's death, as his country's national poet, with the publication of a 'Hymn to Liberty' (1823) which was quickly translated into the languages of western Europe. Soon afterwards Solomós extended his homage to Byron in a fragmentary narrative poem, 'Lámbros', which transplanted the figure of the doomed visionary, made famous through Byron's writings, to Greek soil. During the 1830s Solomós seems to have made a

92

thorough study of the ideas of Schiller and Hegel, and in his fragmentary poems of this and the succeeding decade emerged as the first Greek writer of stature to engage in a serious way with the European Romantic movement in literature.[3]

Literary Romanticism spread quickly in the newly established Kingdom of Greece (1833) as well as in the Ionian Islands which remained a British Protectorate until 1864. The brothers Panayiótis and Aléxandros Soútsos were typical of the intellectual elite of the first generation after Athens was established as the national capital in 1834, and they effectively dominated the literary scene for the following three decades. Their family belonged to Constantinople, to the wealthy and influential circles of the Greek Patriarchate, or *Fanári* as it was popularly called, which had been granted substantial powers of secular administration under the Ottoman Empire. The members of this circle were already known as 'Phanariots', and it is by this name that the cultural leaders of the Greek kingdom during its first fifty years, including the Soútsos brothers, are also known. Panayiótis anticipated the more serious engagement of his Ionian contemporary Solomós with the style and preoccupations of German and Byronic Romanticism with the publication of a long 'dramatic poem', *The Wayfarer*, in 1831, and three years later went on to produce the first modern Greek novel, *Leander*, whose roots in European Romanticism are no less manifest.

With the exception of the realist social criticism of *Thános Vlékas* by Pávlos Kalligás (1855) and the brilliant satire on Romantic fiction and the historical novel in particular by Emmanouíl Roídis in *Pope Joan* (1866), Greek fiction during its first fifty years was dominated by the example of Walter Scott. The poetry that came out of Athens during the same period is largely lightweight and small in scale, in a vein which owes much to Lamartine and French Romantic poetry in general.[4]

After about 1880 the two cultural centres of Athens and the Ionian Islands (especially Corfu), which had maintained distinctive traditions deriving respectively from Ottoman Constantinople and Venetian rule in the previous century, began to draw together. The bombastic nationalist poet Aristotélis Valaorítis moved from Corfu to Athens on the cession of the Ionian Islands to Greece and died there in 1879. Prose after this time moves into the realm of rural realism with a strong admixture of social criticism, and the short stories and novels of this period are only linked to Romanticism in their underlying ideology. In poetry, the lifetime of the true colossus of Greek Romanticism, Kostís Palamás, straddles the turn of the century (1859–1943). In his many and varied works, strands derived from Nietzsche, Greek folk poetry, Greek and European Romanticism, as well as the anti-Romantic movements of the Parnasse and Symbolism, meet in a grandiose synthesis whose dominant obsession is the quest for transcendence through the artistic medium, which of course had been a mainspring of Romanticism from Goethe and Wordsworth onwards.[5] It is worth mentioning that literary Romanticism in Greece has a curiously prolonged afterlife into the twentieth century; the visionary poetry of 'Angelos Sikelianós (1884–1951) and the larger-than-life literary personality of Níkos Kazantzákis (1883–1957) both require to be understood in relation to nineteenth-century concepts of the artist and the literary work.[6]

Romanticism, of course, is much more than a literary movement, although the wider extension of the term implicit in this book makes a reductive definition almost impossible. The rest of this chapter will deal with particular complexes of ideas that have close ideological parallels in western Europe and which also played a key role in determining the course of Greek history in and beyond the nineteenth century. This is not to say that the subject is thereby exhausted, or that a precise definition of Romanticism in a Greek context, which has been evaded here, is necessarily unattainable. The concepts I propose to deal with are the nexus of nationhood and language, and the establishment of cultural identity by appeal to the past, or the concept of 'tradition'.

NATION AND LANGUAGE

Before the outbreak of the war of independence in 1821 there was no clearly defined concept of the nation state among Greeks. Rígas of Velestíno (1757–98), the most influential among the intellectual precursors of the uprising, published a 'constitution' in 1797 which proclaimed a kind of federation of the subject peoples of the Ottoman Empire under the umbrella of a common Greek language and administration, and some such programme seems initially to have been adopted by the expatriate Greeks in Russia who in 1814 formed the 'Friendly Society' whose clandestine activities culminated in the revolt of seven years later.[7] Indeed, at the turn of the nineteenth century there was no single term in common use to define what is meant by 'a Greek' today. The modern word for a Greek is 'Ellinas, a revival of the ancient 'Hellene', which in classical times and until the coming of Christianity had designated not a member of a political entity, but a speaker of a common language. In medieval times 'Hellene' came to mean 'pagan'. The common term for 'a Greek' at the beginning of the nineteenth century was Romiós, which in addition to meaning 'a speaker of Greek' meant an Orthodox Christian – and cognate terms were in use in all the Balkan languages, including Turkish, in which Millet-i-Rum designated the Christian community under the Ottoman Empire.[8]

By 1833 Greece had become an independent nation. The role played in

achieving that independence by western philhellenes, although without the
sanction of their own governments, as well as the anomalous position of
the new state in the balance of power between the European nations and
the still powerful Ottoman Empire, ensured a dominant role for the
western European powers, especially Britain and France, in the political
and cultural emergence of the new state.[9] The peculiar circumstances of
the war of independence made Greece a European country almost overnight, despite the fact that many of its traditional institutions and the
traditional culture of its rural population were often incompatible with
western values. It is an ironic result of the dominance of the European
powers and their ideology over Greece throughout the nineteenth century
that the terms in which the Greeks sought to proclaim their own specific
identity, as distinct from the rest of Europe, were all adopted piecemeal
from the west.

One of these was the concept of the nation. Once a nation state existed
and its citizens had been baptised as 'Hellenes', it remained to define who
or what a Hellene was. Although just about all the citizens of the kingdom,
with the exception of the king and his advisers who came from Bavaria,
were united by the Greek language and Orthodox religion, many more
co-religionists and Greek-speakers lived beyond its boundaries, in territories still under the control of the Ottomans. Since a state now existed,
and the very concept of European statehood had previously been foreign
to traditional Greek perceptions of themselves, it followed that in order to
live up convincingly to that concept, the Greek *state* would have to include
all the *Greeks*. Greek irredentism is therefore as old as the Greek state, a
logical consequence of the Romantic concept of nationhood used to define
that state from the beginning.

The inescapable requirement for the state to incorporate all its
'nationals' within its boundaries in order to justify its own self-definition,
was first articulated in a famous speech to the Constituent Assembly in
Athens in January 1844 by Ioánnis Koléttis, a veteran strategist of the war
of independence and soon to become prime minister:

Greece is geographically placed at the centre of Europe, between East and West,
her destiny in decline [i.e. the decline of *ancient* Greece] to spread light to the West,
but in her rebirth to the East. The former task our forefathers achieved, the latter
falls to us. In the spirit of this oath [i.e. to liberate Greece] and of this *great idea* I
have consistently seen the nation's representatives gathered here to decide the fate
not only of Greece, but of the Greek race [my emphasis].[10]

This is incidentally one of the earliest uses of the Greek word *fylí* (*phyle*),
which in the ancient language meant a tribe or a clan, in its modern sense
of a genetic unity underlying and underpinning the concept of the nation
state. And in the same speech Koléttis also set the slogan which until 1922

became part of the cultural horizon of all Greeks and came to sum up this 'Great Idea': 'There are two main centres of Hellenism: Athens, the capital of the Greek kingdom, [and] "The City" [Constantinople], the dream and hope of all Greeks'.[11]

This 'Great Idea' became the principal motivating force behind all Greek foreign policy during the remainder of the nineteenth century. It was in the hope of realising it that Greece was reluctantly drawn into the First World War, then in 1919 took advantage of a proposal of the Paris Peace Conference to establish a foothold in Anatolia, only to be humiliated by the collapse of the Treaty of Sèvres (drawn up in 1920 but never ratified) and the unforeseen success of the Turkish Nationalists under Kemal Atatürk. In August 1922 the Greek army was driven out of western Anatolia along with those of the Greek civilian population who could escape. In the following year the Treaty of Lausanne provided for an exchange of populations between Greece and Turkey and confirmed frontiers for the Greek state which are more or less those of today. In this way Koléttis' dream was fulfilled, and most of the Greek-speaking Orthodox of the former Ottoman Empire came to be embraced by the nation state, although not in the way he had envisaged.[12]

The identity of the Greeks as a nation, as was to be expected in the century after Herder, was inseparable from their language – the more so in that language had also been the defining criterion of the ancient Hellenes. Their common language, together with religion, was what united the geographically disparate Greek communities of the Ottoman Empire; but the relatively close derivation of that language from classical Greek offered a more stable and prestigious reference point for defining the identity of the new nation state. A consequence of the Romantic ideology that Greece had acquired from the philhellenes who helped her gain her independence, and from the subsequent domination of political life by western governments, was the claim of the modern Greek for special status as the descendant of the Hellene of antiquity. The most tangible link between the modern Greek and a glorious past was his language, and the notorious 'Language Question' that raged among Greek-speakers from even before national independence until 1976 is dependent on two concepts which in their turn are integral to the ideology of Romanticism: that community of language is a defining characteristic of national identity, and that the ancient past is in some way recoverable in the present.

This is not the place to go into the detailed history of the debate about the Greek language, of which concise accounts are available in English.[13] Both in the theoretical polemics and in practical application, the Language Question is best seen as a conflict between opposing *tendencies* rather than between already codified linguistic forms. These tendencies are represented traditionally by the terms *katharévousa* (purifying) and *dimotikí* (demotic, that is, commonly spoken), but these terms gained currency only towards the end of the nineteenth century and a wide range of linguistic practice is covered by each. Each of these opposing tendencies is subsumed in one of the concepts already mentioned as deriving from Romantic ideology: *katharévousa*, as its name implies, proposes a backward progression reversing linguistic development in order to revive past glories; *dimotikí* bases its appeal on the *speech-community* as the ultimate repository of national identity.

However, since the claim of racial kinship with ancient Greece and the ideology of the 'Great Idea' are common to both tendencies in the latter half of the nineteenth century, there is actually a considerable degree of overlap between them. Adamándios Koraís, who first formulated the principle of 'purifying' the modern language to make it more closely resemble the ancient, was in most respects no Romantic, but nonetheless explicitly espoused the ideas of Schlegel and Herder on language as a determinant of nationhood, and in fact depended on them in order to formulate the modern Greek claim to descent from the ancients: the modern Greeks, as a speech-community, have inherited the language of their ancestors.[14] Conversely, the advocates of *dimotikí* never rejected the authority of the past, but sought to demonstrate a continuity of the spirit rather than the letter of an ancient civilisation, as manifested in the customs, beliefs and songs of the peasantry. Certain tenets are therefore common to both sides in the debate; both Koraís for the purifiers and Psicháris for the demoticists almost a century later wished to purge the language of foreign elements, especially Turkish; and both shared an identical organic theory of language. Koraís pays tribute to the 'language which is suckled with one's mother's milk',[15] while Psicháris identifies as one of the abiding characteristics of the Greek his 'love for the language his mother spoke to him as a child'.[16]

For the first fifty years of Greek independence, the purist tendency dominates. Then from about 1880, alongside the discovery of folklore as a repository for ancient customs and beliefs surviving into modern times, comes an interest in the traditional life and particularly in the *language* of the economically backward peasants. The intellectual movement known as 'demoticism' held sway for the following fifty years and, although it failed in its principal aim of making demotic the language of education, it nonetheless decisively shaped the course of modern Greek literature in the twentieth century. Moreover, the concepts of the modern Greek tradition and even national identity as they have tended to be formulated during this century owe an enormous debt to the demoticist movement.[17] The acknowledged hero of demoticism, though not really its instigator, was the expatriate philologist Jean Psichari (or Psichári, as he designated himself simply in Greek), who taught linguistics at the Sorbonne. In 1888 he published, in Greek, a 'novel' called *My Journey*, which is really a lightly fictionalised series of debates and expositions on the Language Question. Psichári' book became the manifesto of the popularising tendency.[18]

In November 1901 rightwing students of Athens University, egged on by some of their professórs, besieged the offices of the newspaper *Akrópolis*, whose editorial had derided opposition to a translation of parts of the New Testament into demotic Greek, that had just been announced. Not content with protest, the students proceeded to wreck the paper's printing presses, and some days later a group of similar protesters clashed with police and a number were killed. The objection to the translation of the gospels was part religious (any translation from the Bible has to be authorised by the Greek Orthodox Church), but still more a protest against the language of the translation.[19] It is interesting to see how closely the Romantic Nationalist ideology of those who protested so violently against this use of the demotic echoes that of Psicháris and many of his fellow-demoticists. (It was only after this time that the Language Question became politically polarised, with demotic becoming the 'official language' of the Greek Communist Party.) On 5 November 1901, a medical student from Anatolia, Ilías Pilarinós, addressed a packed assembly at the University of Athens on the subject of the New Testament translation:

In our veins there must run anything but Greek blood if we permit the holiest and worthiest parts of the *heritage of Hellenism* to be trampled underfoot. Let us not forget, gentlemen, that we are the sole protectors and keepers of the keys of our *ancestral heritage*, that we are the truest representatives of *Hellenism* . . . Let us rise up, friends, and forbid the wretched organ of *anti-national* and diabolical agents from aiming further ridicule at our Holy Gospel and *our exalted language* [my emphasis].[20]

Two years later a similar response to a relatively demotic translation of ancient Greek tragedy (the *Oresteia* of Aeschylus) again provoked violent clashes. A professor in the Faculty of Arts, this time, addresses his class on the subject: 'All peoples possess two foundations for maintaining their identity, Religion and Language, and if they try to corrupt either one of them . . . we have the duty . . . to protest'.[21] From the other side of the controversy, Psicháris had invoked a very similar ideology:

Language and fatherland are one. To fight for one's fatherland or for one's national language, is one and the same fight . . . A nation, in order to become a nation, requires two things: to extend its frontiers and to create a literature of its own . . . Not only its natural but also its intellectual frontiers need to be extended. It is for these frontiers that I am fighting.[22]

The purist links language with religion as the prime constituents of national identity; the demoticist places language alongside the 'secular scripture' of literature, in exactly the same role.

To conclude, both sides in this hotly contested dispute drew on the identity of nation and language and both, it is worth emphasising, were looking to the *past* for prescriptive norms that would at once furnish the nation with a stable linguistic idiom (something not in fact achieved until the 1970s when an act of the Greek parliament declared *dimotikí* the official language of the country) and bring about a revival in the modern Greek nation of the 'glory that was Greece'. To this end the purists sought to reverse linguistic change and revive the latter, while the aim of the demoticists was to privilege the already obsolescent idiom of the rural communities in whose way of life the living spirit of the ancients could be recognised and cultivated.

THE MAKING OF TRADITION

All cultures use their perception of the past to define and validate themselves in the present. Under the impact of Romanticism and the consolidation of nation states throughout Europe in the nineteenth century, perceptions of the past were more radically revised than they had been since the Renaissance. Each nation set about discovering and asserting the value of the *tradition* (or traditions) that in the past had shaped it towards its present condition and in the present continued to guarantee its difference from rivals and its potential for realising its unique aspirations in the future. The cultural tradition of which the Greek language is the focal point has the longest unbroken history of any in Europe. The Greek *state*, however, was newly born out of the conflict of 1821–8 and was without precedent in the history of the Greeks. The newly defined nation therefore had, as a matter of urgency, to *create its own past*, that is, to select and endorse those elements of earlier Greek history which retrospectively could claim to have made the present existence and future aspirations of the nation inevitable. Since the state itself was in many ways the creation of European Romanticism, it was only natural that the means to hand for defining and justifying its existence should derive from the same source.

The formation of a modern Greek tradition covers many aspects of culture, only a few of which can be discussed here. Once again the elements to be treated have been chosen because they are both representative of European traits, and in their particular application to the Greek case produced results that were at once locally influential and to some degree peculiar to that case. The elements to be considered are the formation of a national literature, Romantic historiography and the development of interest in folklore.

Poetry for a new nation

The name of Dionísios Solomós has already been mentioned. Solomós was the first poet writing in Greek to address himself, in his 'Hymn to Liberty', to the Greeks as a free people. As the subject of many of his poems was also the struggle of that people to achieve freedom, it is not surprising that he should have been hailed ever since as the national poet of his country. This tribute was earned in a subtler way too. Solomós was born into the Ionian aristocracy, a community bilingual in Greek and Italian, and spent many of his formative years as a student in Italy. For Solomós, as for many of the educated young men of Zákinthos and Corfu, Greek was not the language of his education. The decision, which seems to have been consciously taken upon his return to Zákinthos at the age of twenty, to write in the language spoken by his countrymen, entailed an even more daunting task than that which faced Wordsworth when he decided to write in the language of 'the middle and lower classes of society'.

Spoken Greek had scarcely been used as a vehicle for sophisticated expression before. Although there were precedents in the form of the elegant ditties of the Phanariot poet Athánasios Christópoulos and the literary experiments in the vernacular by the court physician to Ali Pasha of Ioannina, Ioánnis Vilarás, there was no established literary medium capable of handling the complex ideas of the Romantic thinkers and writers to whose work Solomós had access through Italian. Every literary work depends for a large part of its meaning on its intertextual relationship with other texts, the majority of which one would expect to be written in the same language. Solomós had not only therefore to *learn* his new language and to *create* a poetic idiom based upon it; in order for that idiom to carry the weight of meaning invested in the poems of his European con- temporaries, he had also to create the *intertext* into which his own texts could be inserted, that is, a context made up of previous texts in the same language within which it could acquire more than a superficial meaning.[23]

This he did, after his earlier patriotic and lightweight satirical poems, by turning in the same direction as Wordsworth had done, to the 'lyrical ballads' of the people (in Solomós' case, to Greek folk poetry), and also to the long narrative poem *Erotókritos* which had been written some 200 years earlier in Venetian-controlled Crete under the influence of the Italian Renaissance. Crete had subsequently fallen to the Ottoman Turks in 1669, and many of the educated upper classes fled to Zákinthos and Corfu as the last remaining Greek cultural centres under Venetian control. With them they brought the manuscript of *Erotókritos*, which was later published in Venice.[24] Solomós' own ancestors may also have come from Crete at the same time, and in his poem 'The Cretan' he pays tribute to the achievement of his forebears in creating a literary monument and a powerful literary idiom in *Erotókritos*, and also in preserving it from the national enemy into his own time.[25]

The poem proclaims its intertextual relationship with the 200-year-old romance by adopting its metre and rhyme-scheme and some elements of its language. True to Solomós' patriotic principles, the immediate setting of the poem is the failed Cretan rising that had coincided with the successful revolt on the mainland in 1821; a young unnamed fighter has escaped from the devastation with his fiancée in a boat. The girl, whom he describes as a 'precious burden', dies but at the moment before he is aware of her death he sees her transfigured as a vision 'clad in moonlight', and at this sight and prompted by an ethereal sound which succeeds the apparition, he relives moments of his past life amid the Cretan landscape. The poem is about Romantic transcendence, placed specifically in the context of the Greek struggle for independence; but its intertextual references to *Erotókritos* recreate the particular circumstances in which that poem (whose subjects are love and war) was brought by refugees from Crete and so made available to the later poet. The transfiguration of the girl can also therefore be read as a metaphor for the transcendence into the realm of the immutable and sublime which is sought by the Romantic poet in and through the work of art; a transcendence which in the case of *Erotókritos* is affirmed by the existence and intertextual dependence on it of the present poem.

In an often quoted letter written in 1833, while he was working on 'The Cretan', Solomós declared that the folk poetry of the social bandits of the Greek highlands, the klefts, should not be used merely imitatively by an aspiring national poet: 'Kleftic poetry is fine and interesting as an ingenuous manifestation by the klefts of their lives, thoughts and feelings. It does not have the same interest on our lips; the nation requires from us the treasure of our individual intelligence clothed in national forms.'[26] In his last, uncompleted, poems, Solomós demonstrated to great effect how allusive use of traditional folk poetry could help to create an intertext for the Romantic literature of a new nation.

'The Shark' (1849) uses the same metre as 'The Cretan', but, stripped of the couplet form characteristic of *Erotókritos*, this is now the metre of traditional oral folk poetry.[27] Like 'The Cretan', this poem is in narrative form, and tells of the death of a young English soldier, attacked by a shark while bathing in Corfu harbour. The theme of sudden death interrupting but at the same time sublimating a profound communion of the individual with nature all around him, belongs to European Romanticism. But in the foreign soldier, awakening from his idyllic reverie to the joy of 'his body, naked and free as the lightning' and to the challenge of an unequal fight at whose end 'In a flash of light the young man knew himself', the reader can observe a cosmopolitan and Romantic transformation of one of the most widely loved themes in traditional Greek folk poetry: a young hero, at the height of his physical powers and almost supernaturally attuned to the natural world, is ambushed by the grimly personified figure of Death, Cháros. Rather than submit, the hero challenges Death to a fight according to the heroic code. Cháros is obliged to cheat in order to gain his victory, and so is revealed as unworthy of his human victim, whose heroism reaches its apogee in the challenge to this unequal fight.[28] The assertion of the superior worth of life at the moment of confronting death is the subject of both poems, but Solomós has substituted for the celebration of heroic valour the transcendent moment of self-knowledge experienced by his hero, and has also tacitly inserted the representative of English Romantic poetry (his English hero, communing with the beauties of nature) into the anterior Greek tradition which is radically transformed in the process.

This achievement of Solomós in creating a poetic intertext within which an essentially new tradition could acquire meaning and develop has been recognised, although not explicitly in those terms, by almost all his successors in Greece, and is not matched by any other single writer until the 1880s. This is not the place anyhow to go into the further development of the modern Greek literary tradition, which in the later nineteenth century began to escape the bounds of Romanticism.

Romantic historiography and folklore

The substance of the Greek claim to cultural descent from classical Hellas was afforded by the continuity of the Greek language. But in the discourse of Romantic Nationalism no distinction was made between culture and race. Consequently, from the beginning, the Greeks were committed to substantiating a claim to racial as well as linguistic and cultural continuity from ancient times. This component of the Greek national identity need not have come to the fore had it not been for the theoretical ethnographic researches of the pan-Germanist scholar and historian, Jakob Philip Fallmerayer (1790–1861), who in 1830 published the first volume of a history of the Peloponnese.[29] Fallmerayer purported to prove, largely on the basis of the distribution of placenames, that the population of southern Greece had been made up of Slavs since the sixth century and Albanians since the fourteenth.[30] The appearance of this book constituted an ideological threat to Greece's very existence as a nation state on the European model. So seriously, indeed, was the threat taken, that although Fallmerayer's conclusions have long been discounted by historians, his name continues to send a shudder through Greek intellectual circles to this day.

The response took two forms, both of which went far further in determining and enriching the identity of modern Greece than a mere rebuttal of Fallmerayer's threat. The first was the formulation, between 1852 and 1876, of a two-and-a-half-thousand-year past for the Greek nation; the second the somewhat delayed discovery by Greek intellectuals of the customs and beliefs and songs of rural communities as testimony to an unconscious inheritance from antiquity. The formative phase of this 'discovery' and the development of folklore as a discipline in those terms can be dated to the active career of the founding father of Greek folklore, Nikólaos Polítis, between 1869 and 1921.

Although the development of folkloric researches on a serious scale seem to follow on from the completion of a national history, the two projects were closely linked at their inception. The first attempt at a national history, by Spirídon Zambélios in 1852, actually took the form of an introduction to a collection of folksongs.[31] The introduction is almost 600 pages long; the folksongs take up only a further 150. The writing of history has a practical as well as an intellectual value to Zambélios, indeed the two for him are closely linked. 'The cultivation of the science of history', he writes, 'is as it were a way of measuring the pulse of improvement' (the last word, in Greek, is a metaphor from stock breeding!). 'Every single nation today', he continues, 'presents itself in the arena of civilisation equipped as it were with a historical passport. But we have left ours behind on the field of battle, and have not since taken the trouble to go back and pick it up.'[32]

His reasons for focussing on the intervening historical period between antiquity and the present, namely the middle ages, and for linking historical research with the collection of oral poetry, are similarly linked to the pragmatic function of Romantic historiography. He begins his introduction:

In illuminating this dark and unexplored historical period, in which the most refined race known to civilisation mysteriously progresses from its ancient to its modern stage of liberty . . . we admit that the pen weighs heavily in our hand . . . Just as the life of an author often elucidates passages of his endeavour otherwise inexplicable, so the life of the faceless and anonymous poet, the people, illumines the dark crossings through which the race has passed in the quest for its freedom.[33]

Just as happened in the west, where the middle ages came to be rehabilitated (and named) as an essential period of transition between the glories of imperial Rome and the modern European nations, so in Greece medieval (Byzantine) history becomes a period in which the Greek people 'mysteriously' evolved and struggled towards their present condition. To authenticate such a reading of earlier history, along with historical exposition of the relevant sources, the oral traditions of the present have to be adduced, as the independent record preserved by 'the people'.

A disciple of Solomós, who had first recognised the importance of folk poetry in creating a national literature, Zambélios was one of the first to produce a collection of songs which he had himself collected.[34] But Zambélios' achievement lies principally in his historical work. His mammoth introduction to the folksongs for the first time puts the medieval civilisation of Byzantium on the cultural map of modern Greece. (Greek intellectuals of the Enlightenment, before independence, had reviled Byzantium as theocratic, despotic and obscurantist, in the wake of Gibbon and Voltaire.) In a later book, *Byzantine Studies* (1857), Zambélios went on to spell out the tripartite division comprising a unified Greek history that has remained standard in Greek education and historiography ever since: a division into ancient, medieval and modern.[35]

Zambélios belonged to the Ionian Islands, to the Italian-influenced cultural centre which was not united with Greece until 1864. As a historian he was also an amateur. The task of codifying and conferring scientific authority on Zambélios' intuitions fell to his exact contemporary, Konstandínos Paparrigópoulos (1815–91), who hailed from the other centre of culture for pre-independence Hellenism, Constantinople, and who for forty years held the post of Professor of History at Athens University. Paparrigópoulos' monumental *History of the Greek Nation* was published in five volumes between 1861 and 1876. Aside from the sheer wealth of historical research it contains, and the magisterial style in which it is written, the most radical achievement of Paparrigópoulos' history is implicit in its title: modern nationhood is retrospectively conferred on the Greeks of all earlier historical periods back to classical antiquity. Although late in his life Paparrigópoulos denied that his historical work implied a political programme and declared that 'Nations create History, not History Nations', he nonetheless introduced into his University lectures the Romantic concept of 'national truth'.[36] The reason he gives, in the preface to the final volume of his *History*, for bringing his account of modern Hellenism to a close with the achievement of national independence, is revealing of how this whole monumental recovery and arrangement of the past has been determined by a vision of a specific future which it is required to presuppose. 'It is not yet permissible', he writes in 1874, 'to evaluate the historical worth [of modern Hellenism], since it remains in the initial stage of the mission which it appears destined to fulfil in the East.'[37] The reference, of course, is to Koléttis' 'Great Idea' of Greek irredentism.

The proclamation of a Greek 'nation' with a continuous historical development over two and a half thousand years behind it, and an expansionist destiny awaiting it, was the first consolidated step by which the new state sought to counteract the threat posed by Fallmerayer. The second was announced by a nineteen-year-old undergraduate at the University of Athens, Nikólaos Polítis, in 1871: 'The history of a nation does not consist solely in the narrative of events which have had an influence on the nation's fate. There is a supplementary need . . . also for a precise and detailed knowledge of the character and spirit of that nation'.[38] So begins the preface to Polítis' *Study on the Way of Life of the Modern Greeks*, subtitled, *Modern Greek Mythology*, which inaugurated the systematic exploration by Greeks of their own folklore. Here Polítis has implicitly described his work as a supplement to the achievement of Paparrigópoulos, and he goes on at once to offer his researches as a refutation of Fallmerayer.

Together with a second volume which appeared in 1874, the book provides a detailed account of beliefs and practices current among the Greek peasantry, many of which do indeed bear a relationship, although not always as direct as Polítis would have wished, to those of antiquity. In this way, not just the national language and the nation itself, but that other essential component of Romantic nationhood, 'national character', could be both defined in the present and extended retrospectively to embrace the universally admired civilisation of the ancients. The result of such a systematic study (which Polítis revealingly admits will excise those elements of tradition that are foreign and accidental intrusions, while giving 'a special welcome' to those which bear evident traces of the ancient world) will be that 'we shall behold with wonder and amazement on the one hand the rebirth of ancient mythology, on the other the civilisation of the ancients standing in a closer and more intimate relationship to ourselves'.[39]

In 1882 Polítis embarked on his university career as the first Professor of Comparative Mythology in Greece, and a year later he became a cofounder of the Historical and Ethnological Society of Greece and of its annual *Journal*. Later he went on to found the periodical *Laografía* (*Folklore*) in 1909 and in 1914 published his influential anthology of oral folk poetry, *Selections from the Songs of the Greek People*.[40] Although scientific caution and a prodigious knowledge of the folk traditions of other peoples and of the anthropological theory of the time had by now tempered the enthusiasm with which Polítis had launched his *Modern Greek Mythology*, he could still declare in the preface to that anthology, 'The songs reflect faithfully and perfectly the life and manners, the emotions and the thought of the Greek people and rekindle memories, refined by their poetic invention, of national vicissitudes.'[41]

The search for an ethnographic validation both for the unique 'character' of the Greek people and for their claim to descent from the ancients was not confined to academic folklore. The announcement in 1883 of a competition for a 'Greek short story', to be characterised by 'the representation of scenes from the history or the social life of [the] people, or the psychological description of characters',[42] is thought to have been at least partly the brainchild of Polítis. In any case the competition inaugurated a period of twenty years in which novelists and short story writers turned for their subject matter to the 'lives and manners' of remote peasant communities, and many of these writers also appeared in the journals of the day as regular contributors of folkloric material. The prose fiction of this period turned decisively against literary Romanticism, for which it substituted a realist or even naturalist mode often linked to social criticism, but its underlying ideological impetus remained nonetheless Romantic.[43]

EPILOGUE

The nexus of ideological traits discussed here as representative of Romanticism in the national context of Greece continued to dominate cultural life up until the decisive defeat of Greek irredentism in 1922. That event, and the consequent expulsion of about a million and a half Greeks from Anatolia, has ever since been called simply the 'Catastrophe'. The process of reconstruction and the formulation of a new national identity without the 'Great Idea' and with a reduced dependence on the authority of the ancient past is still not complete, as can be seen in the exaggerated touchiness of Greek diplomatic exchanges with Turkey over the issue of the Aegean seabed in the last ten years, and in the enthusiasm generated by the appeal of a socialist government minister for the repatriation of the Elgin Marbles. Enormous changes have of course come about in Greece in the last sixty years, but in its literature as well as in more pervasive aspects of culture and ideology, the Greek nation today remains very much the heir to the Romantic cultural discourse it inherited from Europe at the same time as it gained its independence in 1821.

NOTES

1 R. Clogg (ed.), *Balkan Society in the Age of Greek Independence* (London, 1981), and *The Movement for Greek Independence, 1770–1821: A Collection of Documents* (London, 1976).
2 See R. Clogg, *A Short History of Modern Greece* (Cambridge, 1986), pp. 16–69; D. Dakin, *The Unification of Greece, 1770–1823* (London, 1972), pp. 20–65; W. St Clair, *That Greece Might Still Be Free* (Oxford, 1972); C. M. Woodhouse, *The Philhellenes* (London, 1969).

3 Most of Solomós' poetry is still unavailable in English. The complementary studies of the poet are R. Jenkins, *Dionysius Solomós* (Cambridge, 1940; 2nd edn, Athens, 1981), and M. B. Raizis, *Dionysios Solomós* (New York, 1972). For Solomós as a Romantic poet see E. Constantinides, 'Towards a redefinition of Greek Romanticism', *Journal of Modern Greek Studies*, 3/2 (1985), 121–36, an article which is of considerable interest for the subject of this paper insofar as it relates to literary Romanticism.

4 See L. Politis, *A History of Modern Greek Literature* (Oxford, 1973), pp. 137–49.

5 See Politis, *History*, pp. 150–85; G. Thomson, 'Introduction', in K. Palamas, *The Twelve Lays of the Gipsy* (London, 1969); and R. Fletcher, *Kostes Palamas: A Great Modern Greek Poet* (Athens, 1984).

6 See, respectively, E. Keeley, 'Sikelianos: the sublime voice', in *idem, Modern Greek Poetry: Voice and Myth* (Princeton, 1983), pp. 31–42; and P. Bien, *Nikos Kazantzakis* (New York, 1972).

7 Dakin, *The Unification*, pp. 29–30.

8 The nuances of the terms 'Hellene' and *Romiós* as used in the nineteenth century are well analysed in M. Herzfeld, *Ours Once More: Folklore, Ideology and the Making of Modern Greece* (Austin, Texas, 1982), pp. 18–21, 31–5. Today although a Greek citizen is officially (and commonly) an *Ellinas* (Hellene), the alternative term is still widely current with subtly differentiated semantic field. See K. Kazazis, '*Ellinas* vs. *Romiós* anecdotally revisited', *Folia Neohellenica* (Bochum and Amsterdam), 3 (1981), 53–5.

9 Clogg, *A Short History*, pp. 70–104; Dakin, *The Unification*, pp. 66–158.

10 K. Th. Dimarás, *Ellinikós Romandismós* (Athens, 1982), p. 406. The series of essays (in Greek) which makes up this volume is of considerable interest.

11 Clogg, *A Short History*, p. 76.

12 M. Llewellyn Smith, *Ionian Vision: Greece in Asia Minor* (London, 1973). The account of these events in A. Toynbee, *The Western Question in Greece and Turkey* (London, 1922), must now be read in conjunction with R. Clogg, *Politics and the Academy: Arnold Toynbee and the Koraes Chair* (London, 1986). The most detailed account of the shortlived Greek administration of Smyrna, with a sympathetic analysis of the reasons for its collapse, is to be found in an unpublished doctoral thesis: V. Solomonidis, 'Greece in Asia Minor: the Greek administration of the Vilayet of Aidin, 1919–1922 (University of London, 1985).

13 M. Alexiou, 'Diglosia in Greece', in W. Haas (ed.), *Standard Languages: Spoken and Written* (Manchester, 1982), pp. 156–92; P. Bien, *Kazantzakis and the Linguistic Revolution in Greek Literature* (Princeton, 1972), pp. 13–146; R. Browning, *Medieval and Modern Greek* (Cambridge, 1983), pp. 100–18; P. Mackridge, *The Modern Greek Language: A Descriptive Analysis of Standard Modern Greek* (Oxford, 1985), pp. 2–14.

14 Bien, *Kazantzakis*, pp. 23; 35–63.

15 *Ibid.*, 43–4.

16 Psicháris, *To Taxídi Mou*, ed. A. Angélou (Athens, 1978), p. 39.

17 See D. Tziovas, *The Nationism of the Demoticists and its Impact on Their Literary Theory (1888–1930)* (Amsterdam, 1986).

18 There is no English translation of this book (see n. 16), although its linguistic programme is discussed in the items listed in n. 13.

19 Bien, *Kazantzakis*, pp. 110–11; K. Th. Dimarás (ed.), *I Metarríthmisi pou den Eyine, B´: 1895–1967* (Athens, 1974), pp. 23–32.

20 Dimarás (ed.), *I Metarríthmisi*, p. 24.
21 G. Mistriótis cited in *ibid.*, p. 36.
22 Psicháris, *To Taxídi Mou*, p. 37.
23 For the theory behind these terms, and related bibliography, see L. Jenny, 'The strategy of form', in T. Todorov (ed.), *French Literary Theory Today* (Cambridge and Paris, 1982), pp. 34–63.
24 V. Kornáros, *Erotókritos*, ed. S. Alexíou (Athens, 1985). A translation by Th. P. Stephanides is published by Papazissis (Athens, 1985), and distributed in England by the Merlin Press, London.
25 R. Beaton, 'Dionysios Solomos: the tree of poetry', *Byzantine and Modern Greek Studies*, 2 (1976), 161–82, includes a slightly abridged translation of the poem. See also P. Mackridge, 'Time out of mind: the relationship between story and narrative in Solomos' "The Cretan" ', *Byzantine and Modern Greek Studies*, 9 (1984–5), 187–208.
26 Cited and discussed in R. Beaton, *Folk Poetry of Modern Greece* (Cambridge, 1980), pp. 8–9.
27 See P. Sherrard, *The Marble Threshing Floor* (London, 1956; 2nd edn, Athens, 1981), pp. 35–7, for summary and translated extracts.
28 See for example Y. Ioánnou, *Ta Dimotiká mas Tragoúdia* (Athens, 1966), p. 30.
29 See Herzfeld, *Ours Once More*, pp. 75–82 and *passim*.
30 J. P. Fallmerayer, *Geschichte der Halbinsel Morea während des Mittelalters* (Stuttgart and Tübingen, 1830–6).
31 S. Zambélios, ´*Asmata Dimotiká tis Elládos* (Corfu, 1852). For an analysis of Zambélios' ideas and contribution to Greek ideology in the nineteenth century, see Herzfeld, *Ours Once More*, pp. 39–52.
32 Zambélios, ´*Asmata*, pp. 7–8.
33 *Ibid.*, p. 5.
34 The first collections of modern Greek folk poetry were made by a German and a Frenchman respectively; the first to be published was C. Fauriel, *Chants Populaires de la Grèce Moderne* (Paris, 1824–5). For the earliest interest in this material in Greek intellectual circles see A. Polítis, *I Anakálipsi ton Dimotikón Tragoudión* (Athens, 1984).
35 Dimarás, *Ellinikós Romandismós*, pp. 463–4.
36 *Ibid.*, pp. 464–5.
37 K. Paparrigópoulos, *Prolegómena*, ed. K. Th. Dimarás (Athens, 1970), p. 155.
38 N. G. POolítis, *Meléti epí tou Víou ton Neotéron Ellínon, Tóm. A': Neoellinikí Mitholoyía* (Athens, 1871), p. i.
39 *Ibid.*, p. 9.
40 For Polítis' career and an analysis of his ideas see A. Kiriakídou-Néstoros, *I Theoría tis Ellinikís Laografías* (Athens, 1978), pp. 99–110, and Herzfeld, *Ours Once More*, pp. 97–122. For a critique of Polítis' anthology see R. Beaton, 'The oral traditions of modern Greece', *Oral Tradition*, 1 (1986), pp. 110–33.
41 Cited in Beaton, *Folk Poetry*, pp. 11–12.
42 The full (Greek) text of the announcement is given in P. D. Mastrodimítris, *O Zitiános tou Karkavítsa* (Athens, 1980), pp. 269–70.
43 See R. Beaton, 'Realism and folklore in nineteenth-century Greek fiction', *Byzantine and Modern Greek Studies*, 8 (1982–3), pp. 103–22.

5

Romanticism in Germany

DIETRICH VON ENGELHARDT

PREMISES

By giving what is commonplace an exalted meaning, what is ordinary a mysterious aspect, what is familiar the impressiveness of the unfamiliar, to the finite an appearance of infinity; thus I romanticise it.

Novalis, *Poeticism*, 1798

Romanticism in Germany does not only refer to literature, painting and music, but equally to science, history, religion and life, none of these, however, in isolation, but always ideally, mutually and intimately interrelated. German Romanticism is universal, encyclopaedic in a specific sense, combining totality and individualism, empiricism and metaphysics, history, the present and utopias.[1] Romanticism in Germany was important only for a short period, from 1797 to the 1830s, varying in length for different arts and sciences, varying in intensity between individual German states and university towns, varying too in its principles and realization. Its early adherents were born in the 1760s and 1770s, the last died after 1860.

It is not always clear who belonged to the Romantic movement, especially regarding several important writers, artists and scientists: Jean Paul, Hölderlin and Kleist in literature; Mesmer, Reil, Purkyně in science are examples of such haziness. What is understood by Romanticism also differs from country to country. Distinctions made in Germany as early as 1800, as well as in later research and in general use today, between Classicism and Romanticism, natural philosophy and Romantic science, were in no way observed abroad. Madame de Staël's categorization of the classical authors Schiller and Goethe as 'Romantic' in her book *De l'Allemagne* (1813) persists to the present day.

Above all in literature, but also in Romanticism in general, three phases can usefully be defined. The first phase is known as Early Romanticism or Old Romanticism. The role of initiator of this phase is played by Wackenroder and Tieck's anonymously published work on the theory of art,

Outpourings from the Heart of an Art-Loving Monk (1797), and the magazine *Athenäum* (1798–1800); its focal points were Berlin and Jena, and it lasted until 1804/5. Wackenroder and Tieck's main adherents were the Schlegel brothers, Novalis and Schleiermacher. The second phase, also called the Later Romantic, High Romantic or Middle Romantic phase, lasted until 1815, and because of its geographical concentration also earned the name Heidelberg Romanticism, although Dresden, Berlin and Munich were also centres of influence during this phase, to which belonged the literary protagonists von Arnim, Brentano, Eichendorff, Tieck, Fouqué, Hoffmann, Chamisso and Zacharias Werner. The influence of philosophers on literature decreased, and music, painting, history and science came to the fore. The third phase – the Late Romantic phase – stretches into the 1830s, in part even into the 1840s and 1850s. Vienna and Silesia, Nuremburg, Munich, Swabia and Berlin were local and regional foci, where alongside literature and art, works of scientific research, medicine, history, society and religion in the Romantic spirit also appeared.

The first definitions of Romanticism in the new and no longer orthodox sense as 'adventurous', 'fanciful', 'at one with nature', 'full of feeling' and 'medieval' are found after the 1790s. It is the 'enthusiastic' sense of 'Romantic' which Werther (1774) has in mind when he writes to Lotte in his farewell letter: 'I want to die, and I tell you that with no Romantic exaggeration.'[2] The complex origins of the genuine Romantic movement in Germany around 1800 were clearly seen by Goethe: 'For us Germans, the move towards Romanticism started from an education acquired first from the ancients, then from the French; it was aided by Christian attitudes and fostered and encouraged by gloomy Northern epic sagas.'[3] In just as decisive and definitive a manner does Goethe, a Classical writer, again stress his distance from Romanticism in a conversation with Friedrich Wilhelm Riemer on his birthday in 1808: 'There is nothing natural or original in Romanticism – rather, it is contrived, affected, intensified, exaggerated, bizarre, even distorted and caricature-like.'[4] Like a magic lantern, Romanticism lent a veneer of wonder to ordinary phenomena, or an appearance of reality to the unreal.

Especially at the beginning, Romanticism in Germany was characterized by an outspoken commitment to philosophy, which has a basic connection with its encyclopaedic-universal character, a hallmark too of the programmatic magazine *Athenäum*. Its dependence on idealistic philosophy, the philosophy of Kant, Fichte and above all of Schelling, is obvious; Friedrich Schlegel is the originator of the revealing aphorism, 'It is just as deadly for the mind to have a system as to have none.' One must therefore resolve 'to combine both aspects'.[5]

NATURE

To integrate nature is the point of his [man's] existence.

J. W. Ritter, *Physics as Art*, 1806

In Germany, one can justifiably speak of Romantic science and medicine side by side with literature and the other arts. This has no equivalent in other countries, although here and there echoes or parallel tendencies can be observed. From the end of the eighteenth to the beginning of the nineteenth century, mainly under the influence of the natural philosopher Schelling but also of other philosophical and theological positions of the past (Plato, Spinoza, Rousseau, Swedenborg, Oetinger, Hemsterhuis), a metaphysical form of scientific research was espoused. This simultaneously implies a particular understanding of human nature while not leaving the other sciences or the arts unaffected,[6] and cannot be adequately understood without it.

Examples of Romantic scientists and medical practitioners are: Eschenmayer, Ritter, Troxler, Kerner, Treviranus, Görres, Schubert, Steffens, Oken, Windischmann, Kieser, Oersted, Carus, and Ringseis, to name but few.[7] Romantic science is not a single entity; various concepts of nature and science are developed; differing conceptual and biographical answers are given for the eventual triumph of empirical-positivist science during the nineteenth century. Goethe's scientific research doubtless comes close to speculative natural philosophy and Romantic science, but differs from these clearly in its specific blend of aesthetics, philosophy and science. Hegel aptly describes Goethe's position as 'thoughtful contemplation of nature', rather than the 'comprehending perception' of natural philosophy; the 'original phenomenon' (*Urphänomen*) provoked a 'twilight, spiritual and comprehensive in its simplicity, visible or tangible in its sensuousness'[8] and in this respect represented a transition from empiricism to philosophy. Hegel sees himself as equally distinct from Romantic science and medicine: their shortcomings were obvious in an unsuccessful 'concept of the idea, the unity of notion and phenomenon as well as the concreteness of the idea'.[9] For his part, Alexander von Humboldt took a position between natural science, natural philosophy and the art of the period. If his aim was, in his own words, an 'empirical view of *nature as a whole* in the scientific form of a *portrait of nature*'[10] then it was expressly neither in the sense of laying a metaphysical foundation for scientific research, nor as the Romantic movement would see it. Finally, indebted as he was to Kant and Goethe, but at the same time sharply opposed to Hegel's natural philosophy (panlogism), as well as to contemporary natural science (materialism), Schopenhauer too occupies a characteristic place in the spectrum of positions around 1800. He likewise cannot be counted among the Romantic scientists in the narrow sense, as he approved of their search for a 'basic type of nature' (*Grundtypus*), but considered their 'hunt for analogies' largely as having 'degenerated into mere witticisms'.[11]

Scientific criticism in the nineteenth century took hardly any notice of the distinctions between Romantic, speculative and transcendental, scientific and aesthetic directions. Romanticism and natural philosophy became a general shibboleth. Hegel, Schelling, Goethe, Schopenhauer, Romantic scientists and even Kant received such unjustified epithets. More than a few scientific historians up till the present have likewise closed their minds to these manifest distinctions – most unconsciously dependent on a positivist concept of science.

Both the Romantic scientists and writers emphasized and justified the move away from the idealism of such as Schelling or, above all, Hegel. For Troxler, the Absolute foundation of both nature and the mind can be grasped neither by 'intellectual appraisal' nor by 'belief in reason'; every word in favour of the Absolute was merely a 'sign' of it.[12] Likewise, Ritter sets an insurmountable barrier in front of human understanding: 'The *highest* deduction is *a priori* a misunderstanding, and man is not its master.'[13] However, the Romantic scientists were not content with limiting human understanding. According to them, faith, feeling and dreams could also help one comprehend nature. Feeling is understood as enthusiasm or inspiration, but, like other psychic capabilities, not in conflict with reason, but as a complement to it; Romantic science, like Romantic literature, is not just a one-sided glorification of irrationality. The doctrine of a limited human awareness corresponds to their literary forms; articles by scientists and medical practitioners, like literary works, often appear in unsystematic, fragmentary, aphoristic, even poetic, form. This form is chosen deliberately, as it is meant to mirror what can be understood of nature. Novalis's precept that 'science's perfect form must be poetic'[14] expresses the aversion to systems common among Romantics, and reflects their efforts to combine science and art.

Central to this is the concept of nature and the mind; the laws of nature should comply with those of the intellect. Eschenmayer's 'Deduction of the living organism' of 1799 is accompanied by the assertion 'that even this object occurs under the necessary conditions of being conscious of itself'.[15] The very fact that nature and intellect are identical increases one's capacity for self-knowledge. Steffens declares: 'Do you want to know nature? Take a look inside yourself, and in your gradual intellectual enlightenment, you may have the privilege of looking on nature's stages of development. Do you want to know yourself? Observe nature, and her works are of the same essence as your mind.'[16]

A prime concept for any understanding of nature is its unity. Tracing natural phenomena back to a metaphysical cause, derivations from vegetable or organic categories, and deductions from mathematical principles, are all different aspects of a concept of unity. Instead of findings in natural science being treated in isolation, Novalis, who admittedly never published any scientific works and who in this respect cannot be counted among the Romantic scientists, called for a study of the interrelationships within nature: 'Up to now, in physics, phenomena have always been torn from their relationships and not investigated in their familiar context. Every phenomenon is a link in an immeasurable chain — which comprehends *all phenomena*.'[17] Romantic science wishes to avoid empirical specialization as much as speculative systematization; however, in practice the danger of formal constructions cannot always be avoided.

Underlying nature and its phenomena is a conflict between opposing principles, whose many manifestations are supposed to have brought about natural processes and phenomena, from protozoa to the highest forms of life. Unity is opposed to polarity, identity to diversity. Apart from identity and diversity, analogy, rank, potency and metamorphosis prove essential to the understanding both of the main fields of nature, and of the individual phenomena of the physical world. All natural phenomena are placed in a relationship of analogy and comparison, and analogies are made in not just one, but many directions. Görres recognizes intellectual elements in nature, and traces natural elements in the mind: 'Thus, what *Reason* is to our personalities, the *Sun* is to nature outside us; here we have ideas, there light: the sun *thinks light*, reason lights up ideas, and sheds bright rays about itself.'[18] Ritter especially makes double and triple as well as many simple analogies: 'The brain of a plant is the earth',[19] he writes in his *Letters from a Dead Physicist* (1810). Also: 'The whole cat species is the human species, and man is but the highest cat, as well as the sun of that species.'[20] The analogies of Romantic scientists stand the test of time particularly badly, often quite rightly so, even if their logic and intentions can still be reconstructed.

For Romantic scientists, life plays a very prominent role; often their proofs of the unity of nature rely on a translation of organic categories into inorganic. Nature attains perfection in living organisms, where the world of physical phenomena overflows into that of the mind; the organism is supposed to portray the essence of nature, and physical, chemical and geological events can be understood according to its logic. Furthermore, the organism becomes a general model for history and society.

Illness and death as the peculiar characteristics of living things are likewise interpreted in a Romantic spirit. Many doctors of the time were inspired by Schelling's natural philosophy, and interpret therapy, as well as the relationship between doctor and patient, metaphysically or religiously, or draw up concepts in which history and medical systems are unified. The subconscious, dreams (Schubert, Carus), every abnormal form of consciousness or awareness are paid particular attention. In Romantic medicine, too, when one looks closely, considerable differences arise with regard to Schelling's, and particularly Hegel's, metaphysical understanding of the organism, its illnesses and treatment.[21]

For Romantic scientists, a hierarchical order in nature implies an ideal and not a real evolution; what is important is the metaphysical context and not the external, historical connections between phenomena. Oken specifically rejects the idea of concrete metamorphosis: 'The expression that earth and metal evolved into coral is hardly to say that the earth as such really changed into coral, just like the above claim that it became metal, or that the air became sulphur . . . everything is to be taken in a philosophical sense.'[22] Romantic evolution is distinct from Darwin's theory of evolution, as well as from Lamarck's theory of development or Buffon's notion of the downfall and revival of species. However, the difference between real and ideal connections is not always consistently observed.

The Romantic scientists did not see natural science as independent or separate from the social world. Rather it should have a practical application, the improvement of external living standards, the social order or people's intellectual education. Not only are concrete and technical applications of natural science not condemned, they even receive theoretical justification, but are nevertheless always subordinate to pure knowledge. Predominantly utilitarian points of view are rejected, although according to Treviranus, pure knowledge always leads back to the practical of its own accord: 'Besides, truth can never be without influence on human well-being. If we manage to discover it, its uses will result without our aid.'[23]

HISTORY

A historian is a prophet facing backwards.   Fr. Schlegel, *Athenäum*, 1798

History, like nature, is a universal principle in Romanticism.[24] People have their individual histories, society is subordinate to history; each area of culture, all the sciences and arts have histories, admittedly history in a particular combination of progression and regression, a timeless ideal state and empirical temporality. History is the history of ideas, and therefore needs to be interpreted. Novalis comments: 'The historian organizes historical entities. The historical data are the raw material which the historian moulds into shape.'[25] Likewise, Steffens sees those historians who only investigate the flow of history 'into the dirtiest puddles', and who do not seek to recognize the true links, as limited: 'and they call that a study of sources'.[26]

Historical knowledge is not simply archive work, not only an account of the past; it has a productive effect; it allows what is past to be seen in a new, truer light. Romantic historical research exceeds the level of any Enlightenment pragmatism – it provides not so much concrete rules for living, or specific instructions for political behaviour, as an understanding of the march of time and world events; it helps one find sense in the past and allows individuals to find a niche for themselves and their existence in the flow of universal development.

Nature has a history, in the same way as history is nature. The historicizing of nature is made one and the same as the historicizing of knowledge about nature.[27] Identity and diversity, expansion and contraction, metamorphosis and comparison are just as valid in nature as in individual and social spheres. According to Steffens, society is driven by the same force 'as the creative force in nature'.[28] Inorganic and technical metaphors are often associated with restriction while images of living and organic things are associated with freedom. Machine man is contraposed to living man; the relationship between individual and state is explained with reference to an organism and its parts; the social hierarchy with reference to hierarchy in nature.

This premise can be reversed, and natural history made dependent on human history. Humanity and nature share a common destiny. With human and natural history reconciled and intertwined, a new epoch for humanity, as well as for nature, could be expected. In the beginning, nature and intellect were one, but then split into natural history and worldly history; this parallel or double development should now pass into a new era of unity. The naturalization of humanity and the spiritualization of nature are supposed to make the exploitation and destruction of nature as impossible as the spiritual warping of humanity and materialistic impoverishment of society caused by the renunciation of nature. The *Guardianship of the Earth*[29] is, for Novalis, humanity's mission. Ritter writes that through and in humanity, nature reaches 'its highest existence and self-perception';[30] its destruction by man is confirmed by Carus in his conviction that 'not only do people need the Earth in which to live and work, but the Earth needs humanity'.[31]

Romanticism brought a renewed interest in history. Attention was paid to all periods of the past, whose unity was central; it was only the context which allowed the essence of history, its universal sense, to become manifest. In the end, one returns to the beginning; the origin is reflected in the realized whole. An understanding of the past is required not from the point of view of the present but from its own perspective. At the same time one should be able to reconstruct the ideal development in the individual events of history. Attention is directed towards irrational or non-rational dimensions, to inspired persons, to chance. Mythology arouses great interest. Creuzer, Schlegel, Görres, Kanne and Schweigger are notable researchers into ancient Indian and Christian traditions.

The Middle Ages were given an approving re-assessment, although negative or separating moments were not overlooked. The past was in no way merely glorified; art and literature were judged not to have attained their full development until the present, and were expected to reach even higher peaks in the future. The Romantic understanding of history as a progressive regression gives new meaning to the seventeenth- and eighteenth-century 'Querelle des Anciens et Modernes'. The French Revolution shattered the Enlightenment fallacy of continual progress, but at the same time confirmed anew the concept of the difference between ideal and factual levels of history. Ideas can neither be denied nor confirmed by events alone.

The concept of progress is more concrete and formal than that of the Enlightenment. The spirit of the populace, of a nation, the state and freedom, should always be understood in a two-dimensional real-ideal perspective. The institutions of family and state, the appearance of peoples and the history of the human race, are applied to the individual and, vice versa, the individual is inextricable from the forces of history and general phenomena. Each person is meant to be 'a hermit and a cosmopolitan', each people national and world-embracing. The state and the family should fulfil the needs of the individual, but at the same time be maintained and realized by him. For Adam Müller, also author of a *Doctrine of Opposites* (1804), statesmanship means 'reconciliation' of science, art and political life, upon the foundation of an organic concept of history (*Elements of Statesmanship*, 1810). The dominance of the principle of the organism in Müller, as in other social theorists of the time, is not simply a translation from the sphere of living things into culture; living things are by now interpreted metaphysically in nature, not just biologically.

The Romantics were committed in their investigations of the social and political relationships of the time. Friedrich Schlegel, in his renowned saying, counted the French Revolution of 1789 along with Fichte's *Doctrine of Science* (1794) and Goethe's *Wilhelm Meister* (1795/6) among the 'greatest tendencies of the age'.[32] Enthusiasm for the revolution was shattered by the political Terror, but the ideas of Liberty, Equality and Fraternity were clung to, once the events in France had been set in a historical-philosophical framework, which anyway aimed far beyond concrete day-to-day politics at an imminent transcendence of history and society. Thus, Novalis's *Christendom or Europe* (1799, published in 1826) is neither an article on empirical mediaeval historiography nor an exhortation to return to that epoch, but a representation of an ideal which is also a pattern for the future development of Europe – totally in the spirit of Friedrich Schlegel's saying: 'A historian is a prophet facing backwards.'[33]

The separation or combination of nationalism or cosmopolitanism can also be understood in this light. Friedrich Schlegel would like to see France and Germany – like the example of Rome and Greece in ancient times – develop a relationship of mutual cooperation and fulfilment. Novalis too wants to overcome national rivalries in a Christian Europe. The magazine *Europa* (1803–5) was also dedicated to the same end. It was edited by Friedrich Schlegel, whose brother August Wilhelm spoke of 'European patriotism'. However, with the expansionism of the Napoleonic empire, nationalistic feelings grew and the Romantics too joined in the 'war of liberation'. Here, as in the criticism of the return of the Bourbons, their idealistic commitment is always overtaken by day-to-day political reality.

Concepts of society and political commitments nevertheless vary considerably between individual Romantics, and also change with time. Oken took part in the Wartburgfest, Eschenmayer gave the Württemberg Constitution legitimacy according to natural philosophy, and, after his conversion to Catholicism, Friedrich Schlegel supported Metternich's politics. The past ideal is seen in various periods: Friedrich Schlegel considers it to be Athenian democracy, Novalis the Christian Middle Ages. More substantial, however, is the hope common to all Romantics of the 'Kingdom of God', 'everlasting peace', the 'golden age'; this hope combines Utopia, history and the present.

The usual alternatives of restoration and revolution, monarchy and democracy, permanence and change, history and progress, do not do justice to the Romantic thinking on history; they cannot readily be assigned one or the other position. They always think of history and systems, immanence and transcendence together, in the field of nature as well as in social and intellectual matters. History is not simply a progression into the future; it restores the origin to its higher position; it actualizes potentiality; it is a progressive regression or regressive progress. In this way, historical knowledge combines with analysis of the present and forecasting of the future; it is the condition of true progress. At the same time it should not be forgotten that the Romantics took up both new and conservative positions in their further development, such as Friedrich Schlegel who turned to Austria, and Adam Müller with his ideas on philosophy of the state. Likewise, one ought not to forget the many misunderstandings and misinterpretations later made of Romantic thinking on history and society, of which National Socialism is the most notorious example. The Romantics, it must be said, felt themselves to be committed to other ideals; their flower is idealistically blue, not politically red or black.

FAITH

Surrounded by the finite, to become One with the infinite and be eternal in one instant, that is the immortality of religion.[34]

> F. Schleiermacher, *On Religion*, 1799

For the Romantics, nature and history have a divine basis. Faith complements reason and sensuality, science and the arts, individual and political life. All the variety and change in nature and history can be traced back to God or the Absolute, the fount of all being, in which the believer is able to take part with his thoughts and senses.

Central to Romantic understanding of religion is Schleiermacher's work *Discourses on Religion* of 1799, with its marked disavowal of the Enlightenment interpretation of religion as a moral standard, and likewise of Deism as an ideal interpretation. With its conviction of transcendence in this world, with its search for piety as emotional perception: 'Its essence is neither in thoughts nor in actions, but in perception and feeling. It wants to contemplate the universe, to listen devoutly to its own representations and actions, to let itself be stirred and fulfilled with childlike passivity by its immediate influences.'[35]

Religion is meant to be compatible with science; God is supposed to appear to humanity in nature, even if the Romantics do not agree on the degree of this manifestation. Schleiermacher, who already showed an interest in natural science and mathematics while he was being educated at the Pedagogical College in Niesky (1783), considered the Romantic Steffens's scientific research to be a suitable complement to his own theology, as Steffens in turn recognizes Schleiermacher's concepts to be the theological counterpart of his observations of nature.[36] Admittedly, according to Schleiermacher, it is not space and the celestial bodies on the visible plane which address our religious sense: 'The eternal laws by which the bodies themselves are created and destroyed show us the Universe at its dearest and holiest.'[37] However, above external nature and its laws is the human soul. It is here that one may truly recognize the world and grasp its divine reason. First of all, friendship and love are the prime medium of the soul, and thus the infinite can and should be experienced in this life and not after death. One should act in religion, not from religion. The community of devout people represents for Schleiermacher the 'true church' rather than institutionalized churches.

All Romantics looked for a combination of religion, philosophy and art, but they could not agree on its content. Friedrich Schlegel, who appreciated Schleiermacher's *Discourses on Religion* as he would a novel, sees philosophy and art as the two elements of religion: 'For if you try to combine the two properly, you will find nothing other than religion.' The proximity of absolute objectivity and absolute subjectivity becomes clear in his saying: 'God is purely and simply the origin and highest part of everything, and thus the individual himself in the highest potentiality.'[38] This religious and often mystical individualization corresponds to a move away from the Bible, which causes Schleiermacher to say: 'He who has religion is not he who believes in the holy scriptures, but he who does not need them, and who could probably write them himself',[39] and which causes Novalis to think of new gospels.

Any enhancement of individual subjectivity cannot do without inter- mediaries to the Godhead. For the Romantic believers, Christ was the prime mediator, but not the only one. Novalis wanted to unite monotheism and pantheism, too: 'As incompatible as they may seem, they can be united, if one makes the monotheistic intercessor into an intercessor for the intermediary world of pantheism, and, so to speak, centralizes them both in him, so that both necessitate each other, although in a different fashion.'[40]

The tendency towards the universal is also found in the field of Roman- tic faith. The differences between religions should be overcome, or super- seded, in an ideal community. Faith is higher than all dogmas or church institutions. The conversions of the Romantics form a link between Protestantism and Catholicism. Those who converted to the Catholic faith retained a memory of Protestantism. The Protestant as well as the Catholic believers display affinities for their respective opposite sides. Schubert was reputed to be a 'crypto-Catholic', August Wilhelm Schlegel 'halfway Catholic'.[41] The mystic path was often chosen; Novalis prays for this in his *Hymns to the Night* (1800), an impressive work. The interest of the Romantics in general in Mesmerism is evidence of this tendency, for example, in Kerner's *Prophetess of Prevorst* (1829), or Brentano's diary sketches of the sufferings and visions of Anna Katharina Emmerick (1818– 24), or Friedrich Schlegel's diary on the magnetic treatment of the Countess Lesniowska (1820–6).

The test of faith is unbelief. This polarity found its sharpest expression at the beginning of the Romantic epoch in Jean Paul's 'Discourse of the Dead Christ from the Top of the World that there Is no God' (*Siebenkäs*, 1796): 'And as I looked up towards the immeasurable world for the divine *eye*, it looked back at me with an empty, bottomless *eye socket*; and eternity lay on top of chaos and gnawed at it and chewed on itself.'[42] The religious nihilism in Jean Paul's novel is admittedly only a dream experience, but it was constantly before the eyes of the Romantics as a looming danger, possible in the human world as well as in nature: 'No one in the universe is quite so alone as he who denies God — he sorrows with an orphaned heart which has lost its greatest father, next to the immeasurable corpse of nature, not moved or held together by any cosmic spirit.'[43]

ART AND LITERATURE

The whole of mankind becomes poetic in the end. New Golden Age.

Novalis, *Heinrich von Ofterdingen*, 1802

An especially high, if not the highest, place is reserved in German Romanticism for the artist and art in all its diversity.[44] Romanticism is often equated with art and literature. Art is meant to be the mirror and culmination of the whole of reality. Romantic poetry is, according to Friedrich Schlegel's well-known definition, 'progressive universal poetry' or, in particular: 'Its vocation is not simply to write diverse poetic genre but to put poetry in touch with philosophy and rhetoric. Its desire and duty is first to mix, then to amalgamate poetry and prose, inspiration and criticism, artistic poetry and natural poetry, so as to make poetry lively and convivial.'[45]

The production of art and literature was always accompanied by reflection. The early Romantics, especially, made some considerable contributions to the theory and criticism of art and literature, whose significance was expressed by Friedrich Schlegel in 1808 with the sentence: 'The distinguishing characteristic of modern writing is its close relationship to criticism and theory, and the determinative influence of the latter.'[46] The close link between production and criticism for the Romantics can be ascertained equally convincingly from the works of the Schlegel brothers and Novalis on literature or literary figures of the past and present, in their reflections on the nature of art, its relationship to life, science and faith. Friedrich Schlegel stresses that literary criticism should itself be literature: 'Poetry can only be criticized by poetry.'[47] Art and science belong together; the history of art constitutes true aesthetics.

At this point we must remember the great achievements of the Romantics as translators and editors of national and foreign literature of the past, such as Tieck's *Folk Tales*, published in 1797 under the pseudonym Peter Leberecht, the collection of songs *The Boy's Magic Horn* (1805/8) by Achim von Arnim and Clemens Brentano and his wife Sophie's editions of Spanish and Italian novellas (1804/6), the collection of *Fairy Tales for Children and the Home* (1812) and *German Legends* (1816/18) by the

Brothers Grimm, the translations of Shakespeare and Calderón by the two Schlegels or Cervantes's *Don Quixote* by Tieck, also the translations of Dante, Boccaccio, Petrarch and Ariosto. Interest in the literature of the past, of the Middle Ages, and of the German development increases or attains perfection in the striving for world poetry as well as the making of the world into poetry.

In artistic and literary works, and even on the level of criticism and theory, nature and science, like illness and medicine, play a central role, as do art and literature in these disciplines. Nature, history, friendship and love are the basic themes in Novalis's *Heinrich von Ofterdingen* (1802) and *The Apprentices of Saïs* (1802). Whereas for Novalis it is the Middle Ages which are central, Tieck in *Franz Sternbald's Wanderings* (1798) and Achim von Arnim in his novel *Crown Warder* (1817) turn to the Renaissance, as does Clemens Brentano in the *Romances of Rosencranz* (1852, written 1803/12). E. T. A. Hoffmann's *The Golden Pot*, *The Magnetisor*, *The Sinister Guest* and *The Vow* have madness and death as their subjects, and their presentation and interpretation are obviously influenced by G. H. v. Schubert and Mesmer, and other medical practitioners of the time.[48] Other Romantic writers also had analogous relationships to the sciences, e.g. Kleist, Brentano, Eichendorff, Jean Paul, Fouqué, as well as Novalis and Achim von Arnim, who themselves took an active interest in the sciences. Split personalities, *Doppelgänger*, the contrast between everyday reality and dreams, consciousness and subconscious, sensuality and reason, bourgeois and artist, society and the individual, crime and virtue, nature and culture, and day and night pervade all Romantic texts, and all have as their basis the Romantic conviction of the ideal-real unity of the world.

Art and literature link faith with life. E. T. A. Hoffmann ends his *The Golden Pot: A Modern Fairy Tale* (1814) with the sentence: 'Is Anselm's saintliness anything more at all than a life in poetry, which opens itself to the holy unison of all creatures as the deepest secret of nature?'[49] Philip Otto Runge claims that painting, like all art, only endures through the painter's awareness of his divine origin: 'For the eternal quality of a work of art is surely only its connection with the talent of the artist, through which it is a picture of the eternal origins of his soul.'[50] Friedrich Schlegel devised the following cosmological formula for Romantic poetry,[51] in which F stands for the fantastic, S for the sentimental and M for mimicry as the presence of the poet in the work:

$$\text{poetic ideal} = \sqrt[\frac{1}{\sigma}]{\frac{FSM^{\frac{1}{\sigma}}}{\sigma}} = \text{God}$$

According to Novalis's slogan 'magical idealism', nature and history are meant to find true freedom in artistic creations, and subject and object manifest themselves as metaphysically identical.

Like the various branches of nature and their corresponding sciences, the different arts are also brought together, are meant to complement each other but at the same time retain their own specific functions: 'All works one work, all arts one art', confirms Friedrich Schlegel in 1801.[52] Individual arts can also be set above one another, as Hoffmann sets music, especially that of Beethoven, at the top: 'It is the most romantic of all art forms, one would almost say the only truly Romantic one, for only the infinite is its theme.'[53] High Romanticism, with its tendency once more to differentiate strongly between the different disciplines, is the first to produce really stage-worthy plays (Kleist).

The metaphysics of nature, concerning death, piety and the isolation of man, also characterize Romantic painting, above all the creations of Caspar David Friedrich and Philip Otto Runge, the former guided primarily by the phenomenon, the latter by reflection. As in other art forms, its resonance depends on the aesthetic positions of the time. Friedrich's *Altar at Tetschen* (1808) is decisively rejected by the Classical art critic F. von Ramdohr: 'How is it possible to mistake the influence that the presently dominant system has had on Herr Friedrich's work! That mysticism which now creeps in everywhere, which wafts toward us from art, science, philosophy, religion, like a narcotic vapour.'[54] All the more enthusiastic is the agreement from the Romantic camp.

LIFE

Let us transform our lives into works of art, and then we can boldly claim to be immortal while still of this Earth.

Wackenroder and Tieck, Fantasies about Art, 1799

In Germany, Romanticism was never understood as a purely intellectual movement, but always as a combination of spirit and life, of universe and the individual.[55] 'Life should not be given us, but rather should be a novel written by us',[56] insists Novalis. 'As his art reached perfection . . . , so his life became a work of art',[57] reads Schlegel's *Lucinde*. Nevertheless, Brentano had to recognize resignedly: 'My life is the most wonderful poem that was ever written. It is approved of neither by me, nor by other people, nor by God.'[58] Romantic existence should be free from all banality and philistine narrow-mindedness. Politics and society are not rejected; rather they are spiritualized in a particular manner in the same way as, vice versa, the poetic spirit is directed towards the social world and the real life of the individual. Understanding and feeling, reason and sensuality, are meant to balance each other; morality should be a matter of inclination, not duty.

The youth of the time must have felt particularly drawn towards Romanticism, as Goethe remarked to Riemer in their conversation of 28 August 1808 on the difference between ancient and modern. He also warned of the possible dangers of Romanticism: 'So-called Romantic poetry attracts young people especially, because it flatters their capriciousness, their sensuousness, their bent for licentiousness, in short, all the inclinations of youth.'[59] Hegel also recognized dangers in the Romantic attitude of mind, as he sets out in a letter of 27 May 1810 to the Romantic medical practitioner Windischmann, who had complained to him of melancholy. He knows this state from his own experience, when one has buried oneself in the 'chaos of events' and has not yet reached the 'clarity and detail of the whole'. He himself had suffered 'from this hypochondria for a couple of years, so that I was quite debilitated'. Each person probably had 'such a turning point in his life, a dark spot where his spirit contracts, through the narrows of which he "must be forced" so as to confirm and ascertain his own self-confidence'.[60] When Hegel again criticizes Romanticism sharply, he is motivated by concern for the endangered individual existence of its adherents, as well as for culture, art and science; the subjective substantialism of his philosophy must have seen its total contradiction in the 'insubstantial subjectivism' or the 'subjective occasionalism' (C. Schmitt) of Romanticism.

Internal and external uncertainty, extreme mood swings, an over-stretched imagination and weakened sense of reality, a broad span of interests and a constantly re-occurring self-doubt characterize and handicap many Romantics. The 'disharmony' constantly felt by Friedrich Schlegel has, for him, a metaphysical-religious reason beyond all physiological-psychological causes: 'For in all things we are narrow, mortal beings, and in only one thing does God make us mortal – in our confusion.'[61] As early as the *Outpourings from the Heart of an Art-Loving Monk* (1797), which heralded the start of Romanticism, a warning picture of the problematical artist foundering on 'the struggle between his ethereal enthusiasm and the base sorrow of this Earth' is found in the literary figure of the musician Joseph Berlinger.[62] In the novels and short stories of E. T. A. Hoffmann, this split is a pervasive theme. It is in this perspective that the Romantics interpreted Hamlet and the entire existence of modern man.

However, true education can overcome or dissipate the dissonances, which have developed mainly due to the Enlightenment and its one-sided emphasis on reason. 'Humanity is torn, art and life are separated',[63] complains Friedrich Schlegel, whose works on the history and theory of literature were always simultaneous criticisms of culture. The memory of Greece could still, however, provide the present with a possible ideal of harmony between culture and existence: 'Art and life were constantly intermeshing, poetry and music were inseparable companions, and harmony, the general characteristic of Hellenic education as a whole, manifests itself here more visibly and is chiefly the property of this era, in which music and gymnastics flowered and friendship and love expressed themselves most wonderfully, in the greatest acts.'[64]

Education is universal education; knowledge of nature is equally indispensable. However, education does not mean an exhaustive knowledge of the details of all subjects and disciplines. According to Steffens, each person should have at his disposal a 'general sense' and in addition devote himself to a specific field of work 'with the strictest renunciation'.[65] Admittedly only an ideal, metaphysical science was meant to be able to improve mental health, give strength and direction to one's thoughts and dispel superstition. Treviranus considered biology as particularly well-suited for educating people. It addressed 'reason and imagination together'; it was particularly suited to 'the relationship between man and humanity'.[66] For Carus, whose *Letters on Landscape Painting* (1831) represent a widely respected Romantic document on the links between science and art, an insight into the beauty and orderliness of nature will inspire people to 'cultivate our own innermost lives to similar levels of harmony and clarity'.[67] 'The key to the true art of life' lay 'in giving *equal appreciation* to Nature and the intellect.'[68]

Life longs for the combination of the finite and the infinite, which can be experienced in friendship and love. All too often, reality for adherents of Romanticism was marked by a dichotomy between bourgeois reality and artistic productivity, and the foundering of personal relationships. The demand, too, for equality of the sexes all too often simply remains literature, despite notable exceptions (e.g. Caroline Schlegel-Schelling). Emancipation is aimed at men as well as women, and is upheld by an ideal of androgyny, which finds an exemplary model in Friedrich Schlegel's novel *Lucinde* (1799) evident in its autobiographical traits (Dorothea Veit), energetically defended against its critic von Schleiermacher in the *Confidential Letters on Lucinde* (1800). According to Schlegel, men should allow feminine qualities to develop and women masculine ones, and both dualisms should complement each other in their different emphases. 'I see here a wonderfully ingenious and meaningful allegory for the consummation of the masculine and the feminine in full, complete humanity.'[69] Higher than friendship – which he experienced in reality first of all with Schleiermacher, Novalis and his brother August Wilhelm – Friedrich Schlegel placed his ideal of 'Symphilosophy' or 'Sympoetry'. However, this ideal did not even find lasting realization with his brother.

The relationship between individual existence and the infinite is described by the terms 'floating intelligence', 'Romantic irony' or 'Romantic wit', which do not refer to subjective arbitrariness or giving the individual an absolute quality, but rather to that very commitment to the tension between reality and the ideal. Irony arises out of 'the combination of a sense of art in life and a scientific intellect, in a meeting between a mature, complete philosophy of nature and a mature, complete philosophy of art. It comprises and gives rise to a feeling of the indissoluble conflict between what is limited and what is not limited.'[70] So says Friedrich Schlegel. Of especial note also are Adam Müller's and K. W. F. Solger's concepts of irony. However, irony can take a negative as well as a positive form, as Schlegel confirmed in his old age: 'True irony – for false irony does not exist – . . . is the irony of love. It arises from a feeling of finiteness and one's own limitations, and the apparent contradiction of this feeling with the idea of infinity inherent in all true love.'[71]

Religion, too, is connected to individual experience. Just as Novalis linked his love for his bride with philosophy – 'Sophie she is called – Philosophy is the soul of my life',[72] her death on 19 March 1797 became for him a religious experience which from then on gave his life its main direction. 'Christ and Sophie'[73] he notes in his diary on 30 June 1797; the dead bride is transfigured as an intermediary between this world and the next. Illness appears not only negative; death not only as the end of life, but as a transition into a higher freedom and harmony. Despair about reality, which greatly contradicts his own ideals of beauty and morality, causes Kleist, too, together with Adolfine Vogel, to commit on 21 November 1811 a suicide 'in which death and love alternate with each other'.[74]

The 'Kingdom of God' was supposed to allow nature and history to achieve unity for man. Friedrich Schlegel saw this as the real aim of modern history: 'The revolutionary desire to make the Kingdom of God a concrete reality is the resilient point of progressive education, and the starting point of modern history. Whatever bears no relationship at all to the Kingdom of God is merely incidental.'[75]

CONCLUSION

We are nothing more, we are worth nothing, we no longer know who we are, we have hardly any idea who we were.

Brentano to S. von Schweitzer, 18 April 1842

Romanticism in Germany implies a combination of nature, history, faith, art, science and life. It is personalized, comprehensive knowledge, or individualized universality. This combination recurs in each respective field. Its all-embracing factor is universal and mutual reflection. For example, the medical practitioners Schubert, Kerner and Heinroth are also writers. C. G. Carus painted as well as practising medicine, Philip Otto Runge produced theoretical essays as well as paintings, Friedrich Schlegel composed the novel *Lucinde*, and like the theologian and philosopher Friedrich Schleiermacher, also concerned himself with mathematical and medical studies. E. T. A. Hoffmann wrote, painted and composed music, like Brentano; Novalis took samples from each discipline and integrated them into his short life.

There remains distance vis-à-vis a clear-cut conceptual hierarchy of the natural and spiritual planes, distance vis-à-vis the speculative deductions of idealistic philosophers. The relationship between phenomena and concepts, detail and totality is unsteady. In contrast to Romanticism in other European countries, German Romanticism is openly philosophical and all-embracing and, despite its tendencies towards history and transcendence, always focuses on the present, and develops concrete utopian proposals. The reasons behind these differences within European Romanticism lie in political relationships, cultural traditions and, not least, education. Therefore, one should speak of Romanticism in the plural rather than in the singular.[76] In her evaluation of the German intellectual movement (*De l'Allemagne*) of about 1800, Madame de Staël emphasizes the links that were already being forged between the various areas of culture as a particular characteristic of Germany: 'Scientists penetrate nature with the help of imagination. Poets find the true beauties of the universe in science. Scholars enrich poets by their recollections, and scientists by their analogies.'[77]

Criticism and agreement, diffusion, decline and continuation all display a common logic, and each occurs in the various arts and sciences affected by the Romantic spirit in its own specific form.[78] Goethe observes that literature is on the decline: 'Romanticism has already followed its course into the abyss; the most hideous of the newer productions can hardly be considered lower'.[79] The leading critics during the latter part of the nineteenth century are Heine and Kierkegaard. The Romantics themselves support this development to a certain extent; in 1808, Friedrich Schlegel demands a reversal: 'This aesthetic reverie, this effeminate, pantheistic humbug, this playing around with forms must cease. They are unworthy of and no longer fitting for this great era.'[80]

Romantic science, too, met with decisive rejection from scientists and politicians and experienced a decline from 1815. As early as 1807 Schelling had publicly renounced further scientific publication, because of numerous attacks and misunderstandings. Steffens had to admit in 1821 that Romantic science had not managed to achieve 'what was promised by its enthusiastic beginnings'.[81] Medicine's final throes are the large-scale presentations of Damerow (1829), Quintzmann (1843) and Isensee (1840/5). Schopenhauer traced the condemnation of Romanticism by the scientists of the positivist century back to the 'pranks of the natural philosophers from the school of Schelling', who had effected such a distaste for all theory and systematization 'that they expect advances in physics from their hands alone, without any contribution from the head, and so would prefer just to experiment, without thinking about it at all'.[82]

Romantic science, political radicalism and atheism are repeatedly equated. Oken was reputed to be one of the 'degenerate professors' who together with their 'corrupted students' had committed vandalism and intolerance at the Wartburgfest.[83] Hegel's summons to Berlin was expressly approved in the perspective of his criticism of Romantic science and the Romantic spirit altogether. In the sharp criticism of the chemist Liebig, for whom Romantic science and natural philosophy represent 'the pestilence, the black death of this century', emphatic reference is made to its destructive effect on the individual existence of its disciples. This movement had cost him 'two precious years' of his life. 'How many of the most talented and gifted I saw perish in this swindle, how many complaints of a totally misspent life did I not later have to hear.'[84]

At the same time the continuing effect of Romanticism cannot be doubted, both in Germany and abroad, and in the diverse branches of science, arts and literature. Coleridge, Keats, and Wordsworth, Balzac, Poe, Dostoevsky and Maeterlinck were all influenced by the science and poetry of German Romanticism. The Symbolism of the turn of the century relates to the Romantic concept of symbols. Thomas Mann, Robert Musil and Gottfried Benn continue the Romantic tradition with their representations of the contradiction between artist and bourgeois, the dichotomy between the particular and the universal, as well as the function of irony. Wilhelm Ostwald sees in 'Classical' and 'Romantic' one of the basic pairs of opposites of the natural scientists. Influences can be observed in anthropological medicine, as well as in the philosophically influenced psychiatry of the twentieth century, also in existential philosophy with its emphasis on the subject and its disowning of speculative-idealistic constructions, or in Jaspers' experience of transcendence in this world (Chiffre). The spiritual roots of the modern ecological movement can be found in the Romanticism and idealistic natural philosophy of around 1800.

There is no doubt that the ideals of Romanticism were not realized, even if they were and still are dreamt of again and again. The hope of self-realization, as well as the preservation of the world, have lost none of their relevance, nor have the hope for union between humanity and nature, science, faith and art, the hope for a compromise between instinct and reason, desire and duty, hope for the unity of history, the present and the future. Romanticism does not have to be in complete opposition to empiricism, but rather it can be understood as its metaphysical correlate, as a complement to Classicism, as Modern is to Ancient. This synthesis is furthermore the central task of the positivist age in which we live, and to which the so-called Postmodernists also still belong, precisely because, according to one of Friedrich Schlegel's sayings, this task can never be completely realized: 'Total coincidence is eternally unattainable.'[85]

•

NOTES

1 On Romanticism in general: R. Ayrault, *La Genèse du romantisme allemand* (Paris, 1961–76), vols. 1–3; A. Béguin (ed.), *Le Romantisme allemand. Textes et études* (Marseille, 1949); R. Benz (ed.), *Lebenswelt der Romantik. Dokumente romantischen Denkens und Seins* (München, 1948); W. Bietak (ed.), *Lebenslehre und Weltanschauung der Jüngeren Romantik* (Leipzig, 1936); R. Brinkmann (ed.), *Romantik in Deutschland* (Stuttgart, 1978); U. Cardinale (ed.), *Problemi del romanticismo* (Milano, 1983), vols. 1–2; H. Eichner (ed.), *Romantic and Its Cognates. The European History of a Word* (Toronto, 1972); W. Emrich, *Der Universalismus der deutschen Romantik* (Mainz, 1964); H. Grassl, *Aufbruch zur Romantik* (München, 1968); R. Huch, *Die Romantik* (Leipzig, 1898/1902, Tübingen, 1964), vols. 1–2; P. Kluckhohn, *Die deutsche Romantik* (Bielefeld, 1924); P. Kluckhohn (ed.), *Charakteristiken. Die Romantiker in Selbstzeugnissen und Äusserungen ihrer Zeitgenossen* (Stuttgart, 1950); H. A. Korff, *Geist der Goethezeit* (Leipzig, 1923), vols. 1–3 (5th–7th edns, Leipzig, 1964), vols. 1–5; A. O. Lovejoy, 'The meaning of romanticism for the historian of science', *Journal of the History of Ideas*, 2 (1941); K. Peter (ed.), *Romantikforschung seit 1945* (Königstein, 1980); L. Pikulik, *Romantik als Ungenügen an der Normalität* (Frankfurt a. M., 1979); H. Prang (ed.), *Bergriffsbestimmung* (Nürnberg, 1966); H. Steffens (ed.), *Die deutsche Romantik. Poetik, Formen und Motive* (Göttingen, 1967, 3rd edn, 1978); Th. Steinbüchel (ed.), *Romantik. Ein Zyklus Tübinger Vorlesungen* (Stuttgart, 1948); Fr. Strich, *Deutsche Klassik und Romantik oder Vollendung und Unendlichkeit. Ein Vergleich* (München, 1922; 5th edn, 1962); M. Thalmann, *Romantik in kritischer Perspektive. 10 Studien* (Heidelberg, 1976); C. Träger, 'Ursprünge und Stellung der Romantik', *Weimarer Beiträge*, 21, 2 (1975), 37–73; R. Ullmann and H. Gotthard, *Geschichte des Begriffes 'Romantisch' in Deutschland* (Berlin, 1927); O. Walzel, *Deutsche Romantik* (Leipzig, 1908; 5th edn, 1923/6), vols. 1–2; R. Wellek, *Konfrontationen. Vergleichende Studien zar Romantik* (Frankfurt a. M., 1964).
2 J. W. v. Goethe, *Die Leiden des jungen Werther*, in Goethe, *Werke* (1774, 1787; Hamburg, 1951), vol. 6, p. 104.
3 J. W. v. Goethe, *Klassiker und Romantiker in Italien*, in *Werke* (1820; Zürich, 1950), vol. 14, pp. 801–2.
4 J. W. v. Goethe to Fr. W. Riemer (letter of 28 August 1808), in *Goethes Gespräche*, ed. W. Herwig (Zürich, 1969), vol. 1, p. 328.
5 Fr. Schlegel, *Athenäums-Fragment 53*, in *Werke* (München, 1967), section 1, vol. 2, p. 173.

6 On natural sciences and medicine in the Romantic period: R. Ayrault, 'En vue d'une philosophie de la nature', in A. Ayrault, *La Genèse du romantisme allemand*, vol. 1, pp. 11–167; Chr. Bernoulli and H. Kern (eds.), *Romantische Naturphilosophie* (Jena, 1926); D. v. Engelhardt, 'Bibliographie der Sekundärliteratur zur romantischen Naturforschung und Medizin 1950– 1975', in Brinkmann (ed.), *Romantik in Deutschland*, pp. 307–30; D. v. Engelhardt, 'Romantische Naturforschung', in D. v. Engelhardt, *Historisches Bewusstsein in der Naturwissenschaft von der Aufklärung bis zum Positivismus* (Freiburg and München, 1979), pp. 103–57; A. Faivre, 'La Philosophie de la nature dans le romantisme allemand', in Y. Belaval (ed.), *Histoire de la Philosophie* (Paris, 1974), vol. 3, pp. 14–45; A. Gode von Aesch, *Natural Science in German Romanticism* (New York, 1941; reprint 1966); A. Grassl, *Die Romantik, ein Gegenpol der Technik* (Bonn, 1954); W. Leibbrand, *Die spekulative Medizin der Romantik* (Hamburg, 1956); K. E. Rothschuh, 'Naturphilosophische Konzepte der Medizin aus der Zeit der deutschen Romantik', in Brinkmann (ed.), *Romantik in Deutschland*, pp. 243–66; P. Schmidt, 'Gesundheit und Krankheit in romantischer Medizin und Erzählkunst', in *Jahrbuch des Freien Deutschen Hochstifts* (1966), pp. 197– 228; H. A. M. Snelders, 'Romanticism and Naturphilosophie and the inorganic natural science 1797–1840', *Studies in Romanticism*, 9 (1970), 193– 215; H. Sohni, *Die Medizin der Frühromantik* (med. Diss., Freiburg i, Br., 1973).

7 Primary sources: M. Heun, *Die medizinische Zeitschriftenliteratur der Romantik* (med. Diss., Leipzig, 1931); E. Hirschfeld, 'Romantische Medizin. Zu einer künftigen Geschichte der naturphilosophischen Ära', in *Kyklos der deutschen Romantik* (Leipzig and Berlin, 1926).

8 G. W. Fr. Hegel to Goethe (letter of 24 February 1821), in Hegel, *Briefe* (Hamburg, 1953), vol. 2, p. 250.

9 G. W. Fr. Hegel, *System der Philosophie, 1, Teil. Die Logik*, in *Werke* (1817; Stuttgart, 1964), vol. 8, para. 231, p. 441.

10 A. v. Humboldt, *Kosmos* (Stuttgart, 1844), vol. 1, p. 33.

11 A. Schopenhauer, *Die Welt als Wille und Vorstellung* (1819; Wiesbaden, 1978), vol. 1, p. 171.

12 I. P. V. Troxler, *Elemente der Biosophie* (Leipzig, 1808), pp. 28–9.

13 J. W. Ritter, *Fragment aus dem Nachlasse eines jungen Physikers* (1810; reprint Heidelberg, 1969), vol. 2, p. 173.

14 Novalis, *Logologische Fragmente*, in *Schriften* (1798; Darmstadt, 1965), vol. 2, p. 527.

15 A. C. A. v. Eschenmayer, 'Dedukzion des lebenden Organismus', *Magazin zur Vervolkommnung der theoretischen und praktischen Heilkunde*, 2, 3 (1799), 334.

16 H. Steffens, 'Ueber die Vegetation', in Steffens, *Alt und Neu* (Breslau, 1821), vol. 2, p. 102.

17 Novalis, *Fragmente und Studien, 1799–1800*, in *Schriften* (Darmstadt, 1968), vol. 3, p. 574.

18 J. v. Görres, *Aphorismen über die Organonomie*, in *Gesammelte Schriften* (1803; Köln, 1932), vol. 1, part 1, p. 175.

19 Ritter, *Fragment aus dem Nachlasse eines jungen Physikers*, vol. 2, p. 46.

20 *Ibid.*, p. 48.

21 D. v. Engelhardt, 'Hegel's philosophical understanding of illness', in R. G.

Cohen and M. W. Wartofsky (ed.), *Hegel and the Sciences* (Boston and Dordrecht, 1984), pp. 123–41.

22 L. Oken, *Abriss des Systems der Biologie* (Göttingen, 1805), p. 53.

23 G. R. Treviranus, *Biologie oder die Philosophie der lebenden Natur für Naturforscher und Ärzte* (Göttingen, 1802), p. 15.

24 On the Romantic concept of history and society: E. Behler, 'Die Auffassung der Revolution in der deutschen Frühromantik', in P. U. Hehendahl *et al.* (ed.), *Essays in European Literature. In Honor of Liselotte Dieckmann* (St Louis, 1972), pp. 191–215; K. Borries, *Die Romantik und die Geschichte* (Berlin, 1925); R. Brinkmann, *Deutsche Literatur und Französische Revolution* (Göttingen, 1974), pp. 172–91; J. Droz, *Le Romantisme politique en Allemagne* (Paris, 1963); H. H. F. Flöter, 'Die Begründung der Geschichtlichkeit der Geschichte in der Philosophie des deutschen Idealismus' (phil. Diss., Halle, 1963); P. Gottfried, 'German romanticism and natural law', *Studies in Romanticism*, 7 (1967/8), 231–42; B. Koehler, *Äesthetik der Politik. Adam Müller und die politische Romantik* (Stuttgart, 1980); Fr. Meinecke, *Die Entstehung des Historismus* (München, 1936; 4th edn, 1959); H. Reiss, *The Political Thought of the German Romantics 1793–1815* (Oxford, 1955); U. Scheuner, *Der Beitrag der deutschen Romantik zur politischen Theorie* (Opladen, 1980); C. Schmitt, *Politische Romantik* (Berlin, 1919; 4th edn, 1982); R. Stadelmann, 'Die Romantik und die Geschichte', in Th. Steinbüchel (ed.), *Romantik. Ein Zyklus Tübinger Vorlesungen* (Stuttgart, 1948), pp. 153–75; see also articles by W. Schieder, G. Birtsch, K.-G. Faber, U. Scheuner and V. Stanislowski, in Brinkmann (ed.), *Romantik in Deutschland*.

25 Novalis, *Vermischte Bemerkungen und Blüthenstaub in Schriften* (1798), vol. 2, p. 454.

26 H. Steffens, *Beyträge zu einer innern Naturgeschichte der Erde* (Freyberg, 1801).

27 D. v. Engelhardt, *Historisches Bewusstsein in der Naturwissenschaft von der Aufklärung bis zum Positivismus*.

28 H. Steffens, 'Über die Bedeutung eines freien Vereins für Wissenschaft und Kunst', in Steffens, *Alt und Neu*, vol. 1, p. 155.

29 Novalis, *Vermischte Bemerkungen und Blüthenstaub*, in *Schriften*, vol. 2, p. 427.

30 J. W. Ritter, *Die Physik als Kunst. Ein Versuch, die Tendenz der Physik aus der Geschichte zu deuten* (München, 1806), p. 14.

31 C. G. Carus, 'Von den Naturreichen, ihrem Leben und ihrer Verwandtschaft', *Zeitschrift für Natur- und Heilkunde*, 1 (1820), 72.

32 Fr. Schlegel, *Athenäums-Fragmens 216*, in *Werke*, section 1, vol. 2, p. 198.

33 Fr. Schlegel, *Athenäums-Fragment 80*, in *ibid.*, p. 176.

34 On religion and Romanticism: K. Lindermann, 'Geistlicher Stand und religiöses Mittlertum. Ein Beitrag zur Religionsauffassung der Frühromantik in der romantischen Religiosität', in *Deutsche Vierteljahrsschrift für Literaturwissenschaft und Geistesgeschichte*, 2 (1924), 367–417; J. H. Randall, 'Romantic reinterpretations of religion', *Studies in Romanticism*, 2 (1963), 189–212; A. Rauscher (ed.), *Deutscher Katholizismus und Revolution im frühen 19. Jahrhundert* (München, 1977); H. Timm, *Heilige Revolution. Das religiöse Totalitätskonzept der Frühromantik* (Berlin, 1978); see also articles by W. Frühwald, H. Timm, E. Stopp, Ph. Schäftr u. B. Casper, in Brinkmann (ed.), *Romantik in Deutschland*.

35 Fr. Schleiermacher, *Reden über die Religion. An die Gebildeten unter ihren Verächtern* (1799; Hamburg, 1958), p. 29.

36 H. Steffens, *Was ich erlebte* (Breslau, 1842), vol. 5, pp. 143ff.

37 Schleiermacher, *Reden über die Religion*, p. 48.

38 Fr. Schlegel, *Athenäums-Idee 46*, in *Werke*, section 1, vol. 2, p. 261.

39 Schleiermacher, *Reden über die Religion*, p. 68.

40 Novalis, *Blüthenstaub*, in *Schriften* (1796), vol. 2, p. 445.

41 J. N. v. Ringseis, *Erinnerungen* (Regensburg, 1886), vol. 2, p. 252, and in *Le Catholique* (1827).

42 Jean Paul, *Siebenkäs*, in *Werke* (1796; München, 1975), vol. 3, p. 273.

43 *Ibid.*, pp. 270–1.

44 On painting and music of the Romantic period: H. Börsch-Supan, *Deutsche Romantiker* (München, 1972); W. Boetticher, *Einführung in die musikalische Romantik* (Wilhelmshaven, 1983); W. Geismeier, *Die Malerei der deutschen Romantik* (Stuttgart, 1984); J. Chr. Jensen, *Malerei der Romantik in Deutschland* (Köln, 1985); K. Lankheit, *Revolution und Restauration* (Leipzig, 1964); H. Schrade, *Deutsche Maler der Romantik* (Köln, 1967); see also titles in n. 1.

45 Fr. Schlegel, *Athenäums-Fragment 116*, in *Werke*, section 1, vol. 2, p. 182.

46 Fr. Schlegel, *Rezension von Goethes Werke, Bd. 1–4, Tübingen, 1806*, in *Werke* (München, 1975), section 1, vol. 3, p. 138.

47 Fr. Schlegel, *Lyceums-Fragment*, in *Werke*, section 1, vol. 2, p. 162.

48 H. Dahmen, 'E. Th. A. Hoffman und G. H. Schubert', in *Literaturwissenschaftliches Jahrbuch der Görresgesellschaft*, 1 (1926), 62–111; M. M. Tatar, *Spellbound. Studies on Mesmerism and Literature* (Princeton, NJ, 1978).

49 E. T. A. Hoffmann, *Der goldne Topf. Ein Märchen aus der neuen Zeit*, in *Werke* (1814; Frankfurt a. M., 1967), vol. 1, p. 204.

50 Philip Otto Runge to D. Runge (letter of 9 March 1802), in Philip Otto Runge, *Briefe und Schriften* (München, 1982), p. 75.

51 Fr. Schlegel, *Literary Note-Books*, ed. H. Eichner (London, 1957), p. 87.

52 Fr. Schlegel, *Über Lessing*, in *Werke* (1801), section 1, vol. 2, p. 414.

53 E. T. A. Hoffmann, *Kreisleriana*, in *Werke* (München, 1960), vol. 1, p. 41.

54 F. von Ramdohr, 'Über ein zum Altarblatt bestimmtes Landschaftsgemälde von Herrn Friedrich in Dresden', in S. Hinz (ed.), *Caspar David Friedrich in Briefen und Bekenntnissen* (1809; München, 1968), p. 141.

55 On the Romantic way of life: see the biographies of individual Romantics and R. Huch, *Die Romantik* (1898/1902; 3rd edn, Tübingen, 1964), vol. 102; B. Krauss, *Das Künstlerideal des Klassizismus und der Romantik* (Reutlingen, 1925); K. Jaspers, *Psychologie der Weltanschauungen* (Berlin, 1919; 5th edn, 1960); K. Lankheit, *Das Freundschaftsbild der Romantik* (Heidelberg, 1952); Fr. Loquai, *Künstler und Melancholie in der Romantik* (Frankfurt a. M., 1984); E. Spranger, *Psychologie des Jugendalters* (Leipzig, 1925; 27th edn, Heidelberg, 1963); B. v. Wiese, 'Novalis und die romantischen Konvertiten', in *Romantikforschungen* (Halle, 1929), pp. 205–42.

56 Novalis, *Poeticismen*, in *Schriften* (1798), vol. 2, p. 563.

57 Fr. Schlegel, *Lucinde* (1799; Stuttgart, 1963), pp. 75–6.

58 Cl. Brentano to Emilie Linder (letter of late 1833), in W. Frühwald (ed.), *Briefe an Emilie Linder* (Bad Homburg, 1969), p. 7.

59 J. W. v. Goethe to F. W. Riemer (letter of 28 August 1808), in *Goethes Gespräche*, vol. 2, p. 329.

60 G. W. Fr. Hegel to Windischmann (letter of 27 May 1810), in Hegel, *Briefe* (3rd edn, Hamburg, 1969), vol. 1, p. 314.

61 Fr. Schlegel, *Briefe an seinen Bruder August Wilhelm* (Berlin, 1890).

62 W. H. Wackenroder and L. Tieck, 'Herzensergiessungen eines kunstliebenden Klosterbruders', in Wackenroder, *Werke u. Briefe* (1797; München, 1984), p. 246.

63 Fr. Schlegel, *Über die Grenzen des Schönen*, in *Schriften* (1794; Paderborn, 1979), section 1, vol. 1, p. 37.

64 Fr. Schlegel, *Geschichte der Poesie der Griechen und Römer*, in *Schriften* (1798), section 1, vol. 1, p. 556.

65 H. Steffens, 'Vorlesungen über die Idee der deutschen Universität', in E. Anrich (ed.), *Die Idee der deutschen Universität. Die fünf Grundschriften aus der Zeit ihrer Neubegründung durch klassischen Idealismus und romantischen Realismus* (1808/9; Darmstadt, 1956), p. 356.

66 Treviranus, *Biologie oder die Philosophie der lebenden Natur für Naturforscher und Ärzte*, p. 15.

67 C. G. Carus, *Lebenserinnerungen und Denkwürdigkeiten* (1855; reprint Weimar, 1966), vol. 1, p. 257.

68 *Ibid.*, p. 238.

69 Fr. Schlegel, *Lucinde*, in *Schriften* (1799; München, 1962), section 1, vol. 5, p. 13.

70 Fr. Schlegel, *Kritische Fragmente, 108, Lyceum*, in *Werke*, section 1, vol. 2, p. 160; see I. Strohschneider-Kohrs, *Die romantische Ironie in Theorie und Gestaltung* (Tübingen, 1960; 2nd edn, 1977).

71 Fr. Schlegel, *Philosophische Vorlesungen insbesondere über Philosophie der Sprache und des Wortes*, in *Sämmtliche Werke* (1828; Wein, 1846), vol. 15, p. 56.

72 Novalis to Fr. Schlegel (letter of 8 July 1796), in *Schriften* (Darmstadt, 1975), vol. 4, p. 188.

73 Novalis, 'Tagebuch' (29 June 1797), in *ibid.*, p. 48.

74 Kleist to M. v. Kleist (letter of 28 November 1811), in Kleist, *Geschichte meiner Seele* (Frankfurt a. M., 1977), p. 401.

75 Fr. Schlegel, *Athenäums-Fragment 222*, in *Werke*, section 1, vol. 2, p. 201.

76 International comparisons: A. Béguin, *L'Âme romantique et le rêve. Essai sur le romantisme allemand et la poésie française* (Marseille, 1937; 2nd edn, Paris, 1946; German edn, München, 1972); E. Behler (ed.), *Die Europäische Romantik* (Frankfurt a. M., 1972); G. Hoffmeister, *Deutsche und europäische Romantik* (Stuttgart, 1978); J. Klein (ed.), *Die deutsche Romantik im Französischen Deutschlandsbild* (Braunschweig, 1957); E. C. Mason, *Deutschland und englische Romantik. Eine Gegenüberstellung* (Göttingen, 1959; 3rd edn, 1970); V. A. Schmitz, *Dänische Dichter in ihrer Begegnung mit deutscher Klassik und Romantik* (Frankfurt a. M., 1974); P. van Tieghem, *Le Romantisme dans la littérature européenne* (Paris, 1940); R. Wellek, 'German and English romanticism', *Studies in Romanticism*, 4 (1964/5), 35–56; see also titles in n. 1.

77 G. de Staël, *De l'Allemagne* (1813; Paris, 1959), vol. 4, p. 270.

78 Ongoing influence: A Geraths, *Epigonale Romantik* (Wiesbaden, 1975); W. Paulsen (ed.), *Das Nachleben der Romantik in der modernen deutschen Literatur* (Heidelberg, 1969); G. Peterli, *Zerfall und Nachklang. Studien zur deutschen Spätromantik* (Zürich, 1958); M. Praz, *La Carne, la morte e il*

diavolo nella litteratura romantica (Milano, 1930; 2nd edn, 1951; English edn, London, 1933; German edn, München, 1963; 2nd edn, 1981); R. Rosenbaum, *Moderne Malerei und die Tradition der Romantik* (München, 1981).

79 J. W. v. Goethe, *Maximen und Reflexionen, no. 865*, in *Werke* (Hamburg, 1953), vol. 12, p. 487; here one can find the well-known definition: 'Klassisch ist das Gesunde, romantisch das Kranke', 'Maximen und Reflexionen, no. 863', in *ibid.*

80 Fr. Schlegel, reivew of A. Müller, *Vorlesungen über die deutsche Wissenschaft und Literatur* (3rd edn, Dresden, 1807), in *Werke*, section 1, vol. 3, pp. 156–7.

81 H. Steffens, 'Über das Verhältniss der Naturphilosophie zur Physik unserer Tage', in Steffens, *Alt und Neu*, vol. 1, p. 67.

82 A. Schopenhauer, 'Parerga und Paralipomena', in *Sämmtliche Werke* (1851, vol. 2; Wiesbaden, 1947), vol. 6, p. 115.

83 K. v. Kamptz, cited in D. G. Kieser, *Das Wartburgfest am 18. Oktober 1817* (Jena, 1818), p. 135.

84 J. v. Liebig, *Über das Studium der Naturwissenschaften und über den Zustand der Chemie in Preussen* (Braunschweig, 1840), p. 29.

85 Fr. Schlegel, *Neue philosophische Schriften* (Frankfurt a. M., 1935), p. 368.

6

Romanticism in Switzerland

CLARISSA CAMPBELL ORR

THEMES AND DEFINITIONS:
THE SWISS AS CULTURAL MEDIATORS

Writing on Switzerland and on Romanticism, both terms elusive of definition, obliges an author to make explicit her working hypotheses from the outset. Taking Romanticism first, then, I follow Isaiah Berlin in believing it to be more than a change of mood and a preoccupation with certain key themes, seeing it rather as a fundamental shift in aesthetic theory and practice from a mimetic to an expressive theory of the arts.[1]

A corollary to this is that the seminal period of European Romanticism is in the decade of the late 1790s and early 1800s; that it is centred on the Jena and Heidelberg groups in Germany; and that it is intimately tied in with a 'nationalistic' reaction to the Napoleonic hegemony, political and cultural, which in France was characterized by a stale if elegant classicism. The generational timelag between German and French Romanticism can be explained in terms of the Napoleonic prolongation of this classical ethos, from which the French did not fully emancipate themselves until c. 1830. A further consequence of this schematization means that the concept of a pre-Romantic period is thrown into sharper relief, a period that can be dated as emerging as early as the 1730s and coexisting with the so-called 'Age of Reason'. Characteristic of this period would be *inter alia* a cult of sensibility and sentiment, a taste for the exotic, a search for the primitive in time and in space; its most familiar manifestations would include the Gothic novel, *Strawberry Hill*, 'Gothick' architecture and decor, 'graveyard' poetry, or the Sturm und Drang movement in Germany. However, it will be argued here that the Swiss contribution to these changing moods and tastes was absolutely seminal, though less familiar. And if the entire period c. 1760–1848 can also be seen in a certain sense as a Protestant, North European emancipation from Catholic, French and Southern European classicism, in its late Baroque and Rococo modes, then again the Swiss have a pivotal role.[2]

It is also important to bear in mind that the term 'Switzerland' designates a changing political entity between these dates. The Confederation, up to 1798, comprised thirteen cantons and their dependent territories, was largely German speaking, and German was the official language. Geneva was an independent Republic; Neuchâtel was a principality of Prussia; the Pays de Vaud, which included Lausanne, was a dependency of Berne; and the Jura, a fief of Basel. The Napoleonic invasions (1798) then created a Republic, 'one and indivisible', whose eighteen cantons were administrative units, not sovereign states in alliance. Geneva became a French *département*, as did part of the Vaud and, later, the Valais; and some of the Italian-speaking areas were absorbed into the Cisalpine Republic. French, German and Italian were now all equally recognized. The Napoleonic mediation of 1803 produced a more federal constitution with greater cantonal autonomy, but the Helvetic Republic was in all essentials a French dependency, and during the latter stages of the Napoleonic era was occupied by Austrian and Russian forces. In 1814 the Swiss Diet reconstituted the country as a federation of nineteen cantons, this time with no subject or associated states; the Treaty of Vienna (1815) recognized Swiss independence and perpetual neutrality; and in the same year the Federal pact was enlarged to include Geneva, Neuchâtel, and Valais as cantons. The external boundaries of Switzerland were then constant for the rest of the period, but as in most parts of Europe the 1830s were a troubled decade, and there were internal constitutional upheavals in many cantons, where there were movements for the 'Regeneration' of cantonal democracy. These liberal movements were succeeded by challenges from Radical parties. In 1847 there was civil war between Liberal and Conservative cantons, the Sonderbund War, after which the constitution was successfully revised in 1848. For the purposes of this essay, I shall use the term Swiss rather loosely, to include areas like the Vaud or Geneva which were not fully part of the Confederation until 1815.

Since the outstanding characteristic of Switzerland as a political entity is that it has nurtured the idea of citizenship as something created by political will, reason and consent, not something inherited organically, as the product of blood, soil and language, it might seem that a sense of Swiss civic identity, with its well-established stance of cherishing unity in diversity, has little to do with Romantic conceptions of the *Volk*, and a lot to do with acquiescence in key historical events and acts, underpinned by liberal constitutional ideas given fresh cogency in the Enlightenment. And this would indeed be true. So if political Romanticism is to be thought of as intensely *völkisch* and monolingual, then it would be absurd to expect Switzerland to conform to this pattern. But as I shall be arguing, political Romanticism can take several forms. The aristocratic liberalism sponsored by the Coppet circle was distinctively Swiss and – in its raising of the banner of protest against Napoleon – dashingly Romantic, even while it was also imbued with a cosmopolitan spirit. Moreover, the diversity of the Confederation notwithstanding, both pre-Romanticism and Romanticism fostered an Helvetism, a cult of Swissness, alongside more localized efforts to cherish cantonal traditions. All the same, it was the fate of the Swiss, susceptible as they were to emigration and permeable as they were to outsiders, to find that even the most 'Swiss' motif of them all, the Tell legend, was a Scandinavian import, and that the story was borrowed and used to inspire the independence struggles of the Greeks and the Hungarians. So even Swiss nationalism was no longer exclusively Swiss.

The essential characteristic of the Swiss contribution to pre-Romantic and Romantic epochs was, then, a mediatory one. The Swiss pioneered the way from classicism to Romanticism, while stopping short of the fully developed Romantic creed associated with Germany – though one of its foremost exponents, A. W. Schlegel, came to reside at Coppet. And as befits a 'nation' facing in at least five different cultural directions – toward Burgundy and the Netherlands; the Rhineland; France and Savoy; Southern Germany and Austria; and Northern Italy – its citizens and guests played a central role in introducing different cultures to each other.

LANDSCAPE, ROMANTICISM, AND EXILE

Above all Switzerland was a *paysage*, a landscape, an archetype of the Romantic vision. What others began to see in this landscape, and what it began to see in itself, created the quintessential Romantic ideal of nature: wild, mysterious, untamed, awe-inspiring; Byron's Childe Harold spoke for all Romantics when he declared that for him 'high mountains are a feeling, but the hum of human cities, torture'. But this cult of landscape would not have emerged had not Rousseau, Geneva's most influential runaway, rediscovered a delight in his native landscape when he returned there in 1754, and, by setting *La Nouvelle Eloïse* in the softer Alpine pastures above Lake Geneva, spread a taste for picturesque natural scenery through the courts and drawing rooms of Europe. Other Genevans, such as Jean-André Deluc, geologist and man of letters, the minister Bourrit, another Alpinist, and the renowned naturalist and geologist Horace Bénédict de Saussure, popularized the Alpine heights in their topographical and geological accounts.[3] Archdeacon Coxe's *Sketches of the Natural, Civil, and Political State of Swisserland* (1779) informed an English audience about the splendours of the glaciers – and the peculiarities of Swiss political life. Turner came to paint the Alpine scenery; Loutherbourg helped to promote the vogue with his sensational panoramas. Alpine scenes became a staple orthodoxy for nineteenth-century Swiss painting until the tradition was transformed by Hodler. The vogue for picturesque landscape provided an additional reason for English Milords to include Lausanne or Geneva as stopping points on their Grand Tours, and the former attracted an international clientèle as a health resort, partly because of the ministrations of the famous Dr Tissot. By the time Wordsworth reacted ecstatically to Switzerland, less well-known Romantic travellers had been doing much the same thing before him, for several decades.

Rousseau's return to his native city was a part of his revolt against Parisian society, and it is a truism that his example was formative in many respects for the later Sturm und Drang. But if Rousseau crystallizes the mood for an entire literary generation in a different language area, his is also an example of how many talented Swiss, then and now, exist in a condition of self-imposed exile that is also nostalgia – a simultaneous pressing against the restrictive boundaries of the native commune or canton, yet an attachment to its virtues once some freedom has been achieved. Gottfried Keller was to portray just such a tension in his *Der Grüne Heinrich* (*Green Henry*), as well as to exemplify it in his life. Rousseau's sense of alienation, of being both *depaysé* and *declassé*, as well as his religious quest in and outside of formal denominational allegiance, was elevated into an existential condition which has come to seem archetypally Romantic, and which also inaugurated the intense subjectivism of pre-Romanticism and Romanticism. But it may be doubted whether he would have reached this stance had he not been born in an independent Republic self-consciously situated between predatory France and Savoy, of parents from a dissimilar social rank; a place where belonging carried so much civic and religious weight, that *not* belonging – running away – had profound metaphysical implications. But Rousseau's plight has many parallels, if not quite the same intensity. Benjamin Constant, for example, belonged to a noble family in the Pays de Vaud, with a tradition of service in Dutch regiments. His life can seem that of the essentially rootless Romantic; his service as Court Chamberlain in Brunswick seems to come straight out of the pages of Schiller's *Kaballe und Liebe*, with its petty formalities and stifling ennui. Yet it is hard to point to where eighteenth-century cosmopolitanism ends and Romantic alienation begins; father and uncle had a not dissimilar pattern, and one cousin was a businessman in China. The combination of attachment to and frustration with the homeland was often rooted in the very palpable limitations on men (the women seem perforce to have stayed put) when it came to finding a livelihood, whether their talents were professional, aristocratic, artistic or artisanal. For centuries the Swiss had been famous as mercenaries; since the Reformation had supplied pastors for the Reformed faith; in the Enlightenment had sent a galaxy of talent to Universities and Courts throughout Europe. Rousseau may have made more of a vocation than most out of exile, but the Romantic quest for fame and fortune away from the *patrie* was more likely to happen to a Swiss than a French or an Englishman.

For those staying at home, the 'cellular' quality of Swiss life[4] meant that intellectual and cultural life was likely to be concentrated in small coteries in the major cities, linked to solitary and isolated parsonages in the countryside – a pattern not dissimilar to the one in Germany. The key centres were thus Zürich, capital of the old Confederation, Berne, Basel, a University town, Neuchâtel, significant for its printing and publishing trade, Lausanne and Geneva – both still important as seminaries for the Calvinist ministry. The first milieu of importance for pre-Romanticism was that of Bodmer and Breitinger in Zürich; the second was the Coppet circle in the Pays de Vaud. Both had an influence on European culture that far transcends their own immediate circle, and both circles show a love–hate relationship for the confines of Swiss life.

BODMER, ZÜRICH, AND PRE-ROMANTICISM

Eudo Mason has described Zürich as 'the fountain-head from which the great revolutionary movement in literature, known to us, though not to the Germans themselves, as Romanticism, was already gradually beginning to spread all over the territories where German is spoken'.[5] Johann Jacob Bodmer (1698–1783) was a man whose influence as a teacher far exceeded his influence as a writer. He is often characterized, not as a pre-Romantic, but as a founding father of the Aufklärung, as for example in the recent analysis of Peter Hans Reill.[6] But this naturally depends on a definition of Aufklärung. Reill, wishing to depart from a narrow focus on Lessing and Kant, stresses as formative influences on German intellectual life the inheritance of Protestant pietism, the willingness to criticize Enlightenment absolutism from a liberal-constitutional standpoint, and the *bürgerlich* status of the Aufklärer; and he challenges the thesis that German historicism dates only from Hegel. I concur entirely with Reill's redefinition and would say only that the literary and artistic culture fostered by the Aufklärung in Reill's sense could equally well be termed 'pre-Romantic'. The pupils of Bodmer, such as J. H. Fuseli, J. C. Lavater, J. Sulzer, J. P. Pestalozzi and J. v. Müller, are virtually a roll-call of Swiss-German pre-Romanticism. It was Bodmer who first introduced an appreciation of English literature to the German public, and began the emancipation of its literature from the sterile orthodoxy of French classicism, as enshrined in the strictures of Gottsched. This rejection stemmed in part from Bodmer's

'Swissness', his awareness of Switzerland's role as a cultural mediator, and his pride in his own roots; according to Reill, these factors predisposed Bodmer to argue that every group of people had its own particular mode of expression.

He and Johann Jacob Breitinger (1701–76) modelled their version of *The Spectator*, *Discours der Maler*, on Addison, but gave to it a particular nationalist twist to highlight the uniqueness of the Swiss character. Bodmer acquainted his readers and pupils with Milton, whom he translated, with Thomson and Young, and then with Shakespeare. Challenged by Gottsched for his praise of Milton, Bodmer developed an analysis of language which stressed the integral and expressive, rather than the merely ornamental, function of metaphor. Reading Blackwell's *Enquiry into the Life and Writings of Homer* (1735) confirmed Bodmer's intuitions about language and national identity, and helped to formulate the idea that each language group follows a similar historical development, which will include an heroic age and the poetic form most expressive of that age – viz. the national epic, product of an age of valour and conflict.

Bodmer went on from there to suggest that German literature, too, must have an epic poem, probably written on the Hohenstaufen epoch. (It is pertinent to recall that Switzerland had legally been a part of the Holy Roman Empire until the Treaty of Westphalia (1648), so Bodmer's medievalism was therefore an enthusiasm for a 'Swiss' past.) Unlike Macpherson, this suggestion did not prompt Bodmer to invent an Ossian that *ought* to exist; instead he and his correspondents initiated a manuscript search throughout Europe. The result was a cargo of rediscovery, including publication of the Minnesänger lyrics, a modernized *Parsifal* (1753), and the *Nibelungenlied*, entirely unknown until 1757. Bodmer interpreted these as historical evidence as well as literary treasure, and idealized the German Middle Ages as an age not of hierarchy but of freedom – a perspective to be shared by the Coppet circle later. Bodmer and Breitinger also delved into the history of Zürich and of the Confederation, helping to found the Helvetic Society and publishing the *Helvetische Bibliothek* (1735–41). But they were never narrowly patriotic; alongside the revaluation of English literature and German medieval writing, came the enterprise of trying to understand Dante in the context of his age. Even if the original poetry of Bodmer's circle is not fully emancipated from a Rococo prettiness, their medievalism, Anglomania and historical explorations emphatically prepare the way for the full-fledged Romanticism of the period 1795–1830.

Bodmer's pupil Johann Friedrich Fuseli (1741–1825) exemplifies very clearly the transitional and mediatory role of Swiss Romanticism. Originally intended by his family, a dynasty of painters and engravers, for the Zwinglian ministry, he was an exact contemporary of Lavater, with whom he conducted a friendship of Wertheresque intensity. He was ordained in 1761 and preached for a year before breaking out of the destiny envisaged for him by his family. But it was not immediately to painting that he turned, but to literature. Fired by Bodmer with enthusiasm for English literature, a role was envisaged for him as a kind of literary/cultural link between Germany, Switzerland and England, and in 1763 he left Zürich for Berlin. Fuseli's companions on the road to Berlin were Lavater and Sulzer, both of whom were to make an impact on European cultural life. Sulzer's aesthetics constitute an attack on materialist epistemology, and explore the concept of artistic genius, thus pointing in the direction of the later, Romantic, cult of the imagination. Sulzer was to make a very successful career in Berlin, and Frederick the Great gave him a Professorship in Philosophy in order to retain him there. Fuseli meanwhile had moved to England through the patronage of the banker Coutts. There he published translations of Winckelmann and of Klopstock's *Messias* (the most important work thus far to have been produced under Bodmer's influence) and a defence of Rousseau.

A future theme of Romantic critical theory was to be the interrelatedness of the arts, and Fuseli typifies this in his shift to painting and the way in which he was to invest his work with literary images and poetic intensity, drawing the viewer into the world of the painting instead of restricting him to detached contemplation. Much of his output consists of illustrations to Milton and Shakespeare, to whom he remained consistently loyal. His reputation as an artist was secured in 1781 with the exhibition of *The Nightmare*, on the face of it an archetypally Romantic painting, prefiguring the later Romantics' exploration of the nature of dreams and the unconscious. But is it really a Romantic piece of work? Art historians rather classify it as typical of an earlier period, and as an essay in the epic mode, depicting a universal predicament while drawing on the European folklore associated with nightmares which was being recorded and explored in the 1770s and 1780s.[7] Fuseli later lectured for the Royal Academy, when he revealed explicitly his adherence to an essentially classical theory of painting. Nevertheless, there is clearly an element in Fuseli that resists being corralled by the term 'classical'. Eudo Mason has aptly characterized his artistic theory as a classical husk, stubbornly maintained while non-classical impulses try to break through. *The Nightmare* may have aspired to epic status, but there is an erotic intensity to the work which was probably due to a frustrated love affair with Lavater's niece, Anna Landolt, who, like Werther's Lotte, was already engaged to a good bourgeois when Fuseli first met her, and he poured out his feelings in letters to Lavater in language characteristic of the Sturm und Drang. Yet, if Fuseli cannot quite be classified as a 'classical' painter, he does not readily fit into

Romantic categories either. He remained outside the literary mainstream of Romanticism after taking up painting, ignoring Herder, Hamann, and Goethe; he did not contribute to the awakening of English interest in German literature in the 1790s, and, aside from his friendship with Blake and the esteem of Byron, had little to do with the English Romantics. Even the noted friendship with Blake was more the encouragement given to a fellow-painter and engraver who needed work than an admiration for a poet, as Fuseli had little time for Blake's mythological epics.

Fuseli in England was known as the 'wild Swiss', and he painted pictures of William Tell, and the Oath on the Rütli, the two cardinal icons of the Helvetic myth. He proudly contrasted Swiss liberty to the petty despotisms of the German nation, and deplored Klopstock's servile flattery of Christian VI of Denmark. He was contemptuous of French classicism as trifling and emptily decorative. It would seem then that Fuseli saw himself as distinctively Swiss, not just Germanic, though his admiration for his homeland contained no illusions. But if he saw himself as Swiss, it is perhaps true that he only enjoyed being Swiss outside Switzerland.

SCIENCE AND SENSIBILITY

His fellow-student and bosom friend, Lavater, spent his life within the Confederation, but he had an international impact on both Romantic 'science' and religious sensibility. His contribution toward the shift from Enlightenment rationalism to that borderland of the mystical and pseudo-scientific, that is a feature of intellectual and court life in the decade prior to the French Revolution,[8] was through his formulation of the science of physiognomy. The science of reading character by means of facial expression was not new, but Lavater tried to put it on a deeper foundation that took structural features into account, and thus would prevent the physiognomist from being deceived by the masks of fashion or hypocrisy.[9] Lavater claimed to be seeing the inner soul, the true self, mirrored in the face, a doctrine bound to attract all those restless characters eager to shrug off the conformities and importunities of social convention in search of true self-expression. His widespread appeal – which attracted interest throughout the Continent – can also be explained by the fact that Lavater managed to suggest his was a fully Christian doctrine entirely separate from astrology, palmistry or the other black arts normally associated with physiognomy, for he enjoyed a high reputation as a Pietistic theologian. The *Physiognomische Fragmente* (1775–8), influenced the European intelligentsia for half a century, and in England their impact was assisted by a sumptuous edition (1789–1810), edited and with engravings by

Fuseli, and Blake. Fuseli also translated the companion piece by Lavater, *Aphorisms on Man* (1788).

As well as fostering a new science, Switzerland produced physicians to minister to the new sensibility. One such was the Bernese physician and man of letters, Johann Georg Zimmermann (1728–95), who also attained international eminence, being appointed Royal Physician in Hanover (1768), and treating Frederick the Great on his death-bed (1786). He typifies the Swiss who pines for larger pastures beyond the stultifying confines of Swiss provincial society, and was relieved when he was able to move to Germany. He was subject to depression, fond of solitude and, socially, rather a bear. A man of the Enlightenment in many respects, like many other Swiss who combined piety with Enlightenment, he deplored the irreligion of the Prussian Court, and later succumbed to persecution mania in the belief that the French Revolution had been brought about by the Illuminati's secret organization, undermining Throne and Altar. From the point of view of Romanticism, he is significant as an explorer of the post-Rousseau sensibility, known throughout Europe for his essay *On Solitude* (1773); his biographer, the equally distinguished doctor, Tissot, wrote that he wished to found a

science of the heart . . . on that noble philosophy which regulates the characters of men, and operating more by love than rigid precept, corrects the cold dictates of reason by the warm feelings of the heart; opens to men the dangers to which they are exposed; animates the dormant faculties of the mind; and prompts them to the practice of all the virtues.[10]

Zimmermann was additionally an enthusiastic supporter of Lavater; it was he who had insisted the latter should publish his theories. Zimmermann also wrote an essay *On National Pride* (1758). This was in many respects a peevish exercise of personal spleen, while castigating aristocratic pride, religious bigotry and narrow xenophobia. Yet he did allow that an appropriate confidence and esteem for past national achievements could foster a healthy sense of national pride, and as an example he cited the Swiss defeat of the Burgundians in 1477; equally he allowed that cultural and literary achievements in the past could help to inspire the present. He thus parallels in an interesting way the cultural nationalism of the Romantic movement, usually associated with Herder and his disciples. The essay breathes a strong distaste for French absolutism, praising Republicanism and constitutional monarchy in a characteristically Swiss fashion.

Zimmermann's other great friend, Simon-André Tissot, was possibly the medical man best known to the literate reading public after he published his *Avis au peuple sur sa santé* (1761), a general medical handbook in non-specialist language which went into numerous editions and was translated into ten European languages. His *Essai sur les maladies des gens du monde* (1771), contrasted the over-indulgent lives of the leisured orders with the wholesome lives of the labouring poor – not those of the cities but the rural worker and skilled artisan – arguing that excess of passion, constrictive dress and rich diet were all detrimental to health. One cannot help surmising that this kind of advice would have been unpalatable had not Rousseau helped form the taste of fashionable Europe, so that it paid lip-service to the notion of the corruptions of worldly society. However, Tissot's recommended regimen was one of moderation rather than austerity. His patients may have read *La Nouvelle Eloïse*, but they did not really want to live like peasants. Tissot's *Avis aux gens de lettres et aux personnes sédentaires sur leur santé* (1768), must surely have flattered all those who fancied themselves persons of taste and literary sensibility. His medical reputation was actually founded on four scholarly volumes on nervous illness, and the rich, idle and fashionable flocked to consult him in Lausanne, where he had been heaped with civic honours. The fact that he accepted the chair of Medicine at Pavia for three years only, so as to return to his political role and medical practice in his native Pays de Vaud, only made him all the more esteemed for his (local) patriotism.

PRE-ROMANTICISM IN THE SUISSE ROMANDE: COLOMBIER AND COPPET

Neuchâtel was the setting for a remarkably individual writer who is as hard as anyone mentioned so far to categorize as either Swiss or Romantic, but who must be included as an important figure of the pre-Romantic era, and in the literary development of the Suisse Romande, although she is also cherished by her fellow-Dutch.

Isabelle de Charrière (1740–1805), first of the two most important women in Benjamin Constant's life, was born Isabelle van Serooskerken Van Tuyll, to a family of impeccable aristocratic credentials in Zuylen, near Utrecht. She was formidably clever, and this conspired to deter all her suitors, together with the fact that she was either too well-born, not rich enough or else Protestant; so all her marriage projects came to nothing. At thirty-three, she staged a showdown with her parents over marrying her brother's tutor, a Swiss gentleman, Charles de Charrière, whom she had known for seven years, or else retiring to a Convent; the former proving more acceptable than the latter, she retired to Colombier near Neuchâtel. Here she mostly remained. The couple wintered in Geneva until 1784, when she fell victim to a violent but unrequited passion for a man very much her junior, and engaged to another. She never revisited the city, but the grief inspired her masterpiece, *Caliste* (1787). It also prompted her dull but well-meaning husband to take her to Paris to cure her melancholy; and it was there that she first met Benjamin. On returning to Colombier she retired almost entirely from society and toward the end of her life never left the estate.

Isabelle de Charrière's impeccable French, and her sensitivity to Vaudois variations, assimilates her more obviously to the literature of the Suisse Romande than to her native Dutch Republic, though it is customary to liken her novellas to Dutch genre painting. The first novel she wrote after settling at Colombier was *Mistress Henley* (1784), a 'feminist' reply to a novel by an uncle of Benjamin, Samuel de Constant, *le Mari Sentimental* (1783). Such novels were enjoying a vogue in Lausanne's literary circles and in spite of her personal aloofness Mme de Charrière was more integrated within Swiss letters than was Mme de Staël. So, she may be accounted as 'Swiss' – but is she a Romantic? She is usually seen as the embodiment of an ironic and almost painfully detached intelligence, as a modern Stoic, as Constant's preceptor in *dédoublement*; yet Stoicism is in itself a stance of extremity, of emotional risk and desperate courage. If she is classical, she is classical in the way that David's masterpieces, like the *Oath of the Horatii*, re-interpret the imperatives of the classical world and point toward the Revolutionary and Romantic epoch. Hers is an uncompromising stance. In 1796 she wrote to Constant: 'In my detachment from you there is something which would make one of the most beautiful attachments one could conceive.'[11] Moreover, there was in Mme de Charrière a well-developed interest in the psychological and moral complexities of *sensibilité*; her Caliste occupies a similar moral universe to Rousseau's Julie: both are women of moral integrity and self-sacrificing duty in spite of also being women who have lapsed from virtue. *Cécile* (1785), a touching portrayal of a mother easing her daughter through her first, and unrequited, attachment, has an astringent element to it but is also sentimental in the best sense of the term.

On the face of it nothing could differ more from Colombier than the château of Coppet during Mme de Staël's legendary 'reign'. Yet even she, in spite of the storms and tempests she generated, could not, any more than could Benjamin or Isabelle, escape wholly from a detached self-consciousness which observed relentlessly without participation. Intellectually, the allegiances of the Coppet circle were more with the Enlightenment than the Romantic movement, the one notable exception being A. W. Schlegel, already one of the most noted theoreticians of the new movement before Germaine swept him up into her circle. Yet although the members of the Coppet circle were in some respects critics of Romanticism – Constant's critique of the Jacobin Republic can also be seen as a critique of Romantic political culture – it is also impossible to portray the European Romantic movement without including their influence as mediators between cultures. And this is an essentially Swiss kind of role.

The Coppet circle is often mentioned in studies of French Romanticism but because Mme de Staël and Benjamin Constant are seen so often in the context of their role as critics of Napoleonic culture and politics, their Swissness can be overlooked. Germaine de Staël, with a Genevan banker who became a French minister for a father, and a mother who was a pastor's daughter from Lausanne, would always have had an insider–outsider relationship to French court life, even had she not become the wife of the Swedish ambassador to Versailles, with all the advantages and immunities of diplomatic status which that provided. Constant's restless wanderings, as I have suggested, are not ascribable simply to Romantic *Weltschmerz* or inherent weakness of character but are part and parcel of a family tradition that was typical of the Swiss; equally typical was his education through private tuition followed by a spell at a Protestant University outside Switzerland – in Benjamin's case, Edinburgh. Neither of the pair had any taste for Swiss scenery; fretting at Coppet under Bonaparte's prohibition, Mme de Staël longed for even the gutter of the Rue du Bac (where the Swedish embassy in Paris was situated), and to relieve the tedium she spent interludes in Geneva and Lausanne – which she was apt to find equally tedious and unattractive. Nonetheless in inheriting Coppet from her father she also became a feudal châtelaine within the seigneurial structure of the Pays de Vaud, and derived some of her income from this position. Moreover, even if she only spent so much time there because Napoleon prevented her returning to Paris, the fact that Coppet was available to her meant that she was able to exercise an influence on a circle of guests who included people with much more integrated links with the Confederation and its literary life than she possessed or wished to nurture. She was one of the most cosmopolitan women in a cosmopolitan age, and she had an outstanding role to play in the development of francophone Romanticism. Paradoxically, being 'free and Swiss' enabled her to have this impact, in spite of lukewarm interest in Swiss affairs. Switzerland's role as neutral host to exiles in the Romantic period begins with Mme de Staël, who was both exile and resident.[12]

Coppet, in its heyday between 1804 and 1810, 'united the qualities of a feudal manor, an aristocratic salon, a bohemian summer colony, a grand hotel, a family seat, and the Isle of Calypso', as J. Christopher Herold observes.[13] What a galaxy of talent was concentrated there! And the guests exemplified fully the intermediary role that characterizes Swiss Romanticism on the larger scale.

First and foremost must be cited Mme de Staël's celebrated *De l'Allemagne* (1813); essentially a critique of Napoleonic cultural orthodoxy, it also served as an introduction not only to German literature and philosophy but also to elements of Danish literature, a facet that is usually overlooked. The connection here was through the Bernese aristocrat and littérateur Charles-Victor de Bonstetten (1745–1823), who had become acquainted with the Danish poetess Frederika Brun in 1791. After the French invasion of Berne in 1798, Bonstetten spent a couple of years in Denmark, living in the Brun household. Frederika in her turn has been described as the Mme de Staël of Denmark; a patroness of all the arts, her chief protégé was the Danish patriot poet Oelenschläger, and both were frequent guests at Coppet after Bonstetten, who had first met Germaine de Staël when she was virtually a child, had introduced them. Oelenschläger wrote a drama on the Tell theme, *Palnatoke* (1808), giving it the Scandinavian setting which was historically more accurate than the Swiss one.

While Brun urged Bonstetten to write in German, Mme de Staël urged him to continue with French. Bonstetten was always something of an elegant dabbler as a writer, but his *L'Homme du Midi et L'Homme du Nord* (1824), should not be slighted as a contribution to the Romantic debate on the idea of two such distinct cultural entities and personalities. If Bonstetten was attracted to Scandinavia, his other love, comparable to that of Goethe's, was for Italy; and his greatest literary success was probably the earlier essay *Voyage sur la scène des six dernier livres de l'Enéide* (1804). Germaine puffed it enthusiastically, having first masterminded its publication. Her own famous novel about encountering Italy, *Corinne* (1807), may owe her self-projection in the character of an *improvvisatrice* to Bonstetten's memories of such a woman, named Corilla, whom he had heard perform in Florence in 1774.

Bonstetten's comparative essay on French, Italian, German, Danish and Swedish literature was the fruit of his Danish and Italian memories and of the balance of his sympathies, poised exactly between the Germanic and Italian worlds; his impartiality mirrors essentially an Enlightened cosmopolitan more than the Romantic national fervour of the nineteenth century. His urbane temper was a survival from a bygone age; but he was not indifferent to his native country. He was sensitive to its picturesque beauty, his first extended work being a series of travel letters on the Swiss *paysage* and customs, *Lettres sur une contrée pastorale de la Suisse* (1793), and he was a member of the Helvetic Society. His patriotism was that of the late Enlightenment: politically reformist, interested in local history and conditions, but not obsessed with altering the international order by nationalistic self-assertion.

Better known than Bonstetten for his advocacy of Italian history and culture is another Swiss protégé of Mme de Staël's, the historian and economist Sismonde de Sismondi (1773–1842), whose family, of Genevese origin, had settled in Pescia. The French regard him as one of the founding fathers of their Romanticism, because of his pioneering work, *De la Littérature du midi de l'Europe* (1813), which introduced the reader to medieval French, Provençal and Italian literature, setting it accurately in the context of social and political events. The ethos of chivalry was seen as the projection of a social ideal not (as was the tendency in German Romanticism) as a description of the social reality of medieval life. Germaine herself has been credited with encouraging the Italians to discover and emulate the new literary movements in the north by her open letter to the Italian people (1816). Drama was also assiduously studied and enacted at Coppet and in this area too there were significant mediations; Schlegel was already well-known for his Shakespeare translations before moving to Switzerland, but once there he translated Calderón, while Constant translated – and in the process classicized – Schiller's *Wallenstein* (*Wallstein*, 1800).

Yet, for all their central importance in furthering an enthusiasm for Romanticism and introducing cultures to each other, it must be repeated that the Coppet circle at best were very hybrid Romantics. Schlegel was indisputably a Romantic, but the rest of the circle had intellectual allegiances strongly rooted in the Enlightenment, even if they led undeniably Romantic lives, in the grip of histrionic passions. Bonstetten was the cultivated, aristocratic, dilettante magistrate typical of the Ancien Régime at its most benign and tolerant; Constant and Mme de Staël owed their conceptions of politics and history largely to the philosophical traditions of Montesquieu and the Scottish Enlightenment; so did Sismondi, who was related by marriage and intellectual affinity to impeccably Whig/*Edinburgh Review* circles. Sismondi's *History of the Italian Republics* (1807–18) is an embodiment of this Swiss aristocratic and Protestant liberalism, which is an important component of the civic tradition in European political thought. It celebrates the specific individuality of each Republic and their common history of 'liberty' – i.e. of freedom from Papal or Imperial control. Because of this slant, the history was a greatly respected text in the Risorgimento. Not for Sismondi any reverence for a medieval mystique of hierarchy and order in Church and Empire, though he had no sympathy with populism either. His belief that his family really were entitled to call themselves 'Sismonde de Sismondi' was utterly sincere, if quite false, genealogically, and he never advocated democracy.

The aesthetic theory of the Coppet circle (again with Schlegel as the exception proving the rule) was equally indebted to Enlightened sources, chiefly Scottish, a reflection in part of Protestant Switzerland's close

relationship with other Calvinist cultures. The group tended to see literature through the lens of an historical theory of the progress of civilization,
which included the refinement of manners, and the extension of the
imaginative sympathies – and thus the moral faculties – through the
medium of literature.[14] Benjamin's *dédoublement Constantien* – his dis-
passionate and relentless irony – is often cited as an un-Romantic characteristic, and the calm yet unremitting irony of his masterpiece, *Adolphe*,
has none of the self-consciousness toward its nature as narrative, often
found in German Romantic novels contemporaneous with it. In form it is
essentially an eighteenth-century type of memoir novel, supposedly found
and published by someone other than the fictional narrator; it has unmistakable affinities with *Caliste*; indeed in many ways it is its masculine
counterpart, having all of Belle de Charrière's classical restraint but with
proportions deriving more from tragic drama than from the genre piece.

And yet, as so often with the Swiss context, even this classification
requires modification. The political values and concepts of the Coppet
circle may have derived from the Enlightenment, but, put into practice,
they constitute, I would argue, a species of political Romanticism that is
characteristically Swiss. The mere celebration of cultural diversity in the
past, the creation of an historiography of freedom that delighted in the discovery of specific liberties and immunities, was a gauntlet thrown down to
the political conformity and cultural aridity of the Napoleonic system. It
was Romantic in contrast to the sterile classicism of his court; though it
was not the Romanticism of the Jacobin Republic either, for to the Coppet
circle this also represented a form of cultural totalitarianism.[15] In showing
how English or German or Italian literature had followed a path dictated
by differing political and social circumstances, Tennenbaum[16]argues that
the Coppet circle pointed to alternative sources of cultural and thus of
political values, revealing that classicism's claims to reflect universal standards was really a mask for French hegemony. This liberal Romanticism,
then, celebrates the political strategies of the middle way, of institutional
checks on despotism, of representative bodies composed of the propertied,
of constitutions and liberties guaranteed by law. In all these respects there
are affinities with the outlook of the Bodmer circle. Coppet's liberalism
could even point toward radicalism; Sismondi's critique of industrial
society and his dissent from orthodox political economy earned him the
respect of Marx, whereas other Swiss critiques of industrialism were to
foster conservative rejections of the new economic and social order.

NATIONALISM AND ROMANTICISM IN THE
SUISSE ROMANDE, 1815–48

The friendship, contacts and preoccupations of the Coppet circle continually spilled beyond their location in the Pays de Vaud; they behaved in ways similar to eighteenth-century cosmopolitans and denizens of the Republic of Letters, although it was Switzerland which gave them a base. But for the most part, Swiss political, cultural and social life went on in other and more local dimensions. The social leaders of these groups might be professors or essayists or magistrates; the hostesses were ladies like two of Benjamin Constant's aunts, Mme de Charrière de Bavois, whose house, La Chaumière, was a beacon to the literati of Lausanne; or the Comtesse de Nassau, likewise in Lausanne. For all that they were *femmes du monde* these two tended to look askance at the irregular passions of Coppet; illustrative of the gap between life at the Château and life lived in tune with the proprieties of Swiss provincial life, is the fact that Mme de Staël was the only person to entertain Byron when he was a visitor to Switzerland in 1816, shortly after the highly publicized separation from his wife. The question therefore arises, how much of a 'native' Swiss Romantic movement was there? And did it foster an enthusiasm for specifically Helvetic – or cantonal – culture and mores?

The question is not an easy one to answer, given that Switzerland is, by definition, polyglot and pluralistic. Moreover, Switzerland had been as much changed as any other country where France had intervened. Its Ancien Régime society had been essentially altered, and the old, loose, defensive Confederation, similar to the Holy Roman Empire in its anomalies and desuetude, had been abolished. The contours of the later Romantic movement in its cultural sense have therefore to be understood within the context of the changed political climate after the Congress of Vienna. The Napoleonic mediation had set the tone for the institution of a much more cohesive confederal structure of cantons possessing equal political status; there were no more subject territories or associated dependencies. Although Swiss neutrality was to be respected, the Confederation was pressurized into becoming a member of the Holy Alliance in 1817, and Metternich's hope was to make Switzerland into an Austrian client-state. At the same time, the Napoleonic occupation had created irreversibly the conditions of bourgeois masculine equality by abolishing feudalism and establishing the idea of personal liberty. The Swiss man was now an individual citizen within a single, equal-ranking canton, though no canton in 1815 allowed for a fully democratic franchise and it was not until 1848 that the revised Constitution gave him the right to settle within any canton in the Confederation. The political struggles of the period up to 1848 largely related to attempts to equalize the political power of the urban centres of the cantons vis-à-vis their rural hinterlands, and to abolish a property qualification for the franchise, while the Swiss woman had to wait until 1971 to attain the vote in Federal elections.

A Swiss man therefore had the task of adjusting to being a new kind of citizen in a new kind of nation; and the question was really, would the liberal aristocratic model of unity and diversity (but not democracy) be followed, or would Switzerland be drawn into the influences prevalent in Germany, Italy and Central Europe to base nationality on ethnic history and language, rather than on a political and rational idea of citizenship? More fundamentally still, could *Kantonligeist* be transformed into a sentimental attachment for the Confederation as a whole?

These questions were of particular relevance for the new French-speaking cantons such as Geneva and the Vaud, who now for the first time had equal political status within the Confederation, but whose cultural sophistication, cosmopolitan connections and love–hate relationship with Catholic France and Piedmont-Savoy, were bound to introduce conflicting cross-currents. How much did the localized institutions, such as the Academies and the Church, or the professional and landed elites, respond to a new cultural movement, Romanticism, that had its origins in Germany but which by the 1820s was making waves in France? How did they feel about being Swiss?

Geneva entered enthusiastically into the new national entity, appropriating the symbols and myths of the older, Germanic cantons. William Tell, the Rütli oath, the Battle of Sempach, etc., were commemorated and pictured; the first two steamboats to ply on the lake were named the *William Tell* and the *Winkelried*. (Not that Geneva's own Republican history was forgotten; it also celebrated the *Escalade* – the famous victory of 1602 against Savoyard attack – and continues to do so to this day.) But it could almost seem as though the new national identity was easier to assimilate than the new taste in arts and letters. Initially the Genevan character and taste seemed inimical to the Romantic movement, as it was developing in France in the work of Hugo, Sand or Lamartine, and they were poorly reviewed in the press. Poetry, to the average periodical-reading Genevan c. 1825, meant the sprightly satiric or patriotic *chanson à boire* of the Caveau circle, led by Chapponnière or Petit-Senn, who were businessmen or *horlogiers* by profession; poetry was a pastime for them, not a vocation.

In 1825 the twenty-year-old Charles Didier tried to introduce the new French school to a Genevan audience. He published his *Harpe helvétique*, a collection celebrating the Swiss alps and Swiss history, following it in 1826 with *La Ruine de Missolonghi*, a theme dear to the Philhellenes of

Geneva. He found that his poetry made little impact of itself, but did initiate a fifteen-year debate on the merits of the new school, conducted in the literary journals and the Société de Belles-Lettres. Disheartened, he dedicated his *Mélodies Helvétiques* (1827) to the French, and left his native city to seek his fortunes in Paris. The same course was followed by Imbert Galloix, whose heroes were Byron and Lamartine. His poems on Swiss history did not meet with great acclaim while his melancholy was simply seen as symptomatic of a soul ignorant of its Saviour. A consumptive, he died in Paris in 1828 at the height of his poetic powers, a mere twenty-one years old. A third poet, Albert Richard (1802–81), proved to have greater staying power. He was convinced that the Swiss national past was an unmined source for epic poetry, and his first effort, published in 1827, celebrated the resistance of Schwyz to the French invasion, and the imaginary experiences of a Swiss mercenary. He spent some time in Paris during the formative years of French Romanticism and attended the famous 'battle' of *Hernani* before returning to Switzerland in 1830. Gradually he attained both esteem for his epics and recognition as a Professor. But the utilitarian and commercial ethos of Geneva, like that of the Netherlands, was not for the most part hospitable to Romantic self-indulgence and melancholy in literature. The drawing rooms of the Upper Town were stiflingly correct, with the men discussing public affairs, the women whispering discreet gossip, and neither sex aspiring to utter a witticism to divert the whole company.

The Genevans took to the new movement more in its musical form; Rossini was always a popular part of the repertoire, not surprisingly, given his opera, *Guillaume Tell* (1829); and Liszt, who chose Geneva as the goal of his elopement with Marie d'Agoult, was warmly regarded as a virtuoso, though not perhaps as a moralist. He had been rapturously received when he had played in Geneva in 1827, aged sixteen, and now he found himself accepted far more than the hapless Byron had been. His arrival in 1835 coincided with the foundation of Geneva's Conservatoire, and Liszt was appointed a Professor. As yet, Switzerland had not produced composers known outside its borders; lacking courts and grand country houses, music had remained, for a much longer time than in the Holy Roman Empire or the Austrian Habsburg lands, the province of the Church, and Calvinism gave less scope than Catholicism or Lutheranism to musical performance. But Xavier Schnyder studied with Beethoven, and Hans Georg Naejeli was extremely active in the choral revival of the 1820s and 30s. Moreover, the Swiss *paysage* and national mythology, mediated through the poetry of Byron and Sénancour, was to inspire Liszt to begin the Swiss 'scenes' of what developed into the *Années de Pèlerinage*, an outstanding example of Romantic musical composition. The eighth study of volume one, *Mal du Pays*, included a melody from Appenzell, first written down in 1710, which (according to Rousseau) was so evocative of their homeland that Swiss mercenaries were forbidden to listen to it lest *heimweh* distract them from their military duties. The early version of the *Années de Pèlerinage* had also included more Swiss folk tunes as a basis for the section *Fleurs mélodiques des Alpes*.

Liszt's visit to Geneva inevitably brought a link with the circle of French Romantic writers in Paris, and his entourage was joined by George Sand and her two children for a visit to Chamonix in 1836. Her account of this is vividly described in Letter 10 of her *Lettres d'un voyageur*, addressed to her erstwhile lover, Charles Didier.[17] The trip also included Adolphe Pictet, of the numerous and distinguished Genevan clan, a Professor, polymath and eccentric, and a translator of the historian Zschokke, discussed below. He left his own *brio* account of the holiday in *Une course à Chamonix*, 1838.

Genevan literary circles were still slow to accept Romanticism as the new creed, however. The new school was satirized by John Rueggiers in a novel similar to those of Thomas Love Peacock, while the popular Genevan *conteur* and critic, Toeppfer, caricatured the Romantics in his *Histoire d'Albert* (1844). The generation of the 1830s persevered nonetheless, publishing two journals, the *Album Littéraire* and *L'Étudiant Genevois*, this time largely devoted to Romantic prose modelled on Dumas, Balzac and Sand, with themes derived from historical legend, Sicilian tales and Swiss historical/patriotic material. The best poet of this generation was Henri Blanvalet. His was a true lyric gift for the poetry not of melancholy or heroism, but of the home, the child and the outcast. Genevan Romanticism was never as passionate or as extravagant as its German or French counterparts. In the longer term, its practitioners did succeed in naturalizing lyric poetry in a culture that had always been better known for serious theological or philosophical debate, and for its contributions to natural science. The appointment of Richard to a Professorship at the Academy to succeed Toeppfer was a belated recognition both of his stature as an epic poet, and of Romantic conceptions of literature.[18]

Lausanne and the Canton de Vaud show a similar mixture of willing embrace of identity within the wider Swiss whole, in tension with the pull of Paris as a cultural magnet. Juste Olivier (1807–78), for example, first made a name for himself with his *Poèmes Suisses* (1830), which gained him a Professorship at nearby Neuchâtel (still nominally a Prussian principality) on the condition that he spend a few months each year in Parisian literary circles. His journal for 1830 consequently has fascinating insights into the 1830 Revolution in politics and letters: he attended the famous first night of *Hernani*, frequented de Vigny's salon, was acquainted with the St-Simonians; he also made friends with Sainte-Beuve, who did not repudiate Romanticism decisively until 1840, although he had his reservations about it already. This did not prevent his rehabilitation of Sénancour's *Obermann* (1804), a powerful expression of the cult of the Alps, based on the author's memories of Fribourg. It was by no means solely the case that the Suisse Romande learnt from Paris. Through his friendship with the Oliviers, Sainte-Beuve came to be visiting Professor in Lausanne from 1837 to 1838 (where Olivier had held the chair of History since 1833), when he gave a course of lectures on Port Royal, the germ of his later *magnum opus*. The sojourn in Lausanne gave him valuable insights into Jansenism, through his acquaintance with Alexander-Rodolphe Vinet (1797–1847) the leading theologian in the canton, known as 'Le Pascal Protestant', and a critic of the pantheism inherent in certain kinds of Romanticism.[19]

Both Juste Olivier and his wife Caroline were poets, publishing a joint volume in 1835, *Les Deux Voix*, and shared an interest in the folklore and customs of the region, which formed the substance of Olivier's Study *Le Canton de Vaud, sa vie et son histoire* (1837). He was a founder member of La Société d'Histoire de la Suisse Romande, dedicated to the publication of old historical sources and of local studies of all kinds. Other members included Felix Chavannes (1802–63) of Vevey, noted for his patriotic songs; Philippe-Syriaque Bridel (1757–1845), later Dean of Montreux, author of popular essays, the *Etrennes helvétiennes*, on Swiss topographical, social and historical subjects, and compiler of a magisterial Glossary of patois spoken throughout the Suisse Romande; and the distinguished historian and liberal politician, Charles Monnard, of whom more will presently be said.

The canton did not confine itself to an interest in its own past and in reviving old customs such as the *Festspiel* – a festival of songs and parades dating back to the annual fêtes of the *vignerons* – in 1819 and 1833. Like Geneva, the canton participated enthusiastically in such events as the *Tir Fédéral* (an annual rifle competition). Another avenue for fostering Federal sentiment was the Société Helvétique de Musique, founded in Lucerne in 1808 to encourage patriotic feeling as well as musical appreciation and education. Every year, a different city in the Confederation would take its turn to hose a concert, largely of amateur instrumentalists or singers. In 1834 an organized attempt began to collect Vaudois folksongs, led by Jean Bernard Kaupers; by 1842 this had grown into the Société Fédéral de Chant. Already in Berne in 1824 a collection of national songs from Cantons Vaud and Fribourg had been published in the original patois with a French introduction, and there were several other collections by mid-century.[20]

How much this kind of antiquarian and regional-historical interest can be attributed to Romanticism can be overestimated, however, for there are important precedents in Switzerland for this which pre-date the Romantic period of post-Napoleonic Europe. The cultural revival in the Vaud, for example, has its roots in Enlightenment patriotism and in the more secular culture of fashionable and leisured society. There had been two abortive attempts already to break the stranglehold of Berne, one in 1723 led by Abraham Davel, and one in 1749 led by Samuel Henzi. Both of these movements can be seen in the light of attempts to reform entrenched oligarchies in a liberal but not democratic direction; there were similar challenges to the narrow oligarchy dominating Genevan politics. By the 1770s such impulses among the educated elite in the Vaud, who had no political power, were finding a focus in the Literary Society founded by Deyverdun in 1772; founder members included Samuel Constant, and the later nationalist leader, Frédérick-César de LaHarpe, whose search for employment as tutor to Catherine the Great's grandson, Alexander, had been prompted partly because the Bernese had reminded him of the 'vassal' status of the Vaudois gentry, underlining the lack of scope for this talented young man in his native land.

One of the papers read at the Literary Society was by the young P.-S. Bridel, 'La Suisse française, a-t-elle une poésie nationale?' He hoped to fill the gap with his own *Poésies Helvétiennes*. There was also a considerable vogue for German literature in translation; Deyverdun translated *Werther*; L.-F. Huber and his wife, the widow of the naturalist Forster, were equally adept at translation from German or French; Tscharner translated Klopstock's *Messias*; Boaton, Gessner's *Idylls*; and Marie-Aimée Steck rendered Haller and English writers like Goldsmith into French. In this way the German and English influences that created and constituted the literature of pre-Romanticism and of the Sturm und Drang, achieved literary currency in the Suisse Romande. It is therefore not surprising that once the area of the Vaud became a full canton, there should have been the basis for a sense of its own cultural and historical identity as well as a willingness, given that a start had been made on removing grievances directed toward Berne, to identify with the whole Confederation.[21]

HISTORY AND PATRIOTISM IN GERMAN-SPEAKING SWITZERLAND C. 1760–1815

There are processes similar to those we have seen in the Suisse Romande to be found at work in the core of the Old Confederation, after the French invasion, and throughout the periods of constitutional change in 1803, the Regeneration of the 1830s and the revolutionary 1840s. There was the same need to forge a new national identity, to accommodate to or else revise the new Federal Constitution, to pick up the threads of cantonal politics interrupted by the Napoleonic epoch and also to take bearings vis-à-vis the cultural and political magnetism of a larger entity – in this case, a still disunited Germany. If anything the pull was potentially stronger, as well as qualitatively different, than that exercised by Paris on the Suisse Romande, for some German patriots believed that the Swiss should be subsumed in a united Germany. But this view met with no real response in Switzerland, and the question of how a writer related to German culture outside the Swiss frontiers was answered on an individual basis. Indeed, by the second half of the nineteenth century, the German Swiss were making the most distinguished contribution to German writing as a whole, in a way reminiscent of Bodmer and his pupils in the eighteenth century.

Alongside the political developments affecting the whole Confederation there remained equally strong instincts of *Kantonligeist* or localism, and in cultural terms this counteracted the magnetism of the other German-speaking lands during their political, economic and cultural evolution. What mattered to Burckhardt, for example, was how he related to his home city, Basel, and then how this fitted in with his attachment to the new Germany of the 1840s, and with his passion for Italy. This differentiated and localized texture to Swiss life makes generalization extremely difficult. It remains true to say that cultural life tended still to be the preserve of the landed and professional elites, to be concentrated in places such as Basel, with its old and distinguished University, or Zürich, by the mid-nineteenth century to become the financial centre of the Confederation; and also within the ecclesiastical structure – the rural parsonage as well as the theological faculties. Publishing opportunities were plentiful and there was a good standard of literacy. The frequency of political change between 1800 and 1850, however, could also mean that constitutional issues and party politics often took precedence over artistic preoccupations. The issues vary from canton to canton, but Hughes has suggested as typical the pattern of

(i) Restoration of a modified old regime in 1813; (ii) Liberal *coup d'état* in 1830–31; (iii) Conservative *coup*, with a lower level of violence, 1837–41; (iv) Transition back to liberalism at an election; (v) Radical rioting threatening a *coup*, followed by a radical victory, 1844–49; (vi) Radical rule with federal backing, 1848–54; (vii) Short period of conservative or liberal rule, accompanied by gesture of accommodation to the radicals, such as the offer of a ministry and a place on the executive council.[22]

Church, writing of the 1830s, has stressed the tensions between urban centres in the cantons where in many cases the old patriciate had managed to recapture its dominance to the detriment of their rural hinterlands, resulting in a pattern of efforts to better the political balance between town and country and make strides toward more directly based popular democracy. Thus the Réveil or Regeneration was seen quite literally as an attempt to restore even older constitutional procedures held to be part of the historical tradition of each canton.[23]

This accent on restoration rather than innovation in political life had also been the keynote of Enlightened political reform. As in the Suisse Romande, the roots of Swiss-wide patriotic feeling are to be found in this period, and are by no means just a response to the experience of being a Napoleonic client-state. In 1762 the Helvetic Society had been formed by intellectuals from Basel, Berne, Lucerne and Zürich, including Bodmer, Lavater and Pestalozzi. Its aim was to nurture a sense of Swiss identity and to regenerate political life, correcting the tendency toward oligarchy; and to accomplish this, it looked, in a manner typical of Enlightened change, to the education of public opinion, and the transformation of sentiments within the ruling elite, rather than to structural political reform.

Given the vested interests of the cliques in power, little was achieved in political terms; yet just as the Revolution in France gave political opportunity to the kind of Enlightened provincial who had become a deputy to the Estates-General, so the French invasion of 1798 gave a similar chance to the Helvetic Society's members, who, instead of convening for their annual meeting, found themselves assembling instead as a legislative assembly for the first Helvetic Republic.

The most distinguished intellectual fruitage of the trends which had given birth to the Society was the work of the great and indefatigable historian, Johannes von Müller, of Schaffhausen, whose work shows affinities with the Enlightenment, but also points toward the Romantic movement in a way that is characteristic of this transitional generation. It was Müller who finally rehabilitated Tell as a noble freedom fighter; up to the eighteenth century the Swiss had not been able to approve of this rebel from the lower orders. Müller took the Rütli oath and the Tell legend as sober history, weaving them into a serious account of the origins of the Confederation in resistance to Austrian Habsburg aggression, and its authority as history was enhanced by Müller's sterling labours in archival sources. Scholarship was, however, balanced by set-piece narrative descriptions, which were later to be admired by French historians such as Michelet. Müller's was no narrow patriotism, however, and his account of Swiss liberty was seen in the tradition of Classical Republicanism (as well as expressing Biblical virtues), a perception shared by his young admirer, Sismondi. Not surprisingly for a native of Schaffhausen, most of Müller's career was spent outside the Confederation, in Berlin, and later as an administrator for King Jerome of Westphalia; but it was Bodmer's circle of pupils in Zürich who facilitated the publication of his *magnum opus*: Fuseli urged it on, and Heinrich Gessner (Salomon Gessner's son and Wieland's son-in-law) actually published the first volume in 1786.[24] It was from Müller that Schiller derived his account of the Tell story. Thus the epic myth of heroic national resistance to tyranny was launched into the wider German-speaking world, soon to be ripe for ousting the French occupation.

Not all Swiss patriots were natives of the Confederation. Müller's successor as eulogist and historian of the Swiss experience was Heinrich Zschokke (1771–1848), who found Swiss liberty more to his liking than Prussian conformity. His Radical views having proved a hindrance to academic advancement in his native Prussia, he settled in the Aarau region and enjoyed a successful career as an administrator under the Directory and then after the Napoleonic mediation, when he became Director of Forests and Mines, a position which left him plenty of free time for journalism. Before settling down in this way Zschokke had wandered around Europe for a while, and written a Gothic melodrama, *Abellino*, the Grand Bandit (1795). This was translated into English by 'Monk' Lewis (1805) as, effectively, his second novel, and is a reminder that Switzerland, one way and another, played quite a part in the 'Gothic' genre, from Deyverdun arranging the publication of Beckford's *Vathek* at Lausanne in 1786, to that stormy summer evening on the shores of Lake Geneva in 1816, when Shelley, Byron and Polidori began to tell ghost stories and Mary Shelley's subsequent nightmare begat *Frankenstein*. He was, it will be recalled, 'by birth a Genevese, and my family is one of the most distinguished of that republic'. All the more horrific that a family such as this – Mary Shelley maybe had the Pictets in mind as a model – should have brought forth such a social outcast!

Zschokke already had an interest in Switzerland before his move, having written on the complex history of the Graubünden (*A History of the Rhaetian League*, 1790); in addition to other cantonal studies he wrote an immensely popular *History of Switzerland for the Swiss People* (1822 and many subsequent editions). Zschokke believed the Swiss needed a greater awareness of being part of the Confederation as a whole, while retaining a respect for and interest in their cantonal identity, and he worked tirelessly as a journalist to this end, founding in 1803 the widely circulating *The Sincere and Well Experienced Swiss Messenger*, and urging Stappfer, the first Swiss Minister of Education and the Arts, to create a Swiss University. Both men were strongly influenced by the pedagogical ideals of Pestalozzi, who believed in contrast to either Jacobins or Conservatives that the individual needed protection from the State's encroachments, however public-spirited and patriotic he might be. This mistrust of the

State belongs unequivocally to Enlightened liberalism, and was emphatically shared by Benjamin Constant and the Coppet circle. Yet unlike the Coppet group, Zschokke was dedicated to the modernizing role of the Enlightenment within a specifically Swiss context. He welcomed the end of feudalism and deplored the Restoration Constitution, which he regarded as illiberal; the revised Constitution of 1848 was to represent what he and other liberals worked for. This contrasts with Mme de Staël's footdragging over the idea of the liberation of the Vaud; it did not escape Republicans there that she was not at all keen to lose her seigneurial income. 'Let them have anything they want except the suppression of the feudal dues' she said, à propos LaHarpe's projected French 'liberation'.[25] Culturally and politically she was too much of a snob to immerse herself in Swiss affairs; she wanted political influence in *La Grande Nation*, and was piqued that Napoleon had no time for her pretensions.

Zschokke, then, was a liberal, and a Swiss patriot by adoption, whose appreciation of the diversity of the Swiss historical tradition was nourished by an imaginative sympathy similar to that of the Bodmer school. He could be classified as pre-Romantic rather than Romantic. Yet, another facet to his career provides a link of a personal kind to the German Romantic movement, for it was the friendship between himself and Heinrich Kleist which was partly responsible for bringing Kleist to Switzerland, in pursuit of Rousseauesque withdrawal to a pastoral idyll. The literary and moral encouragement Zschokke's circle gave this enigmatic genius was invaluable during a formative period of Kleist's artistic development.[26]

PATRIOTISM, NEUTRALITY AND LINGUISTIC PLURALISM THROUGHOUT THE CONFEDERATION, C. 1815–48

Both Müller and Zschokke had been concerned with providing the German-speaking world with an account of Switzerland's past, as a means of encouraging a sense of Swiss nationhood. In the Restoration era it was Charles Monnard (1790–1865) of Lausanne who translated both men into French, and who collaborated on a continuation of Müller's work, thus enlarging the tradition to incorporate the Suisse Romande readership. Monnard was a founder member of the Société d'Histoire de la Suisse Romande, and also belonged to the Helvetic Society, which was revived in 1819. The Société Suisse de Récherches Historiques had been founded in 1811 and the Federal Rifle Club in 1824; these, the enthusiasm for choral singing already discussed, and other learned societies and popular clubs, all tried to foster patriotism, both under the Napoleonic Constitution of 1803, and the politically more conservative Constitution of 1815. Another focus for patriotism was the celebrations of the tercentenary of the Reformation; this brought into being, for example, the Zoffingen Society, begun in 1819 to link together Swiss-German students; Bitzius (who will shortly be discussed) was an early member. Nonetheless, the idea of a Swiss nation meant very different things, according to which epoch is being considered, which canton, and which group within the canton. Liberals like Monnard and Zschokke deplored the attempts of the old elites after 1815 to return to their pre-eminent position, and worked for the kinds of revision that were accomplished under duress in the Regeneration period (c. 1828–33). In conservative Lucerne, the massacre of the Swiss Guard on 10 August 1792 was commemorated by Thorvaldsen's Lion of Lucerne monument, erected in 1821; but while this commemorated Swiss losses, it was also a homage to Ancien Régime society.[27]

While liberals in and out of Switzerland could model their programmes on the ideas of Benjamin Constant (the leading spokesman after 1816 for the opposition to Bourbon legitimism), and also on their own interpretation of their particular cantonal tradition, conservatives and legitimists in the Confederation and elsewhere could look to the ideas of another Swiss, the Bernese patrician Karl Ludwig von Haller (1768–1854). Grandson of the great scientist and conservative politician Albrecht von Haller, he looked back to the kind of aristocratic and benevolent hierarchy that had dominated Berne before the French invasion – in other words to men like Charles von Bonstetten, whom he regarded as a natural ruling elite. He believed authority in society to be divinely based, and inequality to be a function of social differentiation. Ideas such as these, expressed in his *Restauration der Staatswissenschaften* (1817), were music to the ears of men like Metternich, already successfully pressurizing the Confederation to adhere to the Holy Alliance; the book, in a sense, gave Restoration Europe its programme. But actually Haller was also a critic of the expansionism of large states; he had a Swiss respect for small political units, which he regarded as more natural. But this in its turn raised the problem of isolation; for him, the solution was to be received into the Catholic Church, which took place in 1820.[28]

While this may assimilate Haller to the group of conservative political thinkers which includes de Maistre and the Schlegels, and is a contrast to the secular liberalism of Constant and others, who believed in Church–State separation, it is important not to overestimate the differences between the two schools of thought. For the liberals were not democrats, and after the turmoil around 1830, found themselves at variance with Radicals for whom constitutional concessions had been insufficient and who had, like their counterparts in England, social and religious grievances: to take but two examples, in 1845 Olivier left the Vaud in the wake of Radical triumph, and Vinet led a breakaway movement in the

Church because he was critical of what he regarded as political interference with the Church by the new government.[29]

Something of the complexity of these cross-currents can also be seen by
looking at the fortunes of the Tell myth in iconography and ideology. As
we have already seen, it took until the eighteenth century for Tell to
acquire ideological respectability, but he was then regarded as quintessentially Swiss. In 1760, a pamphlet appeared arguing that the Tell story was
really of Danish origin (a thesis which has regained credence in modern
times); a formal protest by the canton of Uri caused the pamphlet to be
banned and burnt. Later, Fuseli's portrait of Tell was seen as a symbol of
Enlightened Republicanism, awakening political life from its torpor and
correcting abuses: Bodmer cited Tell as an exemplar of civic virtue in his
lectures, and the pamphlet which had occasioned Lavater and Fuseli's
departure from Zürich lamented that Switzerland no longer produced men
like Tell.

In the French Revolution, Marat, who was of Swiss origin, could claim
to be Tell's spiritual descendant; French propaganda efforts in Basel and
the Vaud, directed toward encouraging these territories to overthrow their
German-Swiss rulers, made great play of Tell's example in challenging
Austrian interference. After the Helvetic Republic was instituted, Tell's
image became an emblem on all official documents, seals and coins. But
reactionaries who hated French interference in Swiss affairs could equally
well employ the same image for different emotive purposes – as a true-born
Swiss opposing the dragon of the Revolution, for example. After 1815, a
William Tell figure was routinely present in pageants and open-air fêtes;
Keller portrays this type of celebration in his *Der grüne Heinrich*. Tell was
pictured in classical guise, in sentimental Biedermeier mode as an earnest
paterfamilias, or as a dashing Byronic type.

In addition this symbol of national patriotism (however interpreted)
was appropriated by liberation struggles elsewhere. In Geneva, in the
1820s, there was a strong current of Philhellenism, led and generously
financed by a banker, Gabriel Eynard; in Missolonghi, one of the bastions
in the siege was named Byron, another William Tell. His symbol was used
by Kossuth's supporters in Hungary; and by Carlo Cattaneo, a Ticinese by
adoption and the leader of Milanese resistance to Austria. Just as the
mountain scenery represented independence to the native Swiss but
picturesque beauty to the tourist, so Tell was transposed into different
contexts by the exiles who now began to settle in its boundaries.[30]

Switzerland's neutral status meant that after 1815 it had to cope with
the backwash of some of the movements for national unity, especially
those in Germany and Italy, whose ideals were often based on linguistic
considerations. The presence of political refugees made the country as a

whole the target of political interference from Austria, Russia and France, who resented this right of asylum. This was a potent stimulus to defending a conception of national identity based on historical development and political rights – the conception I have characterized as a liberal Romantic one as distinct from a *völkisch* Romantic one – even, or especially, when the movements in Germany and Italy put pressure on Swiss-German or Swiss-Italian sensibilities. These contrasts are illustrated by the Swiss reactions to the presence of Mazzini, the arch political Romantic of the mystical, cultural, linguistic type.

Mazzini fled from Genoa in 1831 and lived clandestinely on the border between Geneva and Piedmont-Savoy, directing the activities of his secret insurrectionary movement, Young Italy. Believing in the historical role of the Italians, Poles and Germans, he also organized Young Europe, to focus the energies of the exiles from the failed movements of 1830, while Young Switzerland was founded to cajole Switzerland out of its neutrality in the conflict which Mazzini believed would soon convulse Europe. While there was some sympathy among Swiss liberals for the plight of subjected peoples, few Swiss wished to see Switzerland's neutrality compromised or the country turned into a convenient location for fomenting violent attacks on their neighbours. Mazzini's antics, such as the farcical attack on Savoy, were deplored by Jacques Fazy of Geneva, the editor, in the 1830s, of *Europe Centrale*, and his counterpart in the Vaud, Henri Druey, editor of the *Nouvelliste Vaudois*, neither of them conservatives, and both later active as Radicals in the 1840s; Fazy was one of the revisers of the Federal Constitution. But to Mazzini, Fazy was a soulless secular materialist, virtually a socialist, with no mystic faith in the regeneration of a people through a confidence in its national genius.

If Piedmont-Sardinia resented the antics of Mazzini, France felt equally sensitive about the presence of Louis Napoleon in Thun, and the conflict over French demands to expel him brought the country to the brink of war – a situation relieved only when Napoleon left of his own accord in 1838. On the whole Switzerland was able to maintain her facility for asylum amidst these buffetings. Two other exiles should be mentioned: the great Polish patriot and Romantic poet, Mickiewicz, who was visiting Professor at Lausanne from 1838 to 1839, and whose *Lausanne Lyrics* were his last published poems; and Alexander Herzen, the great Russian liberal, who stayed in Switzerland on first leaving Russia in 1847. When he had been arrested by the Tsarist police, the fact that Schiller's *William Tell* had been among his books had put him in a most unfavourable light.

It might be expected that as the demands for Italian and German unification grew stronger, there would have been Italian- or German-speaking Swiss who responded to the demand that political entities mirror linguistic distribution more accurately, and who therefore pressed for secession. But this did not really happen while the Romantic movement was at its height. Italian received equal linguistic status within the Republic in 1798 because the Italian-speaking districts of Lugano and Bellinzona, which linguistically and geographically were a part of Lombardy, elected to stay 'free and Swiss' and join the new Helvetic Republic as Canton Ticino, thereby losing their previous status as subject territories of the Old Confederation. The incentive for this was that their previous association had kept the area out of the conflicts of the Lombardy plain; historical experience of settled conditions and benign neglect meant more than linguistic sentiment, or even geographical convenience. In contrast the Italian-speaking areas of the Graubünden welcomed union with the Cisalpine Republic in 1797; their treatment as subject territories had been less happy. In the constitutional discussions in 1815, the Graubünden failed to treat the Italian-speakers of the Valtellina more generously, so it remained part of Austrian Lombardy.

There were Germans outside the Confederation who, as the movement to eject Napoleon from mediatized Germany and the satellite kingdoms gained momentum, thought that Switzerland should join with them in shedding its dependence on France. But Napoleon's mediation in Switzerland had helped to restore cantonal identities for which the Swiss had been pressing, while fostering stronger federal institutions than the Old Confederation had possessed. As in other areas where the Napoleonic occupation had hastened the abolition of feudalism, there were Swiss who had gained from the end of the Ancien Régime. When the constitution was revised there was no question of joining in with the new German arrangements. Thus, the leading Swiss-German writers between 1803 and c. 1848 tended to feel culturally German in the wider sense while being, politically, citizens of their canton and of the Confederation as a whole. This often prompted questions of national identity, but the questions were answered in each individual's way. The same individualism is evident in their lack of self-consciousness toward literary schools and movements. John Peter Hebel (1760–1826), for example, is regarded as the foremost dialect writer of this period. A poor boy from Basel, he rose to eminence in the Protestant Church in Baden. His poems in the South Swabian dialect were acclaimed by the literary stars of Germany – Goethe, Jacobi, Jean Paul. The Romantics' taste for folk tradition meant that his poems obtained a readership among highbrow intellectuals that they otherwise might not have done; but Hebel wrote them as an unpremeditated gesture of affection for the homeland which narrow circumstances had forced him to leave, not because he was a Romantic following Herder or the Grimm brothers in preserving localized culture. Similar considerations would apply to the short stories of Ulrich Hegner of Winterthur (1759–1840) or the dialect poems of John Martin Usteri of Zürich (1763–1827).[31]

SWISS-GERMAN WRITERS AND THE CLOSE OF THE ROMANTIC MOVEMENT

It is as difficult to determine the end of the Romantic movement as it is to determine its beginnings with precision. It is clear for example that such movements such as Dada or Surrealism, with their desire to shock the bourgeoisie, are direct descendants of Romanticism, as are Expressionism, or Art Nouveau, or the Arts and Crafts movement – which in turn cannot be understood without reference to Ruskin's and Morris' Romantic socialism. Granted, there is a distinct movement towards Realism in the arts and literature in the middle of the nineteenth century which challenges Romantic aesthetics, but Romanticism persisted as a formative influence and it is not easy to mark the point where it ends, and the Modern Movement in the arts begins.

German-speaking Switzerland is no exception to this 'untidiness'. None of the three towering figures of mid-century literature and letters, Gotthelf, Burckhardt and Keller, can be easily categorized as Romantics, yet the formative years of each was affected by the movement, and each had also to situate themselves in relation to German culture as well as to their Swiss citizenship and cantonal affiliation. And just as the first stirrings of a new approach to literature had come from Zürich in the 1740s, so it is in its café society at the end of the century that the Romanian exile, Tristan Tzara, helped to define the credo of Dada (and later in Paris, of Surrealism). The reason why the banking and textile centre of Switzerland had spawned such an avant-garde movement cannot be explored within the limits of this essay; though obviously Switzerland's nineteenth-century role as a place of asylum meant that it continued to provide a milieu where artistic and linguistic mediations could be transacted. To conclude this discussion with the ways in which Gotthelf, Burckhardt and Keller came to terms with the legacy of German Romantic literature and philosophy marks only a stage at which the attractions of Romanticism begin to weaken; but in many respects the artist or writer today is still operating in the field of force defined by Romantic aesthetics and bourgeois social dynamics, and the movement does not end conveniently in the 1850s.

Albert Bitzius (1797–1854), better known by his pseudonym, Jeremias Gotthelf, was a pastor and pastor's son from the Emmenthal. He knew the peasant farmer's life intimately, for each parsonage possessed some glebe land for the pastor's use; this knowledge of rural ways, together with a deepening Christian vision, shaped his work, which he saw as an extension of his pastoral and educational role. As a student Gotthelf had read Scott in translation, the writings of Herder and the ballads of Bürger and Schiller, and was a devotee of Müller's history. Later he planned a cycle of legendary and historical stories, not all of which were completed, but at least one, *Die schwarze Spinne*, is an absolute masterpiece of the genre. A plague-story involving a pact with the devil, it is grounded in the naturalistic depiction of a contemporary village christening, where one of the guests recounts the legend of the Black Spider associated with the farmhouse nearby. And it was in stories with a contemporary setting depicting the changing Bernese rural world that Gotthelf really found his vocation as a writer and moralist, not in the Romantic mode; in his humour and vivid characterization he has been compared with Dickens, or, in terms of the moral grandeur with which he invests the lives of 'ordinary' folk, with Tolstoi. In his self-appointed role of conscience to traditional Bernese rural society, he can be likened to the Danish nationalist poet and pastor, Nikolai F. S. Grundtvig, while his critique of mass industrial society would suggest an English parallel with Ruskin, who indeed admired his work and tried to get it translated, or with Carlyle. Gotthelf had been a supporter of liberal reforms during the Regeneration period, but the economic and social dislocations associated with the onset of industrialization, together with the development of Radical mass political movements in the 1840s, alarmed him as much as they alarmed Carlyle, and he became a spokesman for the traditional, rural and patriarchal values. Although Gotthelf experienced these in a very specific context, and portrayed the idiom and customs of the Emmenthal as accurately as Hardy portrayed his native Wessex, the changes to which he was reacting were happening or would happen throughout Europe.[32]

Unique though his artistic achievement was, shaped by his role as a country clergyman in the Bernese Oberland, Gotthelf's outlook can thus be assimilated to a more widespread late-Romantic critique of industrial society. Another pastor's son who was originally destined for the ministry is better known than Gotthelf outside Switzerland for his pessimism about the future of Old Europe in the wake of industrial advance, but the differences between Bitzius and Jacob Burckhardt (1818–97) are greater than their similarities. These differences are in part those of the differences between the Bernese Oberland and the canton of Basel City. Basel had adhered to the Old Confederation in 1501, when it was already an eminent Ecclesiastical City, like Mainz or Cologne, ruled by a Prince-Bishop. Its University, founded in 1460, was the oldest in Switzerland, and from its earliest days was distinguished for its humanist studies: Erasmus and the printer Froben had started their publication of the pagan and scriptural classics in Basel. Occupying a key Rhine crossing-point it was geographically a natural trading centre, and from the Reformation it had been ruled by a patriciate whose origins were in sixteenth-century Protestant immigration. A little detached from the rest of Switzerland, its genius during the Enlightenment had tended to flower in the direction of science rather than the humanities.

Burckhardt's father was not, like Bitzius', a rural pastor, but Dean of the Cathedral, and, again unlike the Bitzius family, which had declined in influence (though the father was still a citizen of Berne), the Burckhardts remained eminent within the patriciate. Growing up in the shadow of the cathedral with its Dance of Death images, Burckhardt early cultivated a sense of the transitoriness and frailty of human life, but this was counterbalanced by the serenity, confidence and detachment imparted by his family tradition. Originally destined by his family for the Church, Burckhardt's faith had faded under the impact of German liberal theology and the controversy in Zürich surrounding the appointment of David Strauss to its new University. Instead he went in 1839 to Germany to study history, where he was strongly attracted to its emergent nationalism. He wrote to a friend in 1841: 'I want to devote my life to showing the Swiss that they are German.'[33]

The idea of culture he acquired at this point was indebted to Romanticism: his teacher, A. Boeckh, a pupil of Hegel, adhered to the notion of each period possessing its own logic of development, and each cultural entity, its own informing spirit or *Geist*. Like many another Romantic intellectual, Burckhardt felt alienated from the excessively staid and bourgeois Basel to which he returned, while his experience of Berlin had also given him a lasting distaste for emergent mass society, with its symbols of the mass-barracks, apartment block and factory. He was appalled at the Radical disturbances of the 1840s, when the proposal to turn the venerable University into a trade school was one of the factors which drove him despairingly away from his role in public life as a journalist. In such a mood, he was ripe to find solace in, and an enduring obsession with, the art and culture of Italy.

Yet in the end Burckhardt found a resolution to the tensions of being Swiss, in a distinctively Swiss way. His final position was one of patrician resignation and detachment from mundane political involvement, coupled with deep attachment to his birthplace, where he settled permanently in 1858, refusing all offers to move elsewhere, and restricting his hope for any influence to the audiences of his lectures and the readers of his books. He lived in an unpretentious fashion, cultivated the Basel dialect, and had already published a volume of melancholy love poetry in it. His vision of the human predicament and his diagnosis of the ills of his age has been compared with Kierkegaard's, while his sense of culture as a barrier to Philistinism resembles Matthew Arnold's; but surely Burckhardt's historical sense of man in variation and sameness, of universality and yet diversity, is one that would come naturally to a Swiss?

Burckhardt's patrician resignation was not achieved without a struggle, for his was an ardent temperament. His contemporary Gottfried Keller (1819–90), on the other hand, was able to resolve the tensions between being Swiss and being German into a more positive civic role, although having made a mess of his schooling he received his real education in Germany, first in Munich, then after a period home in Zürich, in Heidelberg and Berlin. But for Keller, the cultural pull of Germany was not so distracting as it had been for Burckhardt; Germany was the wider cultural homeland, but politically he was a Swiss and a Zürichois. He had no time for mystical or ethnic notions of identity, writing 'Swiss national character does not rest on ancestors nor on patriotic sagas of the country's past nor on anything material; it rests on the Swiss people's love of freedom, on their unique attachment to their small but beautiful and dear fatherland, on the home-sickness which seizes them even in the loveliest foreign lands.' He added that if a foreigner felt politically more at home in Switzerland, this qualified him to feel and to be Swiss more than the question of whether his ancestors had fought at Sempach.[34] He would have thoroughly understood the choices Zschokke had made.

Keller is usually regarded as a writer in the tradition of nineteenth-century Realism, but just as Gotthelf's Naturalism is deepened by his Christian moral vision, Keller's Realism is suffused with a sense of poetry. His greatest work, *Der grüne Heinrich* (1854–5), is indebted to the German Romantic tradition of the Bildungsroman; though it is not as inventive formally as some of these novels, it echoes their theme of the quest for personal and artistic identity. The novel needless to say is based on Keller's experience; he had found the choice between painting and writing a taxing one and had taken years to get into his stride. A child of modest origins, his father being a skilled wood-carver who had married slightly above himself, in his maturity he enjoyed the most distinguished society Zürich had to offer, including the friendship of Liszt's son-in-law, Richard Wagner, whose work he admired, and another composer, Wilhelm Baumgartner, who set Keller's patriotic poem *An das Vaterland* to music. But Keller was not just acclaimed among the Swiss. As Steinberg has pointed out[35] his written German was purer than that of his Prussian contemporary, Theodor Fontane. The esteem in which Keller, Gotthelf and later writers such as Spitteler were held meant that until the flowering of German and Austrian writing at the turn of the century, German-Swiss writers were taking the lead set by Bodmer and his pupils a century before.

Keller also solved the dilemma, felt by many German Romantics, posed by the competing pressures of bourgeois life, and artistic vocation. He received cantonal financial support for the completion of his education, and after he had established himself as a writer he spent fifteen years as

Cantonal Secretary (1861–76), which was no sinecure, resigning in order to complete his final tasks as a writer. Thus the smaller and more intimate scale of cantonal life could make it easier for a variety of roles to be integrated within one personality, in a way that was becoming increasingly impossible in the nineteenth-century national state, with its dehumanizing scale. Romantic alienation and Romantic political attachment were not exclusive choices but simply part of the evolution of a personality.[36]

CONCLUSION

The decentralized nature of German cultural life and the strong cultural traditions prevailing in its several centres of learning, politics and commerce, meant that Swiss-German writers were as likely as any other writer in German to acquire esteem without the stigma of provincialism. By contrast in France, the predominance of Paris over the provinces tended to inflict an inferiority complex over all non-Parisians, including the writers of the Suisse Romande. In France itself, the reaction of those areas that had suffered cultural marginalization was that they became fairly programmatic and aggressive, as witness the demands made by the Félibrigge circle for the recognition of Provençal as a distinct language. In contrast with the cultural hegemony exercized by French speakers within the French State since at least the seventeenth century, there was a far more sympathetic attitude taken by the Swiss Federal government when Romansch speakers started to demand equal recognition in the Confederation. Within seven years of a campaign for status as an official language, the goal was achieved (1938); in the process, many of the strategies familiar in this kind of Romantic, linguistic, nationalism, such as the compilation of glossaries and the composition of a national epic, play a predictable role. The particular nature of the Swiss civic tradition meant that this kind of diversity could be provided for peacefully; unlike their Breton-speaking counterparts, Romansch-speaking schoolchildren were not shamed or penalized for speaking their native tongue.

The mediatory role of Switzerland during the pre-Romantic period also has its counterpart for the second and third generation of the Romantic movement, as it merges into Symbolism and Expressionism, notably in the oeuvre of Ferdinand Hodler (1851–1918). This great painter was of German-Swiss origin but spent most of his career in Geneva, where as a young man he associated with a little group of Symbolists. At the close of his career he was hailed by both Viennese and Berlin Secessionists as a seminal influence. Current revaluations of the contribution of Northern Romanticism to the visual arts are enabling a fresh appreciation of Hodler's stature and distinctive contribution to be made. And there are continuities too with the Zürich circle with which this essay began; for Hodler's reputation was first established with *Night*, whose theme and imagery resembles Fuseli's equally controversial *The Nightmare*. He was often indebted to Blake for his sense of composition, and Blake in turn acknowledged the inspiration of Fuseli.[37]

Both at the beginning and end of Romanticism proper, then, the Swiss situation has been a fruitful source of new directions, as well as showing in the period when nationalistic Romanticism held sway that an alternative, liberal and pluralist sense of culture and national identity was feasible. Moreover, in his love–hate relationship with the confines of the homeland and the search for significant identity, the Swiss artist can be seen to have prefigured the dilemmas of the twentieth century. Adolf Muschg has suggested that in this century, 'with the universal threat of the arms race, destruction of the environment, overpopulation, the economic divide between North and South, there is nothing quaint any more about being Swiss'.[38] In the post-Romantic and post-Modern age, we may be in a better position to give the Swiss Romantic experience its due.

ACKNOWLEDGEMENTS

I would like to acknowledge the help of various friends and colleagues in the preparation of this essay: Dr Clive H. Church of The University of Kent; Dr Jonathan Steinberg of Trinity Hall, Cambridge; Dr T. C. W. Blanning of Sidney Sussex College, Cambridge; Mrs E. Stopp of Girton College, Cambridge; Dr N. Rupke of Wolfson College, Oxford; Dr Paul McHugh of Cambridgeshire College of Arts and Technology; Guus Peek of Utrecht University; Dr Theodora Zemek; Dr A. M. C. Brown; Dr Robert Wokler of Manchester University; and last, but by no means least, my two editors. Particular appreciation is also due to technical staff in the School of Modern Languages and the Computer Centre of Cambridgeshire College of Arts and Technology, for generous assistance in the production of the text.

POSTSCRIPT

While this book was in press, Virgil Nemoianu's book, *The Taming of Romanticism: European Literature and the Age of Biedermeier* (Harvard, Cambridge, Mass., 1984), came to my attention. His discussion of period dynamics and his extension of the term Biedermeier to encompass the culture and society of the Restoration Period, c. 1815–48, is subtle, penetrating and illuminating for the problems of periodization I have touched on in my essay. Though regrettably he overlooks the case of Switzerland as such, assimilating the Coppet circle to France and Keller and Gotthelf to Germany, his discussion would apply particularly well to the timing and character of developments in Switzerland, which could almost be seen as the Biedermeier culture par excellence in his application of the term.

NOTES

1 Among many other discussions see Lillian Furst, *Romanticism in Perspective* (2nd edn, London, 1979); and Hugh Honour, *Romanticism* (London, 1979).

2 This is not to deny that Romanticism, especially during the Restoration period, often fostered conversion to Catholicism; Karl Ludwig von Haller is an example who will be discussed below. But in its formative period Romanticism shared with Protestantism the appeal to subjective and individual judgement and there seems to have been a correlation between a Protestant background and a rejection of French cultural influence. This is a point raised by both Henri Brunschwig, *Enlightenment and Romanticism in Eighteenth Century Prussia*, English translation (Chicago, 1974); and Peter Hans Reill, *The German Enlightenment and the Rise of Historicism* (Berkeley, 1975).

3 Jean-André Deluc (1727–1817) illustrates some of the difficulties presented by trying to place a character within conventional periodization. He was a friend of Rousseau, and in a sense his disciple in idealizing unspoilt rural simplicity in his topographical and geological writings, but equally he was a critic of Rousseau's Deism and attributed it to the malign influence of the Encyclopédists on him. He can be aligned both with the first phase of pre-Romanticism and with the Christian Enlightenment characteristic of Protestant culture in Geneva, Lausanne, Northern Germany, The Netherlands and England. This concept is explored more fully in the companion volume to this series, *The Enlightenment in National Context*, ed. R. Porter and M. Teich (Cambridge, 1981). Deluc played a leading role in the political disturbances in Geneva in the 1760s which are typical of Enlightened attempts to reform oligarchies and can be paralleled elsewhere in Switzerland; see my later comments on Fuseli, and the aims of the Helvetic Society. But Deluc also lived to witness the French Revolution from his vantage point as Reader to Queen Charlotte in England, to make a small contribution in the formation of the Second Coalition against Napoleon, to assist Zimmermann (q.v.) in the preparation of his book arguing the Revolution to be a Masonic conspiracy, and to be the mentor of the Dutch Romantic Bilderdijk, discussed by Nicholas Rupke in his essay in this volume. Longevity turned him from being an Enlightened liberal with sentimental tendencies to being almost a Romantic legitimist. As a geologist he also had a formative influence on 'Catastrophist' theories that can be viewed as Romantic geology. He would have deplored Byron's morals but one of the last glimpses we have of the elderly Deluc is provided by Fanny Burney, recording his homesick interest in Byron's poem *The Prisoner of Chillon*.

4 See Jonathan Steinberg, *Why Switzerland?* (Cambridge, 1976), p. 1.

5 Eudo C. Mason, *The Mind of Henry Fuseli* (London, 1951), p. 14.

6 Reill, *The German Enlightenment*; see also Samuel S. B. Taylor, 'The

Enlightenment in Switzerland', in *The Enlightenment in National Context*, ed. Porter and Teich.

7 See N. Powell, *The Nightmare* (Harmondsworth, 1973).

8 See R. Darnton, *Mesmerism and the End of Enlightenment in France* (Harvard, 1968).

9 See, Roy Porter, 'Making faces: physiognomy and fashion in eighteenth century England', *Etudes Anglaises*, 38 (1985), 385–96; and G. Tytler, *Physiognomy in the European Novel* (Princeton, 1982).

10 See S. A. Tissot, *The Life of J. G. Zimmermann*, English translation (London, 1797).

11 See Harold Nicolson, *Benjamin Constant* (London, 1949), p. 116, and Geoffrey Scott, *The Portrait of Zélide* (London, 1925).

12 See Pierre Kohler, *Mme de Staël et La Suisse* (Lausanne and Paris, 1916).

13 See J. Christopher Herold, *Mistress to an Age* (London, 1959), p. 279.

14 See Susan Tennenbaum, 'The Coppet circle: literary criticism as political discourse', *History of Political Theory*, 1 (1980), 453–74; and Theodora Zemek, 'Mme de Staël and the theory of progress; Scottish social theory in France' (unpub. Cambridge PhD, 1985).

15 See Stephen Holmes, *Benjamin Constant and the Making of Modern Liberalism* (New Haven, 1984). I do not wish to give the impression that this form of liberalism was exactly new. In many ways it derives from the tradition of 'civic humanism' and Classical Republicanism given currency in the Renaissance most notably by Machiavelli; furthered and modified by Rousseau's reinterpretation of Republicanism; and also by Montesquieu and Delolme, the Genevan commentator on the English 'mixed' constitution. The Romantic contribution was to enrich the historical account of this liberal tradition, as well as to adapt theory to the post-Revolutionary age.

16 Tennenbaum, 'The Coppet circle'.

17 Didier's fortunes fluctuated after leaving Geneva. He travelled in Italy and had great success with his novel *Rome souterraine*, an 'inside' view of the underground political movements. His passion for George Sand left him unrequited and disconsolate but he married an heiress and prospered for a while. His later writing met with less acclaim; his eyesight, which had always been weak, failed entirely; and his wife left him. A Republican in the days of his association with Sand, he became an adherent at the end of his life of the legitimist claimant to the French throne, the Comte de Chambord. He took his own life in 1864. See André Maurois, *Lélia, the Life of George Sand*, English translation (London, 1953).

18 For a discussion of Geneva in the Romantic era see Henri Bochet, *Le Romantisme à Genève* (Geneva, 1930), to which the above account is indebted.

19 For Sainte-Beuve and the Oliviers, see Harold Nicolson, *Sainte-Beuve* (London, 1957).

20 Similarly the Liberal Archduke Johann was sponsoring the collection and appreciation of Steierian and Tyrolean folk-music, song, yodelling, etc., as Dr Jonathan Steinberg has kindly informed me.

21 For the literary culture of the Suisse Romande, see Virgile Rossel, *Histoire littéraire de la Suisse Romande des origines à nos jours*, 2 vols. (Geneva, 1889–91).

22 See Christopher Hughes, *Switzerland* (London, 1975), pp. 229–30.

23 See Clive H. Church, *Europe in 1830* (London, 1983), pp. 57–69.

24 *Die Geschichten Schweizerischer Eidgenossenschaft*, first full edition, 5 vols. (Leipzig and Zurich, 1806–8).

25 Cited by Herold, *Mistress to an Age*, p. 176.

26 Joachim Maas, *Kleist, a Biography*, English translation (London, 1983).

27 Church, *Europe in 1830*, provides a useful summary of the Regeneration in its cantonal variations.

28 Haller's relationship to the Restoration period is discussed by H. Kohn, *Nationalism and Liberty: the Swiss Example* (London, 1956); and F. Meinecke, *Cosmopolitanism and the National State*, English translation (Princeton, 1970).

29 Vinet's stance also reminds us not to connect religious revival necessarily with Romanticism and conservatism. The evangelical revival in Geneva, known as the 'Réveil', was of enormous importance within Geneva and the Low Countries and fostered a reactionary social attitude; see Nicholas Rupke's contribution to this collection. But Vinet, of undoubted and piety and with Romantic cultural allegiances, was a critic of this movement.

30 F. R. de Salis (ed.), *Quel Tell? Origine, formation et influence du mythe suisse de Tell* (Lausanne, 1973).

31 See H. and M. Garland, *The Oxford Companion to German Literature* (Oxford, 1976).

32 H. M. Waidson, *Jeremias Gotthelf* (Oxford, 1953).

33 Cited by W. Gilbert, 'The inner necessity', in *Jacob Burckhardt and the Renaissance: 100 Years On* (University of Kansas, Lawrence, 1960).

34 Quoted by Kohn, *Nationalism and Liberty*, p. 93.

35 Steinberg, *Why Switzerland?*, p. 103.

36 For an English introduction to Keller, see J. M. Lindsay, *Gottfried Keller: Life and Works* (London, 1968).

37 See Robert Rosenblum, *Modern Painting and the Northern Romantic Tradition, Friedrich to Rothko* (London, 1975); Sharon Hirsch, *Ferdinand Hodler* (London, 1982); *Dreams of a Summer Night* (Hayward Exhibition Catalogue, 1986). There has not been space to review the development of a Swiss school of Romantic landscape painting in the nineteenth century; but it is part of the story of how Romanticism became a new academic orthodoxy.

38 Adolf Muschg, 'The trouble with good design', *The Times Literary Supplement*, 7 December 1984, p. 1410.

7

Romanticism in Scandinavia

GUNNAR ERIKSSON

In this essay the concept of Romanticism will be related to a current of thought and attitudes permeating the intellectual life of the Scandinavian countries (with a stress on Sweden) roughly between 1800 and 1830. 'Romanticism' in this sense is intended by the author to be a kind of ideal type roughly as Max Weber used the concept. This means that Romanticism is a matter of degree: some authors and thinkers are more Romantic than others, some share only a little of the essential characteristics of the concept, others embrace it wholeheartedly. To find the personalities and attitudes closest to the ideal type one must go to Germany. Schelling, the originator of Naturphilosophie, the Schlegel brothers, critics of culture and literature, Schleiermacher, the philosopher of religion, poets like Tieck and Novalis, all are typical Romantics, of the same kind as those of Scandinavia considered below, and were once greatly influential in this region.

ROMANTICISM AS A WORLD-VIEW

Conceived of in this way, Romanticism is not only a matter of art and literature (in the sense of poetry, prose fiction or drama). It comprehends a whole world-view, including a set of ideas concerning the Universe, Nature, Man, History and God, and of attitudes related to truth, religion and ways of life. In most respects, Romanticism contrasts with the materialism and empiricism of the Enlightenment, convinced as its followers were of the fundamental spirituality of all reality. To the Romantic, nature is a mysterious and sacred, but at the same time 'lower', part of the all-penetrating world-spirit, still unconscious, constituted of forces (not of matter); and man is situated on the Chain of Being at the very border-line between conscious and unconscious within that one and whole spiritual Being. Existence, then, is meaningful, history has a goal, each man and nation fulfils a purpose of the highest dignity, although not fully revealed. Man, in his middle position on the great Chain of Being, cannot have full insight into reality, this insight being reserved for the perfect intelligence of the Absolute at the higher end of the Chain. Epistemology has to recognize that our senses easily deceive us and that our understanding (*Verstand*) is incomplete, but that there is a third way to knowledge, intuition, which in the intellect of the genius may lead to insight into the true nature of existence.

The Romantic conviction is not only, and not always, a result of philosophical construction. It is a way of experiencing, with the totality of one's personality, life as a sacred mystery, nature as a pattern of meaningful but unrevealed signs, and a way of acting according to this experience. True, far from all sympathizers were full Romantics; but to some degree they all shared the same conviction and the same interpretation of existence whether they were professing as poets or scientists, clergymen or politicians.

THE PLACE OF SWEDENBORG

As stated above, this essay will consider Scandinavian Romanticism as a movement basically confined to the period 1800–30. Of course there were Romantic trends outside these strict limits of time. In literary history the concept of 'Preromanticism' is of great importance, and true not least of Scandinavian literature. A brilliant study by a Swedish historian of literature, Martin Lamm, is called *The Romanticism of the Enlightenment* (1918–20). Among phenomena which can be counted as at least 'Preromanticist' in the era of Enlightenment are certain forms of religious mysticism prevailing in Pietist circles, certain kinds of freemasonry connected with occultism, alchemy and other kinds of secret sciences, and, more generally, all manifestations of the platonic-hermetic undercurrent of philosophy which has left its mark upon Scandinavian thought no less than upon that of other areas of the western world. To deal with all these things would be to move the point of gravity of this essay to the second half of the eighteenth century, thus misusing the opportunity to present what in my opinion remains the core of Scandinavian Romanticism. But there is one figure of the Enlightenment who has been so impressive in the international picture of Romantic literature that he, at least, deserves some short comment: Emanuel Swedenborg (1688–1772), the Swedish scientist and founder of an international Christian sect.[1] In Swedenborg's teaching, the theory of correlation between matter, soul and spirit, between earth and heaven, is central and reveals his adherence to the platonist tradition.

In Baudelaire's famous poem, 'Correspondances', this theory has given inspiration to an important Symbolist manifesto, apparently related to what, according to any reasonable standard, must be classified as Romanticism. We also know that Blake, the great poet, was greatly influenced by Swedenborg and there is a discussion about his importance to Schelling, the very founder of the Romantic movement as conceived of here.[2] But in Sweden his immediate influence was not very great. He was no preacher, his message being known solely through his books, written in Latin and published in Amsterdam and London. His sect, The New Church, never numerous, was mainly spread abroad. In his lifetime he had a few adherents among the clergy in Western Sweden (leading to trials brought by the orthodox Lutheran state church), and in Stockholm at the court of Gustavus III where some alchemists and occultists professed themselves Swedenborgians. Among the 'true' Romantics, to be discussed below, authors like Atterbom, Stagnelius and, above all, Almqvist have been inspired by some of Swedenborg's teaching. But, without doubt, they would have adhered to Romanticism in much the same way even without his influence. In Swedenborg's own writings there are unmistakable traces of the Cartesian rationalism which impressed him in his youth, and very little of that mysticist colouring which seems to be such an important ingredient in full-grown Romanticism. Swedenborg does not mark the beginning of Romanticism in Scandinavia.

SCANDINAVIAN HISTORY 1800–30

In trying to trace this remarkable movement in Scandinavia, it is important to stress (for readers not too familiar with Scandinavian history) that this region was, and still is, far from a cultural or political unity. Sweden and Denmark were enemies for hundreds of years and fought numerous wars. During the Napoleonic wars they stood on different sides in the European conflict. Copenhagen, the capital of Denmark, was severely bombarded by the British navy in 1801 and 1807. Sweden, on the other hand, took part in the alliance against Napoleon. The dictatorial king of Sweden, Gustavus Adolphus IV, regarded Napoleon as the monster of the Apocalypse. When, by a *coup d'état*, he was forced to abdicate in 1809, a crown prince of Danish origin was installed in Sweden (an uncle of Gustavus Adolphus being king). He died unexpectedly and surprisingly was replaced by one of Napoleon's own marshals, Jean Baptiste Bernadotte, as king of Sweden (called Carolus Johannes XIV). This strong and ambitious French warrior soon broke with his former sovereign actively to partake in the final wars against the emperor.

All this is intimately connected with the violent changes of the political geography of northern Europe at the beginning of the nineteenth century. In 1800 Norway was part of Denmark, as Finland was part of Sweden. In

1809, after a disastrous war, Sweden lost Finland to Russia, and in the peace of Leipzig in 1814 Denmark had to concede Norway to Sweden. Thereafter Norway and Sweden were bound together in a forced alliance of no impact upon the cultural developments of the respective countries except insofar as it nourished Norwegian patriotism.

The inner politics were perhaps more uniform in the whole region in spite of formal differences. Both Denmark and Sweden were monarchies, where initially the king had all power in his hands. After 1809, Sweden received a constitution not far from the ideals of Montesquieu, the power being shared between king and parliament (Riksdag) and with a free press. Although Denmark remained a monarchy of the old kind, there were reforms, and a relative liberty. For Norway this meant that it shared more or less the same liberty in matters of press and culture under the rule of Denmark as under that of Sweden. The first Norwegian university was founded in Christiania (now Oslo) in 1811 and continued under Swedish sovereignty. When Finland was made subject to the tsardom of Russia it did not lose its former identity altogether. Its official language remained Swedish and the university of Turku (Swed. Åbo) continued its traditions from the Swedish epoch. Even after the disastrous fire of 1827, when the university was moved to Helsinki, it remained true to its own traditions. The rise of a strong nationalist movement among the Finnish-speaking majority came later in the nineteenth century.

STEFFENS' LECTURES

However different the political outlook of the four countries, there is no doubt about what signalled the coming of whole-hearted Romanticism to this part of Europe; it was the lectures held by Henrik Steffens at Elders' Collegium of the university of Copenhagen in 1802. They were a tremendous success. To the majority of intellectuals of the Danish capital, they seemed a revelation of something totally new. Steffens (1773–1845) had returned to Denmark after studying and teaching at the university of Jena, where he had met Schelling.[3] 'It is my intention, Gentlemen,' he began his fourth lecture, 'to demonstrate to you how an organizing and determining Spirit seems to hide behind the seemingly irregular contingency of the productions of Nature, how it reveals itself by the combinations of the reducing observer, and how it is hinting at an infinite context.'[4] Essentially, it was the Naturphilosophie of Schelling, although in a pedagogic and elementary form, that Steffens was expounding.

A skilled geologist, Steffens could use the evidence of the fossil record to connect the apparently living world of men, animals and plants with the seemingly dead world of the geological strata. In his seventh lecture – the last to be printed at the time – he extended the works of the unifying Spirit to the realm of human history. The listening crowd – it more than filled the lecture-room – was left with the impression of having received from the most recent authorities of science and philosophy a message of hope and promise. The era of dry, deadening materialism and threatening atheism seemed to have reached an end; life presented a new meaning. In this crowd were Adam Oehlenschläger, the poet, and N. F. S. Grundtvig, soon to be the leading philosopher, religious thinker and cultural critic of the country.[5] The first-mentioned accepted the message without hesitation; Grundtvig was impressed although not uncritical.

Steffens' lectures demonstrate one way in which a new movement of thought may be distributed broadly and spectacularly in an important area of intellectual culture. His audience comprised not only students and young university teachers but also officials of high order and all sorts of educated people in Copenhagen. But there was another way for the Romantic ideas to penetrate the countries of the north. Important for the German kind of Romanticism was its hard core of post-Kantian philosophy which could probably be absorbed only by specialists trained in the abstract terminology and superintellectual rhetoric of this highly speculative school of thought. There were some philosophers and philosophically minded scientists in both Denmark and Sweden who were open to this more sophisticated and individual influence. In Denmark, the physicist Hans Christian Oersted seems to be a representative of this attitude.[6] He was deeply engaged in the debate concerning the essence of matter, whether constituted by corporeal atoms or by opposing forces, known as the schools of atomism and dynamism. Kant had been a dynamist and one who caused the debate to rage in a number of physical texts and text-books.[7] A work from his late critical period, nowadays often overlooked, was essential for the debate: *Metaphysiche Anfangsgründe der Naturwissenschaft* (1786). Here Kant contended that matter was constituted by two fundamental and opposing forces, the force of expansion and the force of attraction. Everything that we call corporeal is explicable as effects of these two forces. No theory of atoms, logically weak as it must be, is needed. Different states of matter and additional forces may, according to Kant, be explained as modifications of these two basic forces (*Grundkräfte*). In Schelling's famous works in Naturphilosophie from the years around 1800, the Kantian dynamism was further elaborated and modified, the two forces being seen as unified by a third (resulting in a kind of synthesis not far from the conception of Hegel). In this vein Oersted wrote his doctor's dissertation at the university of Copenhagen in 1799: 'Dissertatio de forma elementaris naturae externae'. During a stay on the continent in the following years he met several of the leading scientists of the new movement, among them his compatriot Steffens, the Hungarian chemist Winterl, and the German physicist Ritter. Inspired by the two last-mentioned, he made his scientific debut in Paris with a defence of Winterl's dynamic chemical system. Its harsh refutation by the French chemists was a valuable lesson that taught Oersted to be very careful with his experimental evidence in future. But it did not hold him back from dynamism in general, and evidently impulses from the Romantic world-view played a crucial role in his own personal outlook for the rest of his life. In 1812–13, when a professor of Copenhagen university, he published a work of which the title of the French version reveals his inner conviction: *Recherches sur l'identité des forces électriques et chimiques.* This belief in the fundamental identity of the forces of nature is in full accord with the dynamistic outlook and is crucial for understanding the background of Oersted's most famous scientific achievement – his discovery in 1820 of electro-magnetism, demonstrating an identity of two forces hitherto regarded as absolutely separate.

Oersted's role in Scandinavian Romanticism is not restricted to the domains of physics and chemistry and their theoretical foundations. He was vigorously partaking in the general intellectual debates of the time. In 1812 he had a controversy with Grundtvig, who regarded the German Romantic philosophy more and more sceptically, now criticizing Schelling for his harmonization of the forces of good and evil in history against the mainstream of orthodox Christian belief (in *Kort Begreb af Verdens Krönike, A Short Summary of World Chronicle*). His last work, unfinished when he died, was the widely read *The Soul in Nature*, translated into English shortly after the original Danish edition.[8]

HÖIJER AND GERMAN PHILOSOPHY

A still greater enthusiast for the hard core of post-Kantian German philosophy was a young Swedish philosopher, Benjamin Höijer (1767–1812), studying at Uppsala university in the years around 1800. Throughout his *Avhandling om den filosofiska konstruktionen* (*Treatise upon Philosophical Construction*) (1799), which was translated into German in 1801,[9] he was in the centre of the philosophical discourse of Fichte, Schelling and even Hegel, perhaps influencing the last-mentioned by his concept of absolute self-consciousness.[10] Höijer, who for a while sympathized with the political revolutionary movement in France, was no favourite of the Swedish government which effectively oppressed all conflicting activities, real or imaginary, thereby impeding intellectual life in Sweden and making the first years of the new century some of the most culturally sterile in the modern history of the country. Not until after the

abdication of Gustavus Adolphus in 1809 was Höijer appointed professor
of philosophy of Uppsala university. Meanwhile his private lectures were
attended by a very small but qualified group of students, among them
Geijer and Atterbom, later to be leading figures of the Romantic movement.

Romanticism as a real movement, not only as something individual and
solitary, may be said to have manifested itself in Denmark by 1802
through the lectures of Steffens. In Sweden there was a hidden, preparatory
stage in the years before 1809. Among students in Uppsala certain literary
circles oriented themselves in the direction of the latest German poetry,
absorbing the aesthetics of Schlegel and, in part, the philosophy of
Schelling and his school. Somewhat older students left Uppsala for Stockholm, enrolling in the state offices but still cultivating their intellectual
preferences. So in 1809, when everything changed, there were two headquarters for the Romantic campaign.

LIBERTY OF THE PRESS

Of utmost importance for the change of the Swedish intellectual climate in
1809 was the new law providing liberty of the press. First to take advantage of the new situation was the Stockholm group led by Lorenzo
Hammarskjöld, librarian at the Royal Library, poet and literary critic. In
the autumn of that year he announced the first issue of *Lyceum*, a short-
lived but highly ambitious journal counting among its contributors
eminent men such as Benjamin Höijer and Jacob Berzelius, the chemist. In
the prospectus announcing the new journal there were some lines about
the preceding 'iron years' of Swedish literature which aroused the wrath of
the best renowned of the younger poets of 'the old school', Johan Olof
Wallin. He tried, with little success, to parody the new literary style in a
journal which was intended to serve as the leading organ of the literary
establishment: *Journal för litteraturen och teatern*. Its editor was Per
Adam Wallmark, ironically enough chief librarian of the same Royal
Library where Hammarskjöld was working, and generally regarded as the
chief spokesman of the old school defending the classicist mediocrity of the
Swedish Academy. His journal was the only one of its kind to have been
permitted by Gustavus Adolphus, but its first issue was published after the
end of the old regime. Wallin's parody triggered a new journal from the
Romantic Stockholm camp, the satirical *Polyfem*, which more or less
successfully fulfilled its task for two years.

Contributions to the Stockholm journals also came from the Uppsala
camp but in August 1810 opponents from the university town began publishing the most famous of all Romantic journals, *Phosphoros*. It appeared

in an orange cover, provocative for its time, its vignette showing Orpheus bringing all nature under his lyre in the light of Phosphoros, the Morning Star. In this journal both poetry and prose were published, together with philosophical and scientific articles. All these new journals, an innovation in Swedish culture, struck a vigorous note of disruption and revolt, and polarized the cultural life into two opposing camps, Romantics and Traditionalists. These journals made the total division clear to everyone and the border-line between the two epochs seemed clear-cut. *Phosphoros*, published in ambitious but sporadic issues, was succeeded after two years by *Svensk literaturtidning* (*Swedish Journal of Literature*), which remained the chief Romantic mouthpiece far into the 1820s, when the movement gradually waned.

SWEDISH ROMANTICISM AGAINST CLASSICISM AND ENLIGHTENMENT

Evidently the Romantics waged a war on two fronts. One front was the strictly literary one, separating two ideals of style. In Sweden, at least, the Traditionalist camp kept to the French-classicist ideals of the Swedish Academy, the most powerful literary authority of the country. Moderation, taste and common sense were the leading passwords of academic aesthetics. Among the Romantics, the freedom of genius, the splendour of expression and the wealth of words tended to be given the highest values, but very often the contest was about translating the Greek and Latin classics, the Romantics preferring the original, unrhymed metre and the exact rendering of the original text to the paraphrasing alexandrines of the French classicists. However, their main concern was about the power of poetry to catch the spiritual or, as they preferred to say, the ideal essence of being.

The second front is more important from the point of view of the history of ideas. It was the front against the Enlightenment and its materialistic world-picture and view of man, as well as against its utilitarian, sometimes hedonistic morals. It is most evident in matters of religion. Erik Gustaf Geijer (1783–1847), one of the pupils of Höijer, and later professor of history at Uppsala University, was the author of the most famous pamphlet, announcing the new spirit and condemning the old: *Om falsk och sann upplysning med avseende på religionen* (*Of False and True Enlightenment in Matters of Religion*) (1811). Geijer was no 'phosphorist' (the controversial name for the most extremist Romantics around *Phosphoros*), but he was strongly sympathetic to the new ideas in philosophy and literature. His pamphlet demonstrates his whole-hearted support of the new direction. His main target was the one-dimensional rationalism which had become so popular in the eighteenth century. To make his point clear, Geijer, in a manner characteristic of Romantic philosophy, distinguishes between (practical) common sense and (theoretical) science (the Swedish 'vetenskap' is equivalent to the German 'Wissenschaft', so here 'science' must be understood in that sense). According to Geijer, both are valuable things but they must not trespass on each other's domain. Theoretical science can never in its purity mix with matters of practical life, and common sense has no right to elevate itself to the level of theoretical science. This last is just what happened in the Enlightenment. Its spokesmen tried to accommodate religion to common sense by way of the empirical method as the only source of knowledge, and statements of probability as the only ground of reason, thereby reducing the religious question to a matter of reasonableness. To Geijer, religion represented a different belief from that of the presumptions of common sense, something deeper, more urgent. The heart of Christian belief to him was the atonement of man by the death of Christ, God's son – a doctrine unattainable to common sense. How Geijer looked at the relationship between religion and theoretical science remains unclear. But evidently he supported the absolute claims to true philosophy on certainty in the same way as the German post-Kantian philosophers.

POETRY, PHILOSOPHY AND RELIGION

The contentions of the second front constituted the main theme of Romantic poetry. This does not mean that much of what the authors produced was not from the common ground of lyrics of all time, like the obligatory love poems of the many young men of the new school. But the centre of the new poetry lay always close to philosophy and religion, and in this direction the poets were striving, although painfully conscious of the difficulties of the subject and the danger of maltreating such a sublime theme. In poems like some of Atterbom's prologue and epilogue to the journal *Phosphoros*, 'Diocles and Helidora', philosophy is the main theme, partly treated with immaculate beauty. Atterbom, who was probably the foremost phosphorist poet, has also summarized the Romantic view of nature's continuous chain and ultimate identity with spirit in youthfully luxuriant phrases:

A dormant intelligence, Nature raises out of the sultry sleep of her anorgic Nadir [i.e. the lowest point of inorganic existence] through a chain-walk of more and more light dreams and dream formations, to her heavenly throne, the human organism; from the Olympus of which she, awake, as Reason, overviews herself and the immense, by different shapes replenished space, which all are mirroring her.[11]

Later in the 1810s, Erik Johan Stagnelius (1793–1823), civil servant of the ecclesiastical expedition in Stockholm, in agonizingly beautiful poems formulated his neo-platonist world-view, apprehending external nature as a prison from which the soul longs to be liberated in order to reach its proper home in the world of ideas. In several poems, Stagnelius came close to the convictions of the later Schelling – that the material world could only be understood as a falling away from the spiritual one. Generally the Romantic view of nature was more optimistic.

EVOLUTION IN HISTORY

The idea of history was in accord with the general Romantic convictions. Geijer, who became a professional historian (and professor at Uppsala University from 1817) was constantly underlining the inner intention of history, trying to discern what really happened in what seemed to be happening, to use one of his own expressions. He was constantly focussing his interest on the fate of the state (in his case the Swedish state), because he saw it as the foremost carrier of the inner intentionality. From this vision stems the grandeur of his mighty surveys of Swedish history.[12] Other, more profiled Romantics had a still more ecstatic view of history. A minor but very typical figure is Johan Haquin Wallman (1792–1853), antiquarian and lecturer at a lyceum in the province after his years in Uppsala which ended about 1817. According to his conviction, the first generations of man lived in an earthly paradise, in close contact with the gods and their wisdom.[13] During an era of vast migrations they lost this knowledge, now painfully to be regained. This vision is combined with apocalyptic dreams, announcing a restoration of the first order in the near future. The fact that the Romantic view of history may be combined with this kind of millenarian mysticism, a reminder of radical movements in the sixteenth and seventeenth centuries, is a salutary reminder for those who classify Romanticism as reactionary, however true it may be that some of the leading Romantics of the German type turned very conservative, at least in their old age.

We should not forget that Romantics owed much of their view of history to one of their most important forerunners, Herder. In his *Ideen zu einer Philosophie der Geschichte der Menschheit* (1784) he had pointed to the inner meaning of history and looked at the connection of human history with that of nature, seeing a spiritual design in the fate of the whole world. In Scandinavia, he inspired Niels Treschow (1751–1833), author of *Elementer til Historiens Philosophie* (1811). Treschow was of Norwegian origin and after ten years as professor in Copenhagen returned to Norway in 1812 as professor of philosophy at the new University of Christiania, later becoming Minister of Education. In a remarkable way he was able to mix influences from British empiricism with Romantic traits, which meant that he was a favourite of the ruling establishment but not totally coherent as a philosophical thinker. All the same, his idea of history had a Herderian ring, considering nature as part of history as it did, and, in a Platonist fashion, thinking of all beings as striving to fulfil their ideal, thereby influencing history. As he said:

Is common matter anything but God visible, but a revelation of the supreme Being itself? As the ideas, by His infinite reason, by an eternal birth, evolve themselves, thus the seeds, the basic form of all things, lie enveloped in the bosom of matter, but become, only in time and therefore only gradually, visible images of those patterns which they more and more closely endeavour to express.[14]

Treschow's statement reveals a not uncommon form of Romantic evolutionism including the organic world. This was part – and an important part – of Romantic science. We will now return to this subject, having already presented some of the relevant ideas of the Danish scientists Steffens and Oersted.

DYNAMIC MATTER

The dynamic theory of matter, both in its Kantian and its Romantic form, was also known in Sweden. An early example is Anders Ekeberg (1767–1813), a chemist in Uppsala. In 1806, in his university lectures, he forcefully attacked traditional chemical science which, according to him, had become 'a manufacturist ability, maintained through exactly described manual exercises, man from man in tradition'.[15] At the same time he attacked atomism, declaring dynamism to be the much more satisfactory way of explaining the behaviour of matter in chemical reactions. Ekeberg had several adherents and followers among young physicists and chemists, but the development of a Romantic science of inorganic nature was strongly hampered in Sweden by the great chemist, Jacob Berzelius (1779–1848). He ruthlessly criticized the new ideas as speculative and ill-founded. His research was concentrated on the exact atomic weights of the elements and on their proportions in the chemical compounds, which led him to believe in the atomic theory of Dalton.[16] If sometimes he questioned this theory, he was careful not to let it appear as any positive reflection on Naturphilosophie. Berzelius was an ingenious experimenter, his success depending on the endless toil of weighing and measuring and on the tremendous skill of his hands in the laboratory. By instinct he hated scientists who preferred their own inspired hypotheses to minute empirical investigation. Lorenzo Hammarskjöld, when starting his *Lyceum*, invited Berzelius to become a contributor. His first contribution was also his last, being a stinging account of Winterl and other speculative chemists of the Romantic camp.[17]

In Sweden, the influence of Romantic Naturphilosophie on the biological sciences was far more impressive. The chemist Ekeberg, as we have seen, attacked the routinized traditionalism of his colleagues. Wallman, not only an antiquarian but also a botanist, indicated the same attitude to natural history in a letter of 1813:

It seems to me that the great aim [of the naturalists] is to obtain a universal collection of natural products, and that what they call their scientific endeavours are more or less fragmentary attempts to obtain a neat catalogue of that collection. All *a priori* attempts to construct a science of natural history are therefore, in the eyes of these sensible men, at the summit of all insanity. Nevertheless I know a few aiming at something better, but they are not many and, as usual, their voices are drowned by the screaming masses.[18]

EVOLUTION AND LIVING NATURE

The most renowned Romantic biologists in Sweden were not to be found in Uppsala but in Lund, the small university town of Scania, not far from Copenhagen. Carl Adolph Agardh (1786–1859), professor of botany from 1812, still had direct communication with leading Romantics from the central region of Stockholm–Uppsala.[19] For a while he was a private tutor to the children of von Engeström, the Chancellor of Lund University, who lived in Stockholm. Here, Agardh frequented the circles around *Polyfem*, friend as he was since his student years of the poet and satirist J. Chr. Askelöf. Although he rallied a little with his over-enthusiastic friends, his later writings clearly demonstrate that he was deeply involved in Romantic Naturphilosophie. In a series of botanical aphorisms, of which the first were printed in 1817, he expounds the idea of a ladder of nature, involving stones, plants, animals and men, forming a unity of rising perfection. This fundamental Romantic idea was, of course, much older in western thought than in Romanticism in the sense of this essay, but Agardh expressed its content in an unmistakably Romantic fashion. The unity of the ladder, he says, implies an echoing of one form in another in such a way that lower forms (like mosses) are precursors of more advanced forms (e.g. among the flowering plants), presaging in their appearance that of the later ones. In nature, according to Agardh, polar forces reign: a formative force opposing a reproductive one. The former is creating new forms, the latter imitates the created ones. The higher on the ladder of living forms, the more freedom in the organism; but freedom is always struggling with necessity, dominating the inorganic world. Agardh used these principles in his great taxonomical works on algae which appeared during the 1820s and resulted in international fame in that field of botany.

Agardh had a pupil belonging to a somewhat younger generation, Elias
Fries (1794–1878).[20] His Romantic inspiration is not very evident until the
1820s. It is not completely clear what influenced Fries in his acceptance of
Naturphilosophie. Of course his relationship with Agardh must have been
of importance but we have no source available that can tell us anything
about this. We do know that Wallman, of the Uppsala group (far from
Lund) was visiting Fries in the summer of 1816 in his parents' home deep
in the forests of Småland, a visit that resulted in a frequent correspondence
with Wallman and other naturalist members of the Uppsala group. Fries
was a mycologist, world-famous in his field after the publication of his first
great survey of fungi, *Systema mycologicum* (vol. 1, 1820). It reveals that
he was greatly influenced by the remarkable German Naturphilosoph
Lorenz Oken. Like him, Fries assumed four elements or basic principles in
nature, kept together in a double polarity, and more and more refined at
all levels of the scale of nature. In the realm of fungi those principles,
according to Fries, were at hand as light, heat, air and an organic tendency
to reproduction, specific for organisms. Under the influence of these prin-
cipled, working with varying degrees of strength, the fungi have been
shaped into four classes, each mirroring one of the four principles. The
subordinate groups, orders, genera and species are seen as originating
from the combination of influencing principles: e.g. the class of the fungi
of the light has one order that, besides the light, is most influenced by the
principle of heat, a second by the air, a third by the reproductive tendency,
the fourth, and central, by, once more, the main principle of the class, the
light, etc. This dry scheme becomes deeply Romantic by its deduction from
the central thesis of the spiritual nature of the elements, and by its implication that all nature is One, although manifested by an internal tension
between opposing forces. Later in the 1820s Fries emancipated himself
from Oken in different respects, showing more and more interest in a
Platonist conception of type: all organisms, according to this conception,
belonged to types or ideas which were mirrored by the organisms more or
less perfectly. The types were organized in hierarchical order, all of them
in the end subordinate to the *Ur*-idea of perfection which the naturalist
could trace everywhere, but only to a certain degree reveal.

Very soon it became apparent that Agardh and Fries were following
different paths in the development of their Romantic ideas. Accompanied
by a personal animosity, there is a divergence in their respective views
about the role of logic and freedom in the productions of nature. Perhaps
influenced by Fichte, Agardh stressed freedom, which in the system of
plants was manifested in complicated and unforeseeable relationships
between the different systematic sub-groups within the vegetable kingdom. The strict double-dichotomy in the system of Fries was, according to

Agardh, the result of logical operations of the human reason, no true mirroring of the free operations of nature herself. Fries replied that the regularity of his systematic groups was no result of human logic but the consequence of the infinite reason present in nature.

POLITICAL VIEWS

Romanticism of the kind treated in this essay is known very often to be politically conservative. This is probably true as a generalization in regard to the Scandinavian Romantics. However, the statement has to be qualified. The persons here treated were much more outspokenly conservative in their old age than in their youth. In the first years of the nineteenth century there seems to be some secret connection between the French revolution and the beginning of the Romantic movement. Höijer, the pioneering philosopher, was an active opponent of the ruling power. True, after a visit to Paris, he became sceptical about the political evolution in France, seeing the horrors of the *terreur*, but this is not to say that he adopted conservative ideas. In the 1810s there was an interest among the young Romantic academics in planning secret societies aimed at reforming the nation. These ideas were not necessarily democratic, but it seems incorrect to label them conservative. They seem very often to be connected with religious millenarianism, with apocalyptic expectations. One such plan was sketched in 1816 by Wallman, this secondary but very ideal-typical figure of Swedish Romanticism. In a letter of Atterbom, his close friend and leader of the Uppsala school, he develops some ideas which had been discussed between them the previous autumn about a society able to interpret the secret language of the time and act according to the spirit of that language.[21] He calls it an 'Atlantic society', constituted by two degrees 'like the Pythagorean', one exoteric and one esoteric. In the esoteric degree, the secret source of inspiration, reigns a philosophy 'which originates in the most sacred chamber of the human mind, where knowledge and will in holy accord celebrate their marriage, and the secret paths are opened to the primeval times and to the heavenly countries. Religion is the name of the high priest and intuition [*åskådning*, German: *Anschauung*] the lofty window.' In the exoteric degree it has room for the whole intellectual elite of Sweden. 'An imaginative, symbolic, and meaningful life, electrifying the mind, nourishing imagination, ennobling the actions of every-day life, and furthering a universal culture [*bildning*], influencing thought and action, is our exoteric aim.' Finally, Wallman reminds his friend that this is the time when the wild beast (of the Apocalypse) is rampaging, roaring dreadfully, and raising its banner in the country – time for action by all men of good-will.

Wallman's plan was not unique. At the same time, a young member of the Uppsala circle, Carl Jonas Love Almqvist, later known as one of the foremost writers of nineteenth-century Sweden, was trying to initiate 'Manhemsförbundet' (Manhem, according to the seventeenth-century savant, Olaus Rudbeck, was synonymous with Atlantis, as can be seen in the Swedish version of his famous *Atlantica: Atland eller Manhem*), in the same way aiming at a better and deeper life of the nation, or at least for an elite thereof.[22] More conspicuous was 'Götiska förbundet' (the Gothic Society), founded in 1811. At the same time its aim was much less Romantic, stressing the moral qualities of the heathen Scandinavians, and editing a journal, *Iduna*, for historical-antiquarian essays and poetry, in the spirit of the forefathers (but not exclusively so). Among its most prominent members it counted Geijer and Esaias Tegner, the foremost poet of the time. It could be seen as a somewhat 'Preromanticist' precursor of the later planned societies. In all three cases, however, there is one common ground: nationalism.

NATIONALISM AND NORDIC MYTHOLOGY

Nationalism is often characterized as a typical trait of Romanticism. So far nothing – or almost nothing – can be said against that view. But it is important to remember that the inverse is not valid – that Romanticism should be present in all kinds of nationalism. In fact the nationalism of Scandinavian Romanticism had a form and content of its own, as has already been illustrated to a certain extent. This is not least obvious if we turn, again, to Denmark. Here the influence of Steffens' lectures is the starting point in this respect also. Among his enthusiastic listeners was the poet Adam Oehlenschläger (1779–1850). Inspired by the lectures, and also through personal conversations with Steffens, Oehlenschläger wrote 'Guldhornene' ('The Golden Horns'), a poem which united Nordic mythology with the philosophy of the German Romantic school. This union was possible because of the Romantic conception of mythology. The myths (e.g. those of Nordic pre-Christian religion), according to the Romantics, were symbolic representations of the oldest wisdom of humanity, mirrored in the mentality of every specific people. This wisdom had once in pre-history been the common property of God and man (this was an idea taken from the neo-Platonist tradition) but had been shattered, now to be regained by philosophers and poets of the new generation. Pride in the purity and profundity of Nordic myth was essential to Romantic nationalism in Scandinavia. As the myths stemmed from the past, this kind of nationalism was also historical, and it had an important aesthetical dimension: the Romantics admired the beauty of folk poetry, again tracing behind its apparently simple expressions symbols of eternal wisdom. Even the ethics of nationalism, with its stress on courage as demonstrated in patriotic wars, was amply at hand in the Nordic mythological tradition, uniting past virtues with present demands.

Grundtvig was one of the foremost writers on mythology and at the same time an historian and nationalist, and a very religious man. In that way he may be said to illustrate the typical connection of these areas of ideas and evaluation in Romanticism. At the same time, as we have said, he constantly moved away from this movement. That may tell us something about the limits of Romanticism.

The ideal type (in Weber's sense) of Romanticism was, in contrast to classicism or common sense philosophy, limitless, expansive, without compromise. The poetic style of the Romantics was full of excess; their thought had no measure, they did nothing to avoid bad taste or paradoxes. For most people, even intellectuals, this was hard to follow. Some contradictions were built into the very construction of Romantic mentality. For instance, Romanticism was very nationalist, which contradicted its universalism, equally dear to the members of the movement. A much more difficult problem was religion. Romanticism tried to rescue and revive the values of Christian belief from the Enlightenment attacks. But it admired pagan mythology, and its philosophy of nature tended towards pantheism. Many of the Scandinavian philosophers, however much they admired Schelling, were constantly struggling with this problem, trying to have a personal God as a necessary part of the philosophical construction. This is true not less of Grundtvig than of Geijer or Samuel Grubbe, the professor of theoretical philosophy, who succeeded Höijer at Uppsala.

SOCIAL BACKGROUND

Can these characteristics of the Romantic movement in Scandinavia be linked to social factors likely to explain the appearance of such an extreme current of thought as this one? Let us at the end of our account try to consider the social background common to most Scandinavian Romantics.

At the beginning of the nineteenth century Scandinavia was almost totally agrarian in economic respects. The peasants, constituting about 80 per cent of the population, were ruled by kings who had at their side a well-developed bureaucracy which controlled almost all aspects of men's lives in war and peace. The different branches of economy, for example, the manufacturing sector, the mines, the iron-works and commerce, were controlled by efficient offices, central and local. The controls included distribution of farmland and detailed regulation of markets and taxes. Population statistics were developed in Sweden earlier than perhaps in any other country. This was possible thanks to the organization of the Lutheran state church, which embraced the whole population. In every little parish the vicar kept records of all its inhabitants from birth and baptism to burial. He controlled their ability to read from the Scriptures and had to make certain that representatives from every household were present at the Sunday service. As servant of the state church, he was also a civil servant, his records being used for census and for military recruitment. From his pulpit he had to read all new royal edicts and proclamations. He was an essential part of the intertwined spiritual and political system of these countries.

Most of our Romantics were sons of clergymen. Those who were not had at least, as an alternative outcome of their university studies, a career as clergymen in their minds. This meant a deep consciousness of the role of bureaucracy in the ruling of society. What they had experienced since childhood was an order not unlike that of Plato's Republic, with a vast class of peasants and some industrialists, and a ruling class of academically trained administrators, often spiritual and secular in the same person. This could nourish their adherence to an organicist view of society, in turn serving as a theoretical basis for their self-assurance. As children of Christian preachers they shunned the atheism of the Enlightenment; this made them sensitive to the religious appeal of Romanticism. In agrarian Scandinavia, most parishes were situated in the rural landscape, so most of the Romantics had memories from their childhood of woods, lakes and rivers, of idyllic parsonages and a life close to the common people with their fairy-tales and rich mythology. At the university they could combine what they had experienced in childhood with philosophical speculation and literary analysis. Romanticism is also mainly a university culture from a time when the universities claimed to be the true breeding-places of statesmanship.

To these social considerations we should add the fact that the leading Romantic generation, the one which published its manifestos in 1809 and 1810, was very young indeed. Atterbom, for instance, was not more than 20 when he started his journal *Phosphoros* in 1810. This may partly explain the excessiveness of so many of the Romantic manifestations.

This youthful lack of judgement, combined with over-zealous religious tendencies, may explain some of the main causes behind the revisionist attitudes appearing from the 1820s among most Scandinavian Romantics. Some, like Atterbom and Wallman, grew more and more conservative without keeping the Romantic vision alive. Others began combining a more empirical attitude with political radicalism, like Geijer and Almqvist, who was a latecomer to the Uppsala school and remained one of Sweden's most remarkable writers and poets throughout the 30s and 40s. Romanticism in Norway came late but with a brilliant representative in the poet Henrik Wergeland, who from the beginning (around 1830) demonstrated political radicalism.[23] Scientists like Fries also revised their positions around 1830. They were still idealists but began distrusting speculation. One exception was Israel Hwasser, professor of medicine at Uppsala from 1829, who developed a highly speculative medical system in the 30s and 40s. Romanticism as constituting an epoch ended around 1830 in Scandinavia; Romantic individuals still linger in the Northern forests.

NOTES

1 For Swedenborg's place in the history of ideas, see Inge Jonsson, *Emanuel Swedenborg* (New York, 1971).

2 Ernst Benz, *Schellings theologische Geistesahnen*, Akademie der Wissensch. u. der Literatur. Abh. der Geistes- u. Sozialwiss. Klasse, Jahrg. 1955. Heft 3 (Mainz, 1955).

3 For Steffens, see his autobiography in German: *Was ich erlebte*, 10 vols. (Breslau 1840–5). For a general introduction to Danish intellectual life, in the age of Romanticism, see J. F. Jensen, M. Møller and T. Nielsen, *Dansk Litteraturhistorie*, vol. 4 (Copenhagen, 1983), and S. Auring, S. Baggesen, F. Hauberg Mortensen, S. Petersen, M.-L. Svane, E. Svendsen, P. Aaby Sørensen, J. Vogelius and M. Zerlang, *Dansk Litteraturhistorie*, vol. 5 (Copenhagen, 1984).

4 H. Steffens, *Indledning til philosophiske Forelaesninger*, new edn by B. T. Dahl (Köbenhavn and Kristiania, 1905), p. 42. Here translated from the Danish original.

5 In an international language Grundtvig is treated by Erica Simon, *Réveil national et culture populaire en Scandinavie. La genèse de la höjskole nordique 1844–1878* (Paris, 1960).

6 Biography by L. Pearce Williams in *Dictionary of Scientific Biography*, vol. 10 (New York, 1974), pp. 182ff.

7 This aspect of post-Kantian physics is treated by e.g. L. Pearce Williams, *Michael Faraday, a Biography* (London, 1965).

8 H. C. Oersted, *The Soul in Nature* (London, 1852; repr. 1966).

9 B. Höijer, *Abhandlung über die philosophische Construction* (Stockholm, 1801).

10 K. R. Gierow, *Benjamin Höijer* (Stockholm, 1971), p. 201.

11 Atterbom in *Phosphoros* (1811), cited from H. Frykenstedt, 'Atterbom och nyromantiken', *Ny illustrerad svensk litteraturhistoria*, vol. 3 (Stockholm, 1956), p. 68.

12 E. G. Geijer, *Svea rikes hävder* (1825), *Svenska folkets historia*, 1–3 (1832–6).

13 J. H. Wallman, 'Odhin och Budha', *Iduna*, 10 (1824).

14 N. Treschow, *Elementer til Historiens Philosophie* (Copenhagen, 1811), p. 83.

15 A. G. Ekeberg, Concepts for lectures, University Library, Uppsala, MS D 1502, '1806 d. 1 Oct.'

16 A. Lundgren, *Berzelius och den kemiska atomteorin* (Uppsala, 1979), summary in English pp. 183–96.

17 J. J. Berzelius (anon.), 'Försök till en sammanställning af de viktigare Kemiska

uptäckter, som blifvit gjorde under de sist förflutne åren', *Lyceum*, 2 (1811), 133ff.

18 J. H. Wallman, letter to G. Marklin, University Library, Uppsala MS G 170a, 5 May 1813.

19 Biography by G. Eriksson in *Dictionary of Scientific Biography*, vol. 1 (New York, 1970), pp. 69ff.

20 Biography by G. Eriksson in *Dictionary of Scientific Biography*, vol. 5 (New York, 1972), pp. 190ff.

21 J. H. Wallman, letter to P. D. A. Atterbom, University Library, Uppsala MS G8 e, 12 May 1816.

22 G. Hedin, *Manhemsförbundet* (Gothenburg, 1928).

23 For Wergeland and generally for Norwegian intellectual life at his time, see F. Paasche, 'Norges litteratur fra 1814 til 1850-årene', in F. Bull, F. Paasche, A. H. Winsnes and Philip Houm (eds.), *Norsk Litteraturhistorie*, vol. 3 (Oslo, 1959).

8

Romanticism in The Netherlands

NICHOLAS A. RUPKE

INTRODUCTION

The years 1795–1813 formed the single most ignominious and inglorious period in the history of The Netherlands. During this time the nation's independence was violated by foreign as well as indigenous forces which turned the country into a vassal state of French domination. The political spectrum had become polarised between Orangists, who were loyal to Stadtholder Willem V, and the democratic Patriots. The latter had taken up the banner of French Revolutionary ideas, and when in 1795 the French army invaded The Netherlands, it was welcomed by the Patriotic Party. The Stadtholder fled to England, and prominent Orangists left the country. The new Batavian Republic was in name independent, but in reality no more than a French puppet state. Its democratic ideals bore only meagre results. In 1802 the House of Orange renounced its claims on The Netherlands, and four years later Bonaparte crowned his brother Louis Napoleon King of The Netherlands. The new King turned out to be well-disposed to both democrats and Orangists, but in 1810 the kingdom was liquidated and incorporated into the French empire. Economically, too, these were bleak years.

With the penultimate defeat in 1813 of Bonaparte, the Stadtholder's son returned and was proclaimed sovereign, King Willem I. The new kingdom included the Catholic southern Netherlands, but in 1830 the larger part of these seceded, and Belgium was formed into a separate kingdom. The autocratically minded King abdicated in 1840 in favour of his son, Willem II, who in 1848 granted a new and liberal constitution.

Culturally, too, the late eighteenth- and early nineteenth-century period formed a trough in Dutch history. There were no successors to a Boerhaave in medicine, to a Musschenbroek in physics, no musicians or painters of international repute, virtually no *literati* to lift the national pride. A fashionable deism, imported mainly from France, had spread among the intelligentsia, and especially during the period of French annexation a general apathy prevailed. There existed various societies for the promotion of arts and sciences, but little more was accomplished by these than keeping abreast of foreign developments. Representative of the period was the geologist J. G. S. van Breda (1788–1867), best remembered for his work as secretary to the Hollandsche Maatschappij der Wetenschappen (1838–64).

It must therefore come as no surprise that Dutch names do not occur in the general literature on European Romanticism; none are to be found in Maurice Bowra's *The Romantic Imagination* (1949), none in Mario Praz' *The Romantic Agony* (1956) and none in Hans Schenk's *The Mind of the European Romantics* (1966). Nevertheless, a distinctly Dutch Romantic grouping did form and its main representative, Willem Bilderdijk, deserves European ranking. Although small in number, the Romantics became a major force of political and religious re-alignment in The Netherlands. Given the political humiliation at the hands of the French, the nationalistically inclined Romantics were from the outset anti-French, anti-Revolutionary and more than commonly reactionary. Industrialisation and other contemporary economic developments, which Marilyn Butler so successfully takes into account for England in her *Romantics, Rebels and Reactionaries* (1981), were a minor force in the small Dutch Romantic circle in which personality, political trauma and religious zeal were the prime conditioning forces.

WILLEM BILDERDIJK (1756–1831)

The cultural historian who surveys the Dutch literary landscape, walking through the portals of the eighteenth into the nineteenth century, will see a field covered with a multitude of shrubs, but towering above the shrubbery a single sequoia: gigantic, exotic and Romantic. Dutch Romanticism was dominated, to an exceptional degree, by a single person, Willem Bilderdijk, an approximate contemporary of Germany's Johann Wolfgang von Goethe. No Dutch poet has sent greater shockwaves through politics, religion and literature in The Netherlands than Bilderdijk, and no literary figure has been the subject of as much heated controversy as he, worshipped by a few for his colossal talents and despised by many for his gigantic faults. But whether one loves him or hates him, Bilderdijk was the only Romantic in The Netherlands of European stature, whose international fame has been limited, not by any lack of creative genius, but by the narrow geographical bounds of the only language in which he wrote, his Dutch mother tongue.

Young Willem was a child prodigy who at the age of one and a half read

Jacob Cats and the Heidelberg Catechism. As a two-year-old, the precocious boy desired to be delivered from 'this vale of tears', a dark wish which took approximately three quarters of a century to be granted. In his third year young Willem conducted a secret, slightly erotic correspondence with a girl next door in which the small letter-writer waxed lyrical about the girl's 'little ivory knees'. His talent, however, proved of no use in warding off a rarely interrupted sequence of ill fortune: ailments, sickness, poverty, official neglect and innumerable changes of abode. The darkest times of Bilderdijk's life were two eleven-year periods of isolation and exile which aggravated his prematurely manifested hypochondria. The first period of isolation began when he was only five (some say six) years of age and a severe case of periostitis of part of the left foot made walking impossible. Until the age of sixteen the disabled boy had to stay indoors cooped up with a severe father and an ill-tempered mother, isolated from any playmates. During this long night of exile from the outside world, Bilderdijk withdrew into a fantasy world of books turning into a universal autodidact of exceptional learning.

Finally the inflammation began to heal; but when the shy and socially inept teenager emerged, it was to become a lowly office clerk, a fate which had befallen young Thomas Chatterton about a decade earlier. He overcompensated by nurturing pretensions of nobility claiming to be descended on his father's side from the Earl of Teisterbant and on his mother's from the famed Knight of the Swan. Like the claims of noble parentage by an earlier language genius, Joseph Justus Scaliger, Bilderdijk's claims were in deadly earnest, and at times his genealogical vanity and self-aggrandisement bordered on insanity.

During the period 1780–2 Bilderdijk was permitted by his father to study law at Leyden. He subsequently set up practice in The Hague where he acted as a defence lawyer for the politically oppressed and the socially disadvantaged. One famous case was his defence of the Rotterdam fishwife, nicknamed Kaat Mossel, a staunch Orangist and victim of Patriot vindictiveness. In 1795 all lawyers were required to take the oath of loyalty to the new regime. Bilderdijk dramatically refused. Immediately he was ordered to leave the country, and at the age of thirty-eight a second eleven-year period of exile resulted, this time from his fellow countrymen (1795–1806). The first two years were spent in London where the Stadtholder had taken refuge, the rest in Brunswick where the Stadtholder's brother-in-law, the Duke of Brunswick, resided. Bilderdijk kept himself alive by translations, legal consultations and innumerable tutorials in a wide range of some twenty subjects. He suffered a great deal of hardship, was always overworked and grew addicted to opium (see below).

The Baroness von Berchtolsheim described in her memoirs how 'the brilliant art tutor' and 'famous scholar' Bilderdijk had to teach in order to provide for himself 'and his daughter'. In fact, the girl she referred to was Bilderdijk's mistress. At the age of twenty-eight Bilderdijk had married the beautiful but vulgar Catharina Rebecca Woesthoven. When he left for England, they had suffered ten years of unhappy marriage; she finally divorced him in 1802. In the meantime Bilderdijk had fallen in love with one of his London pupils, the nineteen-year-old Katharina Wilhelmina Schweickhardt, and a Latin notation in his Bible which included the words 'uxorem accepi', indicates that they soon had started a sexual relationship. This 'marriage' was a happy one; Katharina was a gentle and gifted person, herself a poetess of considerable talent who among other things translated Robert Southey's *Roderick* into Dutch. By his wife and his mistress Bilderdijk had thirteen children, but only two survived him; the others died, in most instances in early childhood.

Finally, homesick and filled with a hatred of all things German, Bilderdijk accepted a call for his return to the fatherland. Much had changed, however, and the deeply disappointed patriot now felt alienated from his own country, in exile from a modernised Dutch culture. Although his beloved House of Orange returned, a true Restoration did not take place as the new King, cautiously furthering national unity, tried to have people forget old rivalries. There were some bright times in Bilderdijk's life, but a hoped-for professorship never materialised; Bilderdijk squandered the annuities which he received from Louis Napoleon and later from Willem I; he moved from one city to another suffering damp and squalor, pursued by creditors and forced to sell his library and furniture. His intense feelings had taken the form of a fierce loyalty to his country and the Stadtholder; but his devotion did not find the reciprocal affection he had expected, and a sense of betrayal took the place of his former loyalty. Increasingly he projected his wounded idealism onto far-away places and neglected cultures where his feverish fantasy could rest without the hurt of disappointment.[1]

Although gentle to his family and a few intimate friends, and courteous to the rare visitors from abroad, Bilderdijk's life of alienating vicissitudes led to a chronic hostility towards anything foreign and modern. He attacked his enemies with volcanic outbursts of his exceptional talent for languages, spewing forth words and hurling sentences like boulders at the French and German deists and pantheists, at the modernisers in his own country and at 'the spirit of the age'. His passionate personality grew excessively individualistic, anti-establishmentarian and reactionary, and to the extent that these features were part of a Romantic identity, Bilderdijk was a natural Romantic, and not merely one who followed a fashion.

Notwithstanding his many misfortunes, Bilderdijk's creative output was prodigious. His collected poetry in fifteen volumes contains a total of some

200,000 lines of verse. His prose, mainly about philology, comes to no fewer than thirty volumes. He was a true language magician: his vocabulary was staggering, his ability to versify effortless, his metric technique perfect. His alexandrines especially are above reproach. Bilderdijk experimented with virtually every poetic genre: lyric and didactic poetry, Scottish ballads, medieval romances, pastoral idyls, drama (especially tragedy), epic, love and religious poetry, patriotic songs, proverbs, satire and others, but he saw himself first and foremost as a lyricist.[2]

Bilderdijk's poetry formed the main transition of Dutch literature from the eighteenth to the nineteenth century. In his early years he still followed the classics. Although he later discarded the shallow Neo-classical elegance, a love for the Greek classics stayed with him all his life. Increasingly, however, Bilderdijk began to write medieval ballads and romances, especially translations from Old English and Old Scottish, first from James Macpherson's *Ossian* under the title *Fingal* (1805) (he had previously published translations of Ossian songs in 1799, 1803 and 1804) and later also from Thomas Percy's *Reliques of Ancient English Poetry*. His love for northern, medieval literature was such that he stubbornly defended the authenticity of Chatterton's Rowley and even claimed to have translated Ossian, not from Macpherson but from a Gaelic original. It can be argued though that Bilderdijk's Dutch *Fingal* is superior to Macpherson's English.

Nature and simplicity became the key words of his poetry and the effusion of inner feeling the mark of poetic truthfulness. In poetry and prose, in introductions and annotations, he argued that reason teaches us nothing, that feeling alone puts us in touch with a higher world, with God, from which the material creation derives its harmony and form. Thus all true poetry to him is religious poetry, an outpouring of divinely inspired sentiment. If Bilderdijk disapproved of the ideological colour of a particular literary product, he unhesitatingly dismissed it as 'broddelwerk' (bungled rubbish), whether it showed technical brilliance or not. Thus he expressed his admiration for Shakespeare but used his ready invective on Schiller; or, if he admired a work of literature but wanted to protect his countrymen from its ideology, he translated it into Dutch and simply purged the text in the process of all that he considered damaging. In this way he 'censored' Delille's *L'Homme des Champs* in his *Het Buitenleven* (*Country Life*) (1803) and Pope's *An Essay on Man* in his *De Mensch* (*Man*) (1808), removing all that smelled of deism and reason worship.

During the last three decades of his life Bilderdijk published several major works on the Dutch language dealing with the gender of nouns, grammar and etymology. He objected to the view of Rousseau and others that language is invented, part of a *contrat social*, and that the alphabet is an artificial product of cultural evolution. Bilderdijk believed in the divine origin of language as had a previous generation, for example, of eighteenth-century German Pietists. There is an intimate, organic relation-ship between language and soul, between word and object, between letter and organ of speech. Words to him were not merely sounds based on con-ventions, not mechanical noises like those produced by Wolfgang von Kempelen's speech machine, but emanations of the thing itself. With other Romantics such as Jacob Grimm with whom he corresponded, Bilderdijk believed in the organic nature of language, although he objected to the progressivist anthropology of Herder and others. He stuck to the traditional belief of *origines sacrae*, of a Golden Age, of a Paradise, of a post-diluvial Nordic culture of Hyperboreans. Those had been times of high civilisation and purity. Linguistic change had been a process of degeneration which had occurred since the Fall of Man and since Babel when a single, universal language had existed. Sanskrit not only had the appeal of the exotic, but gave a glimpse of the youthful purity of our own languages. Bilderdijk was the first to translate into Dutch from the Sanskrit *Vedas*. He strongly objected to the spelling reforms of the philologist Matthijs Siegenbeek.

Bilderdijk's most curious linguistic treatise was his *Van het Letterschrift* (*About the Alphabet*) (1820). He argued that not just words, but also letters, are natural in origin, not evolved from Egyptian hieroglyphics. Letters depict the shape of the speech organs at the moment that a particu-lar letter is pronounced. The simplest instances are the capital B which shows the outline of the lips in profile, and the capital M which traces the dividing line between the upper and lower lips, as does the W. The idea was not original; a similar hypothesis, applied to Hebrew characters, had been put forward long ago by the 'Paracelsian' François-Mercure van Helmont; but this treatise does represent a fine example of Romantic organicism, and it was one of the few works by Bilderdijk which was translated into German.

SCIENCE AND SCIENCE FICTION

The contact with Jacob Grimm occurred after Bilderdijk had returned to The Netherlands. Also during his German exile he had met foreigners who influenced and inspired him. Both London and Brunswick were centres for refugees from the French Revolution and the Napoleonic Wars. The displacement of prominent sympathisers with the *ancien régime* had a definite effect on the spread of a form of reactionary Romanticism culti-vated in the cities were exiled scholars were offered the protection or the patronage of a sovereign. Brunswick under the Duke Karl Wilhelm Ferdinand was one such centre where hundreds of aristocrats (together with their servants), clergymen and *literati* had congregated. Apart from Bilderdijk, there were such different figures as Jaques Delille (1738–1813) and Jean-André Deluc (1727–1817).

Bilderdijk and Deluc lived for a time in the same house, and the affectionate support of the older man for the manic depressive poet led to an intimate friendship. Deluc was a Genevan Calvinist who had moved to London where he was appointed Reader to the Queen. On behalf of the British Government he went on a diplomatic mission to solicit the support of the Duke of Brunswick, although ostensibly to take up an honorary professorship at the University of Göttingen where Johann Friedrich Blumenbach worked.[3] Bilderdijk and Deluc had much in common, in particular basic tenets of orthodox Protestant belief. They also shared a strong dislike of the Encyclopédistes. Deluc was an ardent admirer of Bacon and, while in Germany, showed in his *Bacon, tel qu'il est* (1800) how a French translator had wilfully omitted several parts of Bacon's writings which were favourable to revealed religion. He discussed with Bilderdijk another of his Brunswick treatises, the *Abrégé de principes et de faits concernans la cosmologie et la géologie* (1803), in which he referred warmly to Bilderdijk, 'homme de lettres hollandois de beaucoup de mérite et de lumières'.

Deluc awoke in Bilderdijk an interest in geology and turned him into an admirer, not only of Bacon, but also of such contemporaries as Blumenbach, Dieudonné Dolomieu and another Genevan naturalist, Horace Bénédict de Saussure. The fruits of this contact with Deluc became apparent in several of Bilderdijk's works, in particular his *Geologie, of Verhandeling over de Vorming en Vervorming der Aarde* (*Geology, or Treatise on the Formation and Deformation of the Earth*) (1813), which was the first book on geology in the Dutch language.[4]

Geology was the Romantic science *par excellence*.[5] Goethe loved both mineralogy and palaeontology. Novalis, who had been a student at the Freiberg Mining Academy where Werner taught, used geology in his *Heinrich von Ofterdingen*. Byron read Cuvier and worked the new vertebrate paleontology into his *Don Juan* and his *Cain*. Coleridge was fascinated with the relationship of geological with chemical processes; as also was Davy. Constable, too, dabbled in the subject, and so did John Martin whose *The Deluge* showed influences both of Cuvier and the indigenous diluvial geology of Buckland. Many others shared this fascination with geology. It was not just the aspect of geological field work which attracted the Romantics. The period 1790–1820 was the heroic age of geological discovery when the fact of extinction was first established, when monsters from previous worlds were dug up and reconstructed, when the earth acquired a long pre-Adamic history divided into periods, and when the hypothesis was put forward that the present period of human history began after a series of mighty upheavals, the last of which had destroyed the ante-diluvian earth, probably as a result of the close passage of a comet.

This vision of earth history added a dazzling new dimension to the Romantics' love of the past. The pre-historic vertebrates appealed to a taste for the bizarre. The geological catastrophes demonstrated the awesome power of nature and its unpredictable, primeval forces. Moreover, some of the traditionally religious Romantics, especially in England were able to interpret the last of the geological upheavals as the Biblical deluge, and use the new geology to feed their apocalyptic anticipations.[6] 'Diluvial drama' became a successful Romantic literary genre. Byron's *Heaven and Earth* (1823) is a good example. Bilderdijk wrote his highly esteemed *De Ondergang der Eerste Wereld* long before, in 1809 (published in 1820) (*The Destruction of the First World*). Although never completed, it is regarded as his masterpiece, and was an impressive example of apocalyptic diluvialism. The opening stanza (translated into English in 1858) runs as follows (the Dutch original is not in blank verse):

> I sing the doom of the primeval world,
> And of that race, with hell and devils leagued
> In deeds iniquitous, which dared to tempt
> Heav'ns Majesty, and, impious, sought to scale
> The battlements of Paradise; till God,
> Weary of wrestling with sin-ruin'd Man,
> Crush'd and o'erturn'd the guilty world, in wrath
> Hurling creation into chaos back;
> But – in His mercy – from the gen'ral wreck
> One man preserving, to re-people earth
> And raise upon the ruins of the world
> A mortal race, seed for eternity.[7]

The greatest scientist of the Romantic period was Cuvier (although Alexander von Humboldt was the greater as a Romantic), and few *literati* were unfamiliar with his *Discours préliminaire* (1812) which summarised his catastrophist theory of the earth. When Bilderdijk published his *Geologie*, the year after Cuvier's *Essay* had appeared, he was accused of plagiarism; but any similarities between the two books are more likely to be the result of a shared influence derived from Deluc.

Bilderdijk's geological ideas were primarily polemical, written to confute Buffon and other deist and Plutonist authors. He had earlier attacked Buffon in *Het Buitenleven* (*Country Life*) (1803), his translation of Delille's great nature poem. Goethe had followed Werner's Neptunism, and Bilderdijk, too, influenced by Deluc, fell in line with Neptunist theory. The main sources for his geology book were Deluc's *Lettres sur l'histoire de la terre et de l'homme* (1779) and his *Lettres sur l'histoire physique de la terre* (1798). The Biblical creation days were interpreted as geological periods during which chemical precipitation in a primordial ocean produced the greater part of the succession of geological formations. The deluge, probably the result of a passing comet, was caused by the collapse of enormous cavities inside the crust of the earth. These cavities filled with the waters of the primordial ocean, revealing the present continents. Bilderdijk added a mathematical model showing how this transfer of water would have changed the earth's axis of rotation from perpendicular to its present tilted position.

Astronomy, too, attracted the interest of Romantic writers. Several new discoveries were eminently suited to undermine the *Weltbild* of deist rationalism and its love of mathematical elegance and orderliness. Bilderdijk objected to 'Newtonianismus', the mathematical dictatorship over nature, particularly in the area of planetary physics, successfully used for deistic purposes by Voltaire and others. The shackles of mathematical regularity were thrown off, however, by William Herschel's discovery of the new planet Uranus (1781). A few years later (1787) two of its satellites were detected. In quick succession further satellite discoveries followed: in 1789 two new ones around Saturn, and in 1797 more around Jupiter. Most sensationally of all, in 1801 the first two of the minor planets or asteroids were detected (Ceres and Pallas).

Moreover, E. F. F. Chladni proved in 1794 that meteorite falls, which had been derided by Enlightenment savants as the product of superstitious imagination, were in fact real, and during the early nineteenth century a wave of meteorite enthusiasm swept Europe. P.-M.-S. Bigot de Morogues listed no fewer than 130 historical instances of meteorite falls in his *Mémoire historique et physique sur les chutes des pierres* (1812).[8] Freedom for cosmogony at last: more new planets and satellites could be discovered, and the 'Newtonian straitjacket' in which the eighteenth-century *physiciens* had put the planetary system was ripped to shreds. Deluc, who was a friend of Herschel, and knew the astronomer royal Nevil Maskelyne, recorded in a postscript to his *Abrégé* an hypothesis by Maskelyne that even the earth may have more than a single lunar satellite; that very small, sublunary bodies may encircle the earth, too small to be seen by day and invisible by night because their proximity causes them to be eclipsed (but the cause of certain meteoric lights).

Bilderdijk's fertile imagination picked up on Deluc's postscript. Combining astronomical discoveries with the latest balloon technology, he produced a fascinating science fiction story, *Kort Verhaal van eene Aanmerkelijke Luchtreis* (*Brief Account of a Remarkable Air-Voyage*) (1813). The story made use of the balloon travel developed since 1783 when the brothers Montgolfier had launched the first free flight of a hot-air balloon.[9] In the same year J. A. C. Charles had launched the first hydrogen balloon, and Jean François Pilâtre de Rozier conducted the first manned flight. A multitude of sensational developments followed. In 1785 the Channel was crossed by balloon. In the same year the first fatal crash happened. Balloons began to be used for military purposes. Records in flight distance and height were broken. Women took to balloon flight. In Brunswick the wife of a professor was said to have ascended to 8,000 metres.

A balloon craze followed: balloon travel became the subject of innumerable newspaper stories, poems and plays, and it produced a balloon fashion in dress. One of the better known novels using the air balloon was Jean Paul's *Des Luftschiffers Giannozzo Seebuch* (1800). The literary response to this form of new technology was widespread, as Helene Jacobius showed in her *Luftschiff und Pegasus* (1909). Bilderdijk, however, used it to construct a proper science fiction story. Mary Shelley's *Frankenstein* (1818) is often taken as the beginning of genuine science fiction, but Bilderdijk's story pre-dates hers by five years. A summary of the story is nothing less than a catalogue of characteristic features of the Romantic *Weltanschauung*. The origin of the genre itself may be seen as a product of the Romantic mind. The author travels to Persia, the dreamland of many Romantics, where he admires the hospitality of the natives. A sense of alienation makes him think of other worlds. The locals challenge him into making a hydrogen balloon. He ascends too fast and loses consciousness. When he wakes up it slowly dawns on him that he has landed on a small sub-lunary satellite around the earth which he calls Selenion. Its surface features indicate volcanic activity which may be the source of meteorite falls on earth. No indigenous carnivorous animals exist and its paradisiacal state is shown also by the absence of rain as a mist moistens the soil. But an abandoned farmyard indicates that, long before him, someone had landed on Selenion. An inscription with old characters proves that this was Abaris, the Hyperborean. Finally, he tires of his lonely explorations and realises that his excitement is fed by an anticipation of being able to tell his story to those earthlings from whom he had felt so estranged. He manages to repair his balloon and ascend, and he falls back in the Indian Ocean where a Russian ship rescues him.

Bilderdijk's science and technology were accurate, but he did not have the technological fantasy of Jules Verne. His story was more profound than Verne's novels, however, in its use of autobiographical sentiment, of science and history. It records his Romantic agony, his dreaming desire for far-away places, the Orient (he liked to think that he looked Oriental and he often wore a turban), and even for another world, which he then uses as a stage for his anti-rationalistic ideas about a lost paradise, the early height of human civilisation, the superiority of Nordic culture over Greece and Italy, the organic origin of the alphabet, the possibility of

Maskelyne's speculation about sub-lunary satellites and an hypothesis about the origin of meteorites.

Bilderdijk dabbled in other sciences as well, most notably in botany.[10] In *De Dieren* (*The Animals*) (1817) he maintained that animals have souls, a favourite Romantic notion. Medicine he not only wrote about, he occasionally also practised it. His father, Izaäk Bilderdijk, had studied medicine at Leyden, and had been a physician in Amsterdam, known for his ready use of blood-letting. At about the time that Willem was born, father Bilderdijk's medical practice faltered, purportedly because of his Orangist convictions and the enmity of the Patriots, and he was forced to seek employment as a civil administrator. He continued to medicate friends and family, however, and his son Willem later did the same. A large number of prescriptions has been preserved, written by Willem Bilderdijk in apothecaries' Latin, mostly for his own use. From these it appears that the medicine which he 'prescribed' most frequently was opium. He used it for various purposes: as a pain-killer to alleviate head and toothaches, as a soporific to fight insomnia, which he often suffered for several consecutive nights, or to suppress hunger when poverty deprived him of even a simple loaf of bread.

Bilderdijk's use of opium most likely began when he was a student at Leyden, and from that time on it never ceased. On average he used some 130 milligrammes of opium per day, equivalent to approximately 13 milligrammes of morphine. He neither drank it in alcoholic solution, nor smoked it, but consumed opium in the form of pills; on festive occasions he used silver-coated pills. Smoking, in fact, he detested, and he fulminated against it in ''t Nicotiaansche kruid' ('The Nicotine Herb') (1827). Opium, however, he could not do without, and the prospect of having no pills made him tremble with anxiety. There can be no doubt that Bilderdijk became an opium addict, even though he was fully aware of its effects. On one tragic occasion, Bilderdijk's little son Ursinus was given opium as a soporific, and the baby boy, just over one year old, died of an overdose. Bilderdijk described the effects of the drug in *De Ziekte der Geleerden* (*The Scholars' Malady*) (1807), his successful didactic poem which dealt for the most part with psychosomatic problems caused by intense mental exertions. The proceeds of 1,400 Dutch guilders were donated to the victims of the Leyden Catastrophe of 1807 when the explosion of a ship, filled with 37,000 pounds of gunpowder, destroyed half of the old city centre.

The references to opium in *The Scholars' Malady* form a link with such other literary products of the period as Thomas de Quincey's *Confessions of an English Opium-Eater* (1821). Drug addiction was not uncommon among the Romantics; Coleridge, Keats, Shelley, Novalis and several other prominent figures were either in 'bondage of opium' or at least used the poppy product regularly. Alethea Hayter has discussed this phenomenon in her *Opium and the Romantic Imagination* (1968). Following in her footsteps, Boudewijn Büch attributes Bilderdijk's 'religious fanaticism', his 'ink-slinging' and various other Romantic personality features to opium addiction.[11]

The use of drugs may well have enhanced certain visionary aspects of the Romantic imagination. One may even want to list the drug habit of many prominent *literati* as one of the defining manifestations of the Romantic fashion. It would seem to be going too far, however, if one were to claim, as does Büch, that opium addiction was the cause of much that was quintessentially Romantic in Bilderdijk.

BILDERDIJK'S CIRCLE: ISAÄC DA COSTA, GUILLAUME GROEN VAN PRINSTERER AND OTHERS

Bilderdijk's influence, though never wide, was profound. At the age of sixty, having given up the hope of ever being offered a university chair, he decided to start lecturing privately to students. In 1817 he opened a so-called *privatissimum* in Leyden on 'the history of the fatherland'. In his lectures, the anti-Revolutionary Bilderdijk, protester against 'the spirit of the age', gave, as Pieter Geyl puts it, a new lease of life to the Orangist legend, so prevalent in the historical consciousness of the Dutch people, and which was reanimated through the political crises of the French occupation and the subsequent establishment of the new kingdom of The Netherlands. Bilderdijk's history lectures on the *Geschiedenis des Vaderlands* were later edited by his friend H. W. Tydeman and comprised no fewer than thirteen volumes (1832–53). According to Geyl, these were 'a highly seasoned rehash of the Orangist party stuff dished up by eighteenth-century writers'; the *Geschiedenis des Vaderlands* were, he believes, one protracted pamphlet based on very little genuine research.[12] Jan Romein, on the other hand, judges Bilderdijk's history lectures more favourably. He argues that Bilderdijk's Romantic revisionism opened up entirely new vistas to the generation of his students; especially his appreciation of the medieval history of the Low Countries was innovatory.[13]

During the approximately ten years of Bilderdijk's *privatissimum* a total of at most forty students attended; yet among them were several who later became men of consequence, such as Abraham Capadose, Isaäc da Costa, P. J. Elout van Soeterwoude, Guillaume Groen van Prinsterer, the brothers Willem and Dirk van Hogendorp, Jacob van Lennep and others. His relationship with these young men was warm and intimate. None of Bilderdijk's students equalled him as a writer of Dutch poetry or prose, but

Da Costa became known as a poet in his own right and van Lennep as a novelist. In fact, in poetry and prose Da Costa joined Bilderdijk in reminding the nation of its divine mission, and van Lennep's novels helped propagate a form of historical, national Romanticism. Others from the Leyden circle too carried the torch of Bilderdijk's Calvinist-Romantic views of history, religion, political and social affairs.

Closest to Bilderdijk was Da Costa (1798–1862). He and his friend Capadose (1795–1874) were descended from Portuguese-Jewish families, and during their student days in Leyden continued to adhere to the Jewish faith. Influenced by Bilderdijk, however, whose philo-Semitic feelings helped bridge the chasm between the Old and New Testament, the two young Jews converted to Christianity. During an emotional and packed service in Leyden's Dutch Reformed Pieterkerk they were baptised. No sooner had the two friends embraced the Christian faith than they set to work to combat liberalism, irreligiousness and revolution. With all the earnest intensity of the new convert and the uncompromising idealism of his youth (he was twenty-five), Da Costa wrote his sensational *Bezwaren tegen de Geest der Eeuw* (*Objections to the Spirit of the Age*) (1823). This booklet came closer to being the Dutch Romantic manifesto than anything that Bilderdijk had written.

Da Costa's prose was forceful and passionate and his narrative burning with conviction and an eschatological sense of urgency. He believed that the liberal and self-satisfied establishment in Church and state was abandoning God and religion as the source of individual conduct and intellectual creativity. He urged his readers to return to Calvinist orthodoxy, objecting to both Enlightenment deism and the secular metaphysics of the German Naturphilosophen. He detested the non-religious morality of the Encyclopédistes and even of Byron, parts of whose *Cain* he had actually translated into Dutch (albeit with critical commentary).

Da Costa lambasted the fashionable notion of tolerance. In the fine arts he idolised Classical Greece and the Italian Renaissance, Homer and Raphael, but also the Dutch Golden Age of Rubens and Vondel; true art, he argued, came from divinely instilled genius, from an inner source of religious inspiration, not from the new-fangled societies for the promotion of arts, founded by a mediocre and self-satisfied bourgeoisie. The natural sciences, Da Costa maintained, were misused to undermine the Bible, the historicity of creation, deluge, miracles and the reality of a spiritual world. He vehemently objected to Rousseau's *contrat social* and to the concept of a constitutional monarchy; the sovereign's power does not derive from the people but from God; freedom is not a question of political philosophy but of Gospel truth.

The revolution's notion of equality, Da Costa fumed, was an attack on the Providential nature of one's birth; the French Jacobins, who had destroyed the aristocracy, had ended up under the autocracy of Napoleon. That other democratic notion, 'public opinion', had in the past ridiculed Noah and had tolerated the most horrendous vice in Sodom and Gomorrah. Education was failing to preserve the wise understanding of generations of yore and instilling a false sense of progress. 'We are living in an age of enlightenment! . . . Thus boasts in blind conceit an age of slavery, an age of superstition, of idolatry, of ignorance, and of darkness!'

The *Objections to the Spirit of the Age* were like a bombshell exploding amidst a cosy gathering of contented, pipe-smoking and overweight burghers. Their comfort being disturbed, they turned ugly. A rain of pamphlets and newspaper articles came down on young Da Costa. He was attacked, lampooned and ostracised. Bilderdijk came in for a share of the bile and he felt compelled to join the fray with a brochure *De Bezwaren . . . Toegelicht (The Objections . . . Explained)* (1823). He went over the same ground again seeing in all and everywhere signs of degeneration; France and Germany were the worst hot-beds of evil. Bilderdijk's stock of terms of abuse was nearly inexhaustible, but the force of his language was magisterial. Both he and his pupil wrote with the visionary conviction of Biblical prophets, seeing in the post-Revolutionary modernisation of society the apocalyptic decline of a nation that should be the modern-day chosen people (as Israel once had been) and whose origins they perceived in a Calvinist-Romantic haze.

Less sensational, though equally controversial was Capadose's contribution to the 1823 fracas. In 1820 Edward Jenner's method of vaccination had become compulsory. Da Costa raised his voice against this asking indignantly why a child, in order to enter school, should not be asked about whether or not it had been christened but would have to be vaccinated: 'Vaccination replacing baptism.' Capadose, who was a medical doctor, prevaricated, but in 1823 he came out against vaccination, on both medical and theological grounds. In his *Bestrijding der Vaccine (The Fight against Vaccine)* he argued that one should not interfere with divine providence by making children immune to smallpox, and that the government, by forcing parents to do so, was violating parental rights. Bilderdijk added his voice to this duet; in 'De woed der koepok-inenting' ('The Rage of Cow-Pock Vaccination') (1825) he lambasted those who 'drive the flithy cattle poison into children's veins'.

With time Da Costa's language became more moderate, reflecting changes in the orthodox-Protestant movement at large. In 1823 he had objected to the abolition of slavery; but by 1840 he joined the ranks of the abolitionists, and, together with Willem van Hogendorp, initiated protests against the deprivations suffered by many working-class labourers.

Da Costa remained loyal to Bilderdijk, however, whose collected poetry he edited. Less hot-headed than Bilderdijk from the start were both van Lennep and Groen van Prinsterer. In 1826 van Lennep Sr (David) published a paper calling for novels modelled on Walter Scott. His son Jacob (1802–68) responded. Both Bilderdijk and Scott had focused his interest on the Middle Ages, and he wrote four legends in verse, *Nederlandsche Legenden* (*Dutch Legends*) (1828–31), dealing with knights, castles, witchcraft and the like. He had much success with his novel *De Pleegzoon* (*The Adopted Son*) (written in 1827; published 1833) and similar historical novels. Although genre and subject-matter fitted the Romantic fashion, G. P. M. Knuvelder sees van Lennep primarily as a skilful story teller whose lack of passionate identification with his subject matter disqualifies him from having been a quintessential Romantic.[14] Although now little read, Jacob was a prolific writer, and in addition to historical novels *à la* Scott he wrote poetry, drama, librettos and also translated Byron and Shakespeare. For some time he was closely involved with the Amsterdam theatre working together with the successful designer François-Joseph Pfeiffer.

Groen van Prinsterer (1801–76) habitually emphasised his independence from 'the acrimonious Bilderdijk'. Yet as Geyl argues, he acted as the apostle of the older man's view of history. As statesman and effective founder of the Anti-Revolutionary Party, he exerted a greater and longer lasting influence than any other person from Bilderdijk's circle. Groen's work is free from the vehemence and the invective which weighs down Bilderdijk's prose, but it followed the same party line while even more exclusively interpreting historical events from the religious point of view. A series of lectures which he gave in his private library during the winter of 1845–6 to a circle of friends were published as his *Ongeloof en Revolutie* in which he argued that there exists a natural, causal connexion between unbelief and revolution. History to him has not been shaped by a series of actions but by the consequences of ideas. Thus revolution was the result of irreligious scepticism. His heroes were the Englishmen William Pitt Jr and Edmund Burke, who had gone against the French Revolutionary tide. His *Handboek der Geschiedenis van het Vaderland* (*Manual of the History of the Fatherland*) (1846) was, as Geyl put it, a religious epic of the chosen Dutch Republic, elected in order to preserve, under the providential leadership of the House of Orange, a Dutch Reformed people.

THE DUTCH RÉVEIL

One of the distinctive features of the Romantic movement was a renewed respect for the supranatural and religion. Across Europe, many leading

Romantics turned their backs on Enlightenment rationalism and scepticism and returned to the fold of traditional Christianity. One manifestation of this was the intellectual defence of religion in the form of Christian apologetics. A popular example was François René de Châteaubriand's *Le Génie du Christianisme* (1802).

Nowhere was the connexion of Romanticism with religious belief stronger, however, than in The Netherlands. In fact, religion was a prominent defining feature of Dutch Romanticism. Bilderdijk joined the ranks of those who defended with scholarly arguments the historicity of the Bible and the truth of Christianity. He did this by translating into his mother tongue, French, German and English treatises of which he approved. In his geology textbook he defended the historical reality of the Biblical deluge, making ample use of Deluc's *Lettres*. He translated G. E. W. Dedekind's book about spirits, *Ueber Geisternähe und Geisterwirkung*. He also translated Thomas Chalmers' *The Evidence and Authority of the Christian Revelation* which presented the historical argument in favour of the Christian religion.

Romantic religion was far more, however, than an early nineteenth-century form of Christian apologetics. In religion as well as in art, the Romantics emphasised the importance of the human individual, of his subjective experience, his feelings and inner awareness. In the introductions to his apologetic translations, Bilderdijk stressed that the main purpose of external, intellectual evidence of Christianity is to convince unbelievers. Those who already believe will not need such cerebral evidence because the true foundation of their belief is the inner conviction of their hearts. To Bilderdijk the essence of religion was feeling.

This supremacy of inner religious experience did not go hand in hand with doctrinal anarchy, as one might expect. Quite the contrary. The Romantic predilection for what is historical, original and pure manifested itself on the religious level in a return to doctrinal orthodoxy. But this was no simple matter. After all, a return to the source could mean two very different things. On a European scale, it meant a return to the Middle Ages and to Roman Catholicism in the manner of Novalis' *Die Christenheit oder Europa* (1799). On a Dutch national scale, however, it meant a return to the Synod of Dordrecht of 1618–19 with its Calvinist doctrines. Thus Dutch Romanticism was torn between Rome and Dordrecht (colloquially 'Dort').

Bilderdijk clearly felt this pull in the two opposite directions, especially during the 1810s and 1820s. A parallel dilemma was experienced in the 1830s by E. B. Pusey and other members of the Oxford movement. In the end Bilderdijk did not go over to Rome, but his philo-Catholicism was nonetheless strong. He hoped for a re-unification of all Christians to fight the threat of deism. In two public appeals, *Een Protestant aan zijne Medeprotestanten* (*A Protestant to his Fellow Protestants*) (1816) and *Aan de Roomsch-Katholijken dezer Dagen* (*To the Catholics of Today*) (1823), he declared his warm respect for the Catholic Church and objected to the traditional comparisons of the Pope with the apocalyptic beast of the Revelations of St John. To Bilderdijk the Lord's Supper had to be more than a Calvinist feast of remembrance; he believed that there exists a 'hidden relationship' between Christ and the bread and wine. The fact that he wrote a poem about the Virgin Mary, 'Aan de Moedermaagd' ('To the Virgin Mary') in the Reformation Year 1817 was a distinctly philo-Catholic act. In his *Romantiek en Katholicisme in Nederland* (*Romanticism and Catholicism in The Netherlands*) (1926) Gerard Brom saw Bilderdijk as the main Romantic to have contributed to Catholic Emancipation. In a hyperbole worthy of his hero, he described Bilderdijk as a giant Christopher who at the gateway of the nineteenth century carried a childish Christianity across the stream of Revolutionary upheavals.

But orthodox Dutch Protestantism also meant Orangist nationalism, 'the doctrine of our fathers', and the pull of Dort in the end proved stronger than that of Rome. Thus with Bilderdijk, a religion of feeling was grafted upon Calvinist orthodoxy. It appealed to his circle of young Leyden students who were disenchanted with the liberalism of a complacent state Church and its *petit bourgeois* clergy. A religious revival resulted, called the Dutch Réveil, much inspired by analogous developments abroad.

The Réveil was a Protestant revival movement of the first half of the nineteenth century which began around 1810 in the French-speaking part of Switzerland. The originators were students who reacted against the liberalism and rationalism of the Genevan clergy and who were influenced by English Methodism and German Pietism. Prominent figures were Ami Bost, Henri-Louis Empaytez and César Malan. The movement championed a return to orthodox-Reformed belief, to the doctrines of original sin, grace and predestination, but equally emphasised inner religious experience and brotherly love. In 1832 the Société Évangélique was founded with its own theological seminary where J. H. Merle d'Aubigné and others taught. The most important theologian of the Swiss Réveil was Alexandre Rodolphe Vinet.

From Geneva, the Réveil readily spread to other Protestant areas of Europe, in particular to France, Germany and also The Netherlands, a process which M. E. Kluit describes in her comprehensive history of *Het Protestantse Réveil in Nederland en Daarbuiten, 1815–1865* (*The Protestant Réveil in The Netherlands and Elsewhere*) (1970). Bilderdijk is generally regarded as 'the father of the Dutch Réveil'. But also Da Costa's *Objections to the Spirit of the Age* (1823) has been seen as the break-

through of the Réveil movement in The Netherlands. The Dutch Réveil
was centred on Amsterdam and The Hague, and it is true that its leaders
had experienced Bilderdijk's influence during their student years at
Leyden. But the Réveil did not take on any organisational reality until two
clergymen from the Swiss movement, J. D. A. Chavannes and L. G. James,
visited Da Costa in Amsterdam. This contact inspired Da Costa to
organise his renowned Sunday evening Bible-readings. For many years
from 1826, Da Costa opened his house every Sunday to anyone looking for
spiritual renewal and Scriptural instruction. He would read a Bible lesson,
say a prayer and expound.

The Amsterdam circle rapidly expanded and included such other
Romantic *literati* as Abraham Capadose, Willem de Clerq and for a while
Jacob van Lennep. Also A. S. Thelwall, English chaplain and missionary to
the Jews in Amsterdam, was a close associate. In reaction to the rational
religion of the 'brave burger' (worthy burgher), they rediscovered the Old
Testament, Christ and the Jewish people. They too showed a commitment
to Christian philanthropy. This was particularly true for the circle in The
Hague which counted among its members the Bilderdijk students Willem
and Dirk van Hogendorp, Guillaume Groen van Prinsterer, Cornelis
Baron van Zuylen van Nijevelt and several other aristocratic devotees.
They worked for such causes as anti-slavery, poor relief and various other
types of social work. Moreover, in the person of Groen van Prinsterer the
Réveil developed the notion of a Christian statesman, active in education
and politics.

Similar circles spring up in other cities and towns, but in contrast to
Switzerland, no free churches were founded. In 1834, however, in the
northern province of Groningen, the so-called Afscheiding (Secession) was
initiated, led by the Rev. Hendrik de Cock. Its religious aims were closely
related to those of the Réveil. The social composition of the two groups,
however, was very different. Whereas the Réveil was aristocratic in
character, the Afscheiding found its followers mainly among the lower
classes, the majority of them were day-labourers.[15]

NOT A NATIONAL MOVEMENT

In a casual overview of European Romanticism one might be forgiven for
restricting Romanticism in The Netherlands to Bilderdijk and his
immediate circle. If one were to look more closely, such a restriction would
prove to be an unjustified oversimplification. More talented than van
Lennep in developing the literary medium of the historical novel, for
example, was Aarnout Drost (1810–34) who, in spite of a tragically short

life, made a lasting impact with his *Hermingard van de Eikenterpen* (*Hermingard of the Oak Burial Mounds*) (1832). This was not only a fine example of a historical story, but Drost used history as the stage on which to develop religion and morality. Stronger than historical nationalism was Drost's religious commitment in the spirit of the Réveil. Drost also started a new literary journal, *De Muzen* (*The Muses*) (1834). Two men on its staff, the historian R. C. Bakhuizen van den Brink (1810–65) and the writer E. J. Potgieter (1808–75) continued Drost's campaign to improve literary standards in *De Gids* (*The Guide*) (1837), known for its merciless criticism of *bourgeois-satisfait* complacency. Drost's religious idealism also influenced the novelist Anna Bosboom-Toussaint (1812–86), known for the psychological depth with which she described the main characters in her stories.

It has recently been argued that a Romantic fashion was present also in the theatre, especially in the Amsterdam Schouwburg during the 1820s and early 1830s. The popularity of adding music to drama, of the German opera, and the use of new stage *décor* with paintings of ruins, waterfalls or volcanic eruptions were manifestations of a Romantic break-away from the Neo-classical theatre.[16]

In painting, too, a modest Romantic school can be identified. Among its characteristics were a preference for landscapes depicting the primaeval forces of nature in thunderstorms and lightning. Such landscapes were not primarily presentations of nature, but were intended to transmit a feeling about nature. This school took its cue in part from the great landscape painters of the seventeenth century such as Hobbema or Ruisdael, and a recent exhibition catalogue of Dutch painting in the early nineteenth century has been aptly entitled *Op zoek naar de Gouden Eeuw* (*In Search of the Golden Age*) (1986). The leading representatives of Romantic landscape painting were B. C. Koekkoek (1803–62) and Andreas Schelfhout (1787–1870). The latter's pupil, Wijnand Nuyen (1813–39), in spite of his tragically short life, made an unforgettable contribution with, for example, *Schipbreuk op een rotsachtige kust* (*Shipwreck on a Rocky Coast*) (c. 1836).

In science and medicine Romantic elements can be recognised as well. During a recent symposium on 'Romantiek in Nederland (1800–1850)' (1983) H. A. M. Snelders argued that interest in electromagnetism and a use of vitalistic principles were manifestations of a Romantic world view.[17]

But the main conclusion of the symposium was that Romanticism in The Netherlands had been a very limited and half-hearted affair. W. van den Berg expressed his agreement with Gerard Brom's metaphor that Dutch Romanticism flapped its wings but never took off. He maintained that the question of Dutch Romanticism is more whether or not there ever was such a phenomenon than distinguishing its characteristic features. Most of it was not indigenously grown, but imported.[18]

English Romanticism, for example, acquired a genuine following in The Netherlands. Shakespearian drama became popular; Constable and several lesser figures exerted a formative influence on Dutch landscape painting of the period; Scott's historical novels were systematically imitated, and, among the young, 'Byronismus' was for a while a fashionable cult. And all this came over and above Bilderdijk's admiration for Chatterton's Rowley and Macpherson's Ossian. In many more ways the common sense Protestantism of the Dutch was a cousin of English and Scottish culture. (See, however, 'Concluding observations'.)

The French version of the Romantic fashion, however, was regarded as too irreligious and immoral and did not agree well with the ethical partiality of the culturally pervasive 'predikantendom' (Dutch Reformed clergy). German Romanticism in particular was alien to the domestic common sense of the Dutch. It was more readily ridiculed than followed. Snelders shows that German Naturphilosophie had very few followers indeed. To the Dutch physicists, the practical use of science was paramount, not the development of theory, especially not something as speculative and vague as Schelling's philosophy. The Dutch 'national character', the near universal preference for domestic common sense and practicability, simply had little consanguinity with any thoroughbred Romanticism.

C. de Deugd gestures towards Bilderdijk's place among Europe's great Romantics.[19] But even Bilderdijk was poorly known abroad and remained a cultural epiphenomenon in his own country. The few foreigners who visited Bilderdijk did regard him as of European stature, in particular the English poet and historian Robert Southey, who twice visited the Bilderdijk family (1825, 1826), and lavished praise on 'my friend Bilderdijk'. The reason why the Dutchman was not better known in England was, according to Southey, 'the curse that came from Babel, clipt the wings of Poetry', i.e., the fact that Bilderdijk wrote in Dutch. Answering the question 'And who is Bilderdijk?', Southey wrote:

> Right-minded, happy-minded, righteous man!
> True lover of his country and his kind;
> In knowledge and in inexhaustive stores
> Of native genius rich; philosopher,
> Poet, and sage. The language of a state
> Inferior in illustrious deeds to none,
> But circumscribed by narrow bounds, and now
> Sinking in irrecoverable decline,
> Hath pent within its sphere a name, with which
> Europe should else have rung from side to side.[20]

Others, such as John Browning and Hoffmann von Fallersleben, regarded Bilderdijk as the leading literary representative of The Netherlands and wrote admiringly about him.[21] But the reason why the Dutch did not take Romanticism aboard was also the reason why Bilderdijk has never been accepted as a representative national figure. The Byronic self-aggrandisement, the hero-worship, the manic obsessiveness were all features which might have been admired in a country where *Die Leiden des jungen Werthers* led to a wave of suicides among the young, but definitely alienated him from the majority of level-headed Dutch people.

Institutionally too, the Romanticism of Bilderdijk and his circle was markedly anti-establishmentarian. It had no basis in official, public institutions such as the Church, the universities or the societies for the promotion of arts and sciences. When the most prestigious of these societies, De Hollandsche Maatschappij der Wetenschappen, invited Bilderdijk to join, he declined in a typically hypochondriacal letter to the secretary Martinus van Marum. Instead, the small band of dedicated Romantics were informally organised and came together in private circles such as Bilderdijk's *privatissimum*, Da Costa's Sunday evening readings and Groen's private library meetings. Here they nurtured their almost mystical belief in divinely inspired genius.

This separation from the mainstream of Dutch culture did not mean that Bilderdijk had no following. On the contrary. Although the establishment despised him as a nuisance or even as a disfigured madman, a small but devoted following idolised him as Holland's greatest literary genius. Even a few *literati* from outside Bilderdijk's sphere of influence paid tribute to his poetical talent, though such tributes occurred mostly before the 1880s. Among the devotees, already Da Costa, in a book-length essay on 'Bilderdijk en Goethe' (1859) sought to elevate his hero to national prominence.[22] It was particularly the implications of Bilderdijk's views for religion and politics, for Church and state, which determined the nature of his following. In fact, the Bilderdijk heritage was more or less captured by a minority of traditional Calvinists. They were the people who formed the Anti-revolutionaire Partij (1878) and established the break-away free church, Gereformeerde Kerken in Nederland (1892), a fusion of the Afscheiding of 1834 with a later secession from the state Church, the Doleantie (1886). Their leader, the redoubtable statesman, theologian and one-time coalition prime minister Abraham Kuyper contributed to keeping Bilderdijk the partisan property of the Gereformeerden. In 1906, the 150th anniversary of Bilderdijk's birth, Kuyper delivered a lecture on 'Bilderdijk in zijne Nationale Beteekenis' ('The National Significance of Bilderdijk') in which he claimed a place for the poet in Holland equivalent to Byron's in England and Goethe's in Germany. Also in 1906, Kuyper's colleague Herman Bavinck, theologian and member of parliament, wrote his *Bilderdijk als Denker and Dichter* (*Bilderdijk as Thinker and Poet*) in which he placed Bilderdijk in the cultural tradition of Rembrandt because of their having carried the united banners of Christian truth and Dutch art, without Goethe's deification of nature or Schiller's glorification of man.

These and several subsequent hagiographies[23] contributed much to making the Bilderdijk image tailor-fit for the national ambitions of Kuyper and his Anti-Revolutionary political constituency. Pruned away, or at least explained away, were Bilderdijk's eroticism, his sexual escapades, his adultery, his divorce, his occasional opportunism, his ode to the French occupation emperor Napoleon, his philo-Catholicism and verses on the Virgin Mary, his lack of interest in the Church and institutionalised religion, his at times heterodox or at best whimsical exegesis of Biblical texts and his mystical and pietistical predilections. Brom made a valiant attempt to claim a share for the Catholics of the Bilderdijk heritage, blaming Da Costa for blocking a rapprochement to Rome.[24] But it was to no avail. Bilderdijk remained a minority property of orthodox Calvinists, and today some scholars regard it as perfectly acceptable to address the issue of literary Romanticism in The Netherlands without paying the slightest attention to the oeuvre of Bilderdijk and his circle.[25]

DUTCH ROMANTICISM: CONCLUDING OBSERVATIONS

Romanticism in The Netherlands was a minority phenomenon. In its full-grown and purest form it was restricted to a narrow circle of people whose reactionary views grew in the soil of Orangist nationalism and Calvinist orthodoxy. There were, in addition, dispersed traces of a liberal variety of Romanticism, represented by such establishment figures as the statesman Johan Rudolf Thorbecke (1798–1872) whose political science owed much to German Romantic organicism. The liberal variety, however, was a minor late-comer (mainly post-1830). If one were to look at Dutch culture in isolation, without taking the larger European nations into account, one would not see the rich variety of Romantic manifestations that elsewhere in Europe led to the definition of Romanticism as a distinct period of cultural history. As a result, it is difficult to pinpoint either the beginning or the end of the Romantic phase in The Netherlands, although it is clear that the fashion reached its high point during the 1810s and 1820s. Dutch Romanticism had a late start. There were by the end of the eighteenth century several poets, in addition to Bilderdijk, who reacted against Neo-classicism: Hieronymus van Alphen, Rhijnvis Feith, Jacobus Bellamy, Anthonie C. W. Staring. But there was neither the pre-history of the Gothic novel nor that of Sturm und Drang behind them.

If a specific inception date were needed one could take the period during which Bilderdijk was in exile and sent home many Dutch translations of foreign literature, in particular *Fingal*, in 1805, his brilliant rendition of Macpherson's *Ossian*. The year 1850 is sometimes taken as the end of Romanticism in The Netherlands, but this very late date is not chosen because of a manifest persistence of the Romantic tradition, but more for want of a Dutch equivalent to the Victorian phase in England or of the German Vormärz, which started in the 1830s.

The Dutch dependence on a foreign Romantic context, and on an import from abroad, raises the interesting question of how such a cultural transfer took place. One might be inclined to think that a contemporary migration, from one country to another, would have been similar to a migration through time, from one generation to the next, by an admiration for or imitation of the great names of Romanticism. This is not what happened. In fact, the Dutch were unfamiliar with, or effectively ignored, most of the leading foreign Romantics. Examples of unknown or poorly known writers in English were none other than Coleridge, Wordsworth, Shelley and Keats; German examples included Friedrich Schlegel, Novalis, Tieck and Kleist. Conversely, some of the minor English painters (Samuel Prout, James D. Harding, Richard P. Bonnington) had a more direct impact on Dutch landscape painting of the early nineteenth century than had major figures such as Turner (although Constable exerted an influence). In other words, it was more the ideas of Romanticism that were borrowed than its finest fruits, and foreign Romanticism functioned first and foremost as a catalyst for the Dutch variety. A foreign spark was as good as a foreign flame to ignite the small but smouldering stack of native Romantic combustibles.

Even those foreign Romantics who did become well known were adapted to indigenous needs. Bilderdijk's many Dutch renditions of foreign literature were as much filtrations as translations. After all, the Romanticism of Bilderdijk and his circle was unique in that it was grafted upon Orangist nationalism and Calvinist orthodoxy. Not so much Schleiermacher and Kierkegaard influenced their theology, but Merle d'Aubigné and Vinet. The Bilderdijk circle dreamed of a return to an absolute monarchy; they opposed constitutional liberalisation; they detested Rousseau; and they condemned the Greek revolutionaries as a band of plundering Jacobins. They distanced themselves from Byron's heroic self-sacrifice. The nationalism of the Calvinist Romantics went hand in hand, first with philo-Catholicism, but more lastingly with a philo-Semitism embodied by such disciples of Bilderdijk as Da Costa and Capadose. This philo-Semitic commitment should be a caution to those wanting to establish a ready link between the Romantic nationalism of the early nineteenth century and the 'Wagnerian' anti-Semitism later in the century – however much Bilderdijk may have fantasised about superior Hyperboreans.

Finally, a word of caution too about the biographical part of this chapter. Much of what we know about Bilderdijk's life comes directly from himself, and from the biography by his disciple Da Costa, *De Mensch en de Dichter Bilderdijk* (*The Man and the Poet Bilderdijk*) (1859). In other words, the description of Bilderdijk's life is part of the Romantic self-image of the period, a mixture of fact and fiction, a legend to some extent, behind which a more sober reality is likely to be hidden. It therefore has something in common with, for example, Bilderdijk's medieval romance *Elius* in which he celebrated the family legend of his descent from the Knight of the Swan. Just like the later *Life and Letters* of prominent Victorians, Bilderdijk's biography is both an account of historical fact and a document which reflects the fashion and values of the time. This should not be regarded, however, as anything negative; on the contrary, it makes the story of his life even more a source of information about the nature and characteristic features of Romanticism than bare facts would be. A Romantic 'autobiographical' portrait is as useful a defining manifestation of the Romantic fashion as any. The biographical part of this chapter does not therefore try to paint a 'Bilderdijk, tel qu'il est', a 'real' Bilderdijk behind the façade, but quite the opposite: it attempts to reproduce, as reliably as possible, the Romantic self-portrait by Bilderdijk and his group. Bilderdijk's precociousness as a child, for example, may not have been as great as it was made out to be, his youth may not have been as dark, his exile not as alienating and his nationalism not as heroic. But more important than the truth about these matters is another truth, namely that he was portrayed with those Romantic attributes. The latter perception is indispensable for a full and precise account of Dutch Romanticism.

ACKNOWLEDGEMENTS

I am indebted to Francis Warner and to Drs Gerrit Schutte and Mikuláš Teich for helpful suggestions in the preparation of this chapter. Part of the research was carried out with the support of a Humboldt Fellowship at the University of Tübingen where I enjoyed many congenial conversations about Romantic geology with Professor Wolf Freiherr von Engelhardt. It is a particular pleasure to acknowledge an old debt to Dr Jan Wesseling for the effectiveness with which he communicated his interest in Bilderdijk.

NOTES

1 The main secondary sources of information about Bilderdijk's life and work are: I. da Costa, *De mensch en de dichter Willem Bilderdijk* (Haarlem, 1859); R. A. Kollewijn, *Bilderdijk. Zijn Leven en zijn Werken*, 2 vols. (Amsterdam, 1891); Bilderdijk Commissie A.D. MCMVI, *Gedenboek Mr Willem Bilderdijk* (Pretoria, Amsterdam, Potchefstroom, 1906); S. W. F. Margadant, 'Bilderdijk', in *Nieuw Nederlandsch Biografisch Woordenboek*, vol. 2 (Leiden, 1912), pp. 146–66.

Several doctoral theses have examined Bilderdijk's relationship with France, Germany and England: J. Smit, *Bilderdijk et la France* (Amsterdam, 1929); R. Schokker, *Bilderdijk en Duitsland* (Harderwijk, 1933); J. Wesseling, 'Bilderdijk en Engeland' (unpublished doctoral thesis, University of Gent, 1949). See also one of several fine studies by M. J. G. de Jong, *Taal van lust en weelde. Willem Bilderdijk et la littérature italienne* (Namur University Press, 1973). A recent well-told *précis* of Bilderdijk's life is by P. van Zonneveld, 'Ellendig leven. Willem Bilderdijk', *De Gids*, 146 (1983), 183–8.

A large collection of Bilderdijkiana can be found in the Bilderdijk Museum, located in the basement of the Free University in Amsterdam.

2 The standard literary appraisal of Bilderdijk is by G. P. M. Knuvelder, *Handboek tot de geschiedenis der Nederlandse letterkunde*, vol. 3 ('s Hertogenbosch, 1980), *passim*. See also an earlier textbook by J. van der Valk, *Onze letterkunde*, vol. 3 (Rotterdam, 1910), pp. 16–23.

3 P. A. Tunbridge, 'Jean André De Luc, F.R.S.', *Notes and Records of the Royal Society*, 26 (1971), 15–33.

4 H. Blink, 'Mr. Willem Bilderdijk, schrijver der eerste "Geologie" in het Nederlandsch', *Tijdschrift van het Koninklijk Nederlandsch Aardrijkskundig Genootschap*, 2, 13 (1906), 877–918.

5 See for example N. A. Rupke, 'The study of fossils in the Romantic philosophy of history and nature', *History of Science*, 21 (1983), 389–413.

6 N. A. Rupke, 'The apocalyptic denominator in English culture of the early nineteenth century', in M. Pollock (ed.), *Common Denominators in Art and Science* (Aberdeen University Press, 1983), pp. 30–45.

7 Quoted in *Gedenkboek Mr Willem Bilderdijk*, pp. 390–1. Further on science and Romantic literature see J. A. V. Chapple, *Science and Literature in the Nineteenth Century* (London, 1986), *passim*.

8 Rupke, 'The apocalyptic denominator', pp. 33–5.

9 There exists a rich literature on the history of balloon aviation. See for example B. Faujas de Saint-Fond, *Description des expériences de la machine aérostatique de MM. de Montgolfier* (Paris, 1783); G. Tissandier, *Voyages dans les airs* (Paris, 1898); C. C. Gillispie, *The Montgolfier Brothers and the Invention of Aviation* (Princeton University Press, 1982).

10 R. P. W. Visser, 'De dichter Bilderdijk en de plantenanatomie', *Scientiarum Historia*, 14 (1972), 17–28.

11 B. Büch, 'De geopiaceerde wereld van Willem Bilderdijk', in P. van Zonneveld (ed.), *Bilderdijk: 1831–1981* (Leiden, 1981), pp. 12–24. See also W. B. van Staveren, 'Bilderdijk en de geneeskunde', in *Gedenboek Mr Willem Bilderdijk*, pp. 263–332.

12 P. Geyl, *History of the Low Countries* (London, 1964), pp. 150–1.

13 J. Romein and A. Romein-Verschoor, *Ahnherren der Holländische Kultur*

(Bern, n.d.), p. 455. See also H. Smitskamp, 'Bilderdijk historicus', in J. A. L. Lancée (ed.), *Mythe en werkelijkheid* (Utrecht, 1979), pp. 146–58. Bilderdijk's political legacy in the form of the Anti-Revolutionary Party is discussed by G. J. Schutte, 'De ere Gods en de moderne staat', *Radix*, 9 (1983), 73–104.

14 Knuvelder, *Handboek tot de geschiedenis der Nederlandse letterkunde*, p. 317.

15 From the extensive literature on nineteenth-century Church history in The Netherlands see H. Algra, *Het wonder van de egentiende eeuw. Van vrije kerken en kleine luyden* (Franeker, 1965); M. E. Kluit, *Het Protestantse Réveil in Nederland en daarbuiten, 1815–1865* (Amsterdam, Paris, 1970); E. H. Cossee, 'Romantische elementen in kerk en theologie', *De negentiende eeuw*, 8 (1984), 91–107; G. J. Schutte, 'De Afscheiding van 1834 herdacht', *Bijdragen en Mededelingen betreffende de geschiedenis der Nederlanden*, 101 (1986), 400–16.

    See also G. Maury, *Le Réveil religieux dans l'église réformée à Genève et en France (1810–1850)*, 2 vols. (Paris, 1892). About Da Costa, see J. Meijer, *Martelgang of cirkelgang. I. da Costa als joods romanticus* (Paramaribo, 1954).

16 B. Albach, 'De Romantiek en het toneel in de tijd van François-Joseph Pfeiffer', *De negentiende eeuw*, 8 (1984), 130–53; T. van den Berg, 'Romantische decors in Nederland', *ibid.*, 155–62. See also the article on painting by W. Laanstra, 'Romantiek in de schilderkunst', *ibid.*, 109–29.

17 H. A. M. Snelders, 'Romantiek en natuurwetenschappers in Nederland (1800–1850), *ibid.*, pp. 72–90.

18 W. van den Berg, 'Kanttekeningen bij de letterkundige Romantiek', *ibid.*, pp. 53–71.

19 C. de Deugd, *Het metafysisch grondpatroon van het romantische literaire denken* (Groningen, 1966).

20 'Epistle from Robert Southey, Esq. to Allan Cunningham', in A. Cunningham (ed.), *The Anniversary; or Poetry and Prose for MDCCCXXIX* (London, 1829), pp. 9–22.

21 Hoffmann von Fallersleben, *Gesammelte Werke*, vol. 7 (Berlin, 1892), pp. 119–20.

22 I. da Costa, *Bilderdijks epos; of de vijf bestaande zangen van den Ondergang der Eerste Wareld* (Leeuwarden, 1845), pp. 465–519.

23 For example Rudolf van Reest, *'n Onbegriepelijk mensch* (Goes, n.d.).

24 G. Brom, *Romantiek en Katholicisme in Nederland*, 2 vols. (Groningen, 1926), vol. 1, pp. 73–81. Another Catholic admirer of Bilderdijk was J. J. F. Wap, *Bilderdijk, eene bijdrage tot zijn level en werken* (Leiden, 1874).

25 Van den Berg, 'Kanttekeningen bij de letterkundige Romantiek', pp. 53–76.

9

Romanticism in Hungary

MIHÁLY SZEGEDY-MASZÁK

Hungarian literature is generally omitted from comparative discussions of Romanticism as an ideological and artistic movement. One must assume that the reason for this omission is the relative unfamiliarity of the Hungarian language, making it difficult for Western scholars to decide how significant the contribution of Hungarian authors may have been to European culture in a period when lyric poetry, the least translatable of all genres, seemed to be the dominant form of expression. For this reason, the main purpose of this essay will be to introduce and describe in some detail a number of key texts by those Hungarian authors whose work can most readily be discussed in the comparative context of European Romanticism. It should be noted at the outset that these authors did not represent a coherent national Romantic movement, but worked on the whole in relative isolation, and were often neither appreciated nor fully understood by their contemporaries. It has been customary in Hungarian literary history to speak of a broader mainstream Hungarian Romantic 'school' or movement, incorporating the work of a wide spectrum of other more minor writers (Czigány 1984: 120–41), but bearing in mind certain crucial differences between the historical and cultural backgrounds of Romanticism in Hungary and in Western Europe, I do not consider such a grouping to be useful or meaningful in a comparative context. Before going on, therefore, to sketch certain aspects of the historical development of Romantic thinking and writing in Hungary, I should like to draw attention to four of these fundamental differences.

First, the criticism levelled at urban civilization – the belief that 'God made the country, and man made the town', as Cowper put it in the first book of The Task (1783–5) – was considerably less widespread in Central Europe due to the relative backwardness of economic conditions. The Hungarian poet Dániel Berzsenyi (1776–1836), for example, who in the first years of the nineteenth century developed an original metaphoric style in a series of meditative poems about rural retirement, in his later years

217

praised the noise of city life in his epistle *Vitkovics Mihályhoz* (*To Mihály Vitkovics*) (1815). The uniformity of life in the capitals rejected by Rousseau in his *Émile* was unknown to the Hungarian poet whose optimistic view of the advantages of urban life was inspired by a longing for some kind of community. It is not until the middle of the century that we find works about alienation as the individual's sense of uprootedness in a large city.

Secondly, the interrelations between philosophy and literature were considerably less important in Hungary than in Germany, England, or France. Lacking any native tradition in philosophy, Hungarian poets had to borrow most of their ideas from abroad. Both the metahistory and the ontology of German Romanticism becomes widely influential: not only such an important poet, critic, and statesman as Ferenc Kölcsey (1790–1838) assimilated Herder's ideas, but even a minor essayist like Péter Tóth (1813–78), an intellectual of peasant origin who in later life became a Protestant priest and a Utopian Socialist thinker, argued that Fichte provided the key to interpreting the relations between the self and the outside world (Tóth 1984). What is more, the three major lyric poets of the century: Mihály Vörösmarty (1800–55), Sándor Petöfi (1823–49), and János Arany (1817–82) were passionately interested in Romantic conceptions of history. Still, the absence of a fruitful interplay with contemporary philosophers may be responsible for the fact that most Hungarian writers seemed to take less interest in the general conditions of human existence than their greatest contemporaries in Germany, England, or France. The most notable exception was the social thinker and reformer Count István Széchenyi (1791–1860), the author of a *journal intime* and a series of books on economy, culture, politics, and history, whose work comes closest to what may be regarded as philosophy in a Western sense.

A third distinctive feature of Hungarian Romanticism may be identified as a strong resistance to pseudo-scientific ideas anticipating modern psychology. Mesmerism is a case in point. Kölcsey's essays *Levelek a mesmerizmusról* (*Letters on Mesmerism*) (1823) and *Az állati magnetiz-mus nyomairól a régiségben* (*Historical Evidence for Animal Magnetism*) (1828) reflect a Rationalism inherited from the eighteenth century which is at variance with the Romantic cult of the supernatural (*surnaturel*). Most Hungarian writers insisted on preserving the Cartesian opposition between soul and body in an age dominated by monist vitalism. In contrast not only to Western Europe but even to Russia, Hungarians seemed to take little interest in mystic traditions.

This fact will lead us to the fourth and last principal difference between Hungarian and West European Romanticism. While in Germany, England, and France this movement was bound up with a religious revival, no comparable trend can be detected in nineteenth-century Hungary. Neither quietism nor pietism had much impact upon the cultural life of the country, and both Catholic and Protestant theology were at a low ebb. Once again, Széchenyi may be an exception, but in religious matters, as in many other fields, his ideas are often self-contradictory. Sometimes he seems to be a deeply religious writer – in his youth he was acquainted with Adam Müller and Friedrich Schlegel – on other occasions he considers religion a pure convention, in accordance with the rationalistic and pragmatic spirit of the Enlightenment – as in the memorandum sent to Chancellor Metternich, written in German on 11 December 1825:

Bloss in Religions Sachen habe ich keine bestimmte Meinung. Bin vor der unbegränztesten Toleranz, und würde, wie ich es wirklich glaube, wäre ich ein geborner Türke, mit derselben gewissenhaftigkeit fünfmal des Tages meine Füsse waschen, mit der ich nun alle Sonntage regelmässig in die Kirche gehe, und alle übrigen Religions Gebräuche treulich beobachte, die in der meinen vorgeschrieben sind.
(Simply in the matter of religion, I have no set opinions. I have the most unbounded tolerance, and truly believe that had I been born a Turk, I should wash my feet five times a day with the same conscientiousness with which I now attend church regularly every Sunday and faithfully observe all the other religious customs which are prescribed in my religion.)

Széchenyi 1926: 709

Some could, of course, claim that this argument may be in harmony with the Romantic ideal of cultural relativity. Undoubtedly, Széchenyi was fully convinced of the historical nature of values. In general, his views exemplify both the degree of continuity and rupture between the Enlightenment and Romanticism and thus suggest that it is well-nigh impossible to determine when Romanticism began in Hungarian literature.

FROM ENLIGHTENMENT TO ROMANTICISM

It is, indeed, difficult to speak of either of these two terms in the Hungarian context without considerable qualification. The ideas of the English and French Enlightenment did not begin to exert a coherent influence over Hungarian culture until the last third of the eighteenth century, and even then this influence was relatively short-lived. When Maria Theresa established her 'Noble Hungarian Bodyguard' in 1760, the young Hungarian guardsmen not only came into enthusiastic contact with the works of the *philosophes*, but also – inspired to translate these works and to develop an enlightened literature of their own – were forced to recognize the inadequacies of the Hungarian language, and the backwardness (or almost entire absence) of the nation's cultural institutions. Hungarian was not spoken by the greater part of the nobility who constituted the majority of

the reading public at home, and the relatively slow rate of urban development, together with the cultural backwardness of the provinces, meant
that there were few potential centres of literary and intellectual activity.
Enlightened initiatives in Hungary were thus immediately directed
towards language development and reform as a necessary first step
towards a more general national renewal.

The effect of Joseph II's 'enlightened' Language Decree of 1784, making
German the official language of all his peoples, was paradoxically only to
encourage a still more radical insistence on the defence and development
of the Hungarian language, and an increased interest in national traditions. In this way the brief dawning of enlightened thought in Hungary
was rapidly transformed into an awakening of national consciousness
quite alien to the cultural universalism which had played such an important part in the Enlightenment in England and France. If the sceptical, anti-
clerical Voltairean *homme de lettres* had been the ideal of Maria Theresa's
Hungarian guardsmen, Voltaire's influence was soon to be displaced by
that of the more relativistic Rousseau who showed much more interest in,
and sympathy for, the formative role of local traditions.

This shift in emphasis can be clearly seen in the development of the
essayist, poet, and playwright György Bessenyei (1746–1811), the most
accomplished of those Hungarian writers who drew their inspiration and
intellectual bearings from their cultivation as guardsmen at Maria
Theresa's court. While his first major literary achievement, *Ágis tragédiája*
(*The Tragedy of Agis*) (1772), is about the ambiguities of *absolutisme
éclairé*, much in the spirit of Voltaire, the somewhat later comedy, *A
filozófus* (*The Philosopher*) (1777), focuses on Pontyi, a Hungarian squire
whose esteem for local traditions is privileged over his resistance to notions
of international progress – a figure who was to exert considerable influence over Hungarian culture in the next decades. Bessenyei's last major
work, a novel entitled *Tariménes utazása* (*The Travels of Tarimenes*)
(1804), although still in part a tribute to enlightened absolutism, introduces the figure of the Noble Savage, whose embodiment, Kirakades, is
given the following lines: 'the more educated and wise a man is, the less
jovial his life will be; on the other hand, the less reasoning he is, the more
pleasures will accompany him in life' (Bessenyei 1930: 86).

At least as decisive as the influence of Rousseau was that of Herder, who
not only insisted on the importance of preserving and cultivating national
and folk traditions, but also made such imperatives more urgent in
Hungarian eyes by predicting the disappearance of the Hungarian
language (Herder 1965, vol. 2: 272). Furthermore, the French Revolution
had led to a major reaction in the politics of Vienna, and in 1794 many of
Joseph II's leading supporters in Hungary – including the prose writer,

poet, translator, and literary organizer Ferenc Kazinczy (1759–1831), the leading figure in the reform of the Hungarian language at the turn of the century – were sentenced to imprisonment or executed as Jacobins. In this context the confident Rationalist universalism of the West European Enlightenment seemed to have little to offer a Hungarian culture forced onto the defensive. Writers increasingly turned inwards to look for inspiration in the traditions of local culture and for themes relating to the more heroic periods of the national past.

ROMANTIC DRAMA

To see whether the past revealed any values worth preserving, one had to rediscover national history, and the theatre was well suited to that purpose. Bessenyei himself turned to Hungarian history for the subjects of his later plays, and the growing popularity of Shakespeare, as well as the influence of German literature, inspired playwrights to search for the inner logic of Hungarian history. In consequence, Romanticism became the first artistic movement to inspire a comprehensive prolificacy of dramatic writing in Hungarian.

While in the eighteenth century most plays were performed in schools or in the private theatres of aristocratic families, from the turn of the century companies toured the country and permanent theatres were opened in the larger cities. At first, most of the new theatrical institutions had to face financial and professional difficulties, but they produced more and more plays originally written in Hungarian and worked for an audience incomparably larger than the theatre of the Esterházys, who commissioned the best actors of Europe, but showed no interest in plays written in Hungarian.

One of the most significant dramas produced by Hungarian Romanticism was *Bánk bán* by József Katona (1791–1830), a law student who took a passionate interest in both literature and history. This five-act play, written in 1813–14 and based on the story of Bánk as related by Antonio Bonfini in *Rerum Ungaricanum Decades Quattuor et Dimidia* (1487–96) – a work commissioned by the Hungarian king Matthias I – was never fully appreciated in Katona's life-time. It was submitted to a competition calling for a historical drama to mark the opening of the National Theatre in Kolozsvár, the largest city in Transylvania. The first prize was not awarded to any of the plays submitted, and Katona's was not even listed among those deserving praise. Although the author rewrote the text and published it in 1820, his disillusionment was serious enough to put an end to his short career as a playwright. As was the case with some other works of striking originality, the public was not prepared to understand it until some years after its author's death. Its first performance was held in Kassa in 1833, and János Arany was the first serious critic to recognize its artistic merits (Arany 1962: 275–329, 611–15).

In view of the extreme brevity of his literary career, Katona developed very quickly as an artist. His uneven but interesting lyrics show him to be an experimenter with the language of violent emotions. Tormented by a hopeless love for a leading actress, Róza Széppataki, he shared the life of a travelling company. Translating and adapting German plays as well as acting under a pseudonym, he acquired first-hand knowledge of theatrical conventions. The more experience he gained, the more original his writing became, and *Bánk bán* represented the peak of his achievement.

The delayed recognition of this play requires some explanation. The first decades of the nineteenth century saw far-reaching and systematic language reform in Hungary, launched by Kazinczy. To replace Latin terms widely and frequently used by earlier writers, obsolete expressions were revived, dialectal variants standardized, and a great number of new words coined, sometimes with the help of non-existent stems and suffixes. Throughout the country intellectuals were encouraged to enlarge their vocabulary. Many of the neologisms were later integrated into standard usage; others disappeared after a few decades.

In the 1840s a strong reaction set in. The natural ease of spoken language became the model of a new generation led by János Kriza (1811–75), who discovered, collected, and published the Hungarian ballads sung in Transylvania, János Erdélyi (1814–68), an important theoretician of folklore, and the two major poets of the mid-century, Petőfi and Arany. In the light of this change in public taste, many works written in the first decades of the century seem outdated, whereas the reputation of *Bánk bán* rose because it was free of neologisms.

As a result of Katona's disregard for the language reform, the vocabulary of *Bánk bán* is much more limited than that of most literary works composed in Hungary in the early nineteenth century. And yet Katona was none the less an innovator of poetic language: for him, syntactic dislocation and fragmentation, together with metaphor and wordplay, constituted the basic elements of dramatic diction. Aiming to find adequate expression for passionate emotions, moral conflicts, and mental disturbances, he often created an impression of syntactic disorder.

Katona's artistic intention becomes especially clear if we compare his play to other dramatic treatments of the same subject, i.e. the assassination of the wife of the Hungarian king Andrew II in 1213. George Lillo, as the very title of his *Elmerick or Justice Triumphant* (performed posthumously in 1740) suggests, eliminated the conflict by justifying violence. Almost the same could be said of Franz Grillparzer's undoubtedly superior *Ein treuer Diener seines Herrn* (*A Loyal Servant of His Master*) (1828).

The structure and meaning of Katona's tragedy are more complex. Andrew II must go abroad, because his wife Gertrude is ambitious and has urged him to conquer another country. Patriotic nobles led by Petur, a man characterized by violent outbursts and an almost total lack of self-control, decide to oppose the German-born queen, who has too much influence on her husband and makes the country serve purposes alien to its own interests. The conflict is not only between foreigners and natives, but also between central power and feudal anarchy. Bánk must face a dilemma: he is at once the most powerful of the barons and the representative of royal authority in the monarch's absence. The situation becomes further complicated by social conflicts. When Tiborc, a serf, comes to visit Bánk to complain about the heavy taxes peasants must pay towards the upkeep of Gertrude's court, he shows pity and even sympathy, but is reluctant to take action, because as a landowner almost as rich as the monarch, he cannot identify the fate of a country with that of the poor. He learns, however, that the foreign exploiters of the country have also brought him personal humiliation: Gertrude's younger brother Otto has seduced his wife Melinda by using drugs to overcome her resistance. Seeing that shame has driven her mad, and believing, not without good reason, that Otto must have been encouraged by Gertrude, he charges the latter with nepotism and corruption, and when the queen fails to show respect for the dignity of his office, he stabs her. No sooner is the deed done than he realizes that the punishment he has administered is out of proportion with the crime. He is further humiliated when Petur, whose conspiracy against the court has been crushed, curses him as a murderer, immediately prior to his execution by soldiers. The king returns to take revenge, but understands that as a ruler he must blame his wife for her abuse of power. Because of this, he can only make Bánk responsible as a private man. He is just about to do this when Tiborc arrives and informs Bánk of Melinda's assassination by murderers hired by Otto. Recognizing that justice is beyond his power, the king decides not to punish Bánk.

Even such a sketchy summary may suggest that the plot is based on the interrelations of several conflicts. Ethnic and social tensions are combined with moral and psychological oppositions, and a wide range of mental states is presented. In consequence, *Bánk bán* is free of monotony, unlike much Romantic verse drama. Each character speaks a highly idiosyncratic language, and dramatic tension is often heightened by clashes between individual styles. The dialogues between the insane Melinda and her bitter husband, the desperate Tiborc and his aloof or at least seemingly absent-minded lord, the angry Bánk and the haughty Gertrude, are examples of a lack of understanding on both sides which is due as much to widely different states of mind and value systems as to different idioms.

Even minor characters are highly individualized in their speech. Biberach, a vagrant knight who first assists Otto for financial reward, but later informs Bánk about Melinda's shame out of contempt for Otto and for the world into which he has been thrown, speaks a sophisticated jargon, full of twists and ambiguities. His complete negation of all values may remind one of Solver's or Kierkegaard's conception of irony, and his whole character is reminiscent of the demonic *humeur noir* of Beddoes. Stabbed by Otto, his life seems to have been pointless, in keeping with his view that death is not tragic, only ridiculous, because there are no higher values which could give meaning to the life of any individual.

Compared to Katona's masterpiece, most historical tragedies written in Hungarian in the first quarter of the nineteenth century seem to be excessively melodramatic. This is true even of the works of Károly Kisfaludy (1788–1830), who replaced Kazinczy, the last representative of Neoclassical ideals, as organizer of literary life. The younger brother of Sándor Kisfaludy (1772–1844) – the author of *Himfy szerelmei* (*The Loves of Himfy*) (1800–7), a combination of love lyrics and spiritual auto-biography – he showed a keen interest in a number of genres, ranging from the elegy and the ballad to comic narrative in prose. He even tried his hand at the visual arts, and became the earliest of Romantic landscape painters in Hungary. His first play, *A tatárok Magyarországban* (*Tatars in Hungary*), written in 1809 but not performed until 1819, is full of bombastic rhetoric, as he himself admits in an epigram composed in 1825.

More interesting is *Stibor vajda* (*Voivode Stibor*) (1819), a four-act verse drama about Hungary in the early fifteenth century. While in the earlier work conflict is limited to a hostility between the Tatars invading thirteenth-century Hungary and the defenders of the country, in the later play the interrelations between different conflicts create more dramatic tension.

To understand the nature of that interrelation one must be familiar with the historical events referred to by the characters. The Hungarian nobility led by Kont, Voivode of Transylvania, rebel against the absolutism of Sigismond, who is both king of Hungary and the ruler of the Holy Roman Empire. The king, a member of the Luxemburg dynasty and so a foreigner, succeeds in defeating the conspirators, thanks to the financial and military assistance given him by Stibor, a Pole. Kont is executed and Stibor inherits his title, thus becoming the most powerful of the barons, second only to the monarch. The implication may be that the cause of social progress is at variance with that of national independence, and their conflict is further complicated by psychological factors and by the ambiguities of progress. itself: Rajnald, Stibor's only son, falls in love with Gunda, the daughter of a poor serf who has been killed by the soldiers of Stibor. The conclusion is typical of Hungarian Romanticism as a whole: writers in Central Europe had some misgivings about Western models of social organization, wondering whether progress did not imply more oppression.

In Kisfaludy's tragedy, as in *Bánk bán*, the centre of focus is the abuse of power. Although *Voivode Stibor* lacks the close-knit structure of Katona's work, it is more than a didactic parable, because of the complexity of the hero's character. Rich and brave, he is 'part man, part devil', an individual with an egotistical sublime. His view of the world relies on the assumption that there is no higher value than human will. Because he is not afraid of any human being, he is convinced that no one can defeat him. In a sense he is one of the Satanic heroes who have lost their belief in supernatural justice. Ostensibly, he is given punishment when a snake bites him and makes him blind while he is asleep, yet his character retains a sort of sublimity until the very end of the play when, having lost his sight, he commits suicide. His view of existence is not invalidated: even the closure suggests that there are only natural forces at play in the universe.

In sharp contrast to *Bánk bán*, most of Kisfaludy's plays were written for immediate consumption, but later proved to be ephemeral. This is true even of his comedies from *A kérők* (*The Suitors*) (1817–19) to *Csalódások* (*Disappointments*) (1828). Amusing and fresh as these prose dramas may be, they do not show much improvement in dramatic technique upon such earlier works as the unfinished *A méla Tempefői* (*The Dreamy Tempefői*) (1793) or *Karnyóné, vagyis a vénasszony szerelme* (*Mrs Karnyó or An Old Woman's Lover*) (1799), both by Mihály Csokonai Vitéz (1772–1805), the most original poet of the Hungarian Enlightenment. They are hardly more than a set of caricatures loosely knit together. There is only one aspect of Kisfaludy's comedies which affords them unquestionable historical interest: by contrasting an older generation, which observes generally accepted rules of conduct, with younger people, whose ideals are emphatically individual and subjective, they signal a major shift of emphasis in the value system of the age.

NATIONAL CHARACTER AND ROMANTIC IRONY

It has often been maintained that one of the distinguishing features of Hungarian culture is a late survival of the ideas of the Enlightenment (Szauder 1970, Szegedy-Maszák 1982). The example of Károly Kisfaludy would certainly support the thesis that minor talents made use only of the more superficial technical devices of the new trend, without having assimilated the Romantics' conceptions of imagination, nature, and symbol, or the basic assumptions of such thinkers as Herder, Fichte, and Schelling about history and about the relations between the ego and the outside world. Yet the influence of the ideological legacy of the eighteenth century can be felt even in the works of István Széchenyi, one of the major figures in the history of Hungarian culture, and this fact requires a more sophisticated explanation. It reminds us that Romanticism emerged not only as a reaction against the Enlightenment but also as a manifestation of its internal crisis.

This double allegiance is especially clear in *Hitel* (*Credit*)(1830), the first important book which Széchenyi published with the aim of introducing social reforms in his country. Some of its basic points, the attack on prejudice and the idea that government is based on social contract indicate the author's indebtedness to the eighteenth century. Furthermore, the thesis that the criterion of social good is the happiness of the greatest number and the programme asking for market economy, capitalist enterprise, and unlimited property could suggest an unqualified acceptance of Bentham's utilitarianism. The analogy is, however, only partial. Although there is a whole section in *Credit* which could be called almost a translation of various passages from the British theoretician's *The Book of Fallacies* (Széchenyi 1930a: 424–35), Széchenyi's book as a whole outlines a model of desirable society which is different from Bentham's, his conception of liberal democracy is in harmony with some of the basic presuppositions of Romanticism about the autonomous *Bildung* (education or culture) of the human personality.

Having called attention to the etymological structure of the Hungarian word for 'credit' – 'hitel', based on 'hit', meaning 'belief' – he used it not only in a literal, economic, but also in a figurative, moral sense. In his view material growth was important only in so far as it made spiritual progress possible. Man was alterable and education a morally transformative force, a qualitative development, and, as such, the basis of constant changes in society. In accordance with the organic conception of *Bildung*, he called the spiritual independence of the individual the highest of values and argued that the distinguishing feature of a good society was its inclination to encourage individual self-knowledge and self-improvement.

In contrast to Bentham, Széchenyi had a deep historical sense and an awareness of different, sometimes even incompatible local traditions. 'For us black, whereas for the Chinese white is the colour of mourning', he wrote (Széchenyi 1930a: 307), reminding the reader that cultural traditions were the manifestations of the historicity of human experience, and thus their validity was not a question of rationalistic reasoning. In view of the wide range of belief systems and mental habits, our obligation was unlimited tolerance towards others, 'because only posterity can decide if you or I have got closer to the truth', he asserted in *Világ* (*Light*) (1831) (Széchenyi 1831: 54), the book that followed *Credit*.

With the aim of emphasizing the role of traditions in social progress, Széchenyi introduced the idea of national character and the opposition between organic and inorganic cultures, concepts inherited from Rousseau and elaborated by some German Romantics as well as by their Hungarian follower Kölcsey, in his long essay *Nemzeti bagyományok* (*National Traditions*) (1826). An organic culture is in harmony with the character of a nation, while inorganic cultures are imposed on nations. The culture of Hellas, Kölcsey argued, had been a perfect example of organic culture, whereas Roman civilization was imitative and superficial.

Having been familiar with earlier sources from Montaigne to Madame de Staël and from Montesquieu to the German Romantics, Széchenyi started even before Kölcsey, in the 1810s, to speculate about national character in his *journal intime*, written chiefly in German, and between 1831 and 1835 he devoted a whole book, *Hunnia*, to the question.

Echoing Schiller's distinction between naive and sentimental, he resorted to the familiar analogy between the phases of an individual's and a nation's life. Though admitting that a nation may lose certain components of its identity during its evolution, he denied that nations would disappear in some distant future. Unlike some universalist thinkers of the Enlightenment, he did not envisage the disappearance of smaller communities but advocated growing diversity as the necessary precondition for human progress. The belief that progress was the result of mental education rather than of changing circumstances implied for him that higher, i.e. spiritual, values were tied up with the diversity of fully developed cultures. In *Hunnia* he went even as far as adopting the Romantic thesis that language created meaning, and associated the diversity of customs and beliefs with that of languages. If there were no universal rules in language and culture, 'the survival of even the smallest and most primitive nation was of utmost importance' (Széchenyi 1858: 205), a qualitative loss for mankind, because each nation had the task of developing a unique culture.

To avoid simplification, it must be stressed that Széchenyi was aware that national character was as much a fiction as was the personality of a human individual. What is more, he did not seem to believe in the opposition between fact and fiction made by those thinkers of the Enlightenment who asked for objectivity in historical interpretation. Accordingly, taking examples such as the *Essais* of Montaigne or the *Autobiography* of Franklin, he assumed that confessions, the life stories of representative men, had a share in the building of nations. There are signs of such an

awareness in his highly idiosyncratic works, parts of the spiritual autobiography of a personality full of antagonisms. From his works we can
reconstruct the story of how he – the son of Ferenc Széchenyi (1754–
1820), an aristocrat who plotted against the Habsburgs after the death of
Joseph II, employed the most original of the Hungarian Jacobins as secretary, made a plan for social reform in Hungary, and founded the
National Library in Pest – began his career as a handsome Austrian officer
who had been highly decorated in the Napoleonic wars, travelled widely,
had innumerable and complicated love affairs, learned to speak about a
dozen languages, was converted to the cause of Hungarian nationalism,
founded an Academy of Sciences, commissioned two British engineers to
construct the first permanent bridge in the capital of his country, became
member of the revolutionary government of 1848, moved to a lunatic
asylum to escape persecution in the 1850s, and sent articles to *The Times*
attacking Austrian absolutism – the story, that is to say, of an exception-
ally contradictory and eventful life which made Széchenyi a model of the
Romantic character for future generations.

His diary, a *chef-d'oeuvre* of Hungarian Romanticism, not only reveals
a character with a multiple identity, for whom institutions founded by
himself became symbols of his own self, and dreams, hallucinations, phan-
tastic visions were modes of self-knowledge, but also contradicts his published works. To take but a single example, while *Hunnia*, a book which
contains a violent attack upon the advocates of Latin as an international
language, seems to suggest that its author had a language-oriented,
traditionalist approach to culture and looked upon each vernacular as an
inexhaustible array of possible meanings, there is an entry in his diary
which shows a desire for universal grammar that may remind us of the
most ahistorical representatives of Enlightenment universalism:

Aus der Unvollkommenheit der Sprachen entstehet das meiste Übel, und der
grösste Zeit Verlust auf der Welt . . .
   Ich fühle dass man noch eine Arte erfinden wird durch Nummern zu schreiben
– so dass Geschriebene ewig und für alle Begriffe mathematisch stets die selbe
bleiben wird.
(The imperfections of language are the cause of the most harm, and the greatest
waste of time in the world . . .
   I feel that one day, a way will be found to write with numbers – so that in all concepts, the written word will forever stay mathematically the same.)
                                                          Széchenyi 1932: 75

A reader of Széchenyi's works will often encounter alternative meanings, none of which is unambiguously apparent or real, and will be constantly invited to undermine his interpretations. This helps to explain the
great amount of secondary literature on Széchenyi: probably more books

and essays have been written about him than about any other Hungarian statesman or writer, and they contain very different, in many cases quite contradictory, conclusions (Kemény 1851, Szekfü 1920, Barany 1968, Gergely 1972).

Some of Széchenyi's self-contradictions could be explained by the fact that his whole political and cultural activity is marked by a Romantic conception of irony. While the self-defensive *humeur noir* which characterizes Biberach in Katona's *Bánk bán*, or the infinitely regressive negativity underlying the logic of *Vanitatum vanitas* (1823), the most original lyric poem by Kölcsey, seem to be episodic in the work of these authors, in Széchenyi's case the same principle may provide the key for interpreting his *Weltanschauung* from the beginning to the end of his public career.

In his case, as in that of Kierkegaard, the origin of the formation of individual consciousness was a passivity, an inner void. 'What I really lack is to be clear in my mind *what I am to do*', wrote the Danish philosopher in 1835 (Kierkegaard 1959: 44). A similar sense of aimlessness characterized the young Széchenyi twenty years earlier. 'Hab' ich schon einen Weg?' ('Do I yet have a path in life?') he asked in 1815 (Széchenyi 1925: 159). The starting point for him was existential freedom: the mood in the early parts of his journal was determined by that 'infinitely exuberant freedom of subjectivity' which Kierkegaard identified with the source of Romantic irony (Kierkegaard 1966: 223). From 1814 until the early 20s, he presented himself with existential possibilities, life projects. In his journal he recorded how he was struggling with living alternatives that called forth his decision. Viewing subjectivity as free, infinite, and negative, he wrote the following on 27 March 1821:

Was will der Graf S.S. alles werden?
Er will ein berühmter Soldat werden, mit allen Orden ausgezeichnet, und durch alle Zeitungen bekannt.
Er will sein Lebetag reisen, und sich am Ende expatriren.
Er will heirathen und von allen Geschäften frey sich ganz und gar dem gesel[l]enschaftlichen Leben widmen.
Er will ledig bleiben, alle Gesel[l]schaft meiden, und als echter Loup garou Pferden ziehen.
Er will eine diplomatische Carrière machen.
Er will independent von allen Geschäften frey, in der Schweitz, in Frankreich, in England und in Italien sein Leben, im Genuss der Welt beenden.
Er will der Chef einer Parthey werden, und sich ganz dem Recht und Verfassungswesen widmen –
Er will Belletrist werden – Verse und Trauerspiele schreiben.
Dieser Knabe ist in meinem Alter, und da er noch nicht weiss, welche Direction er seinem Leben geben wird – verlegt er sich auf einmahl auf alle Wissenschaften die auf sie Bezug haben – man kann erwarten, sie weit es im jeden Fach bringen wird. –

(Just what does Count S.S. want to be?

He wants to be a famous soldier, decorated with every medal, his picture in all the newspapers.

He wants to spend his life travelling, and end up an expatriate.

He wants to marry, be rid of business matters, and devote himself entirely to social life.

He wants to remain a bachelor, avoid society, and breed horses as a real recluse.

He wants to have a diplomatic career.

He wants to be independent, free of all business matters, to end his life enjoying the world in Switzerland, France, England, and Italy.

He wants to become the leader of a party and devote himself to law and the constitution —

He wants to become an author, and write verse and tragedies.

This lad is my age, and as he still does not know which direction to give to his life, he is tackling each branch of science which might affect it — we can only wait and see how far he will get in each field. —)

Széchenyi 1926: 144

The general laws of the formation of a Romantic ironic consciousness make the world visions of Széchenyi and Kierkegaard comparable in a number of respects. Both had an aristocratic notion of personality, an organic conception of *Bildung*, and a great contempt for Philistine mediocrity. Neither knew the security of any established community. They understood themselves to be fundamentally different from others, and became authors through great inner suffering. They wished to defend an established order, yet always came into conflict with it. There was something similar even in their historical situations and the ways they reacted to them. Both belonged to small nations and criticized provincial-mindedness. One of the sources of the negativity underlying their sense of being was a belief in the historical relativism of traditions. While they had a low opinion of any ignorance of traditions belonging to other nations, they nevertheless assumed that such traditions could be learned only from the inside, by those who shared them. This insoluble dilemma helps to explain the uncertainty of their respective standards of values.

'I am the ultimate phase of the poetic temper on the way of becoming a sort of reformer'. Kierkegaard's self-characterization (Kierkegaard 1959: 129) can also be applied to his older Hungarian contemporary. Like Kierkegaard, he had literary ambitions and liked to think of himself as a poet — he composed verse in German — but was also irritated by the passivity of artists. Consequently, he changed life into a trial, seeking self-inflicted punishments.

His whole career could be described in terms of an infinite polemic with conflicting forces: the establishment of the Habsburg monarchy and Kossuth's struggle for national independence, cosmopolitanism and nationalism, economic radicalism and political gradualism, the ideas of the Enlightenment and Romanticism. Knowledge for him existed always in a condition of hypothetical and fragmented multiplicity. That is why his published books have a conspicuously non-systematic arrangement and his personality found its most appropriate form of self-expression in a *journal intime*, which he started to keep in 1814 and went on writing until a few days before his death.

This work, published posthumously in seven volumes, is similar in its self-irony to the journals of certain German Romantics, or to the comparable works of Kierkegaard and Amiel. An ironic attitude to life does not allow for continuity. Széchenyi was fond of speaking of himself in the third person, and recorded fierce debates between his various selves. As he was constantly under the sway of changing moods, in his journal the most contrary feelings displaced each other in rapid succession. Obsessed with labyrinthine designs, he favoured long parentheses and dislocated structures. The fragmentariness of his text was further complicated by the use of various languages: he quoted conversations in the original (in most cases French, English, or Hungarian), his states of mind he expressed in German, and occasionally he quoted verse in Italian. All these factors contributed to the inconclusive character of his writing. Whenever he pursued an argument, it always tended towards self-cancellation; facetious and serious statements were inextricably woven together.

On many occasions he set himself the task of shocking his audience. He brought confusion in order to stimulate reflection. When in 1844 he opened a session of the Hungarian Academy he had himself founded nineteen years before, he harshly criticized the Reform movement. The Reformists were fighting a desperate struggle for the economic and political independence of Hungary, a struggle largely inspired by Széchenyi's own earlier activity, when he attacked them from behind, reproaching them for their nationalism and lack of tolerance towards ethnic minorities living in Hungary (Széchenyi 1930b: 441–9).

Undeniably, he himself was a social Reformer, but his sense of irony made it impossible for him to be the head of any political party, or join any organized opposition. Kierkegaard's characterization of the Romantic ironist is again true of his growing isolation: 'He stood ironically outside every relationship, and the law governing it was a perpetual attraction and revulsion. His connection with a particular individual was only momentary' (Kierkegaard 1966: 207). This helps us to understand not only the ambivalence of his attitude to the other two important political figures and publicists of his age, the Transylvanian aristocrat Baron Miklós Wesselényi (1796–1850) and Lajos Kossuth (1802–94), the leader of the smaller nobility, but also his reservations about the Liberal opposition organized by these two statesmen and his inconstancy to the bourgeois revolution in

1848. His ironic stance, his lingering between different attitudes can be observed in his account of his first impressions of the outbreak of the revolution:

15ten [March 1848:] Mit meiner Leber . . . infam. – *Heute sehe ich* Ungarn gehet seiner vollkommenen Auflösung entgegen. Ich endige bald.

Das ganze kommt mir vor, wie ein böser Traum! O heilige Nemesis! – Ein Pohle und Kossuth bringen die brennbare Materie in Feuer! Der erste vielleicht ein Abkömmling Sobiesky's . . . der 2te gemartet und zum Narren gehalten. – Armer F[ürst] Metternich – Das System von Kaiser Franz, was zum Absurdum führen musste . . . und die [missing words] brachten Dich zum Fall! –

Was ist zu machen? Louis B[atthyány] und K[ossuth] – muss man souteniren! – Aller Hass, Antipathie, alle Ambit[ion] muss schweigen. Ich werde sie nicht beirren; ob 'Dienen?' Das hängt von meiner Gesundheit ab. – Abend bei Ferenc Z[ichy]. –

'Nous avons vendu le pays pour deux Louis!' – Batthyány és Kos[suth] Lajos. – (15th [March 1848:] With my liver . . . disgraceful. – *Today I see* Hungary approaching total disintegration. I shall die soon.

It all seems like a bad dream to me! O holy Nemesis! A Pole and Kossuth set fire to the flammable material! – The first perhaps an offspring of Sobiesky's . . . the second tortured and held up to ridicule. – Poor C[ount] Metternich – Emperor Franz' system, which had to lead to absurdity . . . and the [missing words] caused your downfall! –

What shall we do? We must support – Louis B[atthyány] and K[ossuth]! – All hate, antipathy and ambit[ion] must be silent. I will not mislead them; whether to 'serve'? That depends on my health. – Evening at Ferenc Z[ichy]. –

'We have sold the country for two Louis! – Batthyány and Kos[suth] Lajos. –)
Széchenyi 1939: 746–7

Finally one year after *Blick* (*Look*) (1859), his satirical pamphlet written against Habsburg absolutism was published in London, Széchenyi yielded to a temptation which Kierkegaard managed to escape by religious conversion. The self-destructive character of Romantic irony manifested itself in an obsession with the idea of suicide, which cast a shadow over the life of both writers. 'Irony is an abnormal growth'; Kierkegaard wrote in 1838, 'like the abnormally large liver of the Strassburg goose it ends by killing the individual' (Kierkegaard 1959: 58).

FROM ROMANTICISM TO POPULISM

If Széchenyi is the central figure of Hungarian Romanticism in the wider context of cultural history, Mihály Vörösmarty occupies a similar position in the more restricted field of poetry.

His career shows the difficult situation in which a Romantic artist found himself in a country where the first half of the nineteenth century was marked by a national upheaval and the beginnings of capitalism. While his talent was for the lyric, social demand compelled him to write epics and historical tragedies. When commissioned to commemorate in hexameters how the seven Hungarian tribes had conquered the Danube basin in 896, he produced a series of lyric passages loosely connected and gave the title *Zalán futása* (*The Flight of Zalán*) (1925) to his work, indicating that the sad fall of the conquered rather than the glory of the conqueror was his true subject. A similar fragmentation characterizes his historical verse plays from *Salamon király* (*King Solomon*) (1827) to *Czillei és a Hunyadiak* (*Czillei and the Hunyadis*) (1840). Although the National Theatre of Pest was opened with his *Árpád ébredése* (*The Awakening of Árpád*) (1837), a short piece about the leader of the conquering Hungarian tribes, none of his dramatic works could hold the stage, because their artistic value was in long and static monologues rather than in dramatic tension.

As a playwright only once did he try to depart from the genre which met with the expectations of his patriotic audience, and his daring experiment, *Csongor és Tünde* (*Csongor and Tünde*) (1928–31), a mixture of dramatic fairy tale and a *Menschheitsdichtung* (poetry of humanity), proved to be a highly original work. György Lukács – who had a very uneven knowledge of Hungarian culture and dismissed many of its products as provincial – called the work the most interesting Hungarian drama ever written. What is more, he suggested that Vörösmarty's play may have been written with a new type of theatre in mind (Lukács 1911, vol. 2: 502–3). There may be a measure of truth in this remark, for *Csongor and Tünde*, while epitomizing the Romantic cult of folklore in general and of the fairy tale in particular, seems also to foreshadow the theatrical conventions of the Symbolistic works of Ibsen, Strindberg, Hauptmann, Yeats, or Synge.

Csongor is a disillusioned wanderer who had travelled the whole world over, unable to find the subject of his dreams. At the end of his wanderings, he meets Mirigy, the elder sister of Time, who is chained to a tree in the middle of a garden which is the property of Csongor's old parents. At night apples grow on this tree of life, but they always disappear before sunrise. Mirigy tells Csongor about the fairy who had planted the tree. She is identical with the subject of his dreams, the old witch argues, and she collects the fruits of the tree at night. In exchange for this information, Mirigy asks Csongor to let her free.

To explain the success *Csongor and Tünde* has had with innovative theatrical artists, we must have recourse to the interrelations and some-times even clashes between different semantic strata in the play. In several cases the same incident can be taken in a metaphorical as well as a literal sense. Csongor's aim is to find what he has seen in his dreams. This abstract ideal is impersonated by Tünde on the concrete level of action. He hides under the leaves of the magic tree, waiting for Tünde to arrive, but she is late, and he falls asleep. When the fairy appears, accompanied by her maidservant Ilma, she awakens him, but their meeting is cut short by Mirigy cutting off a lock of her hair from behind, thus casting a spell over Tünde and forcing her to leave Csongor. While this episode may remind one of the more concrete material of folk tales, the next has an ambiguity hardly found in oral culture. When the hero desperately asks Tünde's down to earth companion, Ilma, where he should search for his lover, she indicates that the middle of three roads meeting on a plain will guide him to his goal. Compelled to continue his wandering, Csongor arrives at the crossroads, only to find that each of them seems to be a middle road. This may be the first hint to suggest that the play is about the loss of purpose in human existence, and thus it reflects a Romantic poet's doubts about historical teleology.

Travellers approach from all three directions, propagating values that contradict each other. The Merchant speaks about material wealth, the Prince is a man of authority and power, and the Scholar has come to the conclusion that he is unable to understand the world, yet his lack of knowledge is superior to all kinds of self-assurance. Csongor's reaction to these interpretations of human existence is characteristically Romantic. The Merchant's basic value is self-reliance. In his view production becomes, as it were, the law of life. Spiritual ambition is hardened into material effort. Such utilitarianism fosters welfare, but also selfishness. Vörösmarty's position is similar to Széchenyi's: the Benthamite model of society is rejected on the ground that it makes no qualitative distinctions between different kinds of pleasure. The poet seems to support a kind of anti-capitalism which many Romantics professed, yet he does not share their illusions about the Middle Ages. This becomes clear when the message of the Prince is also dismissed, because power is viewed as resulting in an inexorable process which leads to destruction. As to the arguments of the Scholar, they are presented as having more validity, yet even his scale of values is rejected on the ground of not giving creative imagination its due. The untenability of three conflicting interpretations of human existence awakens the suspicion in the hero that all such interpretations may be false.

After his encounter with the three wanderers, Csongor undergoes further trials. First he meets Balga, a simple peasant in love with Ilma, who makes devastating comments on Csongor's idealism. Then he makes the acquaintance of three goblins who are quarrelling over an invisible mantle, a running sandal, and a whip. Csongor steals the goblins' inheritance, hoping that with the means of these magic instruments he can leave the prosaic world he inhabits and reach the fairyland in which Tünde resides, but this episode turns out to be just another trap for the hero.

The distance continues to increase between a chaotic existence, afflicted with a basic contradiction between appearance and reality, and a dream-world which knows no ambiguity of values. After having been distracted by a whore, Csongor realizes that all his efforts to reach the land of his dreams have failed. A long time must have passed since his meeting with the wanderers, because now he can hardly recognize them. The Merchant has lost all his wealth in the free competition he used to praise. He is a lame and penniless beggar, deserted by everybody. No less destitute is the Prince, having been dethroned by his people, and even the Scholar is unhappy, tormented by the paradox that a man cannot both live and think, and struggling with the dilemma between a disbelief in God and an inability to accept mortality. Thus, the grave problems of equality, *de jure* power, and nihilism are raised. Simultaneously with Csongor's second encounter with the wanderers, Tünde and Ilma find themselves in a desert and have to listen to the monologue of the Night. This is the climax of the play. Having lost his belief in transcendence, the poet made the Night assert the omnipotence of nothingness surrounding man. Later on Tünde and Ilma catch sight of Csongor's garden, but they can scarcely recognize it, because it has been transformed into a wilderness. Mirigy is digging up the tree of life planted by Tünde.

Whether the closing scene that follows is an organic part of the whole, or an indication of some compromise the poet had to make with his audience has been a matter of some controversy. Mihály Babits, an outstanding poet of the early twentieth century, was probably the first to suggest that the closure was not an integral part of the structure (Babits 1978: 241), a position I myself adopted in my essays on Vörösmarty, written in the 1970s (Szegedy-Maszák 1976: 268, Szegedy-Maszák 1980: 200). It can hardly be denied that on the level of action the happy ending seems to be a kind of *deus ex machina* device: the goblins decide to change sides and capture Mirigy. The magic tree is transformed into a palace, and the lovers are united. It is equally true, however, that while the stylistic complexity of the earlier scenes – a variety of poetic idioms ranging from the tragic sublimity of the monologue of the Night to the vulgar dialect used by Balga or the grotesque nonsense poetry spoken by the goblins – is replaced by a uniform style, this final narrowing of scope is in keeping with the circular structure of Vörösmarty's lyrical drama. The closure echoes the airy style of the beginning, taking us back from the tragic aspects of human existence to the dreamworld of fairy tales.

The fact that Vörösmarty could not overcome his doubts about the optimism of the Enlightenment, expressed in the monologue of the Night, is clear from his later works. Of his three most powerful lyrics, only *A vén cigány* (*The Old Gipsy*) (1854), a highly stylized drinking song in Biblical language, contained a closure promising redemption through suffering. The two other poems transformed recent political events – the repression of Polish rebellions and of the Hungarian revolution by the great powers – into cosmic terms. *Az emberek* (*Mankind*) (1846) is a prophecy about eternal recurrence in history, whereas *Elöszó* (*Preface*) (1850) contains a long apocalyptic vision of cosmic tragedy, preceded and followed by shorter descriptions of an idyllic past and an ironic future. In the later poem the structure is determined by a disturbed solar system: a full summer is suddenly interrupted by a winter of nothingness, and the future is presented as a spring associated not with youth, but with old age, and compared to the face of an old whore who pretends to be a young virgin.

After 1840 Vörösmarty was no longer compelled to touch genres alien to his private vision. As a result of economic and social reforms, a new bourgeoisie began to emerge that wished to see its own everyday life reflected in the arts. Romanticism was rejected as extravagant on both moral and aesthetic grounds. The shift in taste became manifest first in the visual arts. When Miklós Barabás (1810–98), who in Italy had been interested in extraordinary optical effects, as is illustrated by his water-colours *Vesuvius in Eruption* or *The Blue Cave* (both in 1835), came back to Hungary, he was asked to paint portraits and to suggest the jovial character of his models. Almanacs, magazines, and newspapers asked for literature which could be understood by the new public, and a variant of the Viennese *Volksstück* was introduced by Ede Szigligeti (1814–78). His play *Szökött katona* (*The Deserter*) (1843) initiated a form of popular entertainment, a kind of musical *Lebensbild* (genre painting), supplying the half-educated with the clichés of Romanticism: a superficial *couleur locale*, a stereotype representation of gipsy life and of the Hungarian *puszta*, a sentimental imitation of peasant life, and a mannered stylization of inauthentic folklore.

It is against this background that the achievement of the representatives of a much more sophisticated Populist movement should be measured. Liberal publicists wished to make the country aware of the conditions of peasant life, and they found support from some of the leading poets of the new generation. There is a political undertone in both *János vitéz* (*John the Hero*) (1844) and *Toldi* (1846), verse tales by Sándor Petöfi and János Arany. It would be a gross simplification to argue that all the works these two poets wrote in the 1840s represented an anti-Romantic Populist reaction, but their most influential work certainly brought a change in public taste which affected even prose writing: Baron József Eötvös (1813–71), after having given a characteristically Romantic presentation of the emotional conflicts of a French aristocrat in a confessional novel, *A karthauzi* (*The Carthusian*) (1839–41), turned to the didactic portrayal of the social diseases of Hungarian provincial life in *A falu jegyzöje* (*The Village Notary*) (1845).

EPILOGUE: THE ADVENT OF POSITIVISM

It would be tempting to end this survey with the idea that in Hungary the Populist trend assimilated some characteristics of Romanticism and created a new style which anticipated Realism, but such a conclusion would not do justice to the complexity of the historical process involved. Serfdom having been abolished by the revolution, the Populists lost their main political incentive, and the development of capitalism was no longer hampered by the survival of feudalism. Petöfi having died in action in 1849 in one of the last battles fought by the revolutionary army, no one tried to uphold the ideal of a unified national culture. Arany, together with other disillusioned intellectuals, became familiar with the ideas of Positivism propagated in the new periodicals started after the defeat of the revolution. Eötvös devoted most of his energy to writing discursive prose, and a new generation of essayists emerged, who brought most ideas inherited from the Romantics – the concepts of national character and organic culture among them – into question. The ideal of value-free science replaced that of creative originality.

It would be an exaggeration to deny the survival of Romanticism after 1849. Mór Jókai (1825–1904), a writer of exceptional talent but of uneven intellectual control, published more than a hundred volumes during his long life, in which he used some of the superficial technical devices of Romantic fiction. Interestingly enough, his three major contemporaries were not only more susceptible to the influence of Positivism but also had a far deeper understanding of Romanticism. *Az ember tragédiája* (*The Tragedy of Man*) (1859–60), a lyrical drama by Imre Madách (1825–64), is a vast dialogue between Romantic Liberalism and Positivistic determinism, presented in the form of a long series of historical scenes (Lotze 1981). János Arany's whole literary career could be characterized as a life-long struggle with the two ideologies and especially with the question as to whether the laws of nature invalidated those of morality. Among his major poems the dramatic monologue *Az örök zsidó* (*The Eternal Jew*) (1860) is about the loss of teleology, while the ballad *Ágnes asszony* (*Mistress Agnes*) (1853) questions the responsibility of the guilty. Free will and determinism are the two sides of the dilemma underlying the activity of Arany's friend Baron Zsigmond Kemény (1814–75), political thinker, publicist, critic, and fiction writer. The presence of the Romantic heritage is especially obvious in his work: his first published novel *Gyulai Pál* (*Pál Gyulai*) (1847) is an attempt to realize Friedrich Schlegel's ideal of the novel as a synthetic genre, a dialogue of very different discourses; his *Alhikmet, a vén törpe (Alhikmet the Old Dwarf)* (1853) is a *Traumnovelle* (dream novella) inspired by Hoffmann's tales, and his romance *Ködképek a kedély láthatárán (Phantom Visions on the Soul's Horizon)* (1853) combines a consistent use of Romantic irony with the technique of the *Doppelgänger*. It would not be exaggerated to suggest that Kemény was much closer than any other prose writer in Hungary to the mainstream of Romanticism, yet in view of his later career it is clear that for him the Romantic heritage was useful in so far as he could employ it in developing psychological Realism. His anti-revolutionary thought and strong sociological interest, his descriptive essays on politics, culture, history, or literary theory as well as his fiction belong to an age in which Positivism was the dominant ideological movement, and thus they remind us that the suppression of the revolution may have been an important turning-point in the history of Hungarian culture, because it seemed to invalidate most of the ideas cherished by the Romantics.

REFERENCES

Arany, János. 1962. *Prózai müvek*, vol. 1 (Budapest)

Babits, Mihály. 1978. *Esszék, tanulmányok*, vol. 1 (Budapest)

Barany, George. 1968. *Stephen Széchenyi and the Awakening of Hungarian Nationalism, 1791–1841* (Princeton, N.J.)

Bessenyei, György. 1930. *Tariménes utazása* (Budapest)

Czigány, Lóránt. 1984. *The Oxford History of Hungarian Literature: From the Earliest Times to the Present* (Oxford)

Gergely, András. 1972. *Széchenyi eszmerendszerének kialakulása* (Budapest)

Herder, J. G. 1965. *Ideen zur Philosophie der Menschheit* (Berlin-Weimar)

Kemény, Zsigmond. 1851. Széchenyi István. in *Magyar szónokok és statusférfiak (Politicai jellemrajzok)*, ed. Antal Csengeri (Pest), pp. 333–512

Kierkegaard, Søren. 1959. *The Journals* (New York and Evanston)
    1966. *The Concept of Irony: With Constant Reference to Socrates* (London)

Lotze, Dieter P. 1981. *Imre Madách* (New York)

Lukács, György. 1911. *A modern dráma fejlödésének története* (Budapest)

Szauder, József. 1970. *Az estve és Az álom: Felvilágosodás és klasszicizmus* (Budapest)

Széchenyi, Gróf István. 1831. *Világ vagy is felvilágositó töredékek némi hiba 's elöitélet eligazitására* (Pest)
    1858. *Hunnia* (Pest)
    1925. *Naplói*, vol. 1 (Budapest)
    1926. *Naplói*, vol. 2 (Budapest)
    1930a. *Hitel* (Budapest)
    1930b. *Irói és hírlapi vitája Kossuth Lajossal*, vol. 2 (Budapest)
    1932. *Naplói*, vol. 3 (Budapest)
    1939. *Naplói*, vol. 6 (Budapest)

Szegedy-Maszák, Mihály. 1976. Le Rêve et la vision dans la poésie de Vörösmarty. *Acta Litteraria Academiae Scientiarum Hungaricae*, 18: 267–78.
1980. *Világkép és stílus: Történeti-poétikai tanulmányok* (Budapest)
1982. La Poésie hongroise. In *Le tournant du siècle des Lumières 1760–1820: les genres en vers*, ed. György M. Vajda (Budapest), pp. 523–37
Szekfü, Gyula. 1920. *Három nemzedék: Egy hanyatló kor története* (Budapest)
Tóth, Péter. 1984. *Napló (1836–1842)* (Budapest)

10

Romanticism in France

STEPHEN BANN

The debate about Romanticism emerged at a relatively late date in France. In the mid-1820s, the liberal journalist, Etienne Delécluze, confessed that his group of literary friends and associates had been 'chatting for two years about this eternal subject, without ever being able to determine what the Romantic genre consists in'.[1] Although he perhaps contributed more than anyone else to giving content as well as polemical thrust to the movement in France, Delécluze was more than frank about the difficulty of assigning a clear meaning to the concept of 'Romantisme'. In a crucial series of articles which he wrote for the newspaper *Le Globe* in 1825, he reiterated that it would be possible to fill a volume with all the definitions that people had tried to supply, and claimed that he himself could easily find 'fifteen or twenty different meanings'.[2] It is hardly surprising that several of Delécluze's contemporaries at least initially declined to confront the problem. When the poet Victor Hugo engaged in a public debate with a hostile critic in the summer of 1824, his 'Discussion avec Z . . . sur Romantisme et Classicisme' in fact amounted to a refusal to accept the terms of debate. For Hugo, the only satisfactory definition of the 'Romantique' was the one provided by Mme de Staël, presumably in her pioneering work *De l'Allemagne* completed in 1810. To confute his adversary, Hugo provided a detailed proof that all the linguistic usages in his *Nouvelles Odes* which were stigmatised as 'Romantique' could be found in the best of classical authors, and after all, was not the Bible 'un peu *Romantique*'?[3] Looking back on the literary education which he had received at one of the Napoleonic *lycées*, the liberal politician Charles de Rémusat was even more contemptuous of Romanticism's claim to novelty; for him, 'the style named *Romantique*' was one of the styles known to the rhetoricians of the Ancient World. 'Only the name is new,' he wrote, 'and these inventions of the nineteenth century date from the ninety-ninth Olympiad.'[4]

Of course, there were exceptions to this reticence. Another contributor to *Le Globe* when it was founded in 1824 was the future novelist Stendhal, who saw the opportunity to nail his colours to the mast in an open attack on the guardians of the French classical tradition. Stendhal had been vividly impressed by a series of incidents which had taken place in 1822, when a troupe of English actors arrived in Paris to play Shakespeare's *Othello* at the Theatre of the Porte-Saint-Martin. Anti-English sentiment had disrupted their performances, and led Stendhal to publish the first sketches for the work which later became *Racine et Shakespeare*. By the time that the first instalment of the completed text appeared in *Le Globe* in March 1825, Stendhal was not simply concerned to vindicate the claims of a great foreign dramatist over the short-sighted chauvinism of his fellow-countrymen, but he was also replying to an official denunciation of the newly fledged 'Romantisme' which had been delivered in the French Academy on 24 April 1824. Stendhal entitled his lively tract a 'Reply to the Manifesto against "Le Romantisme" pronounced by M. Auger at a solemn sitting of the Institut'. His forceful satire was directed not only against the idiots who had howled down Shakespeare with the accusation that 'he is an aide-de-camp of the Duke of Wellington',[5] but also against the academicians who saw their role as one of proscribing the vigorous new literature being published by young authors like Hugo, Lamartine and Nodier. His formula for defining what he, in deference to the foreign usage, is willing to call 'Le Romanticisme', is a brilliant device for ridiculing the conservatism of the Academy, at the same time as it justifies the young authors by the public esteem which they are beginning to acquire:

Romanticism is the art of presenting people with the literary works which, in the present state of their habits and beliefs, are susceptible of giving them the greatest posssible pleasure.

Classicism, on the contrary, presents them with the literature which gave the greatest possible pleasure to their great-grandfathers.

Sophocles and Euripides were eminently Romantic; they gave to the Greeks assembled in the theatre at Athens the tragedies which, in accordance with the moral customs of that people, its religion and its preconceptions on what gives man his dignity, must have given it the greatest possible pleasure.

Imitating Sophocles and Euripides today, and pretending that these imitations will not make the nineteenth-century Frenchman yawn – this is classicism.[6]

It would be possible to spend a great deal more time tracing the intricate outlines of the debate launched by Delécluze, Hugo, Stendhal and their contemporaries. But for the purposes of this study, it is more important to raise right from the outset the main issues which arise when we stand back from the polemical exchanges and attempt some sort of comparativist view. How far is the agenda for Romanticism in France set by the fact that the Academy had existed, as an official body supervising the production of literature and the purity of language, from the reign of Louis XIV – its power having been shaken by the Revolution, but reconfirmed by the Empire and the Bourbon Restoration? It is indeed striking that all of the authors already mentioned seek not so much to repudiate the classical tradition, but to show themselves better guardians of it than the moribund Academy. If Stendhal pulls off his *coup* by claiming that Sophocles and Euripides, not to mention Racine, were closet Romantics, his successor in polemical criticism, the poet Charles Baudelaire, is no less anxious to demonstrate a quarter of a century later that the classics only wear thin through mindless repetition, and the modern artist will be able to revive their potency.[7]

The question which immediately follows this one is necessarily more far-reaching and difficult to answer. What is the political stake in this literary debate, which obviously has its ramifications outside the specific power nexus of the Academy? I used the word 'liberal' to qualify the position of Delécluze, and indeed the circle of Delécluze has been credited with achieving the 'Genesis of Liberal *Romantisme*'.[8] But the two terms 'liberal' and 'Romantic' are far from being synonymous, and if they became identified with one another in the editorial policies of *Le Globe*, this was not necessarily a foregone conclusion. The ill-mannered audience which disrupted the performances of Shakespeare in 1822 was also in a sense 'liberal', but its xenophobic reaction to English foreign policy fitted very well with a vindication of the classical unities against the unorthodox dramaturgy of *Othello*. The young poet Hugo, who took himself so seriously in 1824 that he tried to exculpate himself at great length from the charge of being a 'Romantic', also published in the same year a rousing Ode to 'La Guerre d'Espagne' which praised the French army's successful reinstatement of the Spanish monarch after a 'liberal' uprising. In 1825, he went so far as to publish a further resonant Ode on the coronation at Reims of the new French monarch, Charles X, claiming the prestige of the legendary Frankish king Clovis for the brother of the guillotined Louis XVI who had spent the greater part of his life in exile.[9] By 1830, admittedly, the situation had changed. When the English actors returned to play Shakespeare in Paris, they found a responsive, indeed an enthusiastic audience. When Hugo's play *Hernani* was first performed in February 1830, it set the seal upon the alliance between an advanced dramaturgy acknowledging the name of 'Romantique', and a liberal, intellectual movement which was to provide the impetus for the unceremonious dismissal of Charles X through the 'July Revolution' of that same year.

On one level, at any rate, the answer to my second question is contained in the material of the two preceding paragraphs. Romanticism in France acquired a political dimension (indeed had never been without it) because art was also a means of *representation*, in the broadest sense of the term.

If Victor Hugo could state that 'political life' and 'literary life' were two sides of the same thing, – which was 'public life' – this was not only because the innovatory writer or artist was bound to confront the vested authority of the academic institutions, delegated to them by the state. It was because the public side of writing – polemical journalism – and the public character of dramatic performances irresistibly drew the new talents into the arena where debates about the values and goals of the post-revolutionary society were taking place. This was indeed particularly true of public drama, which had been well on the way to emancipating itself from official control by the end of the Empire. Ten years before Hugo's *Hernani* caused the most open and vociferous *fracas* on its first night, the young Charles de Rémusat was attending the première of Casimir Delavigne's play *Vêpres Siciliennes* with one eye open for the merits of the performance, and another for the behaviour of the audience, whom he declared to be 'very free from the routines of *l'esprit de parti*', even going so far as to claim that the success of Delavigne's play was 'the first article in the law on the age of deputies'.[10] But if a theatre, like a Legislative Assembly, could be swayed by a new rhetoric and persuaded out of its ancestral prejudices, then was it not possible to see the other, supposedly political events as being annexed to the regime of representation – public life as a succession of different theatrical moments? Hugo was, like his young contemporaries, seduced by the elaborate ritual of the coronation of Charles X at Reims, and poured into his Ode a heartfelt wish for the reconciliation of the old France and the new which the ceremony seemed to satisfy. But the older writer François de Châteaubriand, who had lived through the Revolution and the Empire, was in no doubt that it was not the 'real thing'. As he predicted in a letter of 26 May 1825: 'The present coronation will be the representation of a coronation, not a coronation . . . For whose benefit will this parade be capable of creating an illusion?'[11]

If a coronation can be a representation, then what about a 'revolution'? Châteaubriand thought no more of the 'July Revolution' of 1830 than he did of the ceremony which ushered in the previous reign; he declared that, if the Restoration was a 'stage from which the broad sun had disappeared', its actors were at any rate 'giants in comparison with the society of mites which has come into being'.[12] Indeed his relentless irony at the expense of French public life (in which he himself played a far from insignificant part) seems almost to anticipate the corrosive comments of Karl Marx on yet a further phase in France's post-revolutionary history, in the *18 Brumaire of Louis Bonaparte*. But this is leaping too far ahead. What is important at this point is to proceed in the other direction, and trace some of the characteristic aspects of French Romanticism in the 1820s back to earlier positions which give it its characteristic flavour and approach. Unlike almost all the other national schools of Romanticism, the French school can only be convincingly analysed from the basis of a relatively late, and restricted, period: that of the 1820s. If this implies giving the title of 'precursors' or 'Pre-Romantics' to such figures as Mme de Staël and Châteaubriand himself, then the asymmetry with parallel developments in, say, Germany and Great Britain simply has to be accepted. France, as the nation which experienced in the first degree both the Revolution and the Empire, had a sufficiently distinctive historical experience in the half-century from 1780 to 1830 for the disparities in the history of other European nations to pale into relative insignificance. But this certainly does not mean that it is fruitless to try and reconstruct some of the lines of development which contributed to the characteristic ideology of French Romanticism. If Victor Hugo, the son of a Napoleonic general, was ready to acclaim the coronation of Charles X, this should not be seen simply as a personal lapse from liberal rectitude, soon to be remedied: Hugo's stake in history is a personal one, certainly, but it is also an aspect of the complex and contradictory attitudes to the past which the French historical experience brought into clear relief. Equally, Châteaubriand's *insouciant* attitude to power – at least what we accept as such from the person adopted in the *Mémoires* – derives from a specially turbulent experience of life, which only a Frenchman could have witnessed during this period. But it also acquires particular significance in the light of the doctrine of 'Individualism', usually considered as inseparable from Romanticism as a whole. Châteaubriand supplies an extremely vivid example of the power which a man of letters could exert in the historical period which marked the shift from an *ancien régime* to a modern one.

Travelling back into the *ancien régime* to find the precursors of French Romanticism, we inevitably come up against the prior European movement worthy of a special title, for the French the 'Siècle des lumières', and for the British, the Enlightenment. If Romanticism in France is a late flowering movement, and for that reason not easy to characterise, the French Enlightenment is unquestionably central, to such an extent that a recent editor advertised the need to combat the view that 'the Enlightenment was quintessentially a French bloom'.[13] It would be impossible to trace the complex affiliations between the Enlightenment and the Romantic movement here, if only because the comparative study of the early Romantics on a European basis has rarely been attempted up to now.[14] But one fact stands out. The single most inclusive figure among the European precursors of Romanticism was the French-speaking Jean-Jacques Rousseau, a citizen of Geneva. Rousseau's influence on German and English Romanticism is a crucial one, however hard it may be to pin down.

Within the French context, it is even more dominant. The fact that Rousseau was at one and the same time a political and educational philosopher whose doctrines directly or indirectly influenced the practice of the French revolutionaries, and a confessional, autobiographical writer of unique passion and eloquence, gave him a particularly secure place in the concerns of succeeding generations – though part of his fascination lay in the fact that so large a fish could hardly be swallowed whole.

A carefully balanced estimate of Rousseau's legacy is provided by the young imperial official and intimate of Mme de Staël, Prosper de Barante, writing between 1806 and 1810. For Barante, Rousseau's achievement in the *Confessions* was nicely paradoxical: he had 'persuaded us that he was virtuous while telling us how he was nothing of the kind'. His political and social philosophy was flawed because he had 'lived as a stranger in the midst of society' and hence his enthusiasm for 'virtue and justice' had had the opposite effect from what he no doubt intended, shaking the 'foundation of virtue and justice: the feeling of duty'.[15] Yet Barante, who as a child had witnessed the frightening dissolution of social ties brought about by the Revolution, was fully willing to credit Rousseau as the modern author whose work 'most bears a distinct and native character', and congratulates him for restoring to philosophy 'l'éloquence et le sentiment'. Châteaubriand's testimony is no less clear. Although he decides to pick and choose, and rates Rousseau at his best only in 'about sixty of the letters in *La Nouvelle Héloise*, and a few pages in the *Rêveries* and the *Confessions*', he concedes that in those select passages Rousseau 'arrives at a passionate eloquence unknown before him'. Voltaire and Montesquieu, as Châteaubriand argues, take their stylistic models from the age of Louis XIV, but Rousseau 'creates a language which was unknown in the *grand siècle*'.[16]

Châteaubriand's tribute tells us quite a bit about his own success as a writer. But Barante's reservations also tell us something about the dangers which Rousseau's example held in store for the generation of the Romantics. In a sense, 'Romantic individualism' implied precisely what Barante had identified as Rousseau's fatal flaw: that he 'lived as a stranger in the midst of society'. Of course what Barante is detecting here is in large part a special kind of rhetorical effect: the 'stranger' is also a great writer, possessed of a new, passionate idiom, and he places his inner life constantly before us, with the result that we become incapable of differentiating the historical figure from the larger-than-life experience which we share as readers. Without any doubt, Châteaubriand fits this pattern to a nicety. Born in 1768, and disinherited and bereaved by the Revolution, he began his serious commitment as a writer during a series of picaresque travels which took him to the forests of North America, and the quiet countryside of Suffolk, before returning him to France in 1800, at the beginning of the Consulate. Taken up and subsequently dropped by the Consul and Emperor, whose murder of the Duc d'Enghien he could never forgive, Châteaubriand retained like a secret, ultimate weapon his powerful way with words. Only once did he use it during the Empire, when in 1807 he published a brief but carefully coded paragraph which identified the court of the Emperor Napoleon with that of Nero.[17] Napoleon was far from amused, and closed down the newspaper in which Châteaubriand had made the denunciation. There was no doubt that it had had its effect. During the Bourbon Restoration, when censorship operated less rigorously, he had several further opportunities to prove that a few sentences, a phrase or even a single word could galvanise the attention of his audience. His pamphlet, *De Buonaparte et des Bourbons*, published in 1814 at the outset of the Restoration, not only insisted on the Italianate spelling of the abdicated Emperor's name, but compounded this estrangement effect by referring to him as 'l'étranger'. Louis XVIII himself acknowledged the strong positive effect of this pamphlet in restoring his fortunes.[18] Six years later, after the assassination of the Duc de Berry (a member of the royal house) Châteaubriand penned in his *Lettre sur Paris* the phrase which perfectly epitomised the downfall of the royal favourite, Decazes, which precipitately followed the assassination: 'his feet slipped in the blood'. So rapidly was the phrase taken up by the political opposition that Decazes' complicity with the murder seemed to be attested by the highly charged expression, and Châteaubriand later felt it necessary to explain that he had not intended to accuse Decazes of murder![19]

Undoubtedly it was in part the accidental course of Châteaubriand's biography that helped to give him a certain detachment from the powers that he served. Stendhal's fiction shows that he was fascinated by the notion of a man of great influence, or an officer of state, whose former life simply did not permit him to take the obligations of power seriously. The Marquis de la Mole, in *Le Rouge et le Noir*, has been a penniless exile from France, and regards his present prosperity as liable to vanish as rapidly as it came. The father of Lucien Leuwen, in the novel of the same name, sets up and destroys a ministry with an ironic detachment which Stendhal is thought to have copied from the great survivor of all of France's historical vicissitudes, the Prince de Talleyrand. Châteaubriand did indeed experience a remarkable variety of states of being, from penniless exile under the Revolution to Foreign Minister of France under the Bourbon Restoration. But the important fact was not the experience itself, so much as the sustained capacity to mythologise that experience through a type of autobiographical writing which is distinctively 'Romantic'. Towards the end of the Restoration, when his brief but glorious spell as Foreign

Minister was receding into the past, Châteaubriand was appointed ambassador to Rome, which had been the site of his early diplomatic service under the Empire and was also incidentally the location of his favourite portrait – a memorable image by Girodet which shows the young man musing among the ruins of the Colosseum. Returning to Rome in 1828, Châteaubriand recalls: 'I went to Rome to search among the ruins for my other self (*mon autre moi-même*), since there are in my personality two distinct beings, which have no communication with one another.'[20] Whatever psychological nuance he intends to give to it, this notion of a split personality is perfectly explicable in terms of the gap between the 'lived' and the 'written' life which Châteaubriand's *Mémoires* open up. Not only does he live a life of dramatic contrasts, but he also writes it down – and then returns to it as his own reader. The opening section of his recollections of the Restoration bears the note: 'I have just re-read this book in 1840: I cannot prevent myself from being struck by the continual romance of my life (*ce continuel roman de ma vie*).'[21]

It is indeed quite easy to take the life that Châteaubriand lays out for us at its face value, and forget that it is quintessentially a 'roman', which depends on the writer's capacity to record and dramatise subjective experience. It is also easy to forget that Châteaubriand's incentive to write depended at least in part on a novel arrangement made with his publisher, Ladvocat, during the Restoration. Alarmed by his mounting debts, he made the perhaps unprecedented arrangement to publish his entire *Oeuvres* to date, in a collected edition, and these began to appear in 1826. As a writer who continually needed money, and was forced into increasingly ambitious publishing ventures in order to exploit his market, Châteaubriand suggests a comparison with the most pervasive and prolific of Romantic writers, Sir Walter Scott. But, of course, no one could have been less like the anonymous author of *Waverley* and prudent country squire of Abbotsford than the flamboyant Châteaubriand. During the Restoration, indeed, his effective propaganda on behalf of the Greeks fighting their War of Independence in the 1820s gave him a parallel position to that of Byron in England, though without putting him to the trouble of mounting an armed expedition to Greece at his own expense. Châteaubriand seems quite to welcome the parallel in his *Mémoires*. Named one of the four secretaries of the French Chamber of Peers in 1816, he recalls that Lord Byron was unsuccessful in his early attempt to rouse the consciences of the House of Lords, and abandoned them for ever. I, too, remarks Châteaubriand, 'should have gone back to my deserts'.[22]

If Châteaubriand lived and wrote his life in a picaresque (and sometimes a heroic) mode, Mme de Staël was compelled to adopt a pathetic mode in her *Dix Années d'Exil*. The Emperor, who admired Châteaubriand's talent enough to be wary of him, even when he was out of favour, had no such scruples in dealing with what he regarded as the tiresome behaviour of Mme de Staël. Consequently he took steps to bar her from living in Paris and, after the confiscation of her major work *De l'Allemagne* in 1810, impelled her to travel throughout Europe, as is recorded in *Dix Années d'Exil*. Because of her considerable wealth, her status as a citizen of Geneva, and the vast network of important friends and acquaintances which she maintained throughout Europe, Mme de Staël was potentially a formidable opponent for Napoleon. But, as with Châteaubriand, the real secret of her power lay in the writer's capacity to mobilise deep feelings – in her ability to manipulate the new language of 'passionate eloquence' which was Rousseau's legacy. Redolent with this language is the letter which she wrote to the Emperor to accompany the ill-fated publication of *De l'Allemagne*. Châteaubriand pays her the compliment of publishing it in his own *Mémoires*, and appends to it a comment which shows how very high the Pre-Romantic author was pitching his claims:

Alexander and Caesar would have been touched by this letter of so high a tone, written by a woman so renowned; but the confidence in merit which can assess itself and declare itself equal to supreme dominance, the kind of familiarity of the intelligence which places itself on the level of the master of Europe to treat with him as from crown to crown, these appeared to Bonaparte as merely the arrogance of an unregulated self-esteem. He believed himself to be challenged by everything that had any independent element of greatness . . . he did not know that true talent only recognises Napoleons in the quality of genius; that it has its entrée into palaces as well as temples, because it is immortal.[23]

Châteaubriand's picture of an elite of genius, which treats with the 'master of Europe' on equal terms and has the final trump card of 'immortality' to play in any political contest, is no doubt one that is familiarly identified with Romanticism. It is one that we can recognise in the British tradition, from Shelley to Swinburne. It is generally associated with the political philosophy of Liberalism which developed, in the British context at least, as a natural outgrowth of the eighteenth-century parliamentary system, fuelled by economic interest as well as by the philosophical defence of individual freedom. It is worth recalling that, in the French experience, political development had been anything but continuous. The Revolution had shown how certain assumptions about popular sovereignty could lead to intolerable and oppressive forms of government, and the period of the Empire had shown that equality under a single master was in many respects a more effective and more stable system of government than any which was based on an ill-formulated doctrine of individual liberty. Mme de Staël was fully ready to acknowledge this point, but she was not prepared to abandon the hope that a new rationale for a politics of individual liberty could be formulated. She perceptively summed up the dilemma in these terms:

The Emperor Napoleon's greatest grievance against me, is the respect that I have always felt for genuine liberty. These feelings were handed on to me as an inheritance; and I adopted them as soon as I was able to reflect upon the elevated thoughts from which they spring, and on the fine actions which they inspire. The cruel scenes which dishonoured the French Revolution, being nothing but tyranny under popular forms, were quite unable, in my view, to do any harm to the cult of liberty. At the very most, you could become discouraged on behalf of France; but, if this country was unhappy enough not to know how to possess the noblest of goods, there was no reason to proscribe it over the whole of the earth.[24]

The Liberal movement of the French Restoration owed a great deal to Mme de Staël and her circle – to those who, like Châteaubriand himself, had contrived to play an independent role during the imperial epoch, and acclaimed the return of the Bourbon monarchy with enthusiasm because it offered the possibility of a system of government closer to the English pattern. Admittedly Benjamin Constant, who had begun to write his major political treatise, *Principes de Politique*, towards the end of the Empire, fluctuated in his loyalties and eventually chose an independent political stance rather than lending his full support to constitutional monarchy. But Châteaubriand, struggling as always to conciliate his need for independence with a practical assessment of the political situation, threw in his lot with the new constitutional system which he defined with memorable eloquence in his treatise *De la Monarchie selon la Charte*. Of the necessity for the royal executive power to be limited, and for the newly published Charter to guarantee basic rights like the freedom of the press, Châteaubriand was never in any doubt. Although Mme de Staël herself died in 1817, leaving as a legacy her deeply pondered *Considérations sur la Révolution française*, her distinctive influence was maintained through the political prominence of her close friends, ranging from the royalist and Foreign Minister Mathieu de Montmorency to younger statesmen like her son-in-law Victor de Broglie and Prosper de Barante, both of whom formed part of the liberal pressure group known as the 'Doctrinaires'. All of these figures, who had become thoroughly disillusioned by the last years of the Empire, despite some initial accommodation with Napoleon's regime, were ready to confront the task of forging a new constitutional practice, which would take the safeguarding of individual liberties as its first priority.

Of course it would be wrong to equate the political history of the French Restoration exclusively with the development of liberal theory and the practice of constitutional monarchy. The ferment of ideas released by the Revolution had produced many more exotic growths in political philosophy, ranging from the absolutist dreams of European unity under the Pope cherished by Joseph de Maistre, to the nascent systems of what Marx was to call 'Utopian Socialism' elaborated by Saint-Simon and Fourier. In this respect, the Restoration is merely an interval, though an important one, in the long-term development of political ideas which reach their peak towards the end of the nineteenth century in the philosophies of Communism and Anarchism. Romanticism, in France as elsewhere, is a stage in the preparation of these batteries of ideas. But, in France particularly, the Liberalism to which reference has just been made has a fair claim to be considered the distinctive political expression of Romanticism. It bears the obvious marks of its origins in the experience of a small, but scarcely powerless, elite during the reign of Napoleon, and it is open to the accusation that it enshrines the freedom of the inspired and enlightened artist to publish work as the paradigm case of individual liberty. Charles de Rémusat exposed the flaw in a political practice which neglected its real source of power in the economic interests of the bourgeoisie, when he commented on the writings of Mme de Staël: 'The unfortunate thing about her works is that you must have at the same time liberal ideas and the delicate tastes of good company in order to appreciate them – and the *gens du monde* are not liberal, and the liberals are not *gens du monde*.'[25]

Rémusat himself – a young man during the Restoration who survived to hold office under the Third Republic – could see the drawbacks in a philosophy which took the artist's ego as a paradigm, but also smuggled in implications of social exclusiveness which were a fair reflection of the status of advocates of Liberalism like Constant, Châteaubriand and Mme de Staël. Yet it remains the case that the rhetoric of individual liberty was a powerful and inseparable component of French Romanticism as it gathered its full strength during the 1820s. Victor Hugo is perhaps the prime example of an artist who, unlike those previously mentioned, grows to maturity in the 1820s, and is at first somewhat at sea in the turbulent cross-currents of political debate. In his strange first novel, *Han de l'Islande*, which was published in 1823, Hugo traces the fortunes of a heroic figure transparently based on his own youthful experience, but transposed into the remote domains of seventeenth-century Norway. Towards the end of the work, Ordener has a 'sudden inspiration' – he decides to join a party of rebels who are gathering in revolt to support a disgraced minister, even though he is himself the son of the Viceroy, travelling incognito. The decision is a combination of several things, Hugo tells us: 'all at once . . . a generous desire to get to the bottom of this murky adventure at all costs, mixed with a bigger disgust with life, and with a careless despair for the future'.[26] Ordener changes sides, just as Hugo was to change sides after writing his Coronation Ode, committing himself to a life-long Liberalism which was to lead him into permanent exile after the *coup d'état* of the lesser Napoleon. But we should not expect Hugo's motivation to have been any more clear than that of Ordener. The Romantic Hero may commit himself to liberty, but above all he commits himself to the relentless exposure of the conflicts governing, and sometimes inhibiting, his freedom of action.

The particular timbre which Romantic Individualism acquires in the French context is therefore the direct outcome of France's unique historical experience. In particular, it derives from the fact that the genesis of the literary movement took place, against the odds, while the French were experiencing a regime of unprecedented authoritarian powers, whose eventual decline and fall did nothing to remove the sense that individual wills counted for little against the implacable dictates of fate. Prosper de Barante, an imperial prefect who had spent much of his time in the imperial service trying to palliate the effects of the law of conscription on the local community, wrote to his friend Benjamin Constant in 1813 that he was passing the time by studying the history of the Jesuit missions to China – 'that nation where the life of individuals has been blotted out'.[27] The comparison which he implied with his own situation is underlined by his earlier experience as a literary commentator in the imperial epoch. When he published his pioneering account of the French literature of the previous century in 1808, Mme de Staël reproached him for the fact that 'his manner of seeing seems sometimes to be imbued with the doctrine of fatalism'.[28] Despite the fact that she herself had helped to inaugurate the study of literature in its historical context in her work, *De la Littérature considérée dans ses rapports avec les institutions sociales*, Mme de Staël was uncomfortable with a thesis that seemed to question the influence of writers and philosophers over the events of their times. Barante had in effect taken great care to stress the symbiotic relation of the writer and his age. But the fact that he was still preoccupied with the issue is well attested by the way in which he returns to the subject, at the time of the Restoration, in the 'Life of Schiller' which he published to introduce his translation of Schiller's plays. This brief essay breaks new ground in totally rejecting the French classical criticism based ultimately on Aristotle, and concentrates on 'the relationships which the works of Schiller have with the character, situation and opinions of the author, and with the circumstances which surrounded him'.[29]

Viewed against this background, the discourse of Individualism in France – represented preeminently by such writers as Châteaubriand and Hugo – can be seen as what the psychoanalysts call a 'reaction formation'. It was an assertion of the power of the individual ego in circumstances which were, initially at any rate, extremely unfavourable to its full flowering. This point is strengthened by the countervailing argument that France had to do without the major stimulus to the assertion of *collective* identity which was provided during the Romantic period by the phenomenon of Nationalism. France was indeed the other side of the coin to Romantic Nationalism. As Thomas Nipperdey has explained, the very movement was 'a reaction to French hegemony in Europe, to the cultural predominance of the French-styled Enlightenment as well as to the imperial tendencies of the Jacobins and Napoleon'.[30] Of course various strategies were available to the French which enabled them to fight against this disqualification. They could discover a suppressed 'nation' in the course of recent French history: the region of the Vendée, where royalist and Catholic reaction had been ruthlessly suppressed by the revolutionary armies, could be elevated to mythic status, and celebrated in works like the *Mémoires* of Mme de La Rochejaquelein and Balzac's first novel, *Les Chouans*. Or they could provoke the ire of Napoleon by turning, like Mme de Staël and others of her circle, to a foreign nation like Germany (in Nipperdey's terms, 'the centre of romantic nationalism').[31] Nationalism could be experienced vicariously in the cultural revival of a country, or assemblage of countries, whose history was so vastly different from that of France itself. In the long run, it should be said, France's entire experience during the revolutionary period could be transformed into a Romantic saga, as it was preeminently by Michelet in his *History of France*. But this was a historical recuperation of France's national identity, from Joan of Arc to the Revolution, and should not be confused with the immediate challenge to collective action which existed in such incipient nation states as Germany and Italy.

France's distinctive position in this respect is underlined by the fact that she did not benefit from the intensive research into local culture and language which was, in Germany at least, part and parcel of the national revival. Where the Germans had Grimm, painstakingly collecting vocabulary for his dictionary in order to demonstrate the 'spirit of the language', the French had the revolutionary slogan, 'anéantir le patois' – annihilate the patois. Where the Germans turned inwards to investigate the unique treasure of a national language whose diversity was one of its greatest charms, the French were still attached to the notion of their own tongue as the universal language of polite and intellectual society – a vision given chilling consistency at the outset of the revolutionary period by Rivarol's treatise, *On the Universality of the French Language*. Nevertheless, it would be wrong to go too far in this direction, and convey the impression that France was still the last bastion of Enlightenment thought at a time when the other European nations were experiencing a wholesale transformation of modes of thinking and feeling. The barriers set up by Revolution and Empire were not inviolable, and France did indeed experience some of the broad movements of ideas which proceeded apace elsewhere in Europe. It is worth looking in more detail at two of these deep currents which lie beneath the broad stream of Romanticism, always bearing in mind that they represent different aspects of a single, large-scale transformation. These could be described as the return of religion, and the discovery of the otherness of History.

The return of religion had its political side, as well as its intellectual and emotional sides, in France during the first decade of the nineteenth century. In April 1802, the First Consul signed a Concordat with the papacy which rectified relations between Church and State after the persecutions and confiscations of the revolutionary period. But Châteaubriand's lengthy study, *Génie du Christianisme*, which was published immediately after the Concordat, was no mere *livre d'occasion*. Although Châteaubriand was able to bask temporarily in Bonaparte's favour, he was concerned to deal with more fundamental issues than the modest role of favouring social stability which the First Consul was willing to grant to religious institutions. He places the work fairly and squarely in the ancient tradition of apologetics, arguing that Christianity had always needed to defend itself against its detractors, and Voltaire was hardly more formidable a target than a whole line of anti-Christian polemicists from Julian the Apostate onwards. For Châteaubriand, it is a question of demonstrating the superiority of the Christian religion over the paganism of the Ancient World in virtually every domain of intellectual and cultural endeavour. Christianity not only displays a superior grandeur and beauty in placing mysteries like the Trinity at the centre of its doctrine; it can also be shown to have a superior ethical power, when its teaching is compared with the different religious codes of the entire world, and a superior aesthetic power, when its achievements in poetry, music and the visual arts are compared, point by point, with the greatest triumphs of classical civilisation.

Much of the *Génie du Christianisme* now appears vacuous and naive, as well as intolerably prolix – indeed it had already become quite unpalatable to members of a later generation, like Albertine de Broglie and Alfred de Vigny, by the time of the Restoration. A work of astonishing immediate notoriety, it contained some insights which were very far ahead of its time, like the prescient statement that the Scriptures form 'the basis of the human sciences'.[32] It would, however, scarcely have struck so many responsive chords if a good deal of preliminary work had not already been done to expel the demons of eighteenth-century philosophy and establish a new space for subjectivism. Charles de Villers, a familiar of Mme de Staël's circle, had explicitly accepted the task of mediating Kant's philosophical ideas to a French intellectual community still nourished by the Sensationalism of the eighteenth century. The young Prosper de Barante was able to learn from him that it was not necessary to follow 'the route traced by the science of sensations' which led from Descartes, since Kant had reinstated the primacy of the soul, as being 'inseparable from a number of laws which exist in it, truths which are given to it by its own nature'.[33] For Barante, as for many of the familiars of Mme de Staël, this philosophical legitimation of the 'soul' ('l'âme') made it possible, indeed imperative, to look at religious belief from a new perspective. Even the austere Benjamin Constant, who disagreed with Châteaubriand and deplored the opportunistic use made of the *Génie*,[34] was impelled to begin the study of 'polytheism' which was eventually to be published after his death in 1831: *De la religion*. As he worked on it, from around 1805 onwards, he began to realise that the narrow bounds set for religion by the protocols of the age of reason were totally inadequate, and 'the religious sentiment' in itself required more serious consideration.[35]

It is obvious that this revaluation of sentiment, subjectivity and soul, in the religious context, coincides with the popular estimate of Romanticism's revolt against the eighteenth century. But it is perhaps not so obvious how the point can be extended. Philippe Muray's impressive, if eccentric, recent study, *Le 19e siècle à travers les âges*, locates the founding event of the nineteenth century a few years before 1789: to be precise, on 7 April 1786, when the overcrowding of the Parisian cemeteries was finally recognised as an intolerable hazard to health, and the disinterment of corpses from the central 'cimitière des Innocents' was solemnly initiated.[36] From this stage onwards, Muray argues, France was obsessed with the vision of the return of the dead, which manifested itself not so much in conventional religious practice, as in the steady proliferation of practices relating to the occult. There is indeed a great deal to be said about the burgeoning of interest in irrational and para-normal phenomena from the later eighteenth century onwards, which affected France no less than the other countries of Europe. From Mesmer's experiments with 'animal magnetism' – a practice strongly favoured by the Kantian Charles de Villers – to the spiritualist séances cultivated by Victor Hugo and so many of his contemporaries, the line of descent is a clear one. What Muray does, however, is to endow it with a centrality which historians moderately embarrassed by the para-normal have hesitated to accord it up to now. Indeed Muray goes so far as to invent the word 'ocsoc' for the characteristic combination of belief in the occult and faith in socialism which he sees recurring throughout the century. Victor Hugo is perhaps the figure in whom these twin convictions appear most clearly as two sides of the same coin, and Baudelaire an almost solitary exception to the rule of faith in mysticism and Utopia.

Seen against this context, French Romanticism appears as an annunciatory movement, which is identified with a very broad and substantial change in thought and feeling — hardly less than the shift towards a 'modern' way of thinking which we are only now beginning to examine dispassionately. Michel Foucault has been one of the pioneers in trying to identify this shift which appears to have taken place at the outset of the nineteenth century, and he has not been afraid to acknowledge it as 'the great overturning of the Western epistémè'.[37] Foucault's historical method is complex, and moreover it underwent several crucial changes in the course of his career. But its implications can be clearly seen in the domain which is most relevant to this closing section: that is, a change in the conception of man's relationship to the past which could be qualified as a discovery of the otherness of History. Foucault has a striking way of expressing this change. For him, 'the lyrical halo which surrounded, at that epoch, the awareness of history, the lively curiosity for the documents or traces which time had left behind', was a reaction to an overpowering sense of loss. Man had 'found himself to be emptied of history, but . . . he was already at the task of re-discovering in the depths of himself . . . a historicity which was linked to him essentially'.[38] Eighteenth-century man had begun to discover that the world was not simply an anthropomorphic projection; the beginnings of 'natural history' and scientific practices like geology, even the study of language, were telling him that the world of knowledge featured a large number of autonomous areas, and he merely existed at their intersection. Nineteenth-century man reacted to this predicament by a gigantic act of self-assertion: if he could no longer claim dominion over all these areas, he would colonise the one domain in which he could freely assert his primacy; he would re-invent the past.

France's distinctive history no doubt makes this pattern a good deal clearer than in many other countries. The Revolution had affected the lives of different French citizens in a variety of different ways. But without exception, it had caused a break in political continuity which was liable to be transformed, on the subjective level, into a sense of estrangement and loss. The term 'ancien régime', which became neutral enough when it was adopted by other European nations, had a different resonance in France. When Châteaubriand described, in *Génie du Christianisme*, the effect of entering a Gothic church, he epitomised the experience by the phrase: 'L'ançienne France semblait revivre' — ancient (or former) France seemed to live again.[39] When he wrote a preface for the reedition of the work at the time of the Restoration, he saw this phenomenon of historical recreation taking place not merely in the response to historic buildings, but in the simple reading of the old texts brought together in *Génie*: 'Filled with memories of our antique manners, of the glory and the monuments of our kings, the *Génie du Christianisme* breathed the ancient monarchy in all its fullness.'[40] Châteaubriand was certainly not alone in thirsting for the France that had passed away, and seeking to recreate it in his writings. Prosper de Barante, posted to a Sous-Préfecture in the Vendée by pure coincidence, discovered in 1809 to his delight that this preeminently royalist region of France enabled him to eavesdrop upon the 'simplicity of the good old times', with his fellow-diners telling old-fashioned tales that they had learned by 'tradition', and not out of books.[41] When he determined to edit the memoirs of Mme de La Rochejaquelein, a heroine of the Vendée wars, he was conscious of the fact that the events being retraced, though very recent history, belonged on the other side of an insurmountable divide. As he explained to Mme de Staël, his work was to be 'a last testament of old France'.[42]

During the period of the Restoration, these random indications of a personal response to the past are supplemented and given a context by more far-reaching and systematic attempts to evoke the otherness of the past. Prosper de Barante, himself, deprived of a political career by the fall of the Decazes ministry in 1820, went on to write the substantial *Histoire des Ducs de Bourgogne* (1824–6), whose popularity was due in no small measure to the fact that the narrative was modelled on the 'naive' language of the late medieval chronicler, Froissart. Augustin Thierry, in the Preface to his *Histoire de la Conquête de l'Angleterre par les Normands* (1825), expatiated on the need to retain the original orthography of 'Saxon, Norman and other names' as a condition 'not merely of historic interest, but of historic truth'.[43] Both these historians were well aware that such technical innovations were necessary, not only for the sake of their lucrative market, but because the past had to be perceived in its otherness before it could be recreated by their eager contemporaries. In this respect, there is a worthwhile parallel to be drawn with the historians' direct competitor in the publishing stakes during the period of the Restoration: the historical novelist. Since the historical novel was undisguisedly a model imported from abroad, inevitably associated with the immense European prestige of Sir Walter Scott, the young Romantic authors like Hugo and Alfred de Vigny could not fail to see their successful historical novels as the result of a particular formula, a literary *exercice de style* whose protocols had to be observed in order to obtain a specific effect. One of the earliest of these, Hugo's *Han de l'Islande* (1823), makes so free with its epigraphic references to Shakespeare and Schiller, Spanish drama and the gothic novel, that its intertextual status is clearly acknowledged. It is a literary performance, drawing upon a wide range of prototypes unknown to the French classical tradition. But it is also a device for unlocking the particular springs of feeling which were touched, in this period, by the evocation of a strange and distant past.

Of course historiography and the historical novel are not the only signs of the historical-mindedness of the French Romantics. Hugo showed the continuity between literature and the general cultural environment when he wrote his tirade, 'On the destruction of monuments in France' (1825). As he states the predicament, 'it is necessary for a universal cry to summon the new France finally to the help of the old (*l'ancienne*)'.[44] Scorning the classicist impulse which has filled France with 'bastard edifices', he calls his fellow-countrymen to the rescue of abbeys and castles, dilapidated cloisters and dismantled vaults. When Hugo's pamphlet was finally published in 1829, it certainly did not fall upon deaf ears. Indeed the crucial practical steps were already being taken to safeguard France's artistic patrimony, with a new concern being manifested for the Gothic monstrosities which the polite taste of the eighteenth century had placed beneath serious consideration. The process took place in comparable ways in other European countries. But only in France, perhaps, was a rigidly classical tradition so vigorously contested in favour of a native Romanesque and Gothic tradition which had the force of a revelation. Pierre de Lagarde's useful book, *La Mémoire des pierres*, lists the different types of systematic effort which went into the preservation of the monuments of the past in early nineteenth-century France: from Arcisse de Caumont's conservation societies to Guizot's establishment of an inventory of historical buildings, from Merimée's development of an inspectorate of art treasures to Viollet-le-Duc's pioneering works of restoration.[45] Most significant of all, perhaps, as they belong midway between the 'poetic' recreation of the past and the 'practical' safeguarding of monuments, are the two historical museums which offered instruction and pleasure to French and foreign visitors from the Empire onwards: first of all, Alexandre Lenoir's Musée des Petits-Augustins, and subsequently Alexandre du Sommerard's Musée de Cluny. Indeed the shift in the modes of organising and presenting the vestiges of the past which is perceptible if we compare these two successive institutions is a powerful confirmation of Foucault's thesis that the new 'epistémè' takes its origin from this period.

This essay has developed from the minutiae of literary debate, through the issues of Romantic Individualism and Liberalism, and ends with the wider themes of subjectivity and historicity which are central to Romanticism, but would lead us far beyond it. It has also necessarily concentrated on a few figures who can be taken as emblematic of the French movement: in particular Châteaubriand, Mme de Staël and her circle, and of course Victor Hugo. Châteaubriand can be seen as the best example of a figure whose attitudes are formed before Romanticism becomes a movement in France, but becomes – retrospectively and actually – a focus of so many Romantic themes. Victor Hugo is as good an example as any of the writer who catches the full flood of the Romantic movement in France, but survives into a period when the very word 'Romantic' has come to seem outmoded and even bizarre. Reviewing the Salon of 1859, Baudelaire chose to qualify the landscape painting of Paul Huet as 'the debris of a fighting glory like *Romanticism*, which is already so far behind us.'[46] By this stage, even a Romantic painter could be described as 'a veteran of the old guard'!

NOTES

1 Quoted in Robert Baschet, *E.-J. Delécluze, Témoin de son temps* (Paris, 1942), p. 112. Unless otherwise stated, translations from the French are my own.
2 *Ibid.*
3 Victor Hugo, *Oeuvres complètes*, ed. Jean Massin (Paris, 1969), vol. 2, p. 539. Mme de Staël's well-known definition is provided in a chapter of *De l'Allemagne* entitled 'De la poésie classique et de la poésie romantique', where she notes the recent vogue of the term in Germany and equates Romanticism essentially with the Northern, Christian and medieval spirit as opposed to the Southern and pagan spirit of the Ancient World. See Mme de Staël, *De l'Allemagne*, ed. Comtesse Jean de Pange (Paris, 1958), vol. 2, pp. 127ff.
4 Archives municipales de la Ville de Toulouse, Fonds Rémusat, 5 S 189, Green notebook dated Mardi 9 July 1811, Preface p. 5. Rémusat's manuscript annotations to his school exercise books probably date from the end of the Restoration.
5 Quoted in Stendhal, *Racine et Shakespeare* (Paris, 1936), p. 69.
6 *Ibid.*, p. 33.
7 Cf. Charles Baudelaire, 'The painter of modern life', in *The Painter of Modern Life and Other Essays*, trans. and ed. Jonathan Mayne (London, 1964).
8 Baschet, *Delécluze*, pp. 70–89.
9 Hugo, *Oeuvres*, vol. 2, pp. 493–7, 724–7.
10 *Correspondance de M. de Rémusat* (Paris, 1883–6), vol. 6, p. 172.
11 François de Châteaubriand, *Mémoires d'Outre-Tombe*, Pleiade edition (Paris, 1958), vol. 2, p. 117.
12 *Ibid.*, p. 4.
13 Roy Porter and Mikuláš Teich (eds.), *The Enlightenment in National Context* (Cambridge, 1981), p. vii.
14 See Paul de Man, *The Rhetoric of Romanticism* (New York, 1984), p. 47.
15 Prosper de Barante, *De la littérature française pendant le dix-huitième siècle*, 4th edn (Paris, 1824), p. 231.
16 Châteaubriand, *Mémoires*, vol. 2, p. 129.

17 See *The Memoirs of Châteaubriand*, trans. Robert Baldick (Penguin, 1961), p. 254.

18 *Ibid.*, p. 293. He declared it worth more than 'an army of one hundred thousand men'.

19 Châteaubriand, *Mémoires*, vol. 2, p. 12.

20 *Ibid.*, p. 149.

21 *Ibid.*, p. 53.

22 *Ibid.*, p. 6.

23 *Ibid.*, p. 186.

24 *Mémoires de Madame de Staël* (*Dix Années d'exil*) (Paris, n.d.), p. 204.

25 Quoted in Dominique Bagge, *Les idées politiques en France pendant la Restauration* (Paris, 1952), p. 299.

26 Hugo, *Oeuvres*, vol. 2, p. 305. Jean Massin describes this passage as 'capital for understanding the future options of Victor Hugo' (*ibid.*).

27 Barante to Constant, Bibliothèque de Lausanne, 42865, Co 997.

28 Quoted in Barante, *De la littérature*, p. 348.

29 See Barante, *Mélanges historiques et littéraires* (Paris, 1835), vol. 3, p. 103.

30 See J. C. Eade (ed.), *Romantic Nationalism in Europe* (Canberra, 1983), p. 7.

31 *Ibid.*, p. 8.

32 Châteaubriand, *Génie du Christianisme* (Paris, 1966), vol. 1, p. 358.

33 Barante, *De la littérature*, p. 168.

34 Cf. Benjamin Constant, *De la Religion* (Lausanne, 1971), pp. 141, 250.

35 Letter of Constant to Barante, *Revue des deux mondes*, July–Aug. 1906, p. 246.

36 Philippe Muray, *Le 19e siècle à travers les âges* (Paris, 1984), pp. 23ff.

37 Michel Foucault, *Les Mots et les choses* (Paris, 1966), p. 379.

38 *Ibid.*, p. 380.

39 Châteaubriand, *Génie*, vol. 1, p. 400.

40 *Ibid.*, p. 44.

41 Barante, *Souvenirs* (Paris, 1890–7), vol. 1, pp. 269–70.

42 *Lettres de . . . Prosper de Barante à Mme de Staël* (Clermont-Ferrand, 1929), p. 340.

43 See Stephen Bann, *The Clothing of Clio* (Cambridge, 1984), p. 29.

44 Hugo, *Oeuvres*, vol. 2, p. 569.

45 See Pierre de Lagarde, *La Mémoire des pierres* (Paris, 1979).

46 Charles Baudelaire, *Curiosités esthétiques* (Paris, 1968), p. 108.

11

~~~~~~

Spanish Romanticism

SUSAN KIRKPATRICK

Romanticism in Spain, as in the rest of Europe, is part of a much larger historical process that set up the structures of market capitalism, the modern nation-state, and the forms of thought and daily life that made them viable. It is by now a cliché that Romanticism was a response to such changes, but we must recognize that it also promoted the ideological preconditions, such as nationalism and individualism, that made those changes possible. Certainly the participants in Spain's Romantic movement, which began in the 1830s and ended in the late 1840s, did not see themselves as agents of merely a new aesthetics. Juan Martínez Villergas, a politically radical Romantic writer, remarked in retrospect that 'Romanticism was essentially something more than a literary revolution; it was almost a social revolution.'[1] But, as José Escobar points out, 'the adverb, "almost" with which Martínez Villergas restricts the semantic scope of the syntagma, "social revolution", signals the limits of Spanish Romanticism and those of the Spanish revolution itself'.[2] And indeed, the process that liquidated the ancien régime in Spain, though pressured by the course of European history, was slowed and attenuated by resistant internal social structures; the cultural aspect of this transformation, of which Romanticism was a component, was likewise sporadic, uneven, and incomplete.

ROMANTICISM IN SPAIN'S CULTURAL REVOLUTION

Throughout Europe Romanticism played an important role in the evolution of a new way of representing and experiencing inner life that corresponded to the new world of market capitalism and the bourgeois state. One of the basic common denominators of all the varied aspects of Romanticism is its emphasis on individual consciousness. As Lillian Furst points out, 'it was the real innovation of the Romantics to turn individualism into a whole *Weltanschauung*, to systematize it'.[3] By making the individual subject the standpoint from which the world was viewed,

Romanticism helped to elaborate the ideology of individualism that facilitated and buttressed the new social and economic structures: a language for the experience of the individuated self was worked out in exuberant complexity. The sequence and timing of these developments varied according to the different conditions prevailing in different countries. In England, a culturally active as well as economically powerful bourgeoisie succeeded in establishing the ideological preconditions of the Romantic elaboration of subjectivity – the inviolability of the individual self and the absolute division between the psychological self and the social world – before the end of the eighteenth century. In Spain, however, bourgeois ideas failed to gain hegemony even among the literate classes until well after the turn of the century.

The limitations of the Enlightenment in Spain indicate the weakness of the Spanish bourgeoisie during the period in question. Even the elite that promulgated Enlightenment ideas stopped short of pushing them to their ultimate consequences. In particular, Spaniards resisted those aspects of Enlightened thought that most directly challenged the tenets of Catholicism: the new science was treated as a technological advance rather than as the basis for a materialist epistemology; reason was regarded as the appropriate use of God-given faculties rather than the means of a radical critique of accepted beliefs. The Church remained the hegemonic force in Spanish culture until the beginning of the nineteenth century, effectively limiting the inroads of a secular, bourgeois mentality that might undermine the traditional world view. The lack of any Protestant tradition whatsoever in Spain is, in fact, an important factor in the idiosyncratic development of Romanticism on the Peninsula, for in France, Germany, and England Romanticism developed a set of values already established in Protestant culture.[4]

Political and economic structures changed in Spain during the eighteenth century, but more slowly, less drastically, than in France or England. The impact of the French Revolution on Spain was minimal in comparison to other European countries: it simply threw the Crown and the Church, between whom tensions had developed, into collusion to seal Spain's borders from contamination and frightened the Enlightened minority into even more moderate positions. It was only after the turn of the century that Spanish society suffered convulsions that shattered the monumental structures of the old regime. The Napoleonic invasion of 1808 and the subsequent Peninsular War had far-reaching consequences: it revealed the weaknesses of the monarchy, drew the whole Spanish population into a struggle conceived alternatively as holy war against the French infidel or as a liberal national revolution, and facilitated the independence movements that soon stripped Spain of her overseas empire. This last effect is arguably the decisive one in giving impetus to the revolutionary process. With the colonies, the absolutist state lost a crucial source of income and the commercial and industrial bourgeoisie lost its principal market. The monarchy, absolutist as ever in principle, was forced to seek new revenues by appropriating the property of its former ally, the Church, while the bourgeoisie became increasingly aware that its interests – centrally, the creation of an integrated national market – would best be served by a modern liberal state and the replacement of traditional social relations by forms that permitted more individual autonomy and initiative.[5]

Thus the stage was set for the political struggle of which Spanish Romanticism was a concomitant. Between 1815, when Ferdinand VII, his crown restored by Napoleon's defeat, abrogated the Constitution of 1812 that the liberal parliament of Cadiz had created in his absence, and 1836, when Ferdinand's widow, María Cristina, was forced by a powerful liberal faction to swear allegiance to the same Constitution, the tide turned; the old regime was on its way out in Spain. The diffusion of a new mentality revealed itself in the rising fortunes of Romanticism as a literary school. But before examining the components of the new consciousness, let us see how the erratic progress of Spain's liberal revolution directly affected the rise and fall of its Romantic movement.

For the liberal framers of the Constitution of Cadiz, Enlightenment values such as rationality, measure, and objectivity served as instruments of combat against the baroque cultural forms of the old regime, a means of constructing a secular frame of reference for social relations in the here and now. Thus they greeted with hostility the first appearance of Romantic ideas on the Peninsula, namely an 1814 article by the conservative German, Nicholas Boehl von Faber, in which he summarized and advocated A. W. Schlegel's claims for the superiority of baroque to neo-classical drama. Unable to stomach this exaltation of Calderón's theatre, so closely associated with the absolutist and theocratic regime that Ferdinand had restored, some of Spain's leading intellectuals carried on a bitter polemic with Boehl. To the Spanish liberals of 1814, the organic forms that Schlegel praised as Romantic did not sufficiently contrast with traditional Spanish drama to seem effective in the liberal project of diffusing a new consciousness.

This hostility to Romanticism, known only in its ultra-conservative form, lasted throughout the ensuing decade. Then a dramatic new political event changed the situation. The French invasion of 1823, which restored Ferdinand to absolute power after a brief revolutionary interlude, drove the leading liberal intellectuals into political exile in England or France. In the late 1820s, when Byron's influence was at its height, when Victor Hugo rose to prominence, exiled Spanish writers discovered a European Romanticism more to their liking and within a few years abandoned neo-classical principles to embrace the new aesthetic. While Angel de Saavedra (later the Duke of Rivas) was in France, for example, he wrote the long narrative poem, *El moro expósito* (1834), and the drama, *Don Alvaro o la fuerza del sino* (1835), both clearly Romantic in theme and form. In fact, the former's prologue, written by Antonio Alcalá Galiano, a former anti-Boehl polemicist who became a professor of Spanish literature at London University during exile, was conceived as a Romantic manifesto for Spanish literature. However, Alcalá's conception of Romanticism, strongly influenced by Wordsworth and Coleridge, had little impact on the development of the movement on the Peninsula.

Meanwhile, certain Romantic literary ideas were taking root in the tightly censored Spain of Ferdinand VII. A weekly paper, *El Europeo*, which was published in Barcelona during the winter of 1823–4 by two Catalans, two Italians, and an Englishman, printed articles explaining and advocating the new aesthetics. As the decade wore on, some of these ideas cropped up among the few publications that the censors permitted. For example, in 1828 a treatise by Agustín Durán argued for organic national tradition against the abstract universal standard of neo-classicism, for the representation of passion and psychological particularity, and for a limited historical relativism in moral and aesthetic values. These views were grafted onto neo-classical principles of social unity and good taste in the intellectual formation of the generation that came of age around 1830, a generation that was to be the dominant force in Spanish letters for the next two decades.

The situation in which this new generation turned to writing made Romantic ideas more appealing and acceptable. By the 1830s the economic crisis of the Spanish state and the example of developing capitalism abroad had persuaded the governing elite to accept certain liberal economic and political doctrines, ensuring the eventual defeat of the reactionary faction of don Carlos, Ferdinand's brother, who turned to an armed uprising to challenge the succession of the Infanta Isabel after the king died in 1833. With the end of the Carlist revolt in 1839, there remained no effective alternative to the transformation of the state and the modernization of the economy that was underway. The reactionary factions and the persistent pre-modern structures of Spanish society simply slowed and attenuated such changes. During this decade, then, the mentality that supported a liberal revolution spread and became more secure. These are the conditions in which the Spanish Romantic movement came into existence and rapidly gained momentum; the intellectual vanguard found the Romantic emphasis on nationalism, freedom, and individual subjectivity appropriate to their sense of reality and useful in their struggle to advance the revolution.

The dynastic crisis that followed the death of Ferdinand forced the Queen-Regent to form an alliance with the liberals, initiating a turn of events that gave impetus to the vogue of Romanticism. The exiled political leaders and intellectuals returned to the Peninsula, bringing with them the stimulating models of a more radical Romanticism than Durán's prevailing version. An upsurge of Romantic writing followed the return of the *emigrados* and the gradual easing of censorship that allowed the repressed energies of the new crop of young writers to find expression. José de Espronceda clearly exemplifies this conjunction of forces: although he had the opportunity to read English and French Romantic poets while he was in exile, he continued to write poetry in the neo-classical mode he had been taught at school. Upon his return to Spain, however, he experimented with new poetic language and forms and quickly became the trend-setter among the young poets who declared Romanticism to be their artistic credo. In the theatre, Romantic drama became the vogue for the intellectual, if not for the popular, audience after 1834 and 1835. To further the new artistic movement, the young Romantics founded a journal dedicated to literature and the fine arts, *El Artista*, which published poetry by Espronceda and other new poets, historical novels and tales of fantasy, drama criticism and essays defending Romantic aesthetics, as well as engravings by the artist, Federico de Madrazo, and music criticism by the Romantic pianist and composer, Santiago de Masarnau. Although *El Artista* lasted only a year and a half, it did launch its hitherto unknown young contributors on the literary scene and established the presence of Romanticism as a significant, though not necessarily predominant, style of writing.

In fact, the movement could scarcely be said to have swept the field, as F. Courtney Tarr noted in a seminal article on Spanish Romanticism:

The year 1834 and its successors show, in their literary characteristics and output taken as a whole, but little change in the trends and conditions already established. In the theatre, along with the slow and conditional acceptance of the romantic drama – this was not so much of a departure as it may seem – the vogue of the opera and of translations and adaptations of Scribe . . . and minor French authors of light comedy continued without check; in poetry the flood of mediocre, occasional, patriotic and satiric verse was relieved – at least until 1840 – only infrequently by romantic poems.[6]

The spottiness of Romanticism's hold in Spain reflects the uncertain progress of the bourgeois revolution on all fronts, political, economical, and cultural, faced with the resistance of older forms of thought and social institutions.

The heyday – such as it was – of Spanish Romanticism lasted from 1835 to 1842. These are precisely the years of greatest liberal activism in pushing forward the first phase of Spain's prolonged revolution: irreversible though truncated liberal reforms established constitutional monarchy, abolished aristocratic privilege, and disentailed landed property tied up in aristocratic and ecclesiastical estates. In terms of literary developments, two new dramatists, Juan Eugenio Hartzenbusch and Antonio García Gutiérrez, achieved popular success with a series of Romantic plays. Espronceda reached maturity as a poet, exploring a variety of poetic genres – the short lyrical poems written between 1837 and 1839, the fantasy narrative, *El estudiante de Salamanca* (1837), and the Romantic epic, *El diablo mundo*, which remained unfinished at his death in 1842. Romantic poetry was also published during this period by the Duke of Rivas, Enrique Gil y Carrasco, and Nicomedes Pastor Diáz. Almost all these Romantic writers tried their hand at medievalizing historical novels *à la* Walter Scott. The real innovator in prose was the journalist, Mariano José de Larra, who in the last year of his short life made the newspaper article an instrument of Romantic irony, combining anguished confession with bitter social analysis.

Just as the liberals split into two factions – the progressives and the moderates – during this period, so too marked differences in how Spanish writers viewed the objectives and meaning of the Romantic movement became clear. For many it was the latest literary fashion, a set of glamorous themes and images and, above all, a justification for exalting national tradition. Only a few understood and practised Romanticism as a radical questioning and revision of earlier values. Two sharply distinct tendencies emerged, echoing a political division that appears throughout European Romanticism – the regressive trend that Robert Marrast calls 'nationalist Romanticism', nostalgic, medievalizing, local colourist, and the progressive 'social Romanticism', focused on the contradictions of the present.[7]

In Spain, the close tie between the Romantic movement and politics had a material basis in the fact that almost all the writers of this period were primarily engaged in politics. The easing of censorship after the death of Ferdinand VII permitted a rapid expansion of the press, particularly the periodical press. Writing for the new periodicals, which served mainly as organs of different factions and mixed imaginative writing indiscriminately with political commentary, became the favoured means through which ambitious young men advanced a career in government. A survey of the journalists writing for Madrid papers in the late 1830s shows that as many as 60% were later elected to parliament; of 21 young men from the provinces who moved to Madrid specifically to pursue a career in journalism, 18 either became cabinet ministers or held some other high government office in the following decades.[8] The full significance of this pattern becomes evident when we consider that it holds true for some of the major figures of Spanish Romanticism: Larra was a journalist and was elected to parliament; Espronceda wrote journalism as well as poetry and was elected to parliament; the Duke of Rivas was a cabinet minister, and Martínez de la Rosa was prime minister. For the makers of Spanish Romanticism, then, writing and politics were not strictly differentiated activities.

The Romantic writers' close involvement in political developments helps to explain the general attenuation of the movement after 1843, when liberal advances were halted by a reaction that brought to power the conservative general, Ramón María Narvaez. By this time, Romanticism's initiators had either died, like Larra and Espronceda, or, like Martínez de la Rosa, Alcalá Galiano, and the Duke of Rivas, had repudiated their former credos, both political and literary. The mood of the times was moderate: the aristocracy and the bourgeoisie, both frightened by the disruptive struggles of the thirties, sought social stability in 'middle-of-the-road' political formulas. On the cultural level, likewise, the reigning attitude was 'eclectic', as E. Allison Peers has called the tendency to find a middle road between opposing literary systems.[9] Yet the new writing of the 1840s undeniably incorporated the Romantic paradigms established by the writers of the previous decade. Most of the authors of this second period developed the conservative nationalist line of Romanticism. José Zorrilla had the greatest success in this vein: his enormously popular *Don Juan Tenorio* (1844) epitomizes the 'eclectic' tendency to exploit the sensational aspects of the Romantic hero while neutralizing his rebelliousness through a last-minute religious conversion. However, the Romantic rebellion against the status quo did not entirely disappear during this decade: it surfaced in a new, feminist form in works by two women writers, Gertrudis Gómez de Avellaneda and Carolina Coronado. By 1850, nevertheless, the Romantic flame was spent in Spain. Its aesthetics were superseded, but its vocabulary and the problems it addressed lived on as a legacy assimilated and transformed by the poets and novelists of the second half of the nineteenth century.

A NEW TRUTH FOR A NEW SOCIETY

Romanticism, so closely tied to the course of liberal reform in Spain, can be regarded as central to the cultural agenda of the liberal movement. To understand the connection more fully, we must consider how Romanticism supplied imaginative and emotional meanings for the new structures that the liberals sought to constitute in Spanish society. This connection was drawn explicitly by Larra, the most self-conscious of the

Spanish Romantics. Surveying the course of Spanish literature in his brilliant and influential essay, 'Literatura' (1836), he provided what was in essence an analysis of the state of the cultural revolution in Spain. Noting the failure of the Enlightened vanguard of the previous century to do more than to try to impose foreign tastes on a culture that had developed neither linguistically nor politically to the point of being able to integrate new values and concepts, Larra declares that the present moment is ripe with new possibilities:

Today a numerous young generation rushes anxiously to the sources of knowledge. And at what moment in history? At the moment when intellectual progress, everywhere breaking ancient chains, destroying worn-out traditions and knocking down idols, proclaims in the world moral as well as physical freedom, because the one cannot exist without the other.[10]

We find here the presupposition that grounds the new mentality, or 'intellectual progress', as Larra terms it: the construct of the individual self, that physical and moral unit whose a priori autonomy justifies and demands the freedoms proclaimed in this paragraph. Larra's confidence that the new truth would triumph over the old forms of thought is very much a product of the immediate historical moment: Juan Alvárez Mendizábal, the man whom progressive liberals thought of as their champion, was prime minister and promising miracles of fiscal and legislative reform within months. In Larra's view, 'intellectual progress' was on the verge of carrying the day in Spain, of winning acceptance of the premises of liberal ideology as truth.

Cultural and socio-political transformation were thus closely linked in Larra's mind: 'let us hope that soon we will be able to lay the foundations of a *new* literature, the expression of the *new* society we compose, a literature entirely *true* just as our society is *true*' (pp. 133–4). The anxiety signalled by the writer's emphasis on the two words, 'true' and 'new', reveals the relative insecurity of bourgeois cultural premises in Spain. As a world view not yet sufficiently integrated with social practices to become unconscious, or at least beyond the need for demonstration, it retains for writer and reader the sense of something new, a replacement of something else, and therefore not uniquely uncontestable. Furthermore the use of italics suggests that the 'new truth' refers to a set of concepts for which the language has not yet been fully elaborated; the writer must rely on a kind of gesture to his audience to supplement his meaning. But this is precisely Larra's message: it is time to create a literary discourse that will embody the new truth of the new society.

Larra defines crucial aspects of the 'truth' for us in a passage that reveals both the lucidity and the difficulty entailed by his conscious assumption of an ideology: 'In politics man finds nothing but *interests* and *rights*, that is to say, *truths*. So it follows that in literature he cannot seek anything but *truths* . . . Because man's passions will always be *truths*, because imagination itself, what is it if not a more beautiful truth?' (p. 133). As the common denominator linking politics and literature, the meaning of 'truth' is expanded to include the Romantic values of passion and imagination along with the liberal values of interests and rights. Thus, the new definition of truth implies the basic premise of liberal ideology: the common reality in which society, politics, and literature are grounded is the individual subject. Only by equating truth with the locus where interests and passions meet can we make sense of Larra's argument. And in so doing, this passage articulates the connection between the liberal revolutionary programme and the literary agenda of Romanticism, for the model of the individual subject that underlies 'truth' is to be propagated and elaborated by both movements at different levels of social activity.

In 'Literatura', then, Larra, at the same time that he defines the intellectual and literary project of his generation, locates the place of Romanticism within the political and social transformation he hoped to see carried out in Spain. That this project could not be fulfilled by Larra's generation helps to account for the despair that led to his early suicide. However, Larra's main concerns in this essay – the need for a truly national literature, the truth of individual subjectivity, and the necessity of freedom – identify for us the three interlocking components of Romanticism that played an ideological role in the eventual formation of a modern capitalist society in Spain.

THE VALUE OF 'NATION'

Of all the features of European Romanticism, those centred on the new nationalism were most readily acceptable to Spaniards. Whatever the forces that produced the Spanish people's resistance to Napoleon's occupation, they were interpreted in the decades that followed as a manifestation of essential Spanish independence and dignity. This myth of an inherent national identity functioned as an imaginary compensation for the loss of the overseas empire and offered an image of national unity that was useful to a weakened absolutist regime; less obviously, perhaps, it also served a bourgeoisie whose vital interests lay in consolidating a national market for its products. The related ideas of patriotism, national sovereignty, and popular will also formed a crucial part of the ideological framework to which liberal reformers appealed. Even the reactionaries based their claim to legitimacy on concepts of national tradition and character. Thus, the concept of nation lay at the very core of ideological representations of the political struggles of the Romantic period in Spain, forming the battleground on which contending factions sought to impose their particular definition of what constituted the Spanish nation. In such a context the Romantic exaltation of elements related to nationalism – local custom and landscape, folk traditions, episodes from national history, the high passion of patriotism – had strong appeal for both conservative and progressive intellectuals.

In particular, the implications of Romantic nostalgia for earlier modes of national existence account for the acceptance of some Romantic tenets by a conservative like Durán. His 1828 attack on neo-classical criticism is based on the equation of national literary tradition with the religious and heroic values of medieval Spain; his definition of the national spirit excludes neo-classical aesthetics along with economic progress as anti-national:

Though foreign countries may be ahead of us in industry, we can at least take pride in preserving all the patriotic and religious enthusiasm that even he who dominated all of Europe [Napoleon] could not quell, and in maintaining in all its honour the motto that distinguishes us: *For my God, for my king, and for my lady.*[11]

Conservatives often used this strategy of identifying the Spanish nation with medieval tradition and thus designating modernization as 'foreign'. Durán's commitment to finding the purest literary expression of Spanishness made him one of Spain's first folklorists. His collection of traditional ballads, or *romances*, compiled throughout the Romantic period and published in the 1850s as the monumental *Romancero general*, stands as the great accomplishment of Romantic interest in Spain's oral tradition. The vitality of this tradition contrasts with the artificiality of the poetry that, inspired by the cult of the medieval past, began to appear in the press of the 1830s, starting with *El Artista*. This essentially moderate trend in poetry carried well into the 1840s and peaked in the poetry of Zorrilla that glorified a mythical Spain of heroic knights and virginal ladies.

The new interest in Spain's oral and traditional poetry was not confined to the conservatives. Liberal writers too identified themselves with this repository of popular inspiration. In exile the Duke of Rivas, impressed by the novels of Walter Scott and nostalgic for his homeland, affirmed his national identity in *El moro expósito*, set in a tenth-century Spain divided between Moors and Christians and inhabited by figures from traditional legend. But the poem's narrative structure establishes a distance between Spain's medieval past and the existential uncertainty of the poet's present that Durán would never have admitted. Even Espronceda, though avoiding the usual apparatus of Spanish medievalism in his poetry, drew on Castilian legend for *El estudiante de Salamanca*.

The area in which writers across the political spectrum looked back to remote episodes of national history as their subject matter was in writing historical novels, more or less in imitation of Walter Scott. The authors of these novels undoubtedly hoped to cash in on Scott's popularity while at the same time promoting their vision of the authentic constitution of the Spanish nation. In *El doncel de don Enrique el Doliente* (1834), for example, the liberal Larra represents a legendary twelfth-century page as a kind of bourgeois individualist struggling for his rights against a vicious and tyrannical aristocracy. However, none of these Spanish novels managed to capture the popular imagination as Scott's did.

Jaime Vicens Vives points out that the nostalgic cult of the nation's remote past was an artistic expression of the reformist ideology of the moderate liberals[12] – the middle of the road that formed the meeting place of a reluctant aristocracy and an insecure bourgeoisie. The Romantic image of Spain's middle ages glorified a pre-Habsburg past in which the monarchy's authority had not become absolute and at the same time legitimized the idea of continuity with national tradition. The definition of the Spanish nation that emerged was not in fact reactionary – the very idea of nationality as a bond of language, custom, and character linking people across social strata was modern, implying some degree of popular sovereignty, some other object of loyalty and identity than the feudal clan or village. The Romantic representation of the past was one aspect of a process of self-definition necessary to the establishment of a new nation-state, modern but not radically different in its distribution of power.

An important factor in Spaniards' preoccupation with national self-definition was their consciousness of Spain's image as an exotically 'other' setting for the Romantic fantasy of the rest of Europe. A nationalistic desire to see Spain described and defined by itself instead of by foreigners played into the rise of a genre that gained outstanding popularity in the 1830s – the *cuadro de costumbres* or sketch of manners and types. Ramón de Mesonero Romanos, the enduring master of the genre, justified his project of describing his contemporaries in a series of articles called *The Panorama of Madrid* (1835) by referring to foreign writers' representations of Spain:

The French, the English, the Germans and other foreigners have attempted to describe Spanish customs and psychology; but they have either created an idealized country of romanticism and quixotism, or, ignoring the passage of time, have described her, not as she is, but as she was in the time of King Philip . . . Unable to remain a tranquil observer of such falsehoods . . . , I made up my mind to present to the Spanish public sketches that would offer scenes of our nation's own customs, particularly those of Madrid, which, as the capital and centre of our nation, is the focal point in which those of distant provinces are reflected.[13]

In his bid to portray contemporary Spain 'as it really is', Mesonero deploys an idea of nation that avoids identifying it with either the conservative or liberal definition, thus enabling him to capture a readership from both camps for his articles, which accompanied and promoted the rapid expansion of the periodical press in the wake of Fernandine repression. By representing the nation as centred and epitomized in Madrid, this passage concretizes the abstraction in such a way as to identify the common project that brought together Madrid's literate public against the Carlists and under the Queen-Regent's banner. Regardless of their political affiliation, the upper classes of the capital supported the centralizing and standardizing of the state necessary to the development of modern capitalism. Mesonero's words reveal the important ideological function of 'nation' in his literary project: nationality, 'Spanishness', will be the common factor shared by the diverse scenes he promises, the conceptual frame that will unify the fragmented images of contemporary society.

In Mesonero's practice, as well as his justification of his practice, he goes further in concretizing Spanish identity. Despite the diversity among Spaniards that he acknowledges, and, indeed, shows, Mesonero assures his readers that his object is to depict 'the true colouring of the country, the actions and behaviour common to all classes: nature, in a word, dressed in Spanish form'.[14] Nature appears in Spanish dress, however, predominantly among one particular social group. As he explained to his readers in 1832:

[T]he middle class, because of its extension, variety and different applications, is the one that stamps a people with a particular physiognomy, causing the differences one observes between them. For that reason my pieces give greatest preference to [the customs of] property owners, government employees, merchants, artists and all the classes that form the middle strata of society.[15]

Thus, Mesonero's *cuadros* appropriate the concept of nation for the Spanish bourgeoisie, making in effect the claim that emerging bourgeois life-styles and values constitute the natural, national character of Spain. Apparently politically neutral, his sketches suggest that the growth of capital, industry, and consumer markets comes about naturally: 'The same thing happens everywhere: civilization and culture spawn new needs that, by putting capital in circulation, nurture industry, provide applications for the arts and sciences, and modify and beautify public *mores*' (*Obras*: I, 227). He portrays the triumph of the new regime as gradual and unproblematic, in keeping with the national character, and promoting the prosperity and refinement of all. Consequently, while projecting and supporting a bourgeois perspective, Mesonero in no way threatens the traditional oligarchy nor alienates the moderate sectors of the middle strata. Mesonero, setting the paradigm for the *costumbrista* genre that was to dominate Spanish letters for the next two decades, played a crucial role in the cultural revolution that was underway. His image of Spanish society corresponds to the historical and not easily accomplished task of the Spanish bourgeoisie at that moment – to coalesce as a class. The disparate and divided groups that might ultimately form a bourgeoisie could find in Mesonero's literary representations an ideological identity fusing class and nation.

Larra, younger and more brilliant than Mesonero, was the only practitioner of *costumbrismo* to rival him in importance. Despite significant differences between them – Larra's *cuadros* were more satirical than descriptive, more critical than sentimental – the concept of nation occupied fundamentally the same place in the projects of both writers. In a much anthologized article, 'Marrying Early and Badly' (1833), Larra criticizes the slavish imitation of the English or the French, implying that Spaniards should neither import customs nor adhere stubbornly to ancient Spanish tradition. Instead, he argues for the consolidation of a middle-class Spanish culture, informed by modern values without cutting the roots of its national history. A considerable portion of Larra's literary output was directed toward the promotion of such a culture: his satires of manners, his demands for education, his criticism of the Spanish theatre, and his commentary on leisure activities[16] all hold up the standard of bourgeois values. Larra, then, like Mesonero Romanos identified authentic Spanish nationality with middle-class values. The significant difference is that Larra defined this national core as an absence: his writing addresses precisely the lack of a middle ground of common values and attitudes between the various classes of Spaniards. Larra's lucid assessment of national reality made him unique among his contemporaries; he was the only writer of the Romantic period to acknowledge the mythical status of the idea of nation:

What is generally called society is an amalgam of a thousand societies placed one on top of the other, which only have contact with each other at their mutual boundaries, and which in no country are joined in a compact whole except through the links of a common language and through what men call patriotism or nationalism.

(83)

Thus Larra appears to doubt the real basis for what men call nationalism; yet in his view as in the less self-conscious views of his fellow Romantics, the concept was essential to the coherence of a society torn by civil war and stubborn regional as well as class divisions.

With respect to regional differences, the Romantic cult of nationalism was a double-edged concept throughout Europe, fuelling the resurgence of national identity among smaller cultures subordinated to the central state. In Spain, too, Romanticism was connected with movements in Catalonia, Galicia, Valencia, and Euzkadi to affirm and preserve the uniqueness of their own culture by writing in the vernacular, but these movements did not develop until after 1850, when the Romantic vogue had waned. For example, the Catalan Victor Balaguer published Romantic poetry written in Castilian during the 1840s, but after 1850 he wrote almost entirely in Catalan and became one of the leading promoters of the Catalan Renaissance of the last half of the nineteenth century. It would appear that Romanticism was initially a very centralized movement in Spain, reflecting the political process that drew writers and intellectuals to Madrid in the 1830s and 40s, and was slowly transformed as it diffused outward to the provinces. Thus, Rosalía de Castro, often considered a late Romantic poet, published her first book of poetry (1857) in Madrid and in Castilian; only in the 1860s did she begin to write in the vernacular Galician and publish in Vigo.

THE NECESSITY OF FREEDOM

Another powerful value in the cultural revolution that comprised literary Romanticism and political liberalism was the idea of liberty. To see how this ideal was articulated with nationalism, let us return to Larra's seminal essay, 'Literatura', where he expresses his urgent hope that a new national literature will emerge, one entirely 'true' to the society and history that produces it. In that essay, Larra declares freedom to be the principal factor in the project of reconstituting society, literature, and truth. '*Freedom* in literature, as in the arts, as in industry, as in commerce, as in conscience. This is the standard of our age, this is *our* standard, the gauge we will use to measure' (p. 134). By linking moral and material liberty, he implies the need for freedom from government censorship as well as emancipation from the rules of established literary convention. As the necessary corollary to the economic and political freedoms sought by liberals, freedom of expression was essential to the new young writers whom Larra expected to play their part in the cultural revolution by representing the new truth for the new society.

Formal aesthetic freedom was first decisively claimed for poetry by the Duke of Rivas in *El moro expósito* (1834) and for drama in *Don Alvaro* (1835), which showed the influence of Hugo's assault on the rules of classical restraint in French theatre. However, the thematics of *Don Alvaro* was more subversive than its form in the context of Spanish theatre, from which the open structures of Golden Age drama had never completely disappeared. The play's protagonist, a handsome young gentleman of mysterious origins is ultimately destroyed by the rigid social code of the Calatrava clan, which refuses to admit any of his claims to equality with them. The dramatic conflict thus poses the problem of an *ancien régime* that grants the individual no space for achievement on his own merits or pursuit of his own happiness. Of course, Rivas's own aristocratic bias forecloses the potentially democratic import of such a conflict: don Alvaro, the son of a Castilian nobleman and an Indian princess, turns out to be as high-born as his antagonists by the standards of social rank if not of race.

It was Espronceda who most unequivocally gave poetic expression to the exaltation of freedom as a value, beginning with 'The Song of the Pirate' (1835), a poem that quickly achieved widespread popularity. Declaring 'My treasure is my ship, / Liberty is my god', the pirate captain sings the joys of a freedom unfettered by law or human power as he roams the high seas. Undoubtedly influenced by Byron and French imitations of Byron, this rebel who defies social constraint represents the first appearance in Spanish poetry of the anarchic Romantic hero. The pirate fits in perfectly, however, with the native tradition of popular ballads exalting the outlaw. In presenting this farthest extreme of the concept of freedom, Espronceda reveals its potential conflict with nationalism, for the pirate's 'only fatherland is the sea' – it is precisely his lack of national identity that frees him. The poet explored the tensions between social constraint and individual freedom in a series of other poems written in 1835–6 that adopt the voice of marginalized social types: 'The Beggar', 'The Condemned Man', and 'The Hangman'. The protagonist of 'The Beggar', far from lamenting his lot, celebrates the freedom that his lack of possessions allows him and cynically admits that he lives off the society from whose pre-occupation with wealth he is free. The hangman, in contrast, is totally constrained, his humanity obliterated, by the society that makes him the agent of its vengeance against transgressors of its norms.

In El diablo mundo (1841) Espronceda set out systematically to explore how society limits the individual's freedom. Adam, the epic's main protagonist, imagined as Rousseau's natural man, confronts Spanish society, which immediately claps him in prison, believing his lack of inhibition to be a sign of anarchist tendencies. The metaphor equating socialization with imprisonment is explicitly developed in canto IV, where Adam learns language and strategies of social interaction in prison under the tutelage of an experienced criminal. Society is thus associated with injustice, repression, and violence. The poem represents liberation in terms of the merely temporary escape from the pressure of the social world through erotic union. In his poetry Espronceda expresses a pessimism about the possibility of personal freedom that forms a marked contrast with his optimism as a political activist engaged untiringly in the progressive liberals' struggle to advance the revolution.[17] Though he remained committed to the political ideals of progressive liberalism, his effort to figure these ideals in poetic discourse revealed the elusiveness of that negative abstraction, liberty. Espronceda lacked Larra's unrelenting lucidity, but both demonstrated in their writing the capacity of Romantic thought to call its own premises into question.

The hypocrisies and contradictions of the liberal call for freedom were most poignantly and incisively brought to light, however, by the Romantic writers who found themselves excluded from the liberal programme of political rights and civil liberties – namely women. Unlike England and France, where women began to publish regularly much earlier, it was with the Romantic movement that Spain inaugurated female authorship as a general and growing phenomenon: though women writers appeared singly from time to time in Spanish letters before the nineteenth century, the expansion of the press in the 1830s (which helped to create a growing female readership) and the diffusion of the Romantic ethos of self-expression that gave importance to feeling worked together to draw Spanish women into unprecedented literary activity. A few pieces by women appeared in the early phase of the movement, but the full harvest of woman-authored publication occurred after 1840. The work of the two most outstanding of the new women poets, Gertrudis Gómez de Avellaneda and Carolina Coronado, applied Romantic values to the social situation of women, and in so doing produced a critique of liberalism's failure to address the oppression of those who were not white middle-class males.

The Cuban-born Gómez de Avellaneda voiced women's claim to freedom through the protagonist of her first novel, *Sab* (1841), who denounces the subjugation of both women and blacks in the climactic passage of the narrative. In making two women and a mulatto slave the subjects of a Romantic quest for happiness within a social order that grants only white males the power and freedom to realize their desires, the author created the first abolitionist novel in Spanish. Thus, Gómez de Avellaneda's Romantic protest against the status quo amounts to a plea for extending the right of self-realization, the cornerstone of liberal values, to women and to other races. Her next novel, *Dos mujeres* (1842), specifically indicted society's restriction of the scope of women's experience and activity.

Carolina Coronado also addressed the oppression suffered by women in her society. Even her first collection of poetry (1843), which conformed to the dominant idea of femininity by stressing the poet's girlish innocence, included an angry denunciation of wife-beating. The poetry she wrote between 1845 and 1850 was explicitly feminist, expressing the claustrophobia and anger produced by women's restriction to the domestic sphere. In one poem, 'Liberty' (1846), she gave a woman's perspective on the liberal revolution in Spain, ironically commenting that the newly won freedoms that the men of Spain are celebrating do not include everyone:

'The law belongs to men alone, / For women aren't taken into account / Nor is there a Nation for our sex.' Therefore, she asks, '*Freedom*, what does it matter to us? / What have we gained? What will we have? / Enclosure as our *tribune*? / A needle as our *right*?'[18] The key concepts of liberal ideology – nation, liberty, rights – become objects of critical irony in Spanish Romanticism, then, when viewed, not from the regressive standpoint of nostalgia for the past, but from the perspective of those not yet included in the liberal programme for change.

THE TRUTH OF SUBJECTIVITY

As we have seen, the intersecting values of nationalism and freedom permitted a considerable span of aesthetic concerns and political attitudes in Spanish Romantic writing. There was sharp disagreement about the precise definitions and meanings of those key terms and the lack of consensus made it possible for the most liberal of Spain's Romantics to doubt the reality of change on either the political or the cultural front. However, no such doubts could exist with regard to the idea linking literature with politics that Larra identified as fundamental to the transformatory project of his generation, namely, the idea that the individual subject is the basic social and experiential reality. The assumptions of bourgeois individualism had already taken sufficient hold in Spain to make writers and readers receptive to Romanticism's emphasis on the subjective. It was the lasting achievement of Spanish Romanticism, in turn, to elaborate a language of subjectivity, a discourse of passion and imagination, as Larra would have said, that figured and authenticated the new truth in terms of personal experience.

To trace the shift in mentality that accompanied the Romantic period in Spain, we must go back for a moment to the view of inner experience traditionally maintained and enforced by the Church, which regarded depictions of psychic life to be significant only insofar as they demonstrated moral and metaphysical absolutes. An early Spanish translation of *The Sorrows of Young Werther*, for example, was given the title *Moral Letters on the Passions*. But an 1802 censor, describing his expectations as a reader – which the novel failed to meet – shows even more dramatically how little the traditional mentality was prepared to understand Goethe's innovations in representing subjectivity:

I thought its aim . . . would be to teach men about those movements of the soul that we call passions, showing their origin, their nature, their number and effects, their use, and measures for containing them and subjecting them to the higher faculties and the law, . . . so that men could go from understanding their passions to understanding themselves, and then to understanding God.[19]

To a world view that regarded the representation of the inner self as valid only insofar as it classified the movements of the psyche according to scholastic categories and subjected them to the law of reason and divine order, the Romantic enterprise of expressing the self as autonomous, unique, and potentially transcendent made little sense.

By 1828, when Durán published his treatise on drama, however, it was evident that the traditional mentality had lost ground: conservative though he was, Durán drew on the more modern premises of individualism to defend Spain's literary traditions (which he calls 'Romantic') against the neo-classical critics:

[I]n classical literature man is seen through his external acts alone, and his virtues and vices are considered in the abstract, with no reference to the subject to whom they apply ... The object of the Romantic poets ... is instead to trace the history of the inner man considered as an individual.

(p. 70)

Indeed, the individuality and the interiority of the subject became the measure of verisimilitude in Durán's argument against the classical unities. In this regard he approaches the 'new truth' later identified by Larra. Durán's text is marked as transitional, however, by the imposition of a theological framework upon his argument: in the end he justifies the modern depiction of the inner man by reference to divine truth: 'Let us repeat, in conclusion, that the ideal and sublime beauty of [Romantic drama] is nourished and sustained by ... the submission of human understanding to divine faith' (p. 86). Thus, the continuing force of an older world view makes itself felt in Durán's treatise and in the conservative line of Spanish Romanticism that followed from it, a line that was, as we have seen, medievalizing, strongly nationalistic and resistant to progressive social positions. Nevertheless, even at this least liberal pole of the intellectual elite, individualism and new concern with the interiority of the subject were firmly rooted, providing the basis on which the Romantic cult of the self could develop.

From 1835 on, the idea that subjective reality is the stuff of artistic expression became a commonplace of Spanish literary criticism. During these same years Romantic literary production created concrete models of what emotions were, how they evolved and interacted, how memory, desire, hope, and imagination determined inner reality. This elaboration took place in three main forms: the configuration of the Romantic hero as developed by Rivas, García Gutiérrez, Hartzenbusch, and others; the representation of the lyrical self in the poetry of Espronceda and his imitators; and the subjective narrative *persona* of some of Larra's articles.

The Romantic paradigms of subjectivity that emerged in Spain were to some extent derived from the English and French models for figuring inner life that had already been widely disseminated by the time Romanticism took hold in Spain. Estrangement from the social environment, grandiose Promethean aspiration to break the constraints on human desire, and anguished consciousness of the world's incompatibility with the figures of imagination and desire – all these characterize the Spanish version of the Romantic self. However, certain features reveal a peculiarly Spanish difference: Spanish Romantic literature does not exhibit the triumphantly transcendent self that appears in the image of the poet represented by Wordsworth, Byron, or Hugo. The balance of forces that slowed the bourgeois revolution in Spain had not permitted the individual subject to become enshrined as the unquestioned centre of public and private life; consequently, Spanish writers created images of a self that instead of imposing its values on the world through poetic language, reflected the power of the social context.

The autonomy of the subject was emphasized in Spain as in the rest of Europe by the alienation of the Romantic self, which perceives the surrounding social world as degraded or hostile. For example, the misfortune that pursues Don Alvaro, Rivas's influential version of the Romantic hero, is the dramatization of his alienation. Don Alvaro experienced birth as entry into a hostile and oppressive environment, according to an important monologue, and his death – a suicidal leap over a precipice as he shouts 'I am the exterminating Demon . . . Death and destruction to all!' (V, xi) – acknowledges the collapse of his identity into the negativity that has characterized his relation with the world. Alienation was also a basic characteristic of Larra's representation of subjective experience in the *persona* of Fígaro, the pseudonym and mask that he adopted in his later articles. Characterized as the jokster who makes the world laugh while he inwardly weeps, Fígaro is a figure of alienation that begins as an instrument of satire but becomes the vehicle of self-expression in Larra's final articles. In this version, too, the self has little positive content: Fígaro's subjectivity is produced as a reaction to the corruption and degradation of the social world. Two great essays, 'All Soul's Day, 1836' and 'Christmas Eve, 1836', treat the pain, rage and fevered fantasy that characterize Fígaro's inner landscape as a reflection of the disorder of Spanish society. The only positive value the self brings to its confrontation with the outer world is a despairing lucidity about its own impotence. Larra's suicide within weeks of the publication of these essays dramatized his despair, making his life and death Spain's most widely recognized image of Romantic alienation.

Espronceda represented the self in a similar vein, although he gave the lyrical 'I' constructed in his poetry a positive content, conceiving subjectivity as an ideal potential projected through illusion, hope, and imagination upon the materiality of the world. The material world, usually represented as a woman, is inevitably inadequate as an object of the mind's desire, however, and Espronceda's poetry presents psychic experience as an ever repeated process of desire and disappointment. The positive values of the questing human spirit are never utterly defeated, but never finally triumphant in Espronceda's scheme of the universe. Thus Espronceda's metaphysics of the self is subject to the same uncertain balance of forces as the cultural and political project of the Spanish liberals. Not even the creative powers of the poet, which for Romantic poets of other nations could transcend the gap between subject and object, can construct a coherent vision that subordinates the world to the figures of desire in Espronceda's work. As both *El diablo mundo*'s formal features and its meta-commentary on the poetic process make clear, the best the poet can aspire to do is to duplicate the chaotic, contradictory, and unstable nature of human experience.

Spanish Romanticism gave a unique twist to the elaboration of the self through its women poets who, faced with strongly gendered Romantic paradigms of poetic subjectivity, found it necessary to feminize the subject of desire. In *Sab*, Gómez de Avellaneda puts women (and a mulatto 'feminized' by his social subjugation) in the position of the Esproncedan lyrical subject, showing women's social destiny to be the source of Romantic despair and their subjectivity to be the repository of compassion and love, values ignored or denied by a materialistic world. The female 'I' of Avellaneda's lyrical poetry revises the paradigm epitomized in Espronceda: desire, instead of being the expression, the affirmation of the self and its values, becomes a threat to the autonomy of the subject, reflecting the culture's anxiety about female desire. By fragmenting the lyrical subject, this turning of desire against itself in Avellaneda's poetry anticipates a later age's explosion of the Romantic myth of the coherent, sovereign self. Carolina Coronado revises the predominant version of poetic subjectivity by deemphasizing the distinctions between self and other, attenuating the boundaries between the lyrical 'I' and surrounding nature and thus inverting the general Romantic identification of nature with the feminine 'other'. The social alienation of the female subject becomes a dominant theme, however, when Coronado expresses her explicitly feminist critique of society. The abiding importance of these two Spanish poets is that as unique examples of women poets who became part of the Romantic canon, they illuminate for all of Europe the impact of gender on the Romantic representation of subjectivity.

THE ACHIEVEMENT OF SPANISH ROMANTICISM

The new society whose truth it was the mission of a new kind of literature to represent was not constituted in Spain in 1836, as Larra himself knew only too well, for only a few months after he wrote the optimistic 'Literatura' he complained about 'the inextricable labyrinth in which this paltry revolution is caught, destined it seems never to take a free and unencumbered step, never to give a clear, definitive name to its inept operations'.[20] The process through which bourgeois society was constituted in Spain lasted throughout the nineteenth century; it was only in its erratic and shaky beginnings during the decades of the Romantic movement. The forces that struggled during those years to carry out a liberal revolution were unable to achieve a 'clear, definitive' victory; the class that might have led such a revolution 'did not have enough numerical density or wealth nor a sufficiently clear, solid ideology to triumph'.[21] Thus Spain reached 1850 without the consolidation of an economically progressive commercial and industrial bourgeoisie, or more than a superficial restructuring of relations of production in the predominant agricultural sector. The changes in the structure of political authority were noticeable but also limited: the state was becoming more centralized; the right to political representation for men of the upper classes was established in theory, but in practice the electoral process was manipulated by the great landowning aristocracy through a system of political bosses backed up by military chiefs.

On the cultural plane, where the ideological battles were being fought, the limitations of the revolution were also evident, as we have seen. Romanticism, which in other nations had produced a radically new poetic language, became for the most part in Spain a repertory of imported themes and forms through which progressive and conservative writers attempted to control the meaning of ideas like 'nation' and 'freedom'. In only a few exceptional cases did the works of Spanish Romantic writers reflect a radical rethinking of the status of the subject and its relation to the world, a rethinking necessary to the coming into being of a new social formation. Despite its relative weakness, nevertheless, the Romantic movement, like the liberal movement of its time, introduced lasting changes in Spanish culture. Among other things, it designated and explored new objects of representation – namely individual psychological reality as presented in drama and poetry, and concrete contemporary social reality, as portrayed in *costumbrismo* – that within decades became the primary material of the realist novel, the genre in which bourgeois mentality achieved its most powerful literary expression. Galdós and his generation at last provided the new artistic truth for a new society that Larra had called for 50 years too early.

It is a paradox representative of Spain's historical peculiarities that its most profound and internationally influential exponent of Romanticism's underlying values was not a Romantic poet, but a painter who died before the Romantic movement took form in Spain – Francisco Goya (1746–1828). Though he entered the nineteenth century as a middle-aged man, Goya's artistic production after 1795 heralded the major vanguard movements in art from Romanticism to Surrealism. Romantic painters and critics praised his interest in the popular and his emphasis on emotion rather than aesthetic harmony; the Impressionists found precedents for their own work in Goya's rendering of light and movement; Surrealists considered him a pioneer in exploring the dark caverns of the psyche.[22] Thus in the broadest sense, Goya's art contributed to the coming-into-being of a new age in European culture, registering in a unique way the shift in values that Romanticism also registered. Above all through his concern with the experience of the common man and his cultivation of the artist's subjective vision, Goya participated in a dialectic that emerged with Romanticism. Even though Goya's modernity, the capacity of his work to have meaning for successive generations in the nineteenth and twentieth centuries, may appear to be anomalous in relation to Spanish Romanticism proper, it is not extraneous to his positioning in Spanish culture and history. Goya's most profoundly innovative work was done during a period of cataclismic events in Spanish history, as the violent disparities of his world roused his genius to new creative effort. Goya's vision, so compelling for the new age, was perhaps only possible in Spain, where an intellectual vanguard in tune with the rest of Europe could imagine and desire a revolutionary transformation that in the face of entrenched feudal and oligarchic resistance it could not carry out.

NOTES

1 *Juicio crítico de los poetas españoles contemporáneos* (Paris, 1854), p. 186. Translations of this and subsequent citations of Spanish texts are my own.
2 'Romanticismo y revolutión', unpublished essay (1985).
3 *Romanticism in Perspective* (London, 1969), p. 58.
4 In 'From Protestantism to Romanticism', David Morse summarizes the points of continuity between the two: '[T]he assertion of Protestant values in literature produces all the main components of Romantic aesthetics: the expression of a personal vision; the concern with subjectivity; the belief in a deep self; art as an inward rather than external mirroring; the rejection of rules as a restriction on the freedom of the autonomous self; the belief, as expressed in the Preface to the *Lyrical Ballads* that literature should be more closely related to ordinary life; the concern with spontaneity; and the mistrust of false identity' (*Perspectives on Romanticism* (London, 1981), p. 156.
5 For a lucid account of these processes, see Josep Fontana, *La quiebra de la monarquía absoluta, 1814–1820* (Barcelona, 1971), and 'Formación del mercado nacional y toma de conciencia de la burguesía', in *Cambio económico y actitudes políticas* (Barcelona, 1975), pp. 13–53.

6 'Romanticism in Spain and Spanish Romanticism: a critical survey', *Bulletin of Spanish Studies*, 16 (1939), 19.
7 'Les lignes de force des deux tendances de la littérature espagnole apparaissent donc nettement en 1836. L'une est celle du *romanticismo* ou "national-romantisme" tourné vers la résurrection du passé . . . L'autre est celle du romantisme social . . . représenté par Espronceda et Larra, qui se penchent sur la réalité qui les entoure pour en expliquer et au besoin dénoncer certains aspects dans une perspective progressiste et ouverte' ('The lines of force of the two tendencies of Spanish literature appear clearly in 1836. One is the tendency of *romanticismo* or "national-romanticism", focused on the resurrection of the past . . . The other is that of the social romanticism . . . represented by Espronceda and Larra, who incline toward the reality that surrounds them in order to explain it, and, if necessary, to denounce certain features from a progressive and open perspective.') (Robert Marrast, *José de Espronceda et son temps* (Paris, 1974), p. 505).
8 Anne V. Burdick, 'The Madrid Writer in Spanish Society, 1833–1843' (diss., University of California, San Diego, 1983), Appendix B, pp. 17–18, 25.
9 *Historia del movimiento romántico español* (Madrid, 1954).
10 *Obras de Mariano José de Larra (Fígaro)*, ed. Carlos Seco Serrano (Madrid, 1960), vol. 2, p. 133.
11 'Discurso sobre el influjo que ha tenido la crítica moderna . . . ', in *El romanticismo español – Documentos*, ed. Ricardo Navas-Ruiz (Salamanca, 1971), p. 95.
12 'El romanticismo en la historia', *Hispania*, 10 (1950), 754.
13 *Obras de don Ramón de Mesonero Romanos*, ed. Carlos Seco Serrano (Madrid, 1967), vol. 1, pp. 38–9.
14 From the Prologue to the first edition of *Panorama Matritense* in book form (Madrid, 1835). Cited by E. Correa Calderón in *Costumbristas españoles* (Madrid, 1964), p. xxxii.
15 *La Revista Española*, 2 (10 Nov. 1832). Cited by José Escobar, *Los orígenes de la obra de Larra*, 2nd edn (Madrid, 1973), p. 269.
16 Analysing an article on Madrid's fledgling pleasure gardens, Edward Baker observes: 'What "Public Gardens" announces forms part of the historical project of the "middle class": transforming the ancien régime's forms of leisure onto bourgeois leisure . . . Larra is perfectly aware that the creation of bourgeois leisure is extremely problematical because it depends on the formation of a specifically bourgeois sociability, on forms of behavior scarcely tried in Spain.' 'Larra, los jardines públicos y la sociabilidad burguesa', *Revista de Occidente*, 12 (1982), 51–2.
17 For an analysis of how this contradiction informs the text of Espronceda's poetry, see Thomas E. Lewis, 'Contradictory explanatory systems in Espronceda's poetry: the social genesis and structure of *El diablo mundo*', *Ideologies and Literature*, 17 (1983), 11–45.
18 *Poesías de la señorita doña Carolina Coronado* (Madrid, 1852), p. 72.
19 Anonymous censor's report reproduced in Angel González Palencia, *Estudio histórico sobre la censura gubernativa en España, 1800–1833* (Madrid, 1935), vol. 2, p. 291.
20 'The Mendizábal Ministry', *Obras*, vol. 2, p. 215.
21 Jaime Vicens Vives, *Historia económica de España* (Barcelona, 1959), p. 546.
22 See Nigel Glendinning, *Goya and His Critics* (New Haven, 1977).

BIBLIOGRAPHY

Baker, Edward, 'Larra, los jardines públicos y la sociabilidad burguesa', *Revista de Occidente*, 12 (1982), 43–57.

Burdick, Anne V. 'The Madrid Writer in Spanish Society, 1833–1843' (diss., University of California, San Diego, 1983).

Coronado, Carolina. *Poesías de la señorita doña Carolina Coronado* (Madrid, 1852).

Correa Calderón, E. *Costumbristas españoles* (Madrid, 1964).

Durán, Agustín. 'Discurso sobre el influjo que ha tenido la crítica moderna en la decadencia del teatro antiguo español', in *El romanticismo español – Documentos*, ed. Ricardo Navas-Ruiz (Salamanca, 1971), pp. 54–100.

Escobar, José. *Los orígenes de la obra de Larra*, 2nd edn (Madrid, 1973).
   'Romanticismo y revolución', unpublished essay (1985).

Fontana Lázaro, Josep. 'Formación del mercado nacional y toma de conciencia de la burguesía', in *Cambio económico y actitudes políticas* (Barcelona, 1975), pp. 13–53.

   La quiebra de la monarquía absoluta, 1814–1820 (Barcelona, 1971).

Furst, Lillian. *Romanticism in Perspective* (London, 1969).

Glendinning, Nigel. *Goya and His Critics* (New Haven, 1977).

González Palencia, Angel. *Estudio histórico sobre la censura gubernativa en España. 1800–1833* (Madrid, 1935).

Larra, Mariano José de. *Obras de Mariano José de Larra (Fígaro)*, ed. Carlos Seco Serrano (Madrid, 1960), vol. 2.

Lewis, Thomas E. 'Contradictory explanatory systems in Espronceda's poetry: the social genesis and structure of *El diablo mundo*', *Ideologies and Literature*, 17 (1983), 11–45.

Marrast, Robert. *José de Espronceda et son temps: Littérature, société, politique au temps du romantisme* (Paris, 1974).

Mesonero Romanos, Ramón. *Obras de don Ramón de Mesonero Romanos*, ed. Carlos Seco Serrano (Madrid, 1967), vol. 1.

Morse, David. *Perspectives on Romanticism* (London, 1981).

Peers, E. Alison. *Historia del movimiento romántico español* (Madrid, 1954).

Tarr, F. Courtney. 'Romanticism in Spain and Spanish Romanticism: a critical survey', *Bulletin of Spanish Studies*, 16 (1939), 3–37.

Vicens Vives, Jaime. *Historia económica de España* (Barcelona, 1959).
   'El romanticismo en la historia', *Hispania*, 10 (1950), 745–65.

Villergas, Juan Martínez. *Juico crítico de los poetas españoles contemporáneos* (Paris, 1854).

12

Russian Romanticism

JOHN MERSEREAU, JR, and DAVID LAPEZA

Romanticism in Russia is a topic which seems to defy a confident approach or coherent treatment. We can say that it was essentially an artistic movement, and that its most valuable manifestation was in literature, especially in the 1820s and 1830s. The social and political life of the nation was not moved by Romanticism, and only a minuscule portion of the population had any awareness of the term. Romanticism in Russia was the concern of a mere handful of writers, composers, artists, and patrons of the arts.

At the beginning of the nineteenth century, Russia was a monolithic autocracy whose citizens were assigned places in a hierarchical social structure by birth, whether as serf or sovereign. In between were the 'estates' of the landed gentry, the merchants, the clergy, and the free artisans. There was virtually no movement from one class to another. Both the military and the civil service were organized according to fourteen ranks. Males of gentry status were expected to serve God, Tsar, and Country in some appropriate capacity until retirement. All wore the ubiquitous government uniforms which dominated Russian official and even social life.

All classes were highly conservative, overtly religious, poorly educated, unworldly, untravelled, and apparently content. There were only occasional peasant rebellions in the provinces, which were brutally repressed, as were civil disorders in the cities, which often accompanied the frequent summer plagues of cholera or typhus.

Both education and access to information were extremely limited by a centralized and paternalistic government. Most serfs could not read, and many masters considered literacy pernicious for the 'souls' who served them or worked their land. Even attempts to educate the usually illiterate soldiers were enough to arouse suspicion of conspiracy. The clergy read the publications of their calling, merchants read the Bible and hagiographical works, and the gentry, which read for pleasure, favoured works in French. Appreciation of Russian as a literary language was limited to a very few, at least until the rise of national feelings following the Russian triumphs of the Napoleonic Wars. This was not a market eager for a domestic literary product.

Government policy posed a different sort of problem for the writer or artist. Writers, editors, and theatre directors were obliged to devote a disproportionate amount of time and ingenuity to placating or out-smarting the official censors. After 1828, power was vested in a Directorate of the Censorship, consisting of the presidents of the Academies of Sciences and Arts, the deputy ministers of Education, and representatives of the Ministries of Foreign and Internal Affairs and the Holy Synod. Some censors were sympathetic, even liberal, but others were capricious and paranoid. A poem or article might offend the Tsar or a high official, with the result that the writer, his editor and publisher, and the censor who passed the offending work might be reprimanded, jailed, or even exiled. Musicians and dancers were in an even more precarious position. Musical education meant training abroad; concerts were controlled by the Imperial Theatre Directorate; and musicians were not recognized in the Table of Ranks. Dancers' careers were limited to the Imperial Ballet School, heavily funded from the privy purse, but artistically restrictive, conservative, and favouring foreign stars and foreign music.

Artists necessarily catered to the tastes of a small conservative social élite and a minuscule merchant class still uncomfortable with secular art and western styles. Architects were required to conform to Russian notions of neo-classical propriety, both in the capital, where any building was 'public', and in the provinces, where the prestige of St Petersburg and western pretensions dictated fashion.

In short, the Russian artistic, social, and political environment in the first half of the nineteenth century was so radically different from that in England, Germany, or France, that we must expect a different, slower, or irregular chronology in the development of Russian Romantic arts and ideas. We may also expect completely novel developments, where Russia's late-blooming Romanticism carries its ideas and tastes into the realist period.

LITERATURE

Romanticism in Russian literature has posed problems since it was first discussed in the early 1820s. Prince Peter Vyazemsky, an early proponent of the movement, facetiously compared it with the elusive house spirit of Russian folklore, *domovoy*, noting that everyone was aware of its existence but no one had actually seen it. Almost a century and a half later, there was a vigorous discussion within Soviet criticism concerning the nature and extent of Romanticism, a discussion not greatly illuminated by some critics' efforts to provide political approbation to certain manifestations of the movement: 'progressive' or 'Decembrist revolutionary Romanticism' versus 'passive' or 'aesthetic Romanticism'. These efforts, which were intended to produce a politically acceptable genealogy for Socialist Realism, failed to achieve any conclusive definition, but at least finally legitimized use of the term *Romanticism* in Soviet criticism.

Despite the somewhat ill-defined features of Russian literary Romanticism, we can at least generalize about some of its aspects. Departing from René Wellek's concept of literary periodization, we can see Romanticism evolving from Sentimentalism around 1815, providing Russia's 'Golden Age' of poetry in the 1820s, and laying the foundation in the 1830s for the prose traditions from which Russian Realism evolved in the course of the next two decades. Romanticism did not develop in a vacuum. The second half of the eighteenth century had seen a vigorous effort to develop a Russian neo-classical literature, primarily poetic, which would give Russian letters parity with its European counterparts. Some success had been achieved, particularly by the poet Gavrilo Derzhavin (1743–1816), who celebrated the majesty of Nature and Man in grandiloquent odes to a waterfall and to his sovereign, Catherine the Great. Nonetheless, the literary language was suffering from its dual dependence upon vernacular Russian and Church Slavonic, a variant of medieval South Slavonic dialects, originally used for religious writings. At the end of the century Ivan Karamzin (1766–1826), an adherent of European Sentimentalism, 'reformed' the literary language by attempting to eliminate archaic Church Slavonic elements, borrowing both words and phrases from French, and simplifying literary syntax. His so-called 'salon style' was presumed to please the tender ears of gentry ladies (who, if they read at all, read in French). He enjoyed considerable success with 'Poor Liza' (1792), the tale of a simple peasant girl deceived by a thoughtless officer, and *Letters of a Russian Traveller* (1792), a sentimental account of his journey through Europe.

Karamzin found a number of disciples, as well as antagonists, and for the first two decades of the nineteenth century a battle raged between his followers and the literary and linguistic conservatives, led by Admiral Alexander Shishkov (1753–1841). Karamzin's talented adherents included the poets Vasily Zhukovsky (1783–1852) and Konstantin Batyushkov (1787–1855). An original poet of great gifts, Zhukovsky was also highly successful as a translator of English and German poets, among others, Gray, Thomson, Byron, Scott, Schiller, Goethe, and Bürger. He produced in quantity the melancholy ballads and elegies which typified one line of poetry linking Sentimentalism and Romanticism. Batyushkov favoured Latin and Italian poets, and he was a master of Anacreontic verse celebrating friendship and the pleasures of good living.

Some contemporary poets were not enthusiastic about Karamzin's linguistic innovations. They saw his reforms as restrictive, and correctly so, since he tried to eliminate all Church Slavonic forms not shared with Russian and discarded what he considered substandard or coarse expressions and words. Admiral Shishkov's followers, united in Colloquy of Lovers of the Russian Word, mocked the often ludicrous periphrasis of the Sentimentalists and their unnecessary floridity, which they saw as slavish imitation of western literary conceits.

With the importation of European literary models, Russians became increasingly aware of western political ideologies. With the Russians' defeat of Napoleon, their liberation of Europe and occupation of Paris in 1814, large numbers of young officers became better acquainted with western culture, including concepts of republicanism. Since political discussion was all but proscribed in Russia, concerned citizens met in secret societies to discuss even the most innocuous reforms. Both Freemasonry and European revolutions in Spain, Italy, and Greece were important examples for the radical-minded officers who formed various political brotherhoods, beginning with the Union of Salvation in 1816. The most important of these was The Northern Society, centred in St Petersburg. It favoured establishment of a constitutional monarchy with institutions closely modelled on those of the United States. The Southern Society, which involved officers stationed in Bessarabia and the Ukraine, proposed regicide, democracy, and radical social and economic reforms.

Two major figures of the conspiracy in the capital were Kondraty Ryleev (1795–1826), an official in the Russian-American Company, and Alexander Bestuzhev (1797–1837), an officer in the Dragoons whose several military brothers were also involved. Ryleev, who composed what he termed *dumy* (historical poems) celebrating heroes of the Russian past, and Bestuzhev, an author and poet already known by his (later famous) pseudonym Marlinsky, together edited the very successful literary annual *The Pole Star* (1823–5), whose contents were meant to inspire civic responsibility among the generally indifferent populace. Typical of this effort was Bestuzhev's historical romance *Roman and Olga* which appeared in *The Pole Star* for 1823. The tale is set in Novgorod at the end of the fourteenth century when the republic (the city's princes served at the will of its citizens) faced annexation by Muscovy. The hero, Roman, sacrifices hopes of personal happiness with Olga in order to serve his people; and in the end his patriotism is rewarded with military and matrimonial victory.

Efforts at educating the public to civic responsibility were also undertaken by literary circles and societies, which became particularly numerous in the early 1820s. Among the most important was The Free Society of Lovers of Russian Letters, to which a large number of Petersburg *literati* belonged. The society published an edifying and instructive monthly, *The Emulator of Enlightenment and Charity*. In 1823, in addition to translations of western romances, *The Emulator* carried an important essay in three parts by Orest Somov (1793–1833) entitled 'On Romantic Poetry'. The first two parts of the essay summarized (with credit) Madame de Staël's *De l'Allemagne*; but the final section challenged Russian authors to abandon imitation and create their own distinctive Romanticism, based on Russia's heroic past, its diverse peoples, its native landscapes, and its own rich and sonorous language.

Another important literary society, The Lovers of Wisdom (Liubomudry), promoted German idealistic philosophy in its almanac, *Mnemosyne*. The principal members were the poet and critic Wilhelm Kuechelbecker (1797–1846) and the philosopher and author Prince V. F. Odoevsky (1803–69). Kuechelbecker mocked the endless elegies produced by Zhukovsky's imitators and called for a restoration of the ode and the rehabilitation of Church Slavonic. Odoevsky's reputation was established by a series of *Kuenstlernovellen* (stories about artists) and a Hoffmann-esque cycle of tales entitled *Russian Nights* (1844).

Political liberalism, the new styles of Zhukovsky and Batyushkov, and modern European poets all influenced the young Alexander Pushkin (1799–1837), who was destined to acquire a prestige in Russian literature matching that of Shakespeare in English literature. While still a student in the government Lyceum at Tsarskoe Selo, he composed political epigrams and poems and, in the company of his uncle, Vasily Pushkin, attended some meetings of Arzamas (1815–18), a convivial literary society whose level of seriousness may be judged by its choice of name – a town famous for roast goose. The group included Zhukovsky and Batyushkov, and its principal activity was lampooning the stilted compositions of Shishkov's Colloquy. Following graduation from the Lyceum in 1817, Pushkin was nominally employed in a Petersburg government bureau, which did not interfere with his writing or his social life. In 1820 he published his mock-heroic narrative poem, *Ruslan and Liudmila*, which marked the final victory of the Karamzin–Zhukovsky camp over the literary conservatives. Discovery of Pushkin's political verses resulted in his exile, first to Odessa and later Bessarabia. Later he was put under house arrest in Mikhailovskoe, a family estate near Pskov, where he remained until 1826.

By then, Pushkin had published his southern cycle, three narrative poems in the manner of Byron involving betrayed love, murder, suicide, and exotic settings. Byron was also a significant inspiration for *Eugene*

Onegin (begun 1823, completed 1831), a 'novel in verse' begun while Pushkin was in Kishinev. The verses of the first cantos (called chapters) are properly compared with the effervescence of champagne. It is the tale of a blasé poseur, Onegin, who fails to value the love of a simple but morally superior young gentry girl, Tatiana. Their tale moves from provincial Russia to the brilliant halls of Peterburg's *haut monde*. Pushkin weaves into his narrative fragments of his autobiography, his *ars poetica*, parodies, lampoons, and ironies of all sorts. The work was finished only in 1831, its initial flippancy giving way to a trenchant satirical tone. Although incorrectly lauded as 'an encyclopaedia of Russian life', *Eugene Onegin* does present a broad canvas of contemporary culture, and it is particularly effective in the representation of its hero and heroine. The contrast between the so-called 'superfluous man' and the morally strong woman set a pattern for the Russian novel which was widely copied during the later period of psychological Realism.

The Romantic ideals of liberty, equality, and fraternity which had been nurtured in secret societies, literary circles, and liberal journals and almanacs, achieved momentary expression on 14 December 1825, when a battalion of the Moscow Regiment and some of the Grenadier and Marine Guards occupied Senate Square in St Petersburg in defiance of the newly proclaimed Tsar, Nicholas I (1796–1855). Reluctant to take decisive action, the rebellion's leaders awaited a response from the sovereign, which came in the twilight of the freezing afternoon when Nicholas' artillery cleared the square with cannister shot. Literature, as well as freedom, was a victim. Among those arrested were Kondraty Ryleev, one of five conspirators later hanged, Alexander Bestuzhev and his brothers, Wilhelm Kuechelbecker, and the poet Alexander Odoevsky (1802–39). Although in exile at Mikhailovskoe, Pushkin came under suspicion, from which he was supposedly exonerated the following year during an audience with the Tsar. Over 100 members of Russia's most prominent families were subsequently exiled, and because of the failure of the insurrection government policies for the next thirty years were even more restrictive than before. But so stringent was the censorship and so timid the citizenry that the catastrophe became a non-event as far as public or press discussion was concerned.

In the second half of the 1820s poetry achieved its apogee with the appearance of the so-called Pushkin Pleiad. The best of this constellation included Yevgeny Baratynsky (1800–40), often ranked next to Pushkin himself. His hedonistic early verse gave way to pessimistic philosophical elegies which gained for him the title 'the poet of thought'. In his narrative poems, unrequited love and violent death are major themes. Baron Anton Delvig (1798–1831) produced a small collection of lyrics celebrating the joys of life, a few masterful idylls, and songs in the folk tradition. He is also important as the editor of the literary almanac *Northern Flowers* (1825–32), the most prestigious of the literary annuals, and as editor–publisher of *The Literary Gazette* (1830–1), the newspaper of the Pushkin–Delvig circle. Nikolay Yazykov (1803–46) found his forte in poems celebrating the conviviality of student life (at the University of Dorpat). He was appreciated by his contemporaries for his hedonistic themes, intoxicating rhythm, and verbal fireworks. The Pleiad can be expanded indefinitely to include a surprising number of poets of talent and accomplishment. Several more must be mentioned, both because of their contributions to Russian letters and because of their eternal images in Russian literary history. Dmitry Venevitinov (1805–27), despite his brief career, was recognized by his fellow *literati* as a poet of enormous potential. His work consists of less than fifty poems, but his final verses, concerning unrequited love and hinting at suicide, strengthened the aura of Romantic fatality which surrounded his untimely death (due to a most un-Romantic case of pneumonia). Ivan Kozlov (1779–1840) is remembered for his accomplishments as a translator. By the age of forty he was blind and paralysed but learned English and German and began translating Scott, Byron, and Moore. A Byronic narrative poem, *The Monk* (1825), produced a large number of imitations. Alexander Polezhaev (1805–38) achieved notoriety in 1825 for *Sashka*, a parody of the first cantos of *Eugene Onegin*. Tsar Nicholas was outraged by the salacious content of the poem and sent Polezhaev to the Caucasus as a common soldier. Finally, one must mention Denis Davydov (1784–1839), the poet–partisan who fought against Napoleon and celebrated his calling in poems lauding the pursuits and pleasures of a young hussar.

Fyodor Tyutchev (1803–73) lies outside the mainstream of Russian Romanticism, although unquestionably a part of it. Serving abroad as a diplomat until middle age, he remained virtually unrecognized even after a collection of his poems (signed 'F.T.') were published by Pushkin in 1836 in *The Contemporary*. At the end of the century he was 'rediscovered' by the Symbolists, and today many rank him second only to Pushkin. If Baratynsky merits the apellation of 'the poet of thought', Tyutchev must be considered 'the poet of metaphysics', for much of his poetry is concerned with the hopeless fate of man, caught between the poles of good and evil, eternally isolated. Associated with The Lovers of Wisdom Society while a student, he studied German idealistic philosophy, the influence of which is evident in his many poems on nature. During his assignment in Munich he met Schelling and was close to Heinrich Heine, whom he translated into Russian. Tyutchev's very personal view of the universe, nature, and man, and his unique prosody, establish his place in Romanticism, despite his archaic diction, which reveals ties with the eighteenth century and Derzhavin.

Pushkin's exile at Mikhailovskoe, which he endured with impatience and anger, had some positive effects on his art. His isolation led to long evenings with his old nurse, Irina Rodionovna, who entertained the poet with peasant lore and tales. At one time it was fashionable to credit her with the inspiration for his fairy tales 'Tsar Saltan', 'The Golden Cockerel' and 'The Dead Princess and the Seven Champions' (1831–2), but literary sources have also been identified. Pushkin's interest in history, coupled with a deep enthusiasm for Shakespeare, whom he called 'our father', led to the composition of what he styled a 'Romantic tragedy', *Boris Godunov* (begun 1825, published 1831), which was coolly received by a public accustomed to the three unities. Shakespeare's influence was further evident in the 'little tragedies', studies of obsessive personalities, composed during the unusually productive autumn of 1830 at his father's estate, Boldino. His interest in history and fascination with Peter the Great combined to produce the narrative poem *Poltava* (1828), celebrating the Russian victory over the Swedes, and *The Negro of Peter the Great* (1827), a fictionalized biography of Pushkin's Abyssinian great-grandfather. His investigation of the role of the exceptional individual in historical events led to *The History of the Pugachev Rebellion* (1833) and *The Captain's Daughter* (1833–5), a historical novel in the manner of Walter Scott but without anthropological trappings. Both explored the personality of Pugachev, the illiterate Cossack usurper whose insurgency seriously threatened Catherine the Great. Peter the Great was again a central figure in Pushkin's *chef d'oeuvre*, *The Bronze Horseman* (1833), a narrative poem devoted to the conflict between the rights of the anonymous individual, the outraged but helpless clerk Eugene, and *la raison d'état*, embodied in the equestrian statue of Peter (the work of Falconet, 1765–1782) which dominated Senate Square in St Petersburg. The Boldino autumn also produced *The Belkin Tales*, five short stories with ingenious ironical treatment of literary clichés and types. 'The Shot' probes the mind of a certain Sylvio, who seeks to assert his superiority by adopting a mysterious Byronic mantle and establishing a reputation as a drinker and duellist. When his dominance is challenged by a natural leader, Sylvio plans a vicious revenge, which, unknown to him, fails. 'The Station Master' parodies Karamzin's sentimental tale of 1792, 'Poor Liza', and 'The Undertaker' plays with the theme of the supernatural. 'Mistress into Maid' and 'The Snowstorm' provide variations on the themes of mistaken identity and star-crossed lovers. In 1834 Pushkin published *The Queen of Spades*, perhaps his most famous prose work. The form is that of a society tale, but it parodies stories of the supernatural popular at the time and, like

'The Shot', analyses the obsessions of a would-be superman, Hermann, who became a prototype for Dostoevsky's Raskolnikov.

Pushkin's increasing interest in prose reflects the general orientation of the public during the 1830s. People were satiated with good poetry, and now they desired some new fare. The popularity of Walter Scott and Balzac, who were available in both French and Russian, led to a desire for Russian works on the order of the Waverley novels or *Scènes de la vie privée*. Among the first to respond to this need was Orest Somov (1793–1833). His efforts were limited to short stories and *povesti* (novellas), but with *The Fool in Christ* (1827) he must be credited with one of the first society tales, a genre which became very popular in the thirties. Somov has only recently been rediscovered, and we now are aware that he contributed considerably to the development of the prose literary language and helped 'democratize' fiction by introducing characters from the lower levels of society, in, for example, *Matchmaking* (1830) and *Monster* (1830). Somov's avid interest in the folklore of his native Ukraine led to many tales based on legends, superstitions, and the heroic exploits of dauntless youths combating ghosts, ferocious animals, or brigands. Among these are 'Kievan Witches', 'The Tale of Bone-Breaker Bear', or 'In the Field, Rank Doesn't Count'.

It would not be easy to choose a Russian Walter Scott from among the numerous practitioners of the historical novel. The first to appear was Mikhail Zagoskin (1789–1852), whose *Yuri Miloslavsky, or The Russians in 1612* was published in 1829. In this work he mixed historical personages with fictional characters in recreating life during the 'Time of Troubles' when the Poles occupied Moscow. Ivan Kalashnikov (1797–1863) is remembered for his novels with Siberian settings, particularly *The Daughter of the Merchant Sholobov* (1831) and *The Kamchatka Girl* (1833). Although the stories themselves lack the fascination of Scott's evocation of the past, they are filled with extensive anthropological and geographical details about Siberia, which for Russians of that period was an extremely exotic setting. Ivan Lazhechnikov (1792–1869), a prolific author of considerable talent, created colourful historical pageants permeated with suspense and horror in imitation of Scott and *l'Ecole frénétique*. *The Ice Palace* (1835) concerns the intrigues of Count Biron, lover of the Empress Anna, to discredit his rival Count Volinskoy. The title refers to a structure built in 1739 at the order of the Empress for the wedding of her court jester to a hideously ugly Kalmyk woman.

The end of the 1820s also witnessed the appearance of the first 'best seller' in Russian prose, a moral-satirical novel in four volumes by Faddey Bulgarin (1789–1859), *Ivan Vyzhigin*, which sold over 6,000 copies. Despite the author's assertions to the contrary, the work is hardly original.

Its form is that of a picaresque novel, and some of its incidents come from an eighteenth-century Polish novel, Bishop Krasicki's *Pan Podstoli*. *Ivan Vyzhigin* is a wide-ranging chronicle of its protagonist's rise from gooseherd to aristocrat, with many interpolated tales depicting the depredations of the gentry. The work was considered uncouth by the Pushkin circle, and this probably accounts for their favourable reaction in 1830 to a competitive work by one of their own, *The Convent Girl*, by Alexy Perovsky-Pogorelsky (1787–1836). This was an amusing novel of manners, obviously influenced by Fielding, which treated its Ukrainian characters with friendly irony. The work was important for techniques in delineation of secondary characters later appropriated by Nikolay Gogol. Perovsky had previously established himself with short stories in the style of (or adapted from) Hoffmann which were published in a collection entitled *The Double, or My Evenings in Little Russia* (1828).

While Pushkin's prose remained largely unappreciated, perhaps because of its laconic quality and subtle ironies, the stories of Alexander Bestuzhev were universally popular. Following his conviction for his part in the Decembrist uprising, Bestuzhev was imprisoned and subsequently sent to the Caucasus as a common soldier, a fate shared by some other conspirators. He was permitted to resume publishing under his pseudonym Marlinsky, and his action-filled adventure tales, stressing personal heroism and self-sacrifice, were appreciated for their suspense, their witty dialogue, and their metaphorical elegance. The term 'Marlinism' was coined to describe his colourful and hyperbolic style. His most famous novel, *Ammalat Bek* (1832), with its exotic Caucasian setting and the daring-do of its Circassian hero, exemplified popular notions of that region, where Russia was waging a war of attrition against the Moslem natives. Bestuzhev-Marlinsky was himself a character bigger than life. Exiled Decembrist, student of Caucasian languages and customs (he affected Circassian garb), brave soldier, and popular author, his legendary aura was further enhanced in 1837 when he disappeared in battle during a Russian landing at Cape Adler on the Black Sea. Notwithstanding Bestuzhev's popularity, the critic Vissarion Belinsky (1811–48) evaluated him even before his death as a second-rate author whose heroes were all the same, be they naval captains or Caucasian mountaineers.

Belinsky was the chief critic of *The Telescope*, a Moscow journal which promoted contemporary literary trends. In 1836 it published Peter Chaadaev's *Philosophical Letter*, an essay which averred that Russia was essentially ahistorical because of its failure to embrace the Universal Church (Catholicism), and that it was culturally inferior to the West. The journal was summarily closed and Chaadaev officially declared insane. The essay fomented intense public and private debate about Russia's role *vis-à-vis* the West. Those opposed to Chaadaev argued that Peter the Great's reforms and contacts with Europe had weakened the social fabric of patriarchal Russia and Orthodoxy. These Slavophiles, whose views were curiously intertwined with western Romantic beliefs of nationhood, included persons of liberal political ideology as well as those who were as obscurantist as their government. As a group they were opposed to the so-called Westernizers, among them Belinsky, who called for further adoption of western ideologies and institutions. Belinsky's literary criticism increasingly became a forum for the expression of his liberal political ideas, and he ultimately recanted his art-for-art's-sake stance in favour of one which regarded literature as a tool of social and political reform. He died prematurely in 1848, having firmly established a school of criticism which demanded that writers concern themselves with social issues or ignore them at their peril.

Prince Vladimir Odoevsky (1804–69) was a co-founder of The Lovers of Wisdom Society and one of the major contributors to its journal *Mnemosyne*. A disciple of German idealistic philosophy, he is traditionally linked to E. T. A. Hoffmann, with whom he shared interests in music, the lives of artists, and the supernatural. Odoevsky created his own style of *Kuenstlernovella* in a series of stories on Beethoven, Bach, and Piranesi, whom he used to express his ideas about the lonely mission of the artist. In 'Beethoven's Last Quartet' (1831), for example, the musician is depicted as a decrepit pauper obsessed with composition of a quartet which only he can hear and understand. In Odoevsky's account the great composer, contrary to biographical fact, dies in abject poverty ignored by everyone. The Hoffmannesque combination of genius and madness is also a feature of the tale concerning the architect Piranesi (1832). The story cycle *Motley Fairy Tales* (1833), presented by an impecunious philosopher Iriney Gomozeyko, contains a number of tales satirizing contemporary social values. 'The Fairy Tale About Why It Is Dangerous for Young Ladies to Walk in a Crowd Along Nevsky Prospect' relates how the evil proprietor of a dress shop turns a naive girl into a fashionable but brainless doll. The author's satirical inclination found somewhat more conventional expression in two society tales, *Princess Mimi* (1834) and *Princess Zizi* (1839), the former presenting the ominous portrait of a spinster who controls society through slander.

In 1844 Odoevsky published a collection of ten tales with the format patterned on Hoffmann's *Die Serapionsbrueder*. After each story four friends, led by the author's *porte parole* Faust, seek to find principles unifying science and art while maintaining credence in the supernatural. The work as a whole tends to advance Odoevsky's Slavophile views regarding the superiority of Russian moral values to those of the West.

Nikolay Gogol (1809–52) is one of the major Russian Romantic writers. Born into a Ukrainian family of petty gentry, he first achieved success with *Evenings on a Farm Near Dikanka* (1831), stories collected by the bee-keeper Rudy Panko. Derived from Ukrainian folk tales and the puppet theatre, they feature malevolent and comic devils, witches, ondines, and raucous rustics in improbable but lively anecdotes. These stories reflect Gogol's Romantic interest in the folklore of his native region, probably stimulated by Orest Somov's earlier tales derived from Ukrainian folklore.

One story in this collection is quite unlike the others and presages the vintage Gogol. 'Ivan Fyodorovich Shponka and His Aunt' has as its central character a junior army officer, Shponka, whose entire life has been lacking in any passion whatsoever: he spends his days setting mouse traps or polishing his buttons. His domineering and masculine aunt persuades him to retire to his estate in order to marry him off to a neighbour's daughter; but the vapid and inarticulate Shponka can't even converse with his intended bride. The story dissolves into a dream sequence in which the terrified Shponka is dragged up a belfry and rung like a bell by the aunt, but we never learn the ending because, as Rudy Panko reports, the rest of the manuscript was used by his illiterate wife in baking pies. The absurdity of this conclusion, which mocks the fragmentariness of many Romantic works, should not veil Gogol's didactic intent, which is often obscured by the hilarious content of his stories. Gogol was convinced that the Devil, in whom he firmly believed, was determined to subvert man from his God-given mission by causing people to lead banal lives devoted to triviality and pettiness. These and other concepts are incorporated in the Russian word, *poshlust*, which Vladimir Nabokov, in his book on Gogol, defines as self-satisfied mediocrity, vegetative existence, bogus emotions.

Mirgorod, a collection of four stories, appeared in 1835. It includes a tale of demonic possession featuring the Viy, a folkloric creature of Gogol's invention with eyelids reaching the ground, and the almost equally fanciful *Taras Bulba*, a pseudo-historical novel apotheosizing Cossack vengeance against the perfidious Poles. *Taras Bulba* incorporates numerous elements found in the novels of Walter Scott, but there is no verifiable historical content: indeed, even the century in which the action takes place is unclear. The extensive lyrical content and the hyperbolic nature of the characters and action give this work the quality of a pageant. 'Old World Landowners' and 'The Tale of How Ivan Ivanovich Quarrelled with Ivan Nikiforovich' are trenchant satires on lives devoted to *Poshlust* – the lovey-dovey landowners delighting in a vegetative existence devoted to gourmandizing, and the two 'worthy' Ivans embroiled in a ceaseless, petty, and destructive litigation.

The year 1835 also saw the appearance of the first of Gogol's so-called Petersburg tales, a cycle which ultimately included 'Nevsky Prospect', 'The Portrait', 'Notes of a Madman', 'The Nose', and 'The Overcoat'. The first two are technically *Kuenstlernovellen*. In 'Nevsky Prospect' the Devil lights the street lamps along Petersburg's famous boulevard in order to deceive mortals, among them the artist Piskaryov, who commits suicide when he discovers that his ideal of womanhood is in fact a vulgar prostitute. His tragic fate is parodically contrasted to that of the officer Pigaryov, who is thoroughly thrashed by two artisans named Hoffmann and Schiller, but sensibly determines to ignore their moral insult and proceed to the pleasures of a banal *soirée*. In 'The Portrait' the struggling artist Chertkov becomes the victim of a demonic portrait, his artistic integrity eroded by the temptation of easy success. 'The Nose' satirizes pretensions to rank and wealth, also aspects of *poshlust*, as the self-styled Major Kovalyov seeks a bride with a suitable dowry. His quest is frustrated by his nose, which departs his face for a career of its own and even dares to snub the person of its origin. 'Notes of a Madman', also on the theme of pretension, suggests comparison with Hoffmann, in particular as it includes a correspondence between canines; but, unlike Hoffmann, Gogol never concludes that there is happiness in madness. Here, his protagonist, a miserable petty clerk, goes mad when his hopes to marry his department head's daughter are thwarted; but his compensating delusion that he is the King of Spain ends with quotidien torture by asylum orderlies.

Gogol's comedy *The Government Inspector* (1836) is regarded as one of the best in the Russian repertoire and is regularly performed in the Soviet Union and abroad. The plot hinges upon a vacuous junior clerk, Khlestakov, being mistaken for a government inspector by the officials of a provincial town. With enthusiastic insouciance he accepts their hospitality and bribes and only avoids his comeuppance when his more intelligent servant insists they take French leave. The officials discover their mistake and with righteous indignation blame one another. In the final scene they are literally paralysed with fear when they learn that a real inspector general has arrived. As is typical of Gogol's world, the provincial town is populated with caricatures of humanity who are paragons of mendaciousness, cupidity, stupidity, pretension, and vulgarity. The comedy was allowed to be staged, apparently because the Tsar saw it as a salubrious exposé of bribery. Others interpreted it as an attack upon the social-political structure, while the author apparently intended it as a morality play with the finale as a kind of Last Judgement.

'The Overcoat' (1842) has beguiled generations of readers who persist in seeing it as a philanthropic treatment of a poor clerk, Akaky

Akakievich, who wishes no more than to be a brother to mankind and to enjoy the fulfilment of his modest desire for a new overcoat, only to become the butt of his fellow clerks' teasing, the victim of a coat-snatcher, and the recipient of 'a certain important personage's' tongue-lashing. There can be no sentimental interpretation of this tale if one considers the actual details of Akaky's life and the level of his aspirations. Yet, Gogol's focus upon the downtrodden and his depiction of the seamier aspects or urban life gave rise to the so-called Natural School, which flourished in the 1840s.

Dead Souls (1842) is the last important work of this unique author, whom the critic Belinsky insisted was a Realist devoted to unmasking the evils of Tsarist Russia. Picaresque in form, the novel chronicles the adventures of Pavel Chichikov, a petty schemer, who travels among the provincial gentry seeking to acquire title to deceased serfs, 'dead souls', whom he may mortgage to purchase property and thereby join the landed gentry. The method of stylization initiated in 'Ivan Shponka' is carried to its limits here. Each landowner Chichikov visits typifies one or more mortal sins: avarice, pride, sloth, gluttony, superstition. Ultimately, the hero's scheme is discovered, and following speculations that he is either Napoleon *incognito* or the intended kidnapper of the governor's daughter, he flees town. As in *The Government Inspector*, there is no punishment for the mountebank; Chichikov speeds away, driven by his drunken coachman and accompanied by his smelly servant, while the narrator indulges in an extended hyperbolic metaphor identifying Chichikov's carriage with Russia hastening toward a great destiny to the awe of other nations. One is perplexed as to the meaning of this conclusion: is this irony, or an expression of Gogol's prophetic Slavophilism? Or is it merely grandiloquent loquacity for its own sake, and as such a typical stylistic feature of this unusual author?

Mikhail Lermontov (1814–41) can claim a position as Pushkin's poetic heir and as the author of the first fully developed novel of psychological realism. A quintessentially Romantic figure, his short but brilliant life, characterized by unhappy love affairs, uncompromising opposition to the autocracy, heroism in combat against Caucasian mountaineers, and extraordinary artistic talent, ended with his death in a duel.

Traditional Lermontov scholarship tends to discount almost all of his work before 1837. The large corpus of early lyrics, infused with feelings of alienation, betrayal, and love of nature, suggests mere imitation of Byron. However, Lermontov expressed these emotions long before he became acquainted with Byron in the original, while still a student at the University of Moscow. His early efforts also include plays influenced by Lessing and

Schiller, narrative poems with Caucasian settings deriving from Pushkin and Byron, and an unfinished historical novel featuring a demonic avenger in the style of *l'Ecole frénétique*.

Lermontov left the University of Moscow in 1832 and entered the School of Cavalry Cadets and Ensigns of the Guard in Petersburg. He was commissioned in 1834 and joined the Life Guard Hussars, stationed in nearby Tsarskoe Selo. Lermontov achieved overnight notoriety with his elegy mourning the tragic death of Pushkin, who died in late January, 1837, following a duel with a court favourite, Baron Georges d'Anthès. Lermontov blamed the social circles closest to the Tsar, charging that their members had maliciously intensified the torments which Pushkin experienced in court society, where his talent was scorned. Lermontov was arrested and sent to the Caucasus, the first of three such periods of exile. The second occurred in 1840 following a duel with the son of the French ambassador, and during this period the poet distinguished himself for valour in combat against the Moslem rebels united under the prophet Shamil. His final exile was in 1841, probably as a result of his rudeness to the daughters of the Tsar at a masquerade ball. While en route to a front line regiment, he detoured to Piatigorsk, a spa in the northern Caucasus which served the army for rest and recuperation. There his caustic wit led to a duel with a retired officer, Martynov, whose shot killed Lermontov instantly. It was rumoured that when news of this death reached the Tsar, he remarked 'A dog's death to a dog!'

Officialdom's animosity to Lermontov was due to the poet's implacable hostility to a society whose moral fibre had been destroyed in the aftermath of the Decembrist revolt. His poem on Pushkin's death is one of several which accuses society of frivolity, dishonesty, moral turpitude, and cowardice. The famous 'Meditation' (1838) foresees for his generation 'a future either empty or dark', while 'January 1, 1840' ends with a desire to throw 'an iron verse' into the face of the 'motley crowd'. Personal alienation is the subject of many lyrics, such as 'Alone I Go Along the Road' or 'Goodbye, Unwashed Russia' (both 1841), yet the poet is able to find peace in nature as expressed in 'When Billows the Yellowing Field' (1837). Several poems with religious content have suggested that Lermontov was a poet of reconciliation but such an interpretation would be a gross misrepresentation of such an uncompromising enemy of oppression.

The Song About Tsar Ivan Vasilievich, the Young Bodyguard, and the Daring Merchant Kalashnikov, a unique narrative poem written in 1837, is a veiled account of Pushkin's tragic duel and the circumstances surrounding it. Set in the sixteenth century, the poem contains deliberate anachronisms and other hints to its real subject. Despite its *roman à clé* features, the poem is undeniably the best example in Russian literature of an effort to imitate the Russian historical song.

The most Romantic of Lermontov's expressions are found in two narrative poems, *Mtsyri* and *Demon*. The former is the *profession de foi* of a dying novice who had fled his Georgian monastery for three days of freedom, during which he rediscovered the mountains of his infancy, survived a Caucasian storm, and engaged in mortal combat with a snow leopard. Union with unfettered nature, the thrill of freedom, and nostalgia for his homeland permeate this Romantic extravaganza. *Demon*, on the theme of the love of a demon for a mortal, went through eight redactions from 1829 until the final version of 1838 (perhaps later), indicative of the poet's preoccupation with the theme. Of course Goethe, Byron, Moore, de Vigny, and others had treated this subject, but it had a lasting grip upon Lermontov, whose role in life as outcast, unrequited lover, and *poète-maudit* enhanced his identification with his 'sad Demon, spirit of rejection'.

A Hero of Our Times (1839) is the story of a rebel without a cause, the young officer Grigory Pechorin, who feels himself fated to destroy the happiness or even the lives of others. Lermontov ingeniously used the prose forms common at that time, travel notes, physiological sketch, intensified anecdote, military tale, and society tale to move the reader ever closer to the psychological complexity of the central character. Pushkin's *Eugene Onegin* is also important as a model for psychological portraiture, as consideration of the heroes' names suggests: the river Onega is placid, while the river Pechora is wild and untamed. Alfred de Musset's *La Confession d'un enfant du siècle* is another obvious source: Lermontov's purpose was to disclose the malady of his times, without, he stated, feeling obliged to suggest a remedy.

The five adventures forming the novel depict Pechorin's encounters with smugglers, a Chechan mistress, an old Caucasian army captain, Cossacks, and members of Piatigorsk society. Pechorin's obsessive desire to dominate others leads inevitably to tragedy, but he refuses to accept responsibility for his acts and blames a hostile fate. Despite his fatal effect upon the lives of others, he is engaging and even attractive, and he emerges from the pages of the novel as a 'round' character whose behaviour may surprise us but is always consistent with his personality. Many of the devices for delineation of Pechorin's psychological states became traditional for canonical Realism. Turgenev, Tolstoy, and Dostoevsky all proceeded upon a path explored by Lermontov and depended upon the prose literary language which he developed.

On his final journey to the Caucasus in 1841, Lermontov sojourned in Moscow with literary friends, to whom he expressed premonitions of imminent death. Sometime between May and July he wrote his prophetic 'A Dream', in which he described a vision of himself at the foot of sun-baked cliffs with blood streaming from his breast. Lermontov's foreboding was fulfilled when he was slain at the age of twenty-seven. The recurrence of the fatal duel in the lives of two of Russia's greatest poets, and in their major works, *Eugene Onegin* and *A Hero of Our Times*, is a sad commentary on the Russian social and political system, which fostered boredom, frivolity, and blameworthy behaviour in the upper classes. Onegin and Pechorin won their duels, but remained indifferent and alienated; Pushkin and Lermontov lost their lives. Lermontov's death marked the end of the Golden Age of poetry and, with few significant exceptions, the conclusion of Russian literature's Romantic era.

ARCHITECTURE

Catherine the Great's (1762–96) preference for a severe and impressive Russian variant of Roman architecture dominates St Petersburg and the palaces built for her on the capital's periphery. Such dignified projects as Vallin de la Mothe's Gostinny Dvor (1761–85) and New Holland Gate (c. 1775), Quarenghi's Hermitage Theatre (1783–5), Starov's Tauride Palace (1783–8), the splendid sweep of Velten's granite embankments and the elegance of his gates to the Summer Gardens, and Cameron's Palace at Pavlovsk (1781–96) set standards of proportion, restraint, and taste that were to remain guiding principles of Russian architecture throughout the late eighteenth and most of the nineteenth centuries. These public buildings were conceived as symbols of imperial power and designed to enhance the dignity of the capital. Yet, Catherine's passion for building encompassed projects of another sort.

Sensitive to changes in European taste, Catherine preferred the rambling English garden to the straight allées and canals, geometric basins and prim flower-beds (patterned on Le Nôtre's at Versailles) favoured by her predecessor Elizabeth. From the first decade of her reign, Catherine's plans for Tsarskoe Selo developed in quite another manner. She laid out the ground around the ponds at Tsarskoe Selo as an English park, with irregular paths through 'naturally' wooded slopes (carefully planned to look unplanned), where the contemplative traveller might catch glimpses of pleasure pavilions, rostral columns, obelisks, and arches.

The landscape design itself reflects the 'picturesque' and 'Romantic' attitude toward nature. Yet the garden bears the same relationship to a natural landscape as the temples, monuments, and artificial ruins that ornament it bear to authentic antiquities. This sentimental, frequently literary, architecture was typical of the first phase of Romantic architecture in Russia, as in the West. The familiar antique forms were used as purely decorative objects.

By the mid-1770s, garden caprices became more exotic and appeared in nearly all of the major parks surrounding St Petersburg: an Egyptian pyramid beside the graves of Catherine's dogs, a Chinese village by Cameron, a Chinese theatre and Gothic ship-yard by Neelov (all at Tsarskoe Selo). Quarenghi contributed a Turkish bath in brilliant pastels, a picnic kitchen disguised as an ancient ruin, and the 'Grand Caprice' – an enormous arch cut through an artificial rock wall, surmounted by a pagoda. Larger projects in Turkish and Gothic taste include Velten's Turkish Chesme Palace outside St Petersburg (1770), and Bazhenov's unfinished Gothic Tsaritsyno Palace near Kolomenskoe (work halted 1787). Both reflect Catherine's personal enthusiasms rather than any serious study by the architects of the styles they mimic.

These early manifestations of a Romantic architectural style in Russia produced no immediate effect on the capital. They were a personal affair between the monarch and her servants. There was no broad popular support for exoticism in architecture, and St Petersburg as an architectural ensemble seemed to require adherence to Peter's original plan of rectilinear streets, broad squares, and restrained, uniform façades. The final classical seal was set on the city with a flurry of building under Alexander I (1801–25): Voronikhin's Cathedral of Our Lady of Kazan (1801–11), Zakharov's Admiralty (1806–23), de Thomon's Stock Exchange on the Point of Vasilievsky Island (1805–10), and especially Rossi's ensembles for Palace Square and the General Staff Headquarters (1819–29), and for the Mikhailovsky Palace (1819–25). Country estates and smaller town-houses in the capitals and elsewhere began to acquire the Empire look that was to remain with them until the end of the century.

Yet even in the heart of the classical revival in Russia, the search for exotic styles continued. From garden structures, Romantic eclecticism moved insidiously to more serious building in the capital. Once again, it was at its most experimental when limited to the background or ornament of the neo-classical landscape. Three small suspension bridges designed by Traitteur (after the disastrous flood of 1824, described in Pushkin's *Bronze Horseman*) are a case in point: the Egyptian Bridge over the Fontanka is adorned with sphinxes and obelisks; the Lion's Bridge over the Griboedov Canal is supported by four large beasts, jaws gripping the slender iron chains that sustain the weight of the span (their bodies conceal the system of metal rods to which the chains are anchored); and the Bank Bridge, of similar construction, boasts fantastic golden-winged griffins (all 1825–6). Giant sphinxes adorn the Neva Embankment near the Academy of Arts; and an obelisk formerly stood in the centre of Nevsky Prospekt before the Kazan Cathedral. These and other extravagant additions to St Petersburg's neo-classical façade suggest that, at least by the 1820s, classicism was simply one among many possible Romantic revivals. Indeed, Russia's version of classical norms had taken on a distinctive appearance, marked especially by the decorative, rather than strictly functional, use of windows and columns in the enormous façades of public buildings and palaces, and the obvious fondness for picturesque atlantes and caryatids that support porches, balconies, and porticos throughout the Empire.

The passion for garden caprices continued through the reign of Nicholas I (1825–55). By 1842, this Romantic taste could be ridiculed as affectation in Gogol's *Dead Souls* (in the unflattering characterization of Manilov, whose garden contained a neo-classical 'Temple of Solitary Contemplation'). The last great classical monument, Montferrand's Cathedral of St Isaac (begun 1818) was completed in 1858; yet it was only towards the end of the nineteenth century that Russians succeeded in reviving their own medieval architectural heritage. The Church of the Resurrection exhibits perhaps the first major revival of sixteenth-century forms in St Petersburg; and, with its exotic silhouette and garish ornament of gilded, tiled, and enamelled domes in imitation of St Basil's, it dominates its neo-classical approaches. The neo-Romantic Slavic revival produced such Art Nouveau fantasies as the Moscow Historical Museum on Red Square (1874–83), the Tretyakov Gallery (1901–2) (perhaps the largest of the residences built in medieval style), and Moscow's Kazan station (1914–40) (the latter such an agglomeration of historical souvenirs that its function is completely obscured).

ART

Any analysis of Russian Romantic painting requires the temporary suspension of two widely held assumptions. The first is that the viewer should seek exclusively Russian values in a 'national' school of art. This would, at very least, distort the intentions of both painter and patron. Like other colonial schools, Russian painting aspired to a cosmopolitan finish; and the result is of interest as much for its historical as for its artistic value. The second difficulty is that Romantic painting has been described largely in terms of themes and subject matter. From a society that was both deeply conservative and lacking a long tradition of western art, even of the functional sort (secular portraits, and city-scapes of an impressive and new capital), we can expect an unusual adherence to decorum and prescribed genres. Even minor departures from serviceable neo-classical norms take on peculiar significance, and technical experimentation is unthinkable until the third quarter of the nineteenth century.

Institutional changes also came slowly: Peter the Great's school of drawing at the St Petersburg Printing House was elevated to the status of an independent Academy of Fine Arts only under Catherine II in 1767. The principal rebellion against the 'Academy' (a hallmark of the Romantic movement in the West) did not occur until 1863 (leading eventually to the establishment of the influential Society for Travelling Art Exhibitions in 1870 (Tovarishchestvo peredvizhnykh khudozhestvennykh vystavok – hence the term *Peredvizhniki* for its members)). Even this event never led to a 'Russian School' of painting comparable to those in literature and music, and the *Peredvizhniki* represented trends as disparate as Naturalism, a tendentious 'critical' Realism (to use the Soviet term), Impressionism, and Art Nouveau.

As in architecture, Romantic themes and techniques in Russian painting appeared first in the 'background' – as variants of well-defined genres, often with literary referents, in an 'international' style. Portraiture is perhaps the best example. Vladimir Borovikovsky (1757–1825) made his career with a number of undistinguished state portraits; but his principal work is an astonishing series of likenesses of women and young girls that are, perhaps, the first manifestations of Romanticism in Russian painting. The portrait of Maria Lopukhina (1797, Tretyakov Gallery, Moscow) is typical: the background is hazy, the perspective ill-defined; the subject is in summery, informal dress, with ash-blond curls and languid pose; her large eyes and side-long glance suggest both flirtation and melancholy. The whole is very reminiscent of Reynolds and Gainsborough, but in its mood of self-indulgent sentimentality, we see more of Karamzin.

In Borovikovsky's portraits, sentiment is still an external element. The mood has changed from a neo-classical formality and idealization of the subject, but the form remains eighteenth-century in treatment of space, in pose, and in purpose. With the portraits of Orest Kiprensky (1782–1836), much more than mood was shifted. His handsome portrait of Denis Davydov (1809, Russian Museum, Leningrad) captures the spirit of the hussar-poet, and of the Decembrists' elegant insolence. Symptomatic, too, of Romanticism are Kiprensky's many self-portraits, painted at regular intervals throughout his life. With a gaze fixed on the viewer, he personifies the artist and chronicles the changes in his countenance through the years. The portrait of Catherine Avdulina (1822, Russian Museum, Leningrad) betrays an Italian Renaissance heritage in pose and in finesse of execution; yet the subject's melancholy expression, the stormy sky seen through a window, and the symbolic white hyacinth in a glass on the sill suggest a Romantic text. Kiprensky's sombre portrait of Pushkin (1827,

Tretyakov Gallery) is one of his best-known and most typical works. The poet appears in a static pose, with arms folded on his breast. The restrained colour range and golden aura on the wall behind the subject draw the viewer's attention to the poet's face, which suggests both inspiration and contemplative melancholy. The interest in psychological detail and the classical reference of the statuette of a Muse in the background create that mixture of real and ideal typical of early Russian Romanticism.

Karl Briullov (1799–1852), one of the earliest products of the Russian Academy, and the first Russian painter to enjoy an international reputation, represents a new stage in the development of Romantic portraiture. His portrait of Giovanina Paccini (*The Rider*, 1832, Tretyakov Gallery) presents his subject elegantly perched on a rearing horse. Her cool demeanour is contrasted with the fierce expression of her steed and the searching look of her younger sister. The icy blue and white of her gown is set against the black horse, a stormy sky, and a shadowy façade. A brilliant red curtain appears through a doorway, and the subject's blue and gold veil trails in endless waves behind her. Even more striking is Briullov's portrait of the Countess Samoilova and Giovanina Paccini, her adoptive daughter (before 1842, Russian Museum, Leningrad). The subjects, emerging from a costume ball, are posed against an enormous pillar and a billowing scarlet drape that cuts a strong diagonal line through the canvas. Two (unreconciled) perspectives of an impressive neo-classical interior appear on either side of the curtain, and guests in exotic dress are sketched in the background. Giovanina appears to lean against her mother, while the countess clearly moves in the opposite direction. The subjects are virtually suspended in space, the elaborate textures of their heavy costumes serving in place of a sure footing. In both portraits, perspective and logic fall victim to the artist's concern with strong contrasts in colour and motion.

Exotic landscapes were primarily the products of talented amateurs, officers stationed in the Caucasus or Bessarabia and equipped with a set of water-colours. Lermontov's views of Tbilisi and Piatigorsk, and Nikanor Chernetsov's view of a diminutive, top-hatted Pushkin at Bakhchisaraysky Fontan (1837) may serve as examples. Stylistically conservative, they were meant as realistic records of travel and military exploits on the outposts of the Empire; and they retain the documentary look of postcards.

Marine painting was virtually monopolized by the brilliant Ivan Aivazovsky (1817–1900). In his turbulent canvases, he eliminated first foreground figures, and later all anecdote, to concentrate on light, sea, and sky in the manner of Turner (see *Seashore*, 1840, Tretyakov Gallery; *The Ninth Wave*, 1850, Russian Museum; and *The Wave*, 1889, Russian Museum).

An interest in Russian folk culture is apparent from the third quarter of the eighteenth century, although the market for such paintings was limited. Potential patrons did not care to be reminded that Russian manners and costume were so different from those of western Europe. It was only with the rise of national feeling following the Russian victory in the Napoleonic Wars that genre painting became a major concern. Mikhail Shibanov (active, second half of the eighteenth century), a serf of Potemkin, can be credited with the first Russian painting of manners in his *Celebration of the Marriage Contract* (1777, Tretyakov Gallery). A 'class of domestic exercises' was established at the Russian Academy at about the same time, with the aim of producing a school of genre painters. Alexey Venetsianov (1779–1847) was perhaps the first to benefit. After 1820, he retired to his estate in Tver Province to devote himself to studies of peasant life. The typically graceful peasant girl in *The Field: Spring* (1820s, Tretyakov Gallery) leads two horses across a vast horizon and a pale blue sky interrupted only by fresh greenery. The painting suggests the dignity of labour as well as the subtle beauties of the Russian landscape. Venetsianov's canvases are completely lacking in anecdote, suggesting Vermeer, Chardin, or LeNain, rather than the often tendentious Russian Realists of the 1860s. His simple evocations of the rhythms of country life find their parallels in Pushkin.

Fyodor Tolstoy (1783–1873) (a distant relative of the writer) applied Venetsianov's analysis of everyday life to the Russian 'middle' classes of the capitals. The result was a striking series of interiors – a genre which was very popular in Russia towards the end of the Romantic period. His *Family Portrait* (1830, Russian Museum) betrays a Romantic fascination with both psychological detail and tricks of lighting, perspective, and frames. A couple with their two young daughters are grouped around a table in a dark green room beneath a fashionable moonlit landscape. Husband and wife look intensely at each other, while the girls seem lost in their own melancholy thoughts. The group is off-centre, and the viewer's eye is inevitably led through a doorway to a brightly lit corridor, where impressive sculpture and a lyre-shaped chandelier reflect the Russians' continued fascination with neo-classical decorative art. A seated woman (perhaps the girls' nurse) sits in the distant room beyond. A large mirror in a heavy frame at the end of the corridor echoes and reflects the doorways, endlessly expanding the perspective, and directing the eye back to the green room. (The 'second eye' of mirror and servant is typical of the final stages of Russian Romantic painting.)

The cool detachment of Venetsianov's and Tolstoy's canvases contrasts markedly with the work of their young contemporary, Pavel Fedotov (1815–53). His works are small-scale and theatrical – loaded with gesture, emotion, and details of costume and furnishing. His most famous painting, *The Major's Proposal* (1848, Tretyakov Gallery), depicts the arrival of a middle-aged gentleman of rank but limited means at a rich merchant's home, hoping to improve his circumstances by marrying the merchant's daughter. The major strokes his moustache in the hall; the reluctant bride, in a cloud of white lace, attempts to make her escape, though literally, and firmly, in her mother's grasp; the bewildered father, apparently an Old Believer, confers with a family member, while a servant eyes both bride and viewer. The choice of paintings and prints on the walls of the room, the icons, lamps, and chandelier, the napery and glassware that decorate the scene, speak volumes about the emerging merchant class. The combination of humour and social commentary are suggestive of both Gogol and Hogarth; and in the stifling atmosphere of Nicholas' reign, they were sufficient to call down official censure.

Historical painting in Russia begins with classical, rather than national, subjects. Briullov's *Last Day of Pompeii* (1833, Russian Museum), an enormous canvas inspired in equal parts by the artist's visits to the ruins, a reading of Pliny, and performances of Giovanni Pacini's opera of the same title (1825), is a theatrical extravaganza that was the wonder of the age and secured Briullov's international reputation. Among the crowds that admired and commented on the work, exhibited in Rome, Milan, and Paris before being sent back to St Petersburg, were Pushkin, Gogol, Walter Scott, and Bulwer-Lytton (who wrote a popular novel on the theme). Before our eyes, statues and buildings topple, lightning flashes across a black and red sky, and ash rains on the populace. The melodramatic, not to say morbid, treatment of a classical subject offered enough anecdote for a dozen canvases; a fallen charioteer, a fleeing thief, a family beneath picturesquely billowing drapery; the elderly Pliny carried off by a soldier and young servant, and a pious group with eyes turned to the heavens. The lurid colour, violence, and histrionic effects are skilfully mixed with irreproachably modelled draped and undraped figures reminiscent of David. Yet, unlike classical works, the painting lacks a focal point; limbs of the two central figures (the fallen mother and the charioteer) point to opposite corners of the canvas; to the right and left, the raised arms of Pliny and the fleeing father are symmetrically opposed. In mid-distance, off-centre, the startled face of a beautiful woman stares back at us from the crush, drawing us into the painting and its theatrical vignettes.

Briullov's *Pompeii* became the work to be emulated by a generation of Russian painters – in its scale, complexity, and melodrama. Alexander Ivanov (1806–58) produced the enormous *Appearance of Christ to the People* (1857, Tretyakov Gallery) after nearly twenty years of laborious study. While John the Baptist delivers an impassioned plea, and points to the distant Christ as the Saviour, the emotions of his listeners express doubt, indifference, inspiration, and conviction. For the modern viewer, the classical groupings, idealized nudes, and emphasis on anecdote seem derivative and contrived; while the naturalistic perspective results in a diminutive Christ placed not quite at the centre of the other figures' gaze and gesture, undercutting Ivanov's intention to portray the experience of faith. The canvas failed to achieve the success of Briullov's *Pompeii*, but Ivanov's contribution to Russian painting was in other areas. His innumerable preparatory studies of landscape, nudes, and facial types (on both classical and Byzantine models) were regularly displayed with his Christ. Their casual cropping, brilliant colour, and vague or flat perspective gave new status to sketches lacking the finished quality of the neo-classical 'machine', and paved the way for an understanding of Impressionism.

Vasily Surikov :1848–1916) was the first to turn to Russia's past for historical subjects. Although a Realist in technique, his composition is close to Briullov's and Ivanov's; and his choice of incident indicates a bias toward Romantic literary themes that would dominate Russian history-painting through the first decades of the twentieth century. His most famous works, *The Execution of the Streltsy* (1881); *Menshikov at Beriozov* (1883), a study of Peter's closest associate in exile with his children in Siberia; and the *Boyarina Morozova* (1887), depicting a defiant Old Believer led off in chains (all, Tretyakov Gallery), deal with the theme of personal freedom and the individual's opposition to the state. The colourful palette and saturated detail of the costumery, if not always accurate, at least distracted authorities from any political message. Surikov's lead was followed with historical canvases by Ilya Repin, Vasily Vereshchagin, and Nicholas Gay, through the Art Nouveau fantasies of a mythical Russian past by Victor Vaznetsov and Mikhail Nesterov. There was certainly nothing novel in these paintings; but because of their themes, they remain the most familiar and popular works of Russian art. Romantic in feeling and theme, they never venture far from the safe, prevailing standards of Realism.

MUSIC

Despite the wealth and grandeur of St Petersburg and the Imperial court, foreign composers and performers overwhelmingly dominated the musical life of the capital well into the 1860s. For want of adequate musical training and official encouragement, Russia was unable to produce sufficient native musicians to staff its operas and orchestras, or to provide them with a significant national repertoire. Not until the second quarter of the century did Mikhail Glinka (1804–57) produce the first genuinely Russian operas – *A Life for the Tsar* (1836) and *Ruslan and Liudmila* (1842). Glinka's achievement, however, was not matched by any of his compatriots until the 1850s. In concert music, the situation was even more dismal. Balakirev's musical circle, the so-called Mighty Handful (*Moguchaia Kuchka*), which western listeners most strongly identify as both Russian and Romantic, only gradually took form between 1856 and 1862.

The reasons for this late flowering of Russian Romantic music are manifold. Musical education was perhaps the greatest problem. The first conservatory in the Russian Empire opened in Warsaw in 1861. In the capital, specialized musical education was limited to the Theatre School, which trained musicians exclusively for the Imperial theatres, and for the academy attached to the Imperial chapel, similarly restricted to training singers for the choir of the court chapel. Anyone seriously interested in music as a career was obliged to study abroad or privately. While St Petersburg boasted many piano and voice instructors, lessons in music theory or composition were virtually unknown before 1860.

The Russian legal system did not recognize professional musicians, although from the eighteenth century it had classified painters, sculptors, and actors as 'free artists', with exemptions from the poll tax and military service, and the right to live anywhere in the country. Without independent gentry status, or a nominal government position recognized by Russian law, the professional musician or composer had no more rights than a peasant. Members of the gentry were required to renounce the privileges of their rank as a condition for joining one of the companies of the Imperial theatres.

The Russian taste for bureaucratic centralization also had a stifling effect on Russian music in this period. The Imperial Theatre Directorate controlled all performances in the capitals and from 1846 enjoyed an official monopoly on public entertainments during the winter season (September until the beginning of Lent, usually in March). Effectively, all orchestral concerts were limited to the Lenten season, to ensure that they would not compete with the Imperial opera companies.

The pride of the Theatre Directorate was St Petersburg's Italian Opera, which performed only foreign works, and which enjoyed the enthusiastic support of the royal court (a tradition since the 1730s, when Empress Anna established the first musical theatre in Russian by hiring an Italian opera troupe). Vast sums were spent to provide the Italian Opera with an excellent orchestra, elaborate sets and costumes, and the best foreign artists, often engaged at exorbitant fees. Its performances were as likely to be reviewed in the society columns of St Petersburg's newspapers as by music critics.

Not only in prestige and revenues, but in the quality of its performances, the Russian Opera lagged far behind its Italian counterpart. Although performing in Russian, its repertory came largely from abroad and was not significantly different from that of the Italian Opera, except for a few Russian works and some French and German comic operas. It was frequented by nationalistic opera-lovers, visiting provincials, and students and petty bureaucrats unable to afford the Italian Opera's higher ticket prices.

Concert and chamber music lagged even farther behind. The Philharmonic Society, St Petersburg's oldest concert organization, was founded only in 1802 and gave just three concerts a year to raise money for a musicians' pension fund. The élite Concert Society, frequented only by the highest aristocracy, did not appear until 1850; and the Theatre Directorate's own series of Lenten concerts was not launched until 1859. The one group to escape the ban on private concerts during the opera season was the series of 'Musical Exercises of the Students of St Petersburg University', whose concerts apparently suffered considerably from the musicians' lack of preparation. The repertoire of all groups reflected extremely conservative tastes, relying heavily on eighteenth-century classics, Beethoven, Mendelssohn, and Rossini, interspersed with Strauss waltzes and show-piece arias from Italian operas. In a given year, the four groups together gave only about twenty concerts (of which half were by the University). The two opera companies, by contrast, performed approximately 200 times each season.

In these circumstances, it is surprising only that Russians developed a national repertoire as quickly as they did. Native musicians had begun producing operas for the Imperial court and for the private theatres of the wealthiest gentry as early as the 1770s; but despite certain tendencies to exploit unintegrated folk-song material, the works appear highly imitative of western models. Catterino Cavos (1775–1842), a Russianized Venetian who played a great role in the development of the Russian theatre as a conductor, teacher, and official of the Theatre Directorate for over forty years, was perhaps the first to produce Romantic operas of considerably higher quality. His works reflect two lines of predictable Romantic themes – fantastic tales based on Russian folk songs, legends and fairy tales, and patriotic historical dramas drawn from episodes in Russian history. In both cases, popular sentimental or Romantic literary works usually served as the basis for his libretti (e.g. *Svetlana*, 1822, after Zhukovsky's narrative poem, *The Firebird*, 1822, libretto by Yazykov, and *Ivan Susanin*, 1812, based on Shakhovskoy's play).

Throughout the 1830s and 1840s, Aleksei Verstovsky (1700–1862) wrote on similar subjects. His highly popular *Askold's Tomb* (1835), with its songs and choruses in pseudo-Russian style, and its sentimental airs in imitation of popular urban Romances, remained in the repertoire for more than a decade. Verstovsky was somewhat more successful than Cavos in assimilating Russian folk-song material, yet neither composer fully understood the nature of the folk songs and liturgical music he employed, forcing the characteristic Russian modes into western minor keys. Moreover, neither ever fully escaped from the popular traditions of vaudeville and *Singspiele* in which they first gained popularity. Their operas are really little more than incidental music to Romantic plays. The next major advance was to be Glinka's.

From 1830 to 1834, Glinka travelled in Germany, where he took his first and only serious course in composition, and in Italy, where he met Bellini, Donizetti, and Berlioz. His *A Life for the Tsar* (or *Ivan Susanin*, as it was originally, and subsequently, called) premièred in 1836 and was a spectacular success. Glinka found himself hailed as the leader of the Russian nationalist movement in music. The opera's Russian subject, its sympathetic portrayal of the peasants, and the influence of Russian speech and folk song on the musical style of some scenes made it revolutionary; but, in fact, the opera is in a fairly traditional classical form, based on western models. The overture, especially, with its minimal development and small-scale orchestra, is characteristic of French opera overtures, which Glinka greatly admired. Glinka's second opera, *Ruslan and Liudmila* (1842), based on the Pushkin text, continues the other thematic line already noted in Cavos' work – the fantastic. The work satisfied the tastes and expectations of Glinka's Petersburg listeners with its sensuous and exotic quasi-Russian, quasi-Eastern spectacle; but again, the musical form is closer to Mozart because of the small and colouristic orchestra, and the emphasis on voice over ensemble.

Glinka's characterization is also of interest. It is accomplished not by thematic leitmotifs, but by music appropriate to each character. In *Ruslan*, for example, the evil dwarf Chernomor is wrapped in atmospheric instrumental effects, the witch Naina declaims, and the part of the fantastic talking head is taken by a chorus hidden inside it, while the hero and heroine 'speak' in the 'human' manner of straightforward song. The technique was taken up first by Alexander Dargomyzhsky (1813–69), who also moved toward a more thorough operatic reform: substitution of a continuous expressive line of melodic declamation for the traditional succession of arias and recitative (especially in *Rusalka*, première 1856).

Glinka's taste for the exotic is also reflected in his short orchestral fantasies, *Jota Arragonese* (1845) and *Night in Madrid* (1858–50), and in some of his Romances of the same period. These were the first manifestations of a major new theme in Russian music, Spain. But Glinka's Spain, antique Russia, and exotic East are mostly coloured by his clear-cut forms, bright tone, and an emotional restraint reminiscent of Pushkin.

At Glinka's death in 1857, Dargomyzhsky had already composed his *Rusalka* (1843–55, première 1856, based on Pushkin's play). Yet, it is hard to imagine two contemporary composers more different. In contrast to Glinka's cool melodic lines, Dargomyzhsky's music reflects, on one hand, dramatic conflict, intense passions, and striking contrasts (as in his first opera, *Esmeralda*, 1839, based on Hugo's *Notre Dame de Paris*), and, on the other, biting humour and a sense of the grotesque reminiscent of Gogol (in, for example, his songs and orchestral anecdotes of the late 1850s, *Baba-Yaga*, *The Finnish Fantasy*, *The Old Corporal*, and *The Worm*). Dargomyzhsky's genius was for melodic characterization, which is most impressive in his final opera, *The Stone Guest* (the libretto is Pushkin's 'little tragedy' in verse, based on the Don Juan story). Written in the final years of the composer's life, under the influence of the young composers of the Balakirev Circle (the work was, in fact, completed by Cui and orchestrated by Rimsky-Korsakov, première 1872), the opera reflects both natural speech and Pushkin's poetic Realism in diction and psychology. The manner of expression was totally revolutionary – the familiar characters conduct a passionate melodic dialogue, with no intervening arias. This was the path that Russian Realist opera would follow.

By 1862, the Balakirev Circle had reached its full complement of five amateur composers – Balakirev, Cui, Mussorgsky, Rimsky-Korsakov, and Borodin – marking the beginning of the 'Golden Age' of Russian music. Appropriately enough, that epithet is also used to describe the much earlier period of Russian literary Romanticism, but the term's accuracy lies more in its reference to the establishment of a distinctive national school of the highest calibre than to any purely Romantic traits of the school's artistic products. In music, as in painting and architecture, Russians turned to their own past and folklore relatively late, and only after western European artistic techniques had been fully mastered. Thus, the Balakirev Circle worked simultaneously on contemporary international problems of musical Realism and on the development of a national style, the desire for which was largely motivated by Romantic intellectual tendencies. Operatic texts and words for songs were regularly drawn from the works of the finest poets of the Romantic period, which further confuses the matter. The choice accounts for the presence of Romantic themes, but it was surely motivated in equal parts by the following: (1) at the time, the texts were literary 'classics' and therefore 'safe' for presentation to a conservative public and even more conservative government censor; (2) the subject matter of the texts concerned the Russian past or Russian folklore and was, therefore, appropriate for national treatment; and (3) poetry, more suitable than prose for musical treatment, had been on the decline in Russian since the 1840s. In any case, the spirit of the times demanded that even Romanticism be called Realism in Russia. 'Progressive' thinkers like Apollon Grigoriev, Herzen, and Dobrolyubov applied the same high-mindedness to art that they did to political reform, and subtly bullied the nationalist composers of the Balakirev Circle into thinking of music in terms of its truth value.

Of these Romantic Realists, by far the most original was Modest Mussorgsky (1839–81). His *Boris Godunov* (1868–72, two versions) embodies the most characteristic traits of the 'Golden Age' of Russian music and presages developments through the end of the century. Mussorgsky used strong musical contrasts in theme, style, and instrumental colour to mark not only different characters, as Dargomyzhsky had done, but to characterize different places (Moscow versus Marina Mniszek's court; a monastery versus the crowded coronation scene). His orchestration, like Glinka's, remained lean, relying on clear-cut groupings of instruments and the formation of unexpected, psychologically justified harmonies to achieve its effects, rather than sheer numbers and volume, as in Berlioz and Wagner. The idea that haunted Mussorgsky was that music should reproduce the accents of human speech, raising it to a higher plane, but following its natural rhythm. This was scarcely novel, of course – it was the battle cry of composers from Monteverdi to Wagner, and a concern of Dargomyzhsky's later years – but it led Mussorgsky to a fresh use of Russian liturgical music, especially the 'znamenny' chants (in which the length of each musical phrase is determined by the corresponding length of the verbal phrase, making any metre or predictable rhythm impossible). Finally, Mussorgsky's form was experimental. The opera is written in seven (later nine) scenes (*Kartiny*) covering a period of seven years. While the libretto closely follows the texts of long passages from the Pushkin play, in opera such a disjointed plot, with any possible love interest clearly subordinate to the psychological portraits of Tsar and pretender, was a great novelty.

Mussorgsky's striking characterizations (apparent too in his song-cycle *Songs and Dances of Death*, 1875–7), his ancient harmonies and use of forms ranging from art song to opera to symphonic sketch (e.g., *Night on Bald Mountain*, 1886) anticipated developments in Russian music through Tchaikovsky, Rachmaninov, and Stravinsky.

DANCE

The cosmopolitan audiences of St Petersburg saw not only the most popular Romantic ballets of the day, but the most popular dancers as well. The legendary Marie Taglioni, the creator of the title role in *La Sylphide* (1832) arrived in St Petersburg in 1837, just two years after its St Petersburg première. Fanny Elssler made her debut in *Giselle* in 1848, and Carlotta Grisi in 1850. The Imperial Theatre Directorate was also successful in attracting talented and prolific ballet-masters, most notably, Charles Didelot (1767–1837, in Russia 1801–36), Jules Perrot (1810–92, head ballet-master 1848–59), Jules Saint-Leon (1821–70, in Russia 1859–69), and Marius Petipa (1818–1910, in Russia from 1847, head ballet-master 1869–1903). These four dominated the Russian ballet throughout the century. The composer Cesar Pugni (1802–70) arrived in St Petersburg almost simultaneously with Elssler and Perrot in 1848. Pugni was to spend the rest of his life in Russia, and nearly all of Petipa's and Perrot's ballets were created to his music. Finally, the system was already in place for the training of excellent Russian dancers.

The Imperial Ballet School was generously maintained out of the privy purse, and it shared security and prestige equal to the other national-service academies. By 1815, the school had produced its first great star – Avdotya Istomina (1799–1848), mentioned in Pushkin's *Eugene Onegin* and other works of the period as the very embodiment of Terpsichore.

Except for a brief period in the 1840s, when St Petersburg lacked a brilliant ballet-master and performances fell off (c. 1840–8), there was very little discontinuity in the Russian ballet – in terms of personnel, training, public support, or repertoire. Ballets on Russian themes appeared as early as the 1820s, with *Ruslan and Liudmila* (1821) and *Prisoner of the Caucasus* (1823), both based on Pushkin's works and both produced within a year of the respective publication dates. Saint-Leon's *The Humpbacked Horse* (*Koniok gorbunok*, 1864) is usually credited with being the first 'national ballet', partly due to the ballet-master's own statements to that effect, but largely because it, unlike earlier attempts at Russian themes, remained in the repertoire for a century. Exoticism included such Egyptian extravaganzas as Petipa's *The Pharaoh's Daughter* (1862). However, the most productive thematic line was the fantastic love tale involving sylphs, nymphs or wilis, established by Filippo Taglioni's spectacularly successful *La Sylphide* (1832, St Petersburg première 1835). The sylph's descendants include *Giselle* (1841), *La Péri* (1843), and on Russian soil, Petipa's *Swan Lake* (1895) and Mikhail Fokine's *Les Sylphides* (1909).

Major changes in the Romantic ballet were international and technical: the gradual development of point-work (required of the corps as well as the principals by 1830), and the standardization of the ballet costume (full skirts in layers of white gauze, shortened to show the feet, inspired by Marie Taglioni's costume in *La Sylphide*). Romantic writers' interest in the supernatural, the fantastic, madness, good and evil, and the exotic simply produced a larger fund of extravagant plots with well-known literary referents. Hence to speak of the history of a Russian Romantic ballet is in itself misleading, for in a sense, it was neither exclusively Russian, nor especially Romantic. If the Russian ballet stood out at the end of the century, it was because the Imperial ballet had preserved and nurtured an art form largely ignored throughout the rest of Europe.

A survey of Russian Romanticism cannot end with an elegant colophon. The Romantic movement in Russia presents an unusual, even distorted profile. Western Romantic trends only gradually insinuated themselves into Russian art and political thought; once in place, they did not die a sudden death. In landscape architecture, for example, 'English' gardens and architectural caprices appeared as early as the 1760s; but neo-classicism held sway as the standard of taste for both public and private building through the Revolution. A retrospective 'national-historical' style developed only in the 1880s, already influenced by western Art Nouveau. Painting remained stolidly neo-classical in style until the third quarter of the century; yet portraits from the 1820s already reveal Sentimental and Romantic conceits. Ballet flourished from an early period, heavily supported by the government, and following its own classical style and rigid traditional training; but in the 1820s and 1830s, popular Russian Romantic literary works served as the bases for ballet libretti, often within months of publication. Only literature manifests a more 'typical' time-table. The élite of St Petersburg and Moscow were well acquainted with western literary and philosophical trends by the early 1820s, and by the end of the decade, Russian poets and prose writers had produced a distinctive national Romantic literature. The language, themes, and methods of characterization employed by Pushkin, Gogol, Lermontov, and their contemporaries were to have a huge effect on the Russian Realist writers of the second half of the century. 'National' themes in painting and music produced significant artistic works only decades after literary Romanticism had given way to Naturalist and Realist fashions. The products of Russian Romantic art, disparate in intent, quality, and period, make a comprehensive typology impossible.

BIBLIOGRAPHY

Art and architecture
Hamilton, George Heard. The Art and Architecture of Russia, Pelican History of Art (Harmondsworth, 1964).

Talbot-Rice, Tamara. *A Concise History of Russian Art* (New York, 1963).

University of Minnesota Gallery. *The Art of Russia 1800–1850* (exhib. catalogue) (Minneapolis, 1978).

(Adequate plates of Romantic paintings are readily available in Soviet publications in English, French, and German, concerning pre-revolutionary secular art and the collections of major museums. Soviet works on architecture tend to focus on the development of a city or an architectural ensemble rather than on manifestations of an architectural style.)

Dance

Balet: Entsiklopediya (Moscow, 1981). (The first comprehensive reference work in Russian on the ballet, the encyclopaedia is the only work in any language that details the history of the national ballet.)

Kirsten, Lincoln. *Movement and Metaphor: Four Centuries of Ballet* (New York, 1970; reprint (retitled *Four Centuries of Ballet: Fifty Masterworks*) New York, 1984). (Major sections on ballet in Russia.)

Krasovskaya, Vera. *The Russian Ballet Theatre from its Origins to the Mid-19th Century* (Moscow and Leningrad, 1958).

History

Florinsky, Michael. *Russia: A History and an Interpretation*, 2 vols. (New York, 1953).

Pears, Bernard. *A History of Russia* (New York, 1946).

Seton-Watson, Hugh. *The Russian Empire, 1801–1917*, The Oxford History of Modern Europe (Oxford, 1967).

Literature

Brown, William Edward. *A History of Russian Literature of the Romantic Period*, 4 vols. (Ann Arbor, 1986). (The only comprehensive study of the subject in English.)

Erlich, Victor. *Gogol* (New Haven, 1969).

Fanger, Donald. *The Creation of Nikolai Gogol* (Cambridge, Massachusetts, 1979).

Leighton, Lauren G. *Alexander Beztuzhev-Marlinsky* (Boston, 1975).

Mersereau, John Jr. *Mikhail Lermontov* (Carbondale, Illinois, 1962). (Focuses on Lermontov's prose.)

    Russian Romantic Fiction (Ann Arbor, 1983). (A detailed history of the development of Russian prose in this critical period. Discussion of many authors not available in translation.)

Mirsky, D. S. *Pushkin* (New York, 1963).

Nabokov, Vladimir. *Nikolai Gogol* (New York, 1961). (A succinct and witty scholarly fantasy that captures the life and works of one of Russia's few literary eccentrics.)

Proffer, Carl R. *Russian Romantic Prose: An Anthology* (Ann Arbor, 1979). (A representative sampler of Romantic prosaists and of important short prose forms.)

Pushkin, Alexander. *Eugene Onegin*, translated, with a commentary, by Vladimir Nabokov, 4 vols., Bollingen Series 72 (Princeton, 1964). (Nabokov's three-volume commentary is an encyclopaedia of early nineteenth-century Russian cultural history.)

Rydel, Christine (ed.). *The Ardis Anthology of Russian Romanticism* (Ann Arbor, 1984). (Includes contemporary criticism, literary historical materials and excerpts from rare novels, as well as verse and prose translations from major authors. Detailed commentary.)

Vickery, Walter. *Alexander Pushkin* (New York, 1970).

Music

Newmarch, Rosa. *The Russian Opera* (New York, 1914; reprint Westport, Connecticut, 1972).

Swan, Alfred J. *Russian Music and Its Sources in Chant and Folk-Song* (New York, 1973).

13

The Agony in the Garden: Polish Romanticism

DONALD PIRIE

INTRODUCTION

Prince Józef Poniatowski (1763–1813) was portrayed throughout the nineteenth century in patriotic Polish iconography as leading his troops to heroic death against hopeless odds at the battle of Leipzig (1813). The sequel was less inspiring: his coffin meandered for one and a half years from Leipzig on its way to Warsaw, and was left in a church crypt for fifteen months more. There it would have remained, unceremoniously unburied for years to come, had the Tsar not magnanimously decided to permit its burial with full honours.[1]

It had been a foregone conclusion of the Congress of Vienna of 1815, of which Alexander I (1801–25) was one of the main architects, that Russia would retain the lands of the Duchy of Warsaw, which it had occupied after Napoleon's ignominious retreat from Russia.[2] To a certain extent Alexander was swayed by the arguments of his foreign minister, the Pole Prince Adam Czartoryski (1770–1861),[3] to respect the Poles' distinct identity by retaining the Duchy's separate status and political and legal systems in its new guise as the Congress 'Kingdom of Poland' within the Russian Empire. First and foremost, he was determined to integrate his new Polish subjects into his Empire, and so was willing to accept his role as constitutional monarch in return for the Poles' willing allegiance and total obedience, which to him were not contradictory.

Alexander's reticence as regards permitting the funeral rites of Prince Poniatowski mirrored his discomfort with the Poles generally. Eventually he decided to allow the rites to take place on a grand scale, but wisely, not in Warsaw. With the assent of the two other powers concerned (Austria and Prussia) he asked the Senate of the Republic of Kraków, a tiny island 'republic' at the meeting point of the three vast empires, to make place for Prince Józef in St Leonard's Crypt alongside the sarcophagus of King Jan

317

Sobieski (whose troops had been a major force in the defeat of the Turks at Vienna in 1683).[4] Were the events to cause any demonstrations of patriotism, they would not be taking place on the territory of the Empire. In any case the funeral would testify to the Tsar's subtle understanding of his subjects' sensibilities: he clearly intended that his gesture should be seen as a symbol of reconciliation, and of his desire to be a true King of the Poles. Alexander was after all, depending on how one counts them, the sixth foreign king of Poland since 1572.[5]

Speaking to an Austrian diplomat in 1816, Alexander explained the strategy behind his magnanimous tactics: 'In order to pacify the Poles, we need to flatter their national pride. By indulging them like this at the moment, I'll make Russians of them, though all the while it will seem to them that they are still Polish.'[6] Poniatowski's coffin was allowed to progress in state from Warsaw to Kraków during the spring of 1817, and was finally buried with all the pomp demanded by Catholic ritual and Classical rhetoric, emphasizing the Prince's sense of patriotic duty as a soldier, and his noble code of honour (alibis for the unmentionable circumstances that he had fought against Alexander's forces up to the very last moment of his life).

For the Tsar it was calculated to symbolize the end of 'Polish history'. Yet despite Alexander's calculated magnanimity and the orators' carefully worded eulogies, the Poles read the significance of the funeral rather differently: affirmation of the value of resistance against all odds for national dignity, from 1795 to the Prince's glorious death in 1813.[7]

For the Poles, the symbolism of heroic continuity and inspiration for subsequent generations was then further reinforced by Alexander's proposal that Tadeusz Kościuszko, the virtuous and uncompromising Commander of the 1794 Uprising against foreign (i.e. Prussian and Russian) intervention in the Polish-Lithuanian Commonwealth's affairs, and who died in 1818, should also be buried in the crypt. A sense of unity was forged between the two constituents of the Polish nation, the gentry (*szlachta*) and the peasantry (*lud*): the Prince with his motto, 'honour and the fatherland', a gallant aristocrat always at the head of his troops, and Kościuszko the man from the lesser gentry, who identified strongly with his peasant battalions and to whom the motto 'death or victory' is ascribed. Their experiences and attitudes were obviously different, yet there they lay next to Sobieski, the embodiment of the Polish national spirit.

Thus a period of pessimism and despair had followed Napoleon's total defeat at Waterloo in 1815, with the reimposition of alien rule on the nominally independent Duchy of Warsaw. Yet again the hopes for a resurrected Polish state were dashed: for the rest of the century, the Poles were to be partitioned between a Prussian Sector (the 'Duchy of Posen'), an

Austrian Sector (the 'Kingdom of Galicia and Lodomeria', and after 1846 including the 'Republic of Kraków'), and the Russian Sector, itself divided into two different parts: the 'Western gubernias' within the Russian Empire, and the 'Kingdom of Poland'. If Alexander really imagined he had united his Polish subjects behind him so easily, he was to be greatly disabused. The two funerals kindled a dormant and repressed patriotism. However, it required a force far more powerful than that suggested by the two public funerals to transform such historical figures into mythical heroes, and their deeds into legend. That impetus was Romanticism.

BACKGROUND TO PERIOD

At the beginning of the eighteenth century, Austria was joined by Russia and then Prussia as the major central European powers, while the Polish-Lithuanian Commonwealth with its decentralized form of government and weak army was unable to compete with its powerful neighbours. Its aristocracy (*magnateria*) and lesser gentry (*szlachta*) were exceedingly proud of an anarchic political system which allowed them what they considered a state of 'golden freedom'. The magnates were prone to drawing a certain proportion of their income from the coffers of any one of the three neighbouring states to finance their rule over their local province, so the rule of law was upheld more by local allegiances than decision making in Warsaw. The first half of the eighteenth century saw Russia extend its power over the Commonwealth by redefining the Tsar as Poland-Lithuania's arbiter and protector in 1717 in an act passed by the Polish parliament (the Sejm), supposedly in defence of the *szlachta*'s 'freedoms' and privileges.[8]

The election in 1764 to the Polish throne of the apparently malleable Stanisław August Poniatowski (a courtier to Catherine the Great) seemed to underline the complete subservience of the Commonwealth to Russian interests. But the fop turned and initiated commissions on reforming the Commonwealth's constitution to make it more manageable, and consolidating executive power in the monarchy. The gentry were horrified and called a 'confederation' (a sort of legalized revolt of the whole estate) at Bar in 1766, supported by the Russians, in the name of their traditional privileges and allegiance to Catholicism.[9] It was such violent and concerted opposition, that the King was forced to abandon his 'absolutist' plans and content himself with planning reforms in the economy and education for the next twenty years: in 1773 the three powers had reprimanded the King and his country by forcing him to sign away territory to each of them. This 'First Partition' was to 'pacify' the Poles, and was intended to promote peace and stability. The threat of further such sanctions now loomed over the political horizon.

It suited Russia, Prussia, and Austria to retain a weak Commonwealth as a buffer state, but whenever the Poles attempted to disturb the 'balance of power', the solution was to reduce its territory once more. When Stanisław August recalled the Sejm in Warsaw in 1788 to debate Polish aid to Russia in its war with the Turks, the members instead set about extending the session to four years, and revising the Commonwealth's laws and statutes as the King had originally planned. This culminated in the passing of the enlightened Constitution of the Third of May in 1791.

Aristocrats and conservatives again called on Russian aid to support the attack on their rights, and called the Confederation of Targowice in 1792 to declare the new constitution invalid. This resulted in the so-called 'War of the Second Partition', which saw the King change sides and declare himself for the Confederates in 1793 and a tamer Sejm rescinding the innovative constitution under the shadow of Russian bayonets. Only a few months afterwards in 1794, Tadeusz Kościuszko led another uprising which sought to restore the reformist Constitution of 1791, but was defeated by the combined forces of the traditionalists, and Russian and Prussian troops. On the 25th of November 1795 Stanisław August formally abdicated; and since no separate state or executive existed, no incorporation bill had to be signed. At the final Treaty of Partition signed in St Petersburg in 1797 all three parties pledged that no political entity would ever again be permitted to be called Poland.[10]

News of the French Revolution and the deposition of the French monarchy had overshadowed the dismemberment of the Commonwealth in European news; partition was even commonly justified in Europe by intimating that Jacobin 'ideas' from France had infected the Poles in their drafting of their radical 'Constitution'. No one foresaw the international implications of a revitalized, missionary France bent on exporting revolution. Inspired by Napoleon who was first General, then Consul, and finally Emperor, France's forces not only defeated other armies in order to extend her influence, but promoted the republican ideology of 'liberté, égalité, fraternité' to other states (where it was often taken more literally than Bonaparte wished). Between 1800 and 1810 Napoleon transformed the 'ancien' map of dynastic Europe into the modern map of national Europe.

POLISH ROMANTICISM AND INTERNATIONAL INSPIRATION

The Polish Romantic movement was born in the conservative atmosphere of the 1820s, not long after the pre-Napoleonic dynastic territories had been restored at the Congress of Vienna, and the Polish lands redistributed among Russia, Prussia, and Austria. It would be wrong to consider Polish

Romanticism merely as a literary movement or a fashion, for it corresponded to a protest against foreign occupation. In highly original form, it promoted an awareness of national history among the younger generation.

Three levels of Romanticism can be identified, each encompassing a greater proportion of Polish society and history. As a literary movement it is usually dated (perhaps rather too exactly) from 1822, when a volume of innovative folk ballads and romances entitled *Ballads and Romances*[11] was published in Wilno by Adam Mickiewicz (1797–1855), to the January Insurrection in 1863. As a response to foreign occupation it subsumed all writing, literary or journalistic, until 1918, and as a national paradigm, it survives to this day.

Mickiewicz turned to the model of peasant oral literature based on legend as closer to the spiritual heritage of the nation than the Classicists' irrelevant Latinate rhetoric. In what is regarded as the first ever Polish Romantic poem, entitled *Romanticality*, Mickiewicz explicitly rejects the mechanistic explanation of the world in favour of 'feeling and faith':

> Feeling and faith speak to me more powerfully
> Than the academic's eye-glass or empirical eye.
> You know only dead truths, which the peasants ignore
> You see a world in a grain of powder, and in each sparkle of the stars,
> But you know no living truths, and so will never see the miraculous!
> Take heart, and look into your heart . . . [12]

This argument between rationalism and passion had burst onto the literary scene some few years earlier in the polemic between the liberal Sentimentalist Kazimierz Brodziński (1791–1835) and the conservative Classicist Jan Śniadecki (1756–1830). Brodziński, the first ever lecturer in Polish literature, argued in his essay entitled *On Classicism and Romanticism* (1818), that the Slavs' natural pastoral pacifism required a more immediate and emotional form of expression, and a return to the simplicity of peasant values, and the recognition of the universal worth of finding 'happiness within limitations'. In his most popular work, *Wiesław* (1824), he portrays the sentimentalized love affair between Wiesław and Halina in an idyllic Cracovian village environment: marriage is happiness. For Brodziński Poland still lived on as an inviolable garden of innocence, which no foreign power politics could violate.[13]

His opponent, Śniadecki, was determined to protect the achievements and standards of the Classicist establishment from both weepy sentimentalism and dangerous ardent 'Romanticality':[14]

Let us Poles leave to others the field of glory, let us be humbler in our aspirations, and keep within the bounds of reason. Let us listen to the teachings of Locke in philosophy, heed the rules of Aristotle and Horace in literature, and remember

Bacon's laws in scientific observation and experimentation. Let us flee from Romanticality as a school of treachery and disease!

Romanticality tells us to abandon all the rules of art, to enhance meaning by dispensing with all restrictions; but let us determine to avoid anarchy and flights of fancy, for these lead not to meaning, but to chaos and barbarianism.[15]

In condemning the German Romantics' excessive mysticism, and their glorification of folksy superstitions Śniadecki quite rightly perceived how the proclamation of imagination over reason could undermine the social order.

An anecdotal indication of the confusion in the transitional period between Classicism and Romanticism is the thinking behind the decisions made at the Warsaw Office of Censorship, run by the proto-Hegelian Kalasanty Szaniawski. A one time radical with Jacobin leanings, Szaniawski became one of the most compliant functionaries within the administration of the Congress Kingdom; yet he approved wholeheartedly of Romanticism, as he knew it well in its conservative German guise. Instead he censored the odes and elegies of the liberal veterans of the Polish literary scene, while permitting the publication for many years of the Romantics' subversive anti-establishment works.[16]

Like Mickiewicz, many of the early Polish Romantics were from the Polish-speaking Western gubernias, and they opposed the conciliatory fatalism of the intellectual establishment in the Congress Kingdom. Both the stiff conservative Classicism of Śniadecki and Szaniawski and the compromise liberal position assumed by Brodziński were rejected quite contemptuously by these young innovators, who were not willing to be moulded by their elders, nor prepared to engage in the same arguments with the same terms of reference.

So at this early stage, Romanticism à la polonaise seemed to be developing into a vernacular translation of the general European model, delayed with respect to the German or English chronology, but in step with most of the rest of Europe, and in opposition to the Polish literary establishment. After Mickiewicz's first slim volume of poems had been so enthusiastically received, more and more writers in the Romantic 'style' proliferated as if dry scrubland had been set alight. Mickiewicz's lead was followed by the slightly older Ukrainian Pole Antoni Malczewski (1793–1826), whose *Maria* (1825), a Gothic tale of feuding families, murder, and revenge is set in the evocative and morose landscape of the Steppes in the seventeenth century. Like the German and English Romantics, such as Byron, Herder, Schelling, and Schiller, they began with a reassessment of man's relationship to his natural surroundings: they perceived the uniqueness of the natural environment in an emotional, and not a conventionalized way (and on this Brodziński agreed with the new writers). Secondly, European

Romanticism identified a gulf between the poet (idealized as a supremely sensitive, rebellious being who perceived the true nature of the world by divine intuition) and society, which sought comfort in order, dullness, and philistinism. In his perception of the world's ills the poet took it upon himself to break free from society's oppressive restrictions and guide mankind to the ultimate truths of existence, particularly the coexistence of the visible and 'invisible' worlds. This inherent conflict between an extraordinary individual and his banal society led inexorably to the third and closely related idea of the priority of individual freedom over convention. These core innovations of the European movement dominated the first stage of Polish Romanticism.

It regularly placed its characters (no longer merely heroes) as relatively insignificant beings in the threatening gloom of a hostile and wild landscape where survival depends on instinct and familiarity with nature's moods and incomprehensible extremes. This environmental challenge is seen as being more vital and sincere a challenge than the social conflict that constitutes the second theme: for here, Romantic man develops an awareness of history as an alternation of gradual and violent changes rather than as a recurrent pattern of moral and social choices.[17] The third theme, which portrays freedom as central to human happiness, underlies the psychological insight which is so characteristic of the Romantics. Reacting against what they saw as a repressive and restrictive hypocrisy on the part of their parents, these young men rejected enlightened 'civilization' as a farce, and longed for the uncluttered spontaneity of authentic human feelings among the poor peasants.

This then is why the Romantics' radical aesthetic and philosophical reassessment of the human condition was not welcomed by the cultural establishment in Warsaw or Wilno, Kraków or Lwów, as it implicitly criticized the enlightened liberals as a self-interested, opportunistic group of professionals, who had gained the confidence of the authorities, being equally willing to serve in the administration of the Commonwealth, the Duchy of Warsaw, and then in the posts available in the new Kingdom of Poland.[18]

Yet this aloof withdrawal perplexed the younger generation, who could not accept that such a disillusioned academic withdrawal from political and social issues was justified by the lessons of history. The utilitarian establishment felt these impetuous, inexperienced innovators were undermining their planned concerted effort to ensure cultural standards, even if it had to be in the political context of collaborating with an imposed administration.

The Romantics' rejection of the universalist ideals of the Classicists was not made out of hand: it became more obvious, however, as the young

shifted the emphasis from universal brotherhood and equality to a combination of individual commitment and universal justice within a national
morality, a concept which is so crucial in the later phases of Polish
Romanticism.[19]

THE SECOND STAGE: ROMANTICISM AS SUBVERSION

Polish Romanticism begins to develop its own features when it loses
interest in 'international' Romanticism (for the same reasons that it dis-
trusts the universalism of the Classical Enlightenment) and instead begins
to apply the new aesthetic with its questioning of the cultural status quo to
the specific social realities in which the new wave of writers had to
function. In fact this 'nationalization' of Romanticism is inherent in
Mickiewicz's early *Ballads*, but is foregrounded more clearly with each of
his successive works: in *Grazyna* (published in the second volume of
poetry, *Poetry Volume Two*, 1823) a 'Lithuanian romance' presents a
patriotic wife dying in the place of her treacherous husband when leading
his Lithuanian troops into battle against the Teutonic Knights; in the
Sonety krymskie of 1826, Mickiewicz's exiled alter ego rediscovers his
attachment to his homeland when exposed to the gorgeous but ultimately
alien landscape of the Crimea. This movement towards national
expression in Romantic form culminates in the hugely popular but morally
ambiguous *Konrad Wallenrod* (1828). At the same time this allegorical
poem is symptomatic of the change in direction away from the international model. In it Konrad, the Master of the Teutonic Knights (a
documented historical figure, Master 1391–3), consciously subverts the
Order's military dominance over the Lithuanians because of his own
Lithuanian origins.[20]

Mickiewicz's modification of the foreign prototypes was not immediately obvious. His version of man's close relationship to nature was in
keeping with a more politically active assessment of the peasantry,
exploited under the Commonwealth's feudal social structures. Since the
eighteenth century, many Poles of radical persuasion had worked for the
ideals of 'égalité' between the different classes of Polish society, but the
Romantic cult of the peasantry gave an additional emotional justification:
emancipation was linked to idolization, for the peasantry were the
spiritual backbone of the nation. The only hope for the political independence of Poland lay in the eradication of internal differences in favour of
an all-inclusive definition of nationality.

It was in the individual's relationship to conventional society that
Mickiewicz really made fundamental changes: he translated this into the
individual Pole's opposition to an alien colonial administration, and thus

sanctioned the personal subversion of all established authority which was seen to be imposed against the will of the nation: that the self (ego) should be sacrificed for the higher needs of the collective 'superego' is the central premise of *Konrad Wallenrod*.

This allegorized subversion of established norms by Mickiewicz is calculated to resist the imposition of an imperial colonial cultural model considered superior by the Russian colonial administrations. As a 'literary programme', this parallels the underground political activities of various Masonic lodges, radical student associations, and libertine groups during the early years of the Congress Kingdom, who sought other ways of influencing the Polish population by bypassing the stagnant elite.[21]

Such tactics were the result of the political reality of growing oppression in the Congress Kingdom from the early 1820s onwards. After the initial honeymoon, censorship (imposed by the Tsar's Viceroy, General Józef Zajączek in 1819) and violence, particularly after a campaign against illegal associations in Wilno in 1822–3, were used by all three partitioning powers (and not Russia alone) to control their Polish-speaking subjects. These moves were followed by Alexander's dismissal of the Polish Sejm in 1825. After the repression later that year of the Decembrist Uprising in Russia on Alexander's death, the young radicals could see no alternative to a long-term strategy of subversion to prepare the way for open revolt. Convinced of the moral justice of their cause, this generation matured in a period of creeping intervention and growing repression on the part of their Russian overlords, and as a result redirected their rhetoric of individualism, natural law, and freedom away from their compromised elders against their real political oppressors.

THE NOVEMBER UPRISING – THE 'POLISH REVOLUTION'

Suspicion and tension marked the entire reign of Alexander I's successor, Nicholas, dubbed 'Europe's policeman', whose personal fear of assassination or a coup d'état filtered all the way down through his refined security services and administrative officials. His repressive policies led in their turn to a widening among his Polish subjects of the gap between the liberal conciliators and the radical subversives, and inexorably to the 1830 November Uprising in the Kingdom of Poland, suppressed only after the ten-month 'Polish-Russian War' (1830–1).

Following the July Revolution in France, rumours had swept Warsaw that Nicholas intended to intervene in the events using his Polish armies. On 29 November 1830, a small group of Cadet officers sympathetic to the French revolutionaries, long frustrated by their superiors' conservatism and servility, staged a sudden coup d'état which forced their compatriots

to make a stark choice: allegiance to the cause of Poland or to their constitutional monarch. For most the 'November Night' was too much of a
dilemma, and the necessary unified front came too late in the 'war' to give
the politicians bargaining power to make Nicholas observe the limits set by
the Constitution, or to assure the hitherto independent Polish army of
success in fighting for a totally independent state.

In objective terms, the events of 1830–1 were a disaster for most Poles,
and it is difficult to perceive a clear policy behind the open squabbling and
factionalism that had led to constant changes in the insurrectionary
government. At first sceptical, the older generation had no real choice
other than to support this 'Polish Revolution', and its initial objective –
autonomy within the Empire. But Nicholas' refusal to negotiate led only to
a radicalization of the Polish position, and the official dethronement of the
Tsar on 25 January 1831 by the Sejm in the wake of calls for total independence. The social policies of the predominantly radical provisional governments, such as the emancipation of the peasantry, were not to their elders'
preference for 'order', but the young men had taken the message of St
Leonard's crypt to heart, and were actively revaluating the situation of
Poland in its past, present, and future. Combining the passion of Romanticism with the ideals of the French Revolution, and adding the urge for
national self-determination to the cocktail, these men represented everything that Nicholas and his successors condemned as the legacy of Polish
'anarchy', undermining as it did both the official ideology of Tsarist
absolutism, based on orthodoxy, autocracy, and (Russian) nationality,
and the European balance of power.[22]

LITERATURE AND THE BARRICADES

The origins of insurrection can be traced to two sources: first, as a justifi-
able rejection of tyranny by a whole society, as the French Revolution was
interpreted to have been by many. This was an extraordinary change in
Western culture: history was seen to be progressive (that is transformable,
with a hope of improving man's living conditions) rather than cyclical
(accepting the limitations of class, poverty, illness as constant factors).
What is important in the Poles' case is that the actual move towards revolution took place *after*, and not before the initial thrust of Romanticism had
had its effect. The emphasis on the rights of man as an individual, the
inherent equality of all men, and the promotion of democracy as *political*
justice are therefore subordinated during the 'Polish Revolution' to the
attainment of national equality with other nations, and freedom from the
status of a colony as *historical* justice. But the second, traditional reason
for rebelliousness was the gentry's centuries-old detestation of direction

from the capital: the practice of calling Confederations had been a form of political veto, saying no to 'absolutism'.

For the insurrectionaries, a titanic role-model was that of the now mythicized figure of Napoleon, the quintessential individual and 'genius of his age'. He was seen (particularly in retrospect) as the embodiment of the Romantic ideal: he represented the freedom of all peoples and nations, the individual striding through history and changing its course, all combined to create a nineteenth-century stereotype: the soldier struggling for great ideas, the crusader for equality and freedom.[23] The local Polish adaptation of this cult was the binary legend that Alexander had himself promoted: the twin guiding stars of Poniatowski and Kościuszko. The Romantic insurrectionaries sang songs of their mythical patrons who guided their every move:

> Look down on us, Kościuszko, from heaven,
> When we wade in our enemies' blood:
> We need your sword now
> To liberate the fatherland!
> *Polonaise*, by Rajnold Suchodolski[24]

Surprisingly, the rhetoric of this initially succesful 'Polish Revolution' had to rely on the panegyric models of Classicism (in a sense the Romantic lyric was predicated on failure, sacrifice, and despairing gestures); of Mickiewicz's works the propagandists chose to distribute his *Ode to Youth*, an ode to international brotherhood written in 1820 but censored. It was widely sung during the Uprising, and clearly it had circulated as a key subversive text for years. There were many poets of the moment: the young Juliusz Słowacki (born in 1809 he was some twelve years younger than Mickiewicz), his verse too was somewhat traditional, particularly his *Ode to Freedom*, and his popular *Hymn*, an invocation to the Virgin Mary:

> Oh Mother of God, Oh Virgin!
> Hear our prayer, oh Mother . . .
> This is our fathers' song.
>   Freedom's dawn gleams,
>   Freedom's bell rings out,
>   Freedom's blood boils.
>   Oh, Mother of God,
>   Bring before the Throne of the Almighty
>   The song of a free people.
>
> Raise your heads, oh Knights,
> Let the songs of freedom thunder.
> Moscow's towers will shake
> The Neva's cold granite
> Will I move with this song.[25]

He left Warsaw in the spring of 1831 on a diplomatic mission to the

West, and never returned from exile. Numerous other poets were active as
fighters and writers, but the titles of some collections will suffice to show
the general tone of the year: for example, the second rate poet Franciszek
Kowalski's *Sword and Lute* (1831), or Stefan Garczyński's *War Sonnets*
(not published until 1833 in Paris). Praising the troops' bravery, the reli-
ability of horse or sword in epic fashion, there was also a lyrical strain
which hearkened back to the 'alba' tradition of the young man (soldier)
bidding farewell to his sweetheart. What is interesting, is that in all these
works, the rhetoric was only slightly modified by Romantic diction; in
content, the solitary, doubt-ridden (possibly immoral) Byronic hero disappeared from view.[26]

The most influential figure of all was the critic Maurycy Mochnacki
(1803–34), who announced his rejection of writing for the glory of battle
in the foreword to his masterpiece of Romantic criticism, *On Polish
Literature in the Nineteenth Century* (1830):

It is now time to stop writing about art. We now have something else on our minds
and in our hearts. We have improvised the most beautiful of poems – a National
Uprising. All our life is now poetry. The clashing of arms and the noise of the
cannons – from this moment on that will be our rhythm and melody.[27]

Mochnacki effectively systematized the Polish Romantic movement and
showed how it had prepared the Poles for the Uprising, preparing them as
Wallenrods to become Poniatowskis. He underlined the connection
between national awareness and literature, when he wrote:

Hence literature is . . . a nation's conscience. This leads us to conclude that a nation
without its own original literature . . . is only a collection of people in a space
defined by arbitrary borders, and not yet a moral collective. It is not enough for us
to exist; we have to *know* we exist.

It was Poland's 'consciousness of its physical essence' that meant it would
survive all attempts to destroy it as a nation.[28]

But the Revolution was short lived: imperial Russia did not take kindly
to her recently acquired colony rejecting her protection. After a series of
battles, Warsaw was recaptured in September 1831 by the most able of the
Russian Generals, Paskevitch, who was made the Tsar's *namiestnik* or
Representative in recognition of his services. Paskevitch set about person-
ally supervising the dismantling of all Polish institutions (particularly, of
course, the separate Polish army), and as actual administration now came
direct from St Petersburg, the Kingdom was demoted to the status of a
slightly larger 'gubernia', and imperial Russian now became the Kingdom's official language. Later provisions included the abolition of the
separate Bank Polski and the replacement of the Polish złoty with the
rouble. In the Western gubernias of Russia, where sympathy for the Polish

Revolution had been widespread, the repressions were even harsher, with General Muravev ('the hangman') mercilessly rooting out all dissent.

EMIGRATION

Though thousands of officers and troops were exiled to Siberia or just enrolled in the Russian army in the Caucasus, about 10,000 of the country's elite were able to escape to the West, and were given asylum in a France grateful that the Uprising had prevented Russian interference in the July Revolution. This 'Great Emigration' was to become the centre of all Polish independent cultural activity, and a lobby of the Western powers on what came to be known (and often dismissed contemptuously) as the 'Polish Question'.

Therefore the third and final stage of Polish Romanticism is that which follows the defeat of the Uprising, and covers the years of a separation of the homeland (*kraj*) and the emigration between 1831 and 1864. For all Poles, whether in the three sectors or in exile, Romantic rhetoric and national tragedy became both a refuge and a rallying-call.

In one sense, 'Poland' now lived on in a diaspora. Following the collapse of the 'Revolution' in 1831, and the failure of direct armed struggle, the Poles in emigration debated the successes and mistakes they had made, and tried to reassess their political, social, and historical choices as if the whole nation were on trial. Though there were some who took an objective and quite critical view of events, the most pragmatic predictably being Prince Czartoryski, the self-appointed judges absolved the Poles of all blame, and instead accused the collusion of partitioning powers as led by the Tsar.

The poets in emigration had even greater authority than they had had at home, since so few politicians could provide answers to the nation's broken ideals or register and broadcast the gagged Kingdom of Poland's grief and pain. For the 1830s the spiritual leadership of the nation was considered to have passed to the poets, led by the dominant figure of all Polish literature subsequent to 1822, Adam Mickiewicz. There is no doubt that the texts he published in emigration encapsulated the hope, nostalgia, and anguish of a whole generation and its experience of history. He offered a moral and prophetic interpretation of recent history and a definition of what constituted 'Polishness', equating personal experience with national destiny.

In the disillusionment of defeat, Mickiewicz's works represent both the confession of a Polish exile and a directory of national morality, crowned by the heretical personal vision in the Biblical prophetic tradition, his *The Books of the Polish Nation and Its Pilgrimage* (Paris, 1833). In this work, Mickiewicz as inspired prophet provides an ethical and Messianic programme of 'action', of inner renewal for a nation sent into the desert, and exiled from the garden of Eden; the 'Polish pilgrimage' is ordained by God, part of his incomprehensible, but ultimately just plans for man:

And Jesus said: 'He who would follow me, let him leave his father and his mother, and risk his soul.' And the Pilgrim of Poland says: 'He who would follow freedom, let him leave his homeland, and risk his life.' For he who lives in the Fatherland, and accepts slavery, simply to save his own life, shall lose both his life and his father-land. But he who leaves the fatherland, and risks his life in order to defend freedom, shall gain both the Fatherland, and eternal life.[29]

The Polish myth of national resurrection from the ashes of history is perhaps the most powerful of all the sublimated ideas in this Romantic paradigm of personal and collective response to colonial domination. The purges of the student associations in which he was implicated as a student at the University of Wilno, his arrest and exile, were used by Mickiewicz as a personal analogy of the suffering that followed the collapse of the Uprising (and in which he had not participated) in the dramatized poem *Forefathers' Eve* (publ. Paris, 1833). Mickiewicz's portrayal of the evil empire of the devilish Tsar is centred around an unhappy lover, Gustaw, transformed into poet-cum-warrior Konrad at the behest of God himself, whose purpose in singling out the Poles for suffering and torture is to pre-pare them for their redemptive mission to Europe. Konrad *is* Poland, possessed by the forces of evil and the battleground between Good (Poland/the Virgin/oppressed nation) and Evil (Russia/Lucifer/the Tsar). Once exorcized of these forces, Konrad as horseman of the apocalyptic national liberation goes forth for the cause. *Forefathers' Eve* is the nationalized version of Christ's Agony in the Garden, allegorizing Mickiewicz's own experiences in a dramatized analogical reading of the Wilno trials as a personal November Uprising.[30]

The most powerful passages in the play show Konrad's Franciscan Confessor, Fr. Piotr in a state of trance, and in a vision he is informed that Konrad is the embodiment of the myth of Poland:

> Behold! A child, untouched, grows up as our Defender,
> The Saviour of our Nation!
>
> And his name shall be Forty Four!
>
> Wilt Thou not deign, O God our Lord, to hasten
> His coming, and console my people?
> But no; our race must bear these woes, for woes
> Refine and chasten.
> I see them, tyrannous bandits who have maimed
> My Fatherland! All Europe has come to scoff and shout:
> 'A Tribunal!' to which the murderous mob
> Drags off . . .

Oh Lord, now I see a Cross . . . and how long he must
Bear it!

They gather round – my Nation thrown to penance
Cries out 'I thirst!' So
Rakus gives vinegar and Borus bile,
And Mother Freedom kneeling weeps the while.

My beloved's head has fallen downward on his breast . . .
'Lord, why hast thou forsaken him,
Whom Thou hast blessed?'
It is done, he is at rest . . .

Forefathers' Eve, III, Scene 5[31]

It is in the idyllic epic, *Pan Tadeusz* (1834), that Mickiewicz brought together all these strands in a more digestible form. Different yet again from previous works, it is an 'autobiographical' epic poem, recounting the euphoria of the moment when Napoleon's troops liberated Lithuania en route to Moscow in 1811–12. Superficially a superior satire on the lifestyle of the Lithuanian gentry, *Pan Tadeusz* is also a subtle compilation of most of the themes in previous works, in a threatened Eden. Here, the mythicized 'old country's' virtues and vices are paraded, depicting the xenophobic anarchy that led to the Final Partition of 1795, but the work remains a loving portrayal of the characters, for all their faults. In essence, the message of the poem is the transformation of the gentry's local pride into commitment to the national cause. This Catholic mortality (selfishness replaced by self-sacrifice) is thus the real tenor of the work: the simple faith exemplified by the saint-hero, the Franciscan friar Jacek Soplica (expiating before God and country his youthful treacherous support of the Russians) is matched by the patriotic fervour of his son Tadeusz, who willingly abandons the pastoral innocence of youth to fight in the Napoleonic ranks.

Mickiewicz's works nationalized poetry and catholicized patriotism, and created a model of the ideal patriot to which all who were instilled with Polishness aspired. His works were read by the Polish nation in exile, and when possible, in Poland, as a *truer* picture of its situation and potential than could be formed from economic or political realities. The myth of a Covenant with God promising the resurrection of the Polish nation in body as well as in spirit was a message that permeated through the century down to virtually the whole Polish-speaking population. This prophetic tradition was suspicious of politics or diplomacy as these were seen as an immoral compromise.

In emigration Słowacki became very jealous of Mickiewicz's influence. His *Kordian* (Paris, 1834) is a very different assessment of the underground ferment in the Congress Kingdom during the 1820s to that of

Mickiewicz's evocative drama. Young Kordian embodies the moral and political hesitations of that crucial generation who initiated the 'Polish Revolution'. Kordian is drawn into the conspiratorial underground more out of 'ennui' than conviction, and is selected to assassinate the Tsar but his doubts and fears cause him to fail (Nicholas did indeed come to Warsaw in 1827 to be crowned King of Poland and it was indeed rumoured that a plot had been thwarted). The main character rehearses in his mind contemporary arguments on the justification for regicide versus the need for revolution that eventually led to the Uprising.

More of a poet than a prophet, Słowacki's mature works were rather alien to the emigrés. They did not like his ambiguous idea of the Pole as torn between the laudable aspirations of his 'angelic soul', and the repeated disappointment caused by the selfish demands of a 'coarse body'.[32] Słowacki's concept of transcendence was rather different to that of Mickiewicz. He conceived a very personal philosophical system founded on the revelation that 'all things were created by the Spirit for the Spirit' and the poet's task was to recount the workings of the Spirit, the 'Eternal Revolutionary', whose advance through history is marked by pain and bloodshed. Słowacki's mystical system is presented in the poem *The Genesis from the Spirit* (1844), which explains how the Spirit is moving the world to ever greater perfection, though in creating the imperfect material world it necessarily contradicts its spiritual aspirations. To overcome this imperfection, the Spirit constantly destroys what it has created in order to reconstruct a more perfect version. The Spirit's force in the evolution of the universe is therefore manifest in the succession of ever better reincarnations of matter. To Słowacki the tortured spirits of the Polish nation had gone through the greatest number of 'reincarnations' and were therefore the most advanced along the spiritual path to the 'state of Light'.[33]

Many combinations of Catholicism, Romanticism, and historically determined justice appeared. Particularly striking is the *Undivine Comedy* (1835) of Zygmunt Krasiński (1812–59), the most successful of the tragedies written in Polish in the Romantic period, where Classical Necessitas is replaced by History, and the teeming masses avenge centuries of repression by the decadent aristocracy in an orgy of bloody revolution. But this is certainly no socialist vision. For Krasiński, historical progress cannot bring human perfection or the realization of utopia without Divine Grace, so man is predestined to rebellion and crime, redeemable only through God's direct intervention. Poetry for Krasiński can point to the truth, but cannot redeem. Though the hordes overcome the last bastion of the ancien régime in an orgy of bloodshed and ideology, the appearance of Christ renders the class struggle senseless.[34]

DARKNESS AND DESPAIR

In the Congress Kingdom, the period after 1831 is known as the 'Paskevitch night', and it lasted oppressively until the coincidence of the Tsar's death in 1855 and the Representative's death in 1856. For those twenty-five years the notorious Third Department was relatively successful in tracing small opposition groups, mostly students desperate to prove their radical and conspiratorial credentials. While there was very little public manifestation of Polish national aspirations at all, other than official tolerance of harmless folksy idylls, what little activity there was took place subversively in people's homes, or at best in small clandestine patriotic gatherings, where a sense of national unity was promoted by the recitation of songs and poems of the November Uprising, of the Napoleonic Wars, or even of the patriotic songs from the previous century.

The reading of illegally imported books and pamphlets printed in Paris and elsewhere was in fact an extremely dangerous enterprise, but was quite widespread. Yet the bonds created by participating in such illegal activities caused each household to see itself as a Poland in miniature, and each individual to see himself as a responsible citizen perpetuating the national ethos in every action and statement he made. Thus parents, and to a certain extent the Church, took it upon themselves to provide an alternative system of schooling in a sub-culture based mostly on oral literature and history which was thus difficult for the Tsarist authorities to detect and control, but, because of the emotional complicity, also morally binding on the participants.

As time passed in the Congress Kingdom, a second and third Romantically minded generation appeared, no longer in conflict with Polish Classicism, but struggling for its identity in the face of imperial repression, and rejecting the complacency of the submissive 'salon' society in the 1840s, they tried to encourage their downtrodden compatriots to follow Mickiewicz's programme for internal moral transfiguration, that each Pole should become a Wallenrod. This conspiratorial culture was often in poetic form, being easy to memorize and pass on, and this obviously helped to extend the 'bards'' moral authority among their readers. The main purpose of such poetry was no longer insurrection but propaganda, and hence the criticism that the poetry of the Polish 'underground' was too cliché-ridden and emulative of the emigré models.[35]

Typical of the tone and imagery of the patriotic strain of Polish culture in the mid-century is this section of an unself-consciously dreadful and long patriotic work by the mediocre poet Franciszek Morawski (1783–1861), *My Grandfather's Estate*, written in 1851:

In Polish blood there is that valiant spark,
A holy, all-powerful, immortal spark
Smouldering in its secretive ardour,
Turning a threatening red hot at the mention of 'fatherland'
A spark that flares up at words from the heart,
Or visions of the soul, in those who lie
In chains, or beneath the executioner's axe . . .
That selfsame spark that burned in the bosom
Of our fathers and grandfathers, and now smoulders
In us, their sons, and will enflame their grandsons.
Crush it beneath gravestones, or mountainous force,
And yet it shines on, through tombs and darkest night![36]

THE PHILOSOPHICAL RESOLUTION

While literary life in the Congress Kingdom stagnated in the 1830s and
1840s, an alternative, more integrated and reflective response was
developing in the Prussian Sector, where the lead was taken by the
philosophers. In *Features of the National Soul*, published in Paris in 1847,
Bronisław Trentowski (1808–69) advocated that the spiritual leadership
of the nation should be taken away from the irresponsible poets, and given
to philosophers, thereby paving the way to true independence through
inner liberation.[37]

Here was a Hegelian synthesis of two distinct schools: the French
'philosophy of action' and the German idealist 'philosophy of thought';
out of this there developed a Polish philosophy of praxis, which envisaged
a gradual change of the world in the desired direction, starting with the
moral conversion of mankind, and ending in the emancipation of the
Polish nation. This could only realistically come about after philosophy
applied itself to solving practical problems: the education of the nation,
and the improvement of welfare, dubbed 'organic work'. The main concerns also included the reconciliation of philosophy with religion, as it was
reasoned that religion was the main world view of the masses, and that any
transformation of the national predicament would reuire the masses' participation. The natural religious wisdom of the peasants would provide a
firm base for changing the world's consciousness. This approach conveniently bypassed the issue of the widespread disaffection with the
Catholic hierarchy's disinterest in the lot of its congregations, while recognizing that Poles were beginning to identify with their Catholic heritage in
order to withstand the pressures on the part of the Orthodox Russian and
Protestant Prussian authorities. Only in the Austrian Sector was Catholicism a hindrance rather than a support to the Polish cause. As in France
and Italy, where many emigrés were based, progressive social ideas were
often integrated with Catholic populism.[38]

The most impressive convergence of these ideas can be found in the work of the prolific writer August Cieszkowski (1814–94), editor of the *Warsaw Library*, a journal that was central to the intellectual life of the Kingdom after 1831. In his desire to transcend the idealism of philosophy, he promoted the association of different parties within the 'Society of the Friends of Progress' in Posen in the Prussian Sector when he moved from Warsaw in 1842. His work *Our Father* (publ. Paris, 1848) was completed only at the end of the century, based on his interpretation of the Lord's Prayer as revelation: he divided history into three ages, that of Father, Son, and Holy Spirit. In the last age, the age of action and emancipation, 'Christianity is by no means the final and absolute sphere of the development of the human spirit.'[39] He explicitly criticizes the Christian world picture, as it 'divorces man from his positive qualities', ascribing them to God, and thus creating an unbridgeable chasm that by definition accepts the existence of evil and unhappiness as natural. His new 'religion of the Holy Spirit' aimed at the moral education of collective man in peace and in his diversity. Cieszkowski rejected revolution as retrogressive barbarianism, and instead looked forward in almost millenarian terms to a new society. This was a programme equal to Mickiewicz's in its vast aspirations, but could not equal it in popular attraction:

The differences between Mickiewicz's and Cieszkowski's Messianisms reflects the difference between the two basic trends in nineteenth-century Polish political life: the insurrectionary (or if the social emphasis was strong enough, the revolutionary) trend, and the trend which saw the way to national regeneration in the legal 'organic progress'. Seen in the broadest perspective, the two Messianisms were in fact two solutions (heroism or anti-heroism) to the Polish dilemma.[40]

It is in the poetic legacy of Cyprian Kamil Norwid (1821–83) that the arguments for the anti-heroic solution come to the fore. Though he published (at his own expense) a thick volume of poems entitled simply *Poems* in 1863, their dense, ornate, and parabolic stylization and opaque didacticism proved to be too great a change of direction from the obligatory national Romantic rhetoric that had by then dominated Polish culture for forty years. Norwid's impressionable adolescence was spent in Paskevitch's Warsaw, and the covert imagery that was criticized as a 'mannered unclarity of thought' was in fact an alternative response to repression, a search for a new idiom. For Norwid, Romanticism had deflected the national cause by creating a fictitious and overwhelming concept of the 'suffering nation' to the detriment of day-to-day 'humanity'. Only the lesson of the Christian Gospel showed the way out of the mental cul-de-sac to which the three 'bards' (Mickiewivz, Słowacki, and Krasiński) had led the Poles: in the equation of morality and politics made by the Romantics he reminded them of the superiority of personal over national morality, of the dignity of work over the conspiratorial ethic.

When he left the Congress Kingdom in 1846 to live abroad, settling eventually in Paris, Norwid tried to revise the dangerously attractive conclusion that the Polish experience was a universal one. His writing encompasses Romanticism, Realism, and Symbolism, and his main concern is not the 'Poles' but man and the illusory fictions and ideologies he creates to substantiate his inadequacies. Like many of his contemporaries, Norwid sought to find the mechanism that directed human affairs (he termed it 'Providence'), and his techniques of investigation (irony, unspoken conclusions, allegory, and a revaluation of the meaning of silence) attempt to locate the source and implications of the 'invisible and silent interior truths of the universe'.

Abstract, archaic, and complex with multiple significances, Norwid demanded a high intellectual interaction from his readers which was usually beyond them. Undoubtedly a more original thinker and poet than his predecessors, Norwid's apparent crankiness and seeming criticism of the Romantic ethos led to his being shunned by the emigré community in Paris. He died in a poor-house in 1883 his work forgotten until rediscovered in the twentieth century.[41]

By the late 1850s, following the deaths of Tsar Nicholas and Novosiltsev in the Kingdom, a fleeting opportunity for independence was seen in the Crimean War of 1855–6 (during which Adam Mickiewicz died attempting to set up a Polish legion in Istanbul), and it seemed as if a wind of change might sweep the Empire and improve the fortunes of the unhappy Polish subjects of the new Tsar, Alexander II. Though he warned them he had no intention to grant anything approaching autonomy in his apocryphal words 'Pas de rêveries, messieurs', nonetheless a significantly more liberal climate followed his accession.

The loosening of control did lead to a rise of patriotic feeling in the Kingdom, and the conspiratorial underground saw hope of extending its influence and eventually organizing another national uprising. Until the late fifties, other than some sparse activity by the Poles in the Austrian Sector and Prussian Sector in 1846 and 1848, the divided Polish populations had been somewhat reticent to expose themselves so soon after the catastrophe of 1831. Particularly the events in Galicia in 1846, when an uprising of the Polish gentry was bloodily hacked to pieces by the local peasantry (paid by the Austrian authorities for each 'rebel' head they brought in), called into question many Romantic assumptions about the peasantry's natural pride in its Polishness. The Tsarist authorities tried to preempt the plotters by implementing a general conscription of all able-bodied young men on 13 January 1863, but as the police and security agencies were as rife with double agents as the underground, the conspirators ordered the young men into the forest a day early, and long drawn out guerrilla war followed that was doomed to failure, however well organized it seemed. The repressions that followed in 1864 after all the leaders had been rounded up and executed were harsher even than those in 1831. The Congress Kingdom was reduced to a border province, and for forty years Russian imperial 'realism' was imposed on a disillusioned population, which turned to 'organic work' and the anti-heroism of the 1840s' philosophers to disperse its national energy in welfare, education, and industry.

National Romantic idealism underpinned all the moves made towards self-determination in the nineteenth century, symbolized by the dates 1830, 1846, 1848, 1855, 1863, and in part also (in the Congress Kingdom) in the Revolution of 1905. Despite superficial changes in literary taste or artistic style, the *content* of Polish nineteenth-century culture was always the same: national Romanticism. It varied of course from individual to individual, but even organic work was a sublimated form of conspiracy predicated on the ultimate goal of the Polish pilgrimage: liberation and freedom. While not successful as an active insurrectionary tactic, Romantic subversion consolidated the national identity and outlived the colonial structures of repression and subjection.

CONCLUSION

The Polish Romantics' conception of history is rather different from that of the Western Romantics. It is not a continuous sequence which is open to interpretation. Even today, Poles are essentially unanimous about their historical heritage: a closed, repetitive cycle of dates and actions affirming their moral right to be an independent nation against often insurmountable opposition from their neighbours, and disinterest on the part of countries further away. In their view, history is not an objective set of facts, but a *morality play* like *Forefathers' Eve* that revolves around the same truths: the victimization of the Poles, and their collective struggle to resist national extinction. History is therefore a parable on self-sufficiency, self-determination, and self-definition. This is why the Polish experience has created an enclosed culture making use of the Romantic paradigm and perceiving the world exclusively through that struggle for nationhood and national dignity.

One of the conclusions of Polish Romanticism is that no individual can be truly free if he does not belong to a nation that is independent. Their sensitivity to both the subtle and brutal methods of foreign intervention and control has not surprisingly made the Poles distrust 'objective', foreign interpretations of their history. Critical accounts of their struggles and their achievements remind them of the concerted campaigns of Russification and Germanization in the second half of the last century. On the other hand objectivity undermines the emotional, subjective (not to say 'Romantic') attachment of each Pole to the national cause, and questions his identity. These two reasons cause the Poles strongly to resist any historical analysis that does not support the idealized vision of Polish suffering and resurrection.

It might seem that there are few parallels to the partition of the Poles which was the coincidental environment in which Romanticism developed, for the Poles maintain that their experience was and is unique. While this may be true within Europe, the examples of nations being arbitrarily divided by (European) colonial powers for the sake of peace, or the balance of power, are manifold. The history and development of the Kurds and Armenians, of the Indian subcontinent and the whole of Africa are a constant reminder of the damage such expansionism can do to smaller nations. A useful parallel might be that of the Somalis, who are divided to this day as a result of the Berlin Conference that parcelled out Africa's territories among the European powers in 1888: today's Republic of Somalia comprises former British Somaliland and Italian Somaliland, while former French Somaliland now has separate political status as Djibouti (Somalis still comprise significant minorities within the artificial post-colonial states of Kenya and Ethiopia). The conclusion of one commentator, that 'the Somalis' dream of independence was in part a dream of unification'[42] equally encapsulates the essence of all the aspirations that the Poles voiced during the nineteenth century. The Kingdom of Poland, the Kingdom of Galicia and Lodomeria, and the Duchy of Posen were similarly states of colonial convenience and political mystification whose duration (even when renamed) has had typical consequences for the post-colonial independent state: a tension between colonial inertia and the need for national collective enthusiasm.

Nineteenth-century colonialism, the era of the 'territorial imperative' distrusted the concept of nation so consistently promoted by the Romantics, and instead preferred to promote a sense of duty to the imperial state, ensured by a whole series of measures and controls: in the various Polish-speaking territories of the three empires after 1831 competence was required in the relevant imperial language, as the monopoly of control and information resided with the native speakers of the imperial power, thus rendering entire populations dependent on the metropolitan centre. More disturbing, perhaps, is the morality of colonialism, which holds its cultural and social model to be more sophisticated than those it replaces. Such a superiority complex not too surprisingly initiated 'cultural warfare' between the indigenous, traditionally anarchic, multicultural decentralized structures of the former Commonwealth, and the new masters' alien, monolithic, centralized autocracies. As the century progressed, particularly in Russia and Austria, the obsession with security and control of their multicultural empires gained such priority over efficiency, education, and integration that the results were mismanagement, tensions between the nationalities, and corruption. These stagnant societies based on the myth of imperial magnanimity, and, in effect, racial superiority, refused to deal with the real needs of those nations for whom they had become responsible. This created immediate resentment and hatred, which the arbitrary generosity founded on 'divide et impera' could not contain.[43]

The resilience of Polish culture to alien pressures is due primarily to the recognition of a specific national identity defined by language and traditional values which Romanticism (despite its initial destabilization of the Classicist order) successfully deepened and broadened: 'In the final analysis, the shallowness of the imported institutions was due to the culture gap between the new structures and the ancient values, between alien values and the ancestral tradition.'[44] It is this conflict that is resolved in works such as *Forefathers' Eve*.

The triple heritage of Polish culture is a complex of Catholic morality, republican anarchy, and the unique experience of inner-European colonialism. Romanticism erupted at the moment when the Poles and the Russians were exchanging roles: from monolithic to multicultural, dominant to secondary state, a process that had begun far earlier, and which was not completed until 1945. While Russia grew thanks to aggressive, all-powerful Tsars, the aesthetics of Imperialism saw Russia, like Rome subjugating Greece, wanting at first to acquire some of the Poles' sophistication once the Polish territories had been acquired by political ruthlessness and military power. In one sense, therefore, the final partition did not take place until 1831, delayed in part by the Napoleonic episode, and Alexander's pseudo-liberalism and magnanimous gestures.

It was thus within this imposed order that a subversive strategy of Polishness was adopted (national Romanticism), which ensured the permanence of the identity of the Poles far from the idyllic garden of innocence, in the political and cultural wilderness. Polish Romanticism's concept of personal experience as the reflection of national (and, by curious extension, universal) history substantially revised the cliché of the conflict between the artist and society, and instead substituted the model of the artist/poet and society in conflict with an alien administration. This subversive formula underpinned much of nineteenth-century Polish culture and insurrectionary action. The Poles, like the Somalis, were a stateless nation, given coherence through poetry, for underneath the structures of control, means to realize Alexander's intention to 'make Russians of them', the Poles developed a 'culture of cooperation' based on the collective dream of independence and reunification for which the medium was Romanticism.

NOTES

This article concentrates mainly on events within the Russian Sector (the Congress Kingdom and the Western gubernias) and the emigration in Paris, because these were the centres of Polish cultural geography during the first half of the nineteenth century. Detailing political, social, and cultural variations in the Austrian and Prussian Sectors would have made the article more unwieldy than it is at present.

1 A. Kijowski, *O dobrym naczelniku* (Warszawa, 1984), p. 35. For biographical details of Poniatowski in French, consult S. Aszkenazy, *Le Prince Joseph Poniatowski* (Paris, 1921).

2 The historical background can be read in English from the following sources: *The Cambridge History of Poland*, vol. 2: *From Augustus II to Pilsudski. 1697–1935*, ed. W. F. Reddaway *et al.* (Cambridge, 1941); A. Zamoyski, *The Polish Way* (London, 1987); and I would particularly recommend the informative volume by Piotr Wandycz, *The Lands of Partitioned Poland, 1795– 1918* (Washington, DC, 1974).

3 See particularly Marian Kukiel, *Adam Czartoryski and European Unity 1770–1861* (Princeton, NJ, 1955), and Patricia K. Grimstead, *The Foreign Minister of Alexander I* (Berkeley, California, 1969).

4 Sobieski's life is treated in J. B. Morton's *Sobieski, King of Poland* (London, 1932).

5 The other five kings would include, in my reckoning, Henri de Valois (1573–4, French); István Báthory (1575–86, Transylvanian); Sigismund Vasa (1586– 1632, half-Swedish, half-Polish); and Augustus II and III of Saxony (1697– 1733 and 1733–64, respectively).

6 Quoted in Kujowski, *O dobrym naczelniku*, p. 36.

7 *Ibid.*, p. 38.

8 For general background on the Polish-Lithuanian Commonwealth, the most recently published works in English include: Norman Davies, *God's Playground* (Oxford, 1981), the whole of vol. 1 deals with Polish history up to the Final Partition in 1795; and *A Republic of Nobles: Studies in Polish History to 1864*, ed. J. K. Fedorowicz, M. Bogucka, and M. Samsonowicz (Cambridge, 1982).

9 The 'Confederation of Bar' is still hotly disputed among historians, as to whether it was patriotic or reactionary, since it provoked both Russian military intervention and a Ukrainian national uprising. Essentially it was both, and Stanisław August underestimated the resistance to both his new centralism and the new imported 'foreign' liberal ideology that lay behind reform. Perhaps he played his hand too early. See particularly W. Konopczyński, *Konfederacja Barska*, 2 vols. (Warszawa, 1936–87); the introduction to a selection of the vast literature produced by the Confederates is also very informative, written by J. Maciejewski in *Literatura barska* (Wrocław, 1976).

10 Davies, *God's Playground*, vol. 1, pp. 541–6.

11 Mickiewicz's *Ballads* are mentioned for the first time en passant in John Bowring's early anthology of Polish poetry, *Specimens of the Polish Poets* (London, 1827); a translation of the *Ballads* was not, however, made until 1925, when a team of translators under George Rapall Noyes produced *Konrad Wallenrod and Other Writings of Adam Mickiewicz* (Berkeley, California). It also includes a translation of the later *Books of the Polish Nation and Polish Pilgrimage*.

12 *Romantyczność*, lines 64–9. It is available in translation in the Rapall Noyes edition.

13 Brodziński was the first lecturer in Polish literature at the recently established University of Warsaw (founded 1817). His 'Arcadian' sentiment was attacked particularly violently by the Romantic critic, Maurycy Mochnacki (of whom more later on); Mochnacki decried Brodziński's 'effeminate pastoralism', pointing to the repressions in the real Congress Kingdom as a 'serpent that has crept into the garden, since when thorns, thistles, as well as parasitic weeds grow where once milk and honey flowed so generously' (*Kurier Polski*, 1830, no. 159).

14 Many of the plans of the Enlightenment's luminaries were paradoxically realized *after* 1795, such as the founding of Towarzystwo Przyjaciół Nauk (The Society of the Friends of Learning) (1800) and the University of Warsaw (1817). The establishment's liberal Classicist programme saw its primary task as laying firm foundations for Polish education and philosophy, and the undoubted achievements of a period all too easily dismissed by the victorious Romantic camp as dull and conciliatory includes the publication of St B. Linde's monumental *Słownik języka polskiego* (*The Dictionary of the Polish Language*), which appeared in 1807–14.

15 Śniadecki, *O pismach klasycznych i romantycznych*, in *Dziennik Wileński*, 1 (1819), vol. I, 25. Mickiewicz's attack on the staid rationalism of the academic in his poem *Romantyczność* (quoted above) has always been read as a personal reference to Śniadecki.

16 Andrzej Walicki, *Philosophy and National Romanticism: The Case of Poland* (Oxford, 1982), p. 102.

17 Maria Janion and Maria Żmigrodzka, *Romantyzm i historia* (Warsaw, 1978), pp. 134–9. The authors consider that Romantic individualism had two distinct faces: 'a nostalgic (selfish) negation of history, condemning all of society and progress, and based on purely intimate, private experience, or it could be (and in Poland usually was) a passionate desire to participate in the historical process, searching for the ultimate source of human dignity' (p. 139).

18 See Alina Witkowska, *Literatura romantyzmu* (Warsaw, 1986), pp. 5–17.

19 The introduction to a selection of polemical texts from the 1820s made by Stefan Kawyn, *Walka romantyków z klasykami* (Wrocław, 1960), pp. iii–lxxxviii, is extremely informative for those who read Polish; otherwise, the résumé in Piotr Wandycz's chapter, 'The era of late Classicism and early Romanticism', in his *The Lands of Partitioned Poland 1795–1918*, pp. 92–102, can be recommended.

20 Adam Mickiewicz and his works are discussed in English in David Welsh's volume, *Adam Mickiewicz* (New York, 1966).

'21 See A. Kamiński, *Polskie zwigzki młodzieży w pierwszej połowie XIX*, 3 vols. (Warszawa, 1959–68).

22 Davies, *God's Playground*, vol. 2, pp. 85–6.

23 Janion and Żmigrodzka, *Romantyzm i historia*, pp. 213–43.

24 *Ibid.*, p. 97. Suchodolski died in the final defence of Warsaw, in September 1831.

25 *Hymn* (1830), lines 1–15, quoted also in Janion and Żmigrodzka, *Romantyzm i historia*, p. 433.

26 Witkowska, *Literatura romantyzmu*, pp. 74–5.

27 M. Mochnacki, *O literaturze polskiej w dziewiętnastym wieku* (Warsaw, 1830; reprinted Łódź, 1985), p. 39.

28 *Ibid.*, pp. 66–7.

29 A Mickiewicz, *Księgi narodu i pielgrzymstwa polskiego* (Paris, 1833), Book VII, verses 1–3.

30 Analogical thinking is gradually being seen as the key to Mickiewicz's literary transformation of the Biblical and patriotic materials into his various works. In the introduction to *O dobrym naczelniku*, Andrzej Kijowski gives a fascinating (though wordy) explanation of analogy as the medium by which patriotic Romanticism used history to create a sense of national identity: 'A hero is a social creation, produced at a moment when history affects all members of society; it is the moment when a nation's future is seen to hang in the balance, and which by virtue of its content and tone is easily associated with the past; in other words, this is the moment of historical relevance. Actions and people caught up in these events seem familiar, as all those participating seem to be transported to another dimension. They dress up in costumes, and in word, gesture and behaviour act out the roles they have learnt from history. Thus this is a crucial moment, when societies are capable of great efforts when lent wings by their historical memory, and because they are conscious of their role, and are enriched by identifying with their forefathers. Thus society is brought together as a nation (societies are not automatically nations, entities defined by a common past and future).

    'A society's sense of identity can become stronger than its instinct for survival, when the models from the past gain greater authority than living leaders, who in turn can only gain authority in as much as they identify with those models. This society, overcome by a "psychosis of history", is not held back by the need to make great sacrifices, since its members are determined to conform to the analogies which have imposed themselves (or more frequently, are imposed on them by others). This is both a great and dangerous moment, for historical analogy obscures the capacity either of individuals (even leading figures) or the collective as a whole to assess a situation pragmatically; this produces stereotypical thoughts and emotions which lead to spontaneous reactions that can have catastrophic consequences. The nation and its leaders behave as if on stage, playing their roles imposed on them by history in front of an audience of posterity, whom the nation is determined to impress, rather than showing concern about immediate advantages and risks.' *O dobrym naczelniku*, pp. 14–15.

31 *Dziady III*, scene V, lines 20–59. One explanation of how myth is connected to the creation of a national Romantic ethos is furnished by Kijowski further on in the same introduction: 'Myth tells of events as they should have happened, to fulfil their salutary purpose; the forces of good do battle in myth with those of evil, the way things should have happened is in conflict with the way they actually did occur: a fundamental source of myth is thus a faith in the eternal ascendancy of good and its certain ultimate victory: this is why myth

treats history as a value system which expresses itself in the archaic language of the fable or fairy tale.' *Ibid.*, p. 29.

32 J. Słowacki, *Podróż do Ziemi Świętej z Neapolu* (*A Journey to the Holy Land from Naples*), canto VIII, lines 91–6. Canto VIII was published in Paris in 1840 as *Grób Agamemnona* (*Agamemnon's Tomb*); the rest of the *Journey* was not published until after the author's death.

33 J. Słowacki, *Genezis z Ducha* (Paris, 1844).

34 Janion and Żmigrodzka, *Romantyzm i historia*, pp. 161–4.

35 The whole problem of Romanticism as a 'style' in the Congress Kingdom, particularly after 1831, was considered during a Conference held in Warsaw on 6–7 December 1982, published as *Style zachowań romantycznych*, ed. Maria Janion and Marta Zielińska (Warszawa, 1986), pp. 15–121.

36 F. Morawski, *Dworzec mojego dziadka*, written 1851, lines 881–90, published in *Pisma zbiorowe wierszem i prozą*, ed. St Tarnawski, 4 vols. (Poznań, 1882).

37 B. Trentowski, *Wizerunki duszy narodowej* (Paris, 1847).

38 Walicki, *Philosophy and National Romanticism*, pp. 242–6.

39 A. Cieszkowski, *Ojcze nasz* (Poznań, 1922), vol. 3, p. 279.

40 Walicki, *Philosophy and National Romanticism*, p. 207.

41 Norwid's work is discussed in English in Jerzy Peterkiewicz's excellent essays, 'Introducing Norwid', in *The Slavonic and East European Review*, 27, 68 (1948); and 'Cyprian Norwid's vade-mecum: an experiment in didactic verse', in *The Slavonic and East European Review*, 44, 102 (1966), 66–75. A complete study of Norwid in English is by George Gömöri, *Cyprian Norwid* (New York, 1974).

42 A. Mazrui, *The Africans*, BBC Publications (London, 1986), p. 71.

43 'It would be wrong to see the hundred years between the Napoleonic wars and the Great War of 1914 purely in terms of conspiracies and insurrections. Oppressed peoples do revolt, but they also carry on eating, working and breeding, and it is these unspectacular activities which absorb the overwhelming share of the national effort at all but the most critical times. The Poles were no exception, and their instinct was to get on with life as best they could. It was the inability of the three Powers to provide a congenial framework within which their new subjects could live that kept the Polish problem in an explosive state. Moral considerations aside, they cannot escape the charge of extraordinarily inept colonialism. During a century when states like Britain and France could easily and profitably control vast and populous continents, the three greatest Powers of the European mainland devoted incomparably greater resources in troops, funds and gigantic bureaucracies to policing a small, thinly populated and easily accessible country in their midst, with lamentable results. The only thing that made Poland a difficult country to colonise successfully was that the legacy of the Commonwealth did not include a native civil service or police force which would have been employed by the new masters. The entire apparatus of social control had to be imported, with the result that authority never lost its alien garb': Zamoyski, *The Polish Way*, p. 301.

44 *Ibid.*, p. 20. Further information on Somali literature and culture can be found in *Literatures in African Languages. Theoretical Issues and Sample Surveys*, ed. B. W. Andrzejewski, S. Piłaszewicz and W. Tyloch (Warsaw, 1985). B. W. Andrzejewski's survey of Somali literature is fascinating in the context of the oral transmission of much of Polish Romantic nationalism (pp. 337–407). It

also contains a useful bibliography. Note also B. W. Andrzejewski's 'Poetry in Somali society', in J. B. Pride and J. Holmes (eds.), *Sociolinguistics: Selected Readings* (Harmondsworth, 1972), pp. 252–9.

Index

absolutism: Austrian, 228; enlightened, 220; Tsarist, 326
aesthetics: in Germany, 111–12; reverie, 126; in Switzerland, 140; in Spain, 260–3; freedom of expression, 273; Spanish painting, 281
Agardh, C. A., 183–5
Alexander, I, Tsar, 137–8, 325, 327, 339
Alexander II, Tsar, 336, 339
Almquist, C. J. L., 174, 186, 188
Amsterdam, 174, 202; theatre in, 205, 209; Jews in, 208
ancien régime, Introduction, *passim*, 45, 159, 196
ancient civilisation, in Greece, and of Greek descent, 97–111
Andrew II (of Hungary), 222–3
Anglo-Irish, 62, 69–71, 74–6, 79, 82–4
Annally, Lord, 80–1
anti-Romantic movements, in Greece, 93
anti-Semitism, 214
Arany, J., 218, 222, 236–7
architecture, Russian, 300–2, 311
Arnim, A. von, 110, 120–1
Art: modernist, 40; paintings in London, 57; German Romanticism and science, 109–12; Romanticism of, 118–27; and faith, and science, 120; theory and criticism of, 120–1; Classical, 122–4; German Romantic painting, 125–6; Swiss patronism of, 146; Modern Movement, 163; Swiss painting, 167; fine arts in Spain, 264; in Spain, 281; in Russia, 284
artists: painters, 109–10, 121, 126; Swiss, 140; Russian, 302–7, 311
Art Nouveau, 163, 302–3, 307, 314
atheism, 188; in Germany, 127
Athens University, 104–5; and professors, 98

Atterbom, P. D. A., 174, 178, 180, 185, 188
Aubigné, J. H. Merle d', 207, 213
Avellaneda, Gertrudis Gómez de, 266, 275, 279

Babits, M., 235
Bach, J. S., 294
Bacon, F., 197, 322
Balakirev, M. A., 311
Balakirev circle, 308, 311–12
ballet, Russian, 312–14
Balzac, H. de, 127, 252, 292
Baptists, in Wales, 10; Welsh minister, 16
Batthyány, Count L., 232
Batyushkov, K., 286, 288
Baudelaire, C., 173, 242, 255, 258
beauty, in Keats' poetry, 61; of nature, 124; ideals of, 125
Beddoes, T. L., 224
Beethoven, L. van, 122, 294, 309
Belinsky, V. G., 293–4
Bentham, J., 226
Berchtolsheim, Baroness von, 193
Berlin, 110
Berlinger, J., 123
Berlioz, H., 1, 9, 310, 312
Bernadotte, Marshall J. B., *see* Carolus Johannes XIV
Berzelius, J. J., 182
Bestuzhev, A., 287–8, 293
Bible, 25, 54, 57, 98, 119, 240
Bilderdijk, I., 201
Bilderdijk, W., 192–214 *passim*; *About the Alphabet*, 196; *The Animals*, 201; *Brief Account of a Remarkable Air-Voyage*, 199; *To the Catholics of Today*, 207; *Country Life*, 198; *The Destruction of the First World*, 198; *Elius*, 214; *Fingal*, 195, 213 (*see also* Macpherson, J.

Bilderdijk, W. (*cont.*)
(*Ossian*); *Geology . . . of the Earth*, 197;
The History of the Father Lands, 202;
The Objections . . . Explained, 204; *A
Protestant to his Fellow Protestants*, 207;
'The Rage of Cow-Pock Vaccination',
207; *Romanticism and Catholicism in the
Netherlands*, 207; *The Scholars' Malady*,
201
Blackwell, T., 46
Blair, H., 44–7
Blake, W., 2, 3, 32, 37–41, 46–51, 141–2,
168, 174
Blumenbach, J. F., 197
Bodmer, J. J., 139–40, 148, 155–8, 160
Bonaparte, *see* Napoleon
Bonnington, R. P., 213
Borodin, A. P., 311
Boswell, J., 18, 44
bourgeois, bourgeoisie: in German litera-
ture, 121, 127, 166; Fuseli and Switzer-
land, 140; masculine equality, 149;
Spanish Romanticism, 260; in Spain,
266–8
bourgeois revolution, 231
Brentano, C., 110, 119–22, 125–6
Briullov, K. D., 304, 306–7
Brom, G., 207, 209
Brunswick, 196, 200
Büch, B., 202
Buckland, F. T., 197
Buffon, G. L. L., Comte de, 114
Burckhardt, J., 155, 163–6
Bürger, G. A., 286
Burke, E., 3, 52–3, 72, 205
Burney, F., 62
Burns, R., 56, 63
Byron, G. H., Lord, 7, 37, 41, 56–60, 92–3,
136, 141, 149, 151, 157, 160, 197, 203,
205, 211, 247, 262, 274, 278, 290,
297–9, 322; *Cain*, 197, 203; *Don Juan*,
197; *Heaven and Earth*, 198
Byzantine, 103–4

Calderón (de la Barca), P., 121, 147; theatre
of, 262
Calvinism, in Wales, 27
Capadose, A., 202–4, 208, 213
capitalism, 232, 237
caricature, German Romanticism, 110
Carolus Johannes XIV (of Sweden), 174
Carus, K. G., 111, 114–15, 124, 126
Catherine the Great, 286, 291, 300–1, 319
Catholic, Catholicism, 69ff., 117, 119, 134;
in Ireland, 84–6; in France, 252; in Spain,
261

Cavos, C., 309–10
Celts, 53, 77–8
Cervantes, S. M. de, 121
Chaadaev, P., 293–4
Chardin, J. B. S., 305
Chartists, in Wales, 34
Châteaubriand, F. R. de, 3, 6, 243–58; *La
Génie du Christianisme*, 206
Chatterton, T., 45–6, 56, 193, 210
Chavannes, J. D. A., 208
Christians, 27, 32, 49–50, 58; Greek, 59; in
England, 61; in Greece, 94; attitudes of,
110; tradition of, 116; in Europe, 117; in
Switzerland, 141; in France, 253; in
Spain, 269
Church of England, 26, 45
Cicero, 42
Cieszkowski, A., 335
civil war, 41, 70; in Ireland, 78; in Switzer-
land, 135; in Spain, 272
Clare, J., 63–4
Classicism: in Germany, 109, 128; Classical
Republicanism, in Switzerland, 156;
neo-Classicism, 212; in France, 241
Cobbett, W., 60
Cock, H. de, 208
Coleridge, S. T., 1, 3, 7, 37–40, 53–4, 60–1,
72, 127, 197, 201, 213, 263
Constable, J., 20, 197, 210, 213
Constant, B., 137, 143–5, 148–9, 158–9,
249–51, 254
Copenhagen, 174, 181, 183
Coppet circle, 136–9, 143–9, 158
Coronado, C., 266, 275, 279
Crabbe, G., 51–4, 63
Cronin, J., 85
Cui, C. A., 311
cultural identity, in Greece, 94–6
Cuvier, G. L.-C.-F., Baron, 197
Czartoryski, Prince A., 317, 329
Czokonay, Vitéz, M., 225

Da Costa, I., 202–5, 211–14; *Objections to
the Spirit of the Age*, 203, 205, 207
Dada movement, 163
Dante, A., 121, 139
Dargomyzhsky, A., 310–12
Darwin, E., 38, 57, 114
Davis, T., 72–3, 76–8, 82
Davydov, D., 290
death: as personified in Greek poetry, 102;
as freedom, 125; suicidal leap, 278
Decembrist revolt, 289, 298, 325
Dedekind, G. E. W., 206
Dee, Dr J., 11
Defille, J., 195, 197

Deism, 118, 194–5, 199, 203
Delécluze, E., 240–2
Deluc, J. A., 136, 197–9, 206
De Quincey, T., 61, 201
Derzhavin, G., 286, 291
Dissenting academies, in England, 60
Dobrolyubov, N. A., 312
Doppelgänger, 121, 238
Dostoevsky, F. M., 127, 292, 299
drama, 173, 205, 209, 221, 233
dreams, and Romantic scientists of German
    Romanticism, 112; and the subconscious,
    114; reality and, 121
Drost, A., 208–9
Druids, Druidism, 14, 20–1, 28, 30–2, 43,
    49–50, 56
Dryden, J., 41

Edgeworth, M., 62, 71–2, 79–81
education, 110, 124, 204, 208, 226, 284;
    Hellenic, 124
Eichendorff, J. von, 110, 121
eisteddfodau, 11–34
Ekeborg, A., 182–3
Empaytez, H.-L., 207
empiricism, 109, 111, 128, 172, 182
Engels, F., 16
Engeström, L. von, 183
Enlightenment, 3, 4, 6, 12–15, 18, 29, 32, 92,
    115–16, 118, 123, 172–3, 179–80, 186,
    188, 199, 203, 206, 219, 221, 225–8,
    231, 252; 324; Enlightenment thinkers,
    38; in Europe, 138; and Lavater in
    Switzerland, 141; in Switzerland,
    146–65; in Britain and France, 244; in
    Spain, 261
Eötvös, Baron, J., 236–7
Erdélyi, J., 221
Eschenmayer, A. K. A., 111–12
ethnography: ethnographic researches,
    102; Historical and Ethnological Society
    of Greece, 105
evangelicalism, in Wales, 16, 25, 27
Evans, E., 9, 28, 47
Evans, J., 9–16
exile, and Switzerland, 136
Expressionism, 163, 167

Fabvier, C., 92
faith, 118–20; and Romantic scientists of
German Romanticism, 112; in Germany,
125; self-realization, 127; Christian and
Jewish, 203; in French socialism, 254; *see
also* religion
Fallmerayer, J. P., 102–5
fatalism, in Irish writing, 71, 76; in French

writing, 251
Faust, 81
feeling: and scientists within German
    Romanticism, 112; in German writings,
    123
Ferdinand VII, 262–5
Ferguson, A., 44–6
Ferguson, Sir Samuel, 72–3, 79, 82–4
feudalism, survival of, 237
Fichte, J. G., 110, 116, 177, 184, 218, 226
folklore, folktales, folksongs, 17–18, 23;
    Greek folk poetry, 93, 99, 101–6;
    German folktales, 120; Swiss folklore,
    140, 152–3; Spanish folklore, 269
Foucault, M., 255–7
Fouqué, F. H. K. de la Motte, 110, 121
France, 11, 18, 26, 41–4, 49, 54, 57, 95,
    134–6, 149–50, 156, 161, 167, 262;
    French theatre, 273
Freemasons, Freemasonry, 173, 287; in
    Wales, 10, 32
Freiberg Mining Academy, 197
French Revolution, 3, 11, 14, 17, 29, 31, 40,
    46, 48, 51, 57–9, 116, 141–2, 160, 185,
    196, 220, 242, 248, 255, 261, 320, 326
Friedrich, C. D., 121–2
Fries, E., 184–5, 189
Fuseli, J. H., 138–42, 157; portrait of Tell,
    160; *The Nightmare* (painting), 168

Gaelic, 70–89
Gay, N., 41–2, 307
Geijer, E. G., 178–81, 185, 187–8
Geneva, 207
geology, 197–8
Gibbon, E., 4, 38, 57, 104
Gilpin, W., 20, 54
Glinka, M. I., 307–8, 310–12
God, 40, 58, 118–20, 122–3, 261, 276;
    Kingdom of, 117, 125; *see also* religion
Godwin, W., 38, 57, 62–3
Goethe, J. W. von, 7, 37–8, 94, 109–12, 116,
    123, 126, 141, 162, 192, 197, 212, 276,
    299; and Romanticism, 110, 123, 126;
    and Schlegel, 116; and Bilderdijk, 211;
    Die Leiden des jungen Werthers, 211;
    Wilhelm Meister, 116
Gogol, N. V., 293, 295–7, 306, 310, 314;
    and Briullov, 306; *Dead Souls*, 297; *The
    Government Inspector*, 296
Goldsmith, O., 52, 70, 154
Görres, G., 111, 113, 116
Gothic: fiction, 37; English, 69; novel and
    architecture, 134; church, 255; novel,
    256; tradition of, 257
'Götiska förbundet' (Gothic Society), 186

Goya, F., 6, 281
Gramsci, A., 12
Gray, T., 41–3, 47, 52–3, 286
Griffin, G., 72, 84–5, 88
Grimm, J., 196
Grimm brothers, 17, 31, 121, 162, 252
Grubbe, S., 187
Grundtvig, N. F. S., 176–7, 186
Gustavus III (of Sweden), 174
Gustavus Adolphus IV (of Sweden), 174, 178
Gutiérrez, A. G., 265

Haller, K. L. von, 159
Hammarskjöld, L., 178, 182
Hardiman, J., 72, 82, 84
Hartman, G., 40
Hartzenbusch, J. E., 265
Hauptmann, G., 233
Haydn, F. J., 9, 21
Hazlitt, W., 57, 50–61
Hegel, G. W. F., 3, 93, 111–12, 114, 123, 127, 138, 165, 176–7
Heine, H., 126, 290
Heinroth, J. C. A., 126
Herder, J. G., 97, 141, 162, 181, 196, 218, 220, 226, 322; *Ideen zu einer Philosophie der Geschichte der Menscheit*, 181
heroic figure, in Greek and English folk poetry, 102; in Victor Hugo's literature, 250–1; Spanish Romanticism, 266, 274, 277–8
Herzen, A. I., 312
history: German Romanticism, 109–11, 114–15, 117–18, 121–2, 126–7, 172, 176–7, 181–2, 191, 197, 218–19, 321; and nature, 115; Switzerland, 154, 157–8; of ideas, 179; evolution in, 181ff.; pre-Adamic, 197; of culture, 238; France, 253; Foucault's historical method, 255; Spanish Romanticism, 281
Hodler, F., 137, 167–8
Hoffmann, E. T. A., 110, 121, 123, 126, 238, 293–4, 296; German tales, 63
Hogendorp, D. van, 202, 208
Hogendorp. W. van, 202, 204
Höijer, B., 177–8, 185, 187
Hölderlin, J. C. F., 6, 109
Hollandsche Maatschappij der Wetenschappen, 192, 211
House of Orange, 191, 194
Hugo, V., 317, 240–4, 250–1, 254, 256–8, 262, 273, 278, 311
Humboldt, A. von, 111, 198
Hume, D., 4, 38, 57
Hunt, L., 57, 60

Ibsen, H., 233
idealism(sts): in England, France, Germany, 92; in Germany, 117; religious, 209
identity and diversity, 113, 115
Impressionists, 281, 303
Indians: Welsh-Indians, 12; ancient, 116
individualism: in France, 251, 257; in Spain, 260–1, 264, 267–8, 274, 276–7
inspiration, in German Romanticism, 111, 120
irony, 125, 127, 224–5, 232, 238, 293, 336
irrationality, 112
Ivanov, A., 306

Jacobins, 3, 32, 53, 157, 204, 213, 221, 228, 320; Welsh, 10; anti-Jacobin, 13; Robert Southey, 58; Republic, 148; French-styled, 252
Jacobites, in Ireland, 79, 84, 87
Jaspers, K., 127
Jena, 110, 175
Jews, 49–50
Johnson, S., 18, 30, 41, 44–5, 47
Jones, W., 12–13
Joseph II, 220, 228
journals and magazines: *Athenäum*, 110, 114; *The Contemporary*, 290; *Cylchgrawn Cymraeg*, 15–16; *Dublin University Magazine*, 73, 82; *El Artista*, 264; *The Emulator of Enlightenment and Charity*, 288; *Europa*, 117; *Gentleman's Magazine*, 56; *De Gids*, 209; *Iduna*, 186; *Journal för Litteraturen och teatern*, 178; *The Literary Gazette*, 290; *London Magazine*, 61; *Lyceum*, 178, 182; *Mnemosyne*, 288, 294; *De Muzen*, 209; *Northern Flowers*, 290; *Phosphoros*, 178–80; *The Pole Star*, 287; *Polyfem*, 178; *Svensk literaturtidning*, 179; *The Telescope*, 293; *The Times*, 228; *Warsaw Library*, 335
Judaism, 32
July Revolution (France), 325, 329

Kalashnikov, I., 292
Kant, I., 110–12, 138, 176, 253–4) *Metaphysische Anfangsgründe der Naturwissenschaft*, 176
Karamzin, I., 286–8, 291, 303
Karl Wilhelm Ferdinand (Duke of Brunswick), 193, 196–7
Katona, J., 221–5
Kazinczy, F., 221–2
Keats, J., 37, 46, 58, 60–1, 63–4, 127, 201, 213
Keller, G., 137, 163, 166

Kemény, Baron Z., 237–8
Kempelen, W. von, 196
Kerner, J. A. C., 111, 119, 125–6
Kierkegaard, S., 126, 165, 213, 224, 229, 231
Kiprensky, O., 303–4
Kisfaludy, K., 224–5
Kleist, H. von, 3, 109, 121–2, 125, 158, 213
Knight of the Swan, 193, 214; *see also* Bilderdijk, W.
Knuvelder, G. P. M., 205
Kölcsey, F., 218, 227, 229
Koléttis, I., 95–6, 104
Kościuszko, T., 318, 320, 327
Kossuth, L., 230–2
Kraków, 318, 323; republic of, 317
Krasiński, Z., 332, 335
Kuechelbecker, W., 288–9
Kuyper, A., 211–12

Lamarck, J.-B. de, 114
Lamb, C., 61, 63
landscape: Switzerland, 136; French painting, 258; Spain, 269
language: Greek, 94, 96, 98, 99, 105; Swiss, 135, 161, 167; Spanish, 270
Larra, Mariano José de, 265–80
Lavater, J. C.: in Switzerland, 138–41, 156; science, 141; physiognomy, 142
Lennep, D. van, 205
Lennep, J. van, 202–3, 205, 208
Lermontov, M. I., 6, 297–300, 314; exile, 298; and Pushkin, 298; and Martynov (duel), 298; as painter, 304; *A Hero of Our Times*, 299–300
Lessing, G. E., 297
Leyden, 193, 207
Lhuyd, E., 27
Liberalism, 207, 213, 237, 288, 294
liberty, equality, fraternity: 'war of liberation', 117; in Switzerland, 135; in Britain, 248; French Restoration, 249; in France, 257; in Spain, 262–3, 265, 268, 273–4; Spanish female writings, 275
Liebig, J., 127
literature, 109–12, 120–1, 126–7, 172, 179, 192, 213, 217, 219, 221, 285, 288; theory and criticism of, 120, 294; and philosophy, 210, 218; neo-Classical, 286; as national (Polish) consciousness, 328; *see also* drama, poetry, prose
London, 71, 174, 193, 196–7; literary society, 42; Shakespeare Gallery, 48; literary figures, 57; House of Lords, 247; University, 263
London-Welsh, 9, 11–12, 14–15, 19, 24, 32

Louis Napoleon (King of The Netherlands), 191, 194
Lukács, G., 233

Macpherson, J., 44–6, 48–9, 52–3, 75, 84, 139; *Ossian*, 195, 210, 213
Maeterlinck, M., 127
Mangan, J. C., 72, 79, 88
Mann, T., 127
Maria Theresa, 219–20
Marum, M. van, 211
Marx, K., 16, 38, 148, 243, 250
materialism, 2, 111, 127, 176
Matthias I (of Hungary), 221
Maturin, C., 81–2, 84
medicine, 111, 121, 191, 200; in German literature, 110; medical systems in German Romantic thought, 114; medical practitioners in Germany – melancholy, 123; illness as negative, 125; German medical studies, 126–7
medieval period, 110; Wales, 13; Plantagenet kings, 53; Spain, 269
melancholy: in English poetry, 61; 'chaos of events', 123; Isabelle van Serooskerken Van Tuyll, 143; in Swiss poetry, 151; love poetry, 165
Mendelssohn, J. L. F. (Mendelssohn-Bartholdy), 309
Mesmer, A., 109, 121, 218, 254
Mesonero Romanos, Ramón de, 270–2
metaphysical: in German literature, 109, 111, 122; -religious, 123; science, 124; in Spanish writings, 276
Methodists, in Wales, 9–11, 16, 23, 25, 26, 27
Metternich, Prince K., 219, 232
Mickiewicz, A., 6, 321–2, 324, 329–33, 335–6; *Books of the Polish Nation and Its Pilgrimage*, 329; *Forefathers' Eve*, 330; *Konrad Wallenrod*, 324–5; *Ode to Youth*, 327; *Pan Tadeusz*, 331
Middle Ages, 30, 103, 116–17, 121, 139, 205–6, 234, 270
Milton, J., 48–50, 58, 60, 139–40
Montaigne, M. de, 227
Montesquieu, G. L. de S., 175, 227
Moore, T., 57, 59, 71, 74, 79, 83, 85–8, 290, 299
Morgan, Lady, 70–9
Morganwg, Iolo (Edward Williams), 9, 13, 23–4, 27–31, 33–5, 49–50
Moscow, 299, 314
Mossel, Kaat, 193
Mozart, W. A., 310
Müller, Adam, 116–17, 125, 219

Müller, Johannes, von, 138, 156–8, 163
Munich, 110, 290
music, 109–10, 124, 126, 294; opera, 209;
    Russian, 307–12; Golden Age, 311–12
Mussorgsky, M. P., 311–12
mysticism, 122, 173, 181
mythology, 38, 60, 188; Welsh, 11; English,
    49, 57; Greek, 58, 105; German, 116;
    Swiss, 141, 151, 156; Nordic, 186–7;
    French, 246; Spanish, 279

Napoleon, 6, 58, 117, 134–5, 145, 148–9,
    154–8, 162, 174, 191, 204, 240, 246–52,
    261, 268, 287, 290, 317, 320, 326; defeat
    of, at Waterloo, 318
Napoleonic Wars, 92, 174, 196, 228, 285,
    305, 333
Nation newspaper, 69, 73, 77, 79
national character, 227, 237
nationalism: in England, 42; in Ireland, 77,
    88; Turkish, 96; Greek, anti-, 98, 102,
    106; in Germany, 116–17; Swiss, 139,
    149, 156, 161, 165–7; in France, 252;
    Spanish, 260ff.; Orangist, 213; in
    Russia, 285; Polish, 321ff.
nationhood: in England, 41, 51; in Greece,
    94–7, 104
natural philosophy, 109, 111, 113, 117, 127
nature: in English Romantic poetry, 102; in
    German Romanticism, 110–13, 121–3;
    and history, 115; spiritualization of, 115;
    in Spanish Romanticism, 271
Naturphilosophie, 6, 172, 175–6, 182–4,
    203, 210
Nicholas I, Tsar, 289–90, 306, 325–6, 332,
    336
Nonconformity, in Wales, 26
Normans, 79, 256; Norman Yoke, in
    Wales, 12
Norwid, C. K., 335–6
Novalis (Hardenberg, F. L. von), 109,
    112–15, 117, 119–22, 124–6, 172, 201,
    213; *The Apprentices of Saïs*, 121;
    Christendom or Europe, 117, 207;
    Heinrich von Ofterdingen, 197; *Hymns
    to the Night,* 119
November uprising ('Polish Revolution'),
    325ff.

Odoevsky, Prince V. F., 288–9, 294
Oehlenschläger, A., 176, 186
Oersted, H. C., 111, 176–7, 182
Oken, L., 111, 114, 127, 184
oral literature, 103, 105; Spanish tradition
    of, 269
Orthodox Church, 92, 94–8

Ottoman period, 92–100
Owenson, R., 74–5

Paganism, 53; in England, 54–8; medieval
    period, 94; in Switzerland, 164; in France,
    253
painters, *see* art, artists
pantheism, 119, 194
Pantycelyn, W. W., 9, 25–7
Paris, 185, 287, 333; Peace Conference, 96
Parnasse, in Greece and Europe, 93
Parry (Blind) John, 19–21
Paskevitch, General I. F., 325, 328;
    'Paskevitch night', 333
Patriarchate, 92–3
patriotism: in England, 41–51; in Ireland,
    78, 83–4; in Greece, 101; in Switzerland,
    154–60; in Spain, 268–9
Paul, Jean, 109, 119–21, 162, 200; *Des
    Luftschiffers Gianozzo Seebuch,* 200;
    Siebenkäs, 119
peasants: life of, 236; rebellions, 284;
    Polish, 318ff.
Pennant, T., 114, 20–1, 24
Percy, T., 12, 17, 47, 195
Pest: Academy of Sciences, 228, 231;
    National Library, 228; National Theatre,
    231
Pestalozzi, J. P., in Switzerland, 135, 156–7
Peter the Great, 291, 294
Petöfi, S., 218, 221, 236–7
philosophy, 110–11, 117, 119–20, 122–3,
    176–80, 185–7, 218, 290, 334; specu-
    lative natural philosophy, 111 (*see also*
    Naturphilosophie); of nature, 125, 186;
    of art, 125; existential, 127; of religion,
    172; *philosophes,* 4–5, 219
physics, 113, 176, 182, 191, 199
physiognomy: and Lavater, 141; and
    Spanish Romanticism, 271
Pietism, 173, 196, 206, 219
poetry, 120, 123, 127, 172, 178–80, 185–8,
    194–5, 202–3, 205, 210, 232, 289–90,
    292, 328, 330; Golden Age of Russia, 300
politics, 117, 122, 208, 218, 220, 238;
    political life, 116, 284; radicalism, 188–9;
    philosophy, 203; political brotherhoods
    (Russia), 287
Polítis, Nikólaos, 103, 105–6
Poniatowski, Prince J., 317–18, 327
Poniatowski, King Stanislaw August (of
    Poland-Lithuania), 319–20
Pope, A., 41–2, 195
Populism, 233–7
Positivism, 237–8
post-Kantianism, 39–40

Potemkin, G. A., 305
Priestley, J., 9, 16, 134
Prinsterer, G. Groen van, 202, 205, 208, 211
prose, 120, 172, 179, 195, 202–3, 220, 224, 237–8, 292–3, 299
Protestantism, 70, 73–81, 119, 134, 197, 207, 210, 218, 219; Welsh, 11, 16, 25; Irish, 69, 82–3; and Pietism, 138; and liberalism, 147; in Spain, 261
Psichari, Jean, 97–8
Pugachev, E. I., 291
Puritans, 25, 97–8
Purkyně (Purkinje), J. E., 109
Pushkin, A. S., 6, 288–93, 298, 311, 314; exile, 288, 291; and Irina Rodionovna, 291; Baron G. d'Anthes (duel), 298; and K. P. Briullov, 306; *The Bronze Horseman*, 291, 301; *Eugene Onegin*, 288–90, 300; *The Queen of Spades*, 291
Pushkin, V., 288

Quitzmann, E. A., 127

Rachmaninov, S. V., 312
radicalism: in Germany, 127; in Switzerland, 134, 159–65; in Spain, 280
Raphael (Santi), 203
rationalism, 174, 179, 199, 206–7, 218
Realism, 163, 166, 307; psychological, 238, 289; Socialist, 286; Russian, 286, 312; canonical, 299; 'critical', 303; mystical, 311
Reformation, in Switzerland, 137–8
Reil, J. C., 109
Reill, P. Hans, 138–9
religion, 109–10, 118–18, 122, 179–80, 185, 192, 205–6, 208, 334; Afscheiding, 208, 211; Calvinism(sts), 197, 204, 211–12; Calvinist doctrines, 206; Calvinist orthodoxy, 213; Catholic(ism), 117, 119, 206, 212, 293, 319, 334; Catholic Church, 207, 333; Catholic theology, 219; Church Slavonic, 286–8; Doleantie, 211; Dutch Réveil, 205, 207–9; Free Churches, 208; Gereformeerde kerken in Nederland, 211; Holy Synod, 285; Lutheran State Church (Sweden), 188; Methodism, 207; New Church, 174; Orthodoxy, 294, 326; Oxford movement, 206; 'predikantendom', 210; Protestant(ism), 119, 197, 207, 210, 218; Protestant theology, 219; Société Evangélique, 207; Swiss Réveil, 207
Renaissance, 99–100, 121, 203, 273, 303
Reynolds, Sir Joshua, 20, 303

Riemer, F. W., 110, 123
Rimsky-Korsakov, N. A., 311
Ritter, J. W., 111–13, 177
Rome, 206–7, 212
Romein, J., 202
Rossini, G. A., 309
Rousseau, Jean-Jacques, 38, 75, 111, 136–40, 142, 152, 195, 203, 220, 227, 244–5, 248, 274; *Emile*, 219
Royal Academy of Arts, and J. H. Fuseli, 140
Royal Irish Academy, 82
Rozier, J. F. Pilâtre de, 200
Rudbeck, O., 186
Runge, P. O., 121–2, 126
Ryleev, K., 287, 289

St Petersburg, 285, 288–9, 306–8, 312–14, 328; Academy of Arts, 285, 301, 303, 305; Academy of Sciences, 285; Imperial Ballet School, 285, 313; The Northern Society, 287; The Free Society of Lovers of Russian Letters, 288; The Lovers of Wisdom, 288, 290; School of Cavalry Cadets, 298; Nevsky Prospekt, 301–2; Theatre School, 308
Saussure, H. B. de, 197
Saxons, 256; in Wales, 12, 14; massacre, 33; Anglo-Saxons, 53
Schelling, F. W. J., 1, 5, 110–14, 126–7, 172, 174–8, 181, 187, 210, 226, 290, 322
Schiller, 37, 93, 109, 137, 147, 157, 161, 163, 195, 212, 227, 251, 256, 298, 322
Schlegel, A. W., 116–17, 119, 124, 136, 144, 147, 262
Schlegel, F., 5, 38, 40, 97, 116–17, 119–28, 213, 237
Schlegel brothers, 110, 120–1, 159, 172
Schlegel-Schelling, Caroline, 124
Schleiermacher, F., 110, 118–19, 124, 126, 213
Schopenhauer, A., 111–12, 127
Schubert, G. H. von, 111, 114, 119, 121, 126
science, 103, 109–14, 116, 118, 120–7; and art, 112, 120; metaphysical, 124, 173; and Lavater, 141, 176, 180, 182–3, 192, 200; and technology, 200
science fiction, 199–200
Scott, Sir Walter, 7, 9, 18, 21, 52–3, 61–2, 72, 93, 205, 210, 247, 256, 265, 269, 270, 290–2, 295; and K. P. Briullov, 306
sensationalism, French, eighteenth century, 254
sentimentalism(ists): poetic ideal, 121, 286–7, 321
serf(dom), 237, 284

Shakespeare, W., 48, 60, 121, 139–40, 195, 205, 221, 241–2, 256, 288, 291
Shelley, Mary, 57; *Frankenstein*, 62, 157, 200
Shelley, P. B., 3–4, 37–8, 41, 56–60, 210, 213, 248
Shishkov, A., 286–8
Slavophiles(ism), 294, 297
Słowacki, J., 327, 331–2, 335; *Genesis from the Spirit*, 332; *Kordian*, 331; *Ode to Freedom*, 327
Snelders, H. A. M., 209–10
Sobieski, King Jan (of Poland), 232, 317–18
Solger, K. W. F., 125, 224
Somov, O., 288, 292, 295
soul, artist, 121; philosophy of life, 125; physiognomy, 141; Kant's representation of, 254; passions, 276
Southey, R., 3, 53–4, 58–9, 194, 210
Spain, 10–11, 18–19, 41; drama in, 256
Spenser, Edmund, 43, 48, 59, 64, 71–2, 80–3
spiritualization: of nature, 115; poetic, 122; idealistic *philosophes*, 126; seances in France, 254
Staël, Madame de, 109, 126, 145–7, 158, 227, 240, 244–58; *De l'Allemagne*, 109, 126, 288
Stagnelius, E. J., 174, 181
Steevens, G., 48
Steffens, H., 111–12, 115, 118, 124, 126, 175–8, 182, 186
Stendhal, F. de, 1, 6, 240–6
Stockholm, 178, 183
Sturm und Drang, 2, 37, 134, 137, 140, 154, 212
Sulzer, J., 138–40
Surrealism, 163, 281
Swedenborg, E., 111, 173–4
Swedish Academy, 178–9
Swift, J., 41–2, 70
Symbolism(ists), 93, 127, 167, 290, 336; works, 233
Széchenyi, Count I., 218–19, 226–32, 234; *journal intime*, 218, 227, 231; *Credit*, 226–7; *Hunnia*, 227–8; *Light*, 227; *Look*, 232

Tell, William, 141, 146, 150; legend of, 156–61
theatre, 221, 233; of the Esterházys, 221; puppet, 295
Thelwall, A. S., 208
Thomson, James, 41–3, 48, 53, 63–4, 286
Tieck, L., 109–10, 120–2, 172, 213
Tolstoy, F., 305

Tone, Wolfe, 77
tradition, 94, 99; Greek concept of, 105; Swiss, 158; British, 248; Spanish, 269, 272
Treschow, N., 181–2
Treviranus, G. R., 11, 114, 124
Tsarskoe Selo, 288, 298, 300–1
Turner, J. M. W., 1, 21, 136, 213, 304

unity: concept of, 113; ideal conviction, 121; history of, 127
Universities: Christiania (now Oslo), 175, 181; Copenhagen, 175–7; Dorpat (now Tartu), 290; Göttingen, 197; Helsinki, 175; Leyden, 201–3; Lund, 183; Moscow, 297–8; Turku (Abo), 175; Uppsala, 177–9, 181–2, 189; Wilno (now Vilnius), 330
Uppsala, 183–6, 188–9
Utopia, 109, 117, 255

Vaznetsov, V., 307
Vereshchagin, V., 307
Verne, J., 200
Verstovsky, A., 309–10
Vienna, 110, 220, 318; Congress of, 317, 320
Vinet, A. R., 207, 213
Vogel, A., 125
Volney, Constantin François Chassebeuf de, *Ruins of Empires*, 15–16, 57–8
Voltaire, F. M., 104, 199, 220, 245, 253
Vondel, J. van der, 203
Vörösmarty, M., 218, 232–5
Vyazemsky, Prince P., 285

Wackenroder, H. W. F., 109–10, 122
Wallman, J. H., 181, 183–6, 188
Wandering Jew, 81
Warsaw, 316, 320, 325, 327–8, 335; conservatory (music), 308; Duchy of, 316, 323
Weber, M., 173, 186
Werner, A. G., 197–8
Werther, 110, 140, 154
William I (King of The Netherlands), 191, 194
William II (King of the Netherlands), 191
William V (Stadtholder), 191, 193
Williams, Edward, 49
Windischmann, K. J. H., 111, 123
Winterl, J. J., 177, 182
witch-hunts, in Wales, 13
Woesthoven, Catharina Rebecca, 194
Wordsworth, W., 1, 3–4, 37–42, 46, 52–61, 64, 94, 100, 127, 137, 213, 263, 278

Yazykov, N., 290, 309
Yeats, W. B., 89, 233

Zambélios, Spiridon, 103–4

Zhukovsky, V., 286, 288, 309
Zimmermann, Johann Georg, 142
Zorrilla, José, 266